D0712965

Battleground:
The Autobiography of Margaret A. Haley

Battleground:

THE AUTOBIOGRAPHY OF
Margaret A. Haley

EDITED BY
Robert L. Reid

University of Illinois Press
URBANA CHICAGO LONDON

Frontispiece: Margaret A. Haley, December, 1910
(courtesy of the Chicago Historical Society)

This book is printed on acid-free paper.

Library of Congress Cataloging in Publication Data

Haley, Margaret A.
Battleground: the autobiography of Margaret A. Haley.

Includes bibliographical references.
1. Haley, Margaret A.   2. Educators—United
States—Biography.   3. Chicago Teachers' Federation
—History.   I. Reid, Robert L., 1938-
II. Title.
LA2317.H26A32   331.88'113711'00977311 [B]   81-12930
ISBN 0-252-00913-4   AACR2

Contents

Editor's Introduction

Margaret A. Haley called her autobiography *Battleground* and opened with the disclaimer, "I never wanted to fight." After telling her story of "forty fighting years," she concluded, at the age of seventy-five, that "fighting Irish I am yet." Had her name been Michael or John, this theme of combat would have suggested the life history of a military hero or prize fighter. But her name was Margaret, or "Maggie" to her close friends. She was a diminutive female with blazing blue eyes which reflected her Irish Catholic temper. Her narrative is that of a grade school teacher, a social reformer, and a labor advocate. Her opponents were neither soldiers nor boxers; they were tax-dodging corporate businessmen, corrupt politicians, and autocratic school administrators. As the leader of the nation's most militant teacher organization, the Chicago Teachers' Federation, Haley fought to advance the cause of public education and to improve the well-being of the women grade teachers of Chicago.

The narrative encompasses that period which historians describe as the years of modernization. She was born on November 15, 1861, the first year of the Civil War administration of Abraham Lincoln, and died on January 5, 1939, during the New Deal era of Franklin D. Roosevelt. She witnessed the transformation of America from a rural, agrarian society of relatively independent geographic areas to the highly complex, interdependent industrial-urban nation of the twentieth century. Woven through her life story are contemporary American themes: urbanization, bureaucratization, feminism, and professionalism.[1]

---

[1] These themes are discussed in greater detail in Robert L. Reid, "The Professionalization of Public School Teachers: The Chicago Experience, 1895-1920" (Ph.D. diss., Northwestern University, 1968) (hereafter cited as Reid, "Professionalization"). Robert H. Wiebe, *The Search for Order, 1877-1920* (New York: Hill and Wang, 1966) and David B. Tyack, *The One Best System: A History of American Urban Education* (Cambridge, Mass.: Harvard University Press, 1974) are valuable accounts (hereafter cited as Tyack, *One Best System*).

Haley fashioned her story in chronological order. Her earliest recollections were of life on a farm located on the Illinois prairie between Morris and Joliet. Her father, Michael Haley, had come to the Midwest as a boy to work on the construction of the Illinois and Michigan Canal. When she was ten, he left farming to operate a stone quarry and the family moved to the village of Channahon. The quarry business did not succeed and his disappointments provided Margaret lessons in the workings of the economic and political system. The failure of another quarry firm in which her father was a partner coincided with Margaret's graduation from a convent school in Morris. As the oldest child, she was obliged to help the large Haley family. She selected the calling which was most open to women—that of schoolma'am.[2] At the age of sixteen she began teaching at a country school near the village of Minooka. Next Haley taught in the town of Joliet and in 1882 moved to the city of Chicago. She obtained a position as a sixth grade teacher at the Hendricks School, located in the turbulent stockyards district, where she served for the rest of her teaching years. From farm to village to town to city, the pattern of urbanization which she experienced belonged as well to the society at large.

In January, 1900, Haley left the classroom to become the paid business representative of the Chicago Teachers' Federation. She held this assignment until her death. Through her leadership, the CTF played a significant role in the progressive reform movement which took place in the nation's second largest city. In Chicago, as in other urban areas, city and state government struggled to provide services, extract necessary revenue in the form of taxes, and bring order and regularity to emerging municipal social and economic systems.

The public schools were Haley's most important concern. The school system was the city's largest employer and required the greatest share of the public budget. When she arrived in Chicago in the early 1880s, the city's population was one-half million, 59,562 pupils were crowded into the public schools, and the city's annual educational expenditure was one million dollars. In 1939, Chicago was a city of more than three million, and the schools served approximately 400,000 students at a cost in excess of seventy million dollars.[3] Apart from the issue

---

[2]The introduction of the system of progression through grades, the rise of co-educational normal schools, and the manpower shortage brought on by the Civil War were factors which contributed to the feminization of teaching. Women constituted approximately two-thirds of the nation's teaching force by the late 1860s. U.S. Commission for Education, *Report for the Year 1867-1868* (Washington, D.C.: Bureau of Education, 1868), pp. 649-50. See also Willard Elsbree, *The American Teacher* (New York: American Book Co., 1939), pp. 17-31.

[3]Mary J. Herrick, *The Chicago Schools: A Social and Political History* (Beverly Hills, Calif.: Sage Publications, 1971), pp. 403-6 (hereafter cited as Herrick, *Chicago Schools*).

of the nature and quality of the education provided, these statistics introduce significant concerns related to the size, complexity, and costs of the educational system. The political question, Who governs? and the economic query, Who pays? were real problems confronting the teachers, taxpayers, and citizens of Chicago. The growth of the city brought concentrations of power and of wealth as well as of people. Given a complex system which located authority in a twenty-one member school board appointed by the mayor, depended on the city council for its financial needs, and was subject to state legislation, the public schools were very much a part of the political experience of the city. Fundamentally important to Haley were those issues related to the political control and the financial support of the schools. These remained paramount throughout her public career. Haley's participation in civic reform continued unabated until the mid-1930s when problems of failing health and old age forced her to slow the pace. Then she turned her attention to composing her life story.

An autobiography is a selective recreation of experience and resembles a work of fiction in the careful shaping of the narrative. In selecting episodes from her youth, Haley called forth a set of values which reflected the reform urgings of the Gilded Age. These included a belief in the workings of democracy, an understanding of the relationship between taxation and social justice, a respect for the dignity of all human beings including those of the feminine sex, and a strong faith in the importance of education and the common schools. She wrote that discussions in the home between her father and his friends alerted her to the political movements, both in America and Ireland, of the late nineteenth century. A Greenback pamphlet on the money question and the reading of Henry George's *Progress and Poverty* introduced economic issues. She recalled an incident in which her father led the Haley girls from a public lecture hall when the speaker "spoke sneeringly of Susan B. Anthony." She remembered her mother, who valued education "as only the Irish, who had been denied the full measure of education, could value it" and who taught Margaret the old Irish maxim, "Educate in order that your children may be free."

Probably each ethnic group in America had its own version of this Irish saying on the relationship of education and freedom. Certainly the advocates of the common school movement in the nineteenth century successfully used this popular understanding to establish a network of schools which were locally based, controlled and supported by the citizenry, and assimilated pupils from diverse backgrounds. Convincing evidence of the broad consensus which provided the essential support for public education could be found in the pervasive one-room schools of the villages and townships of Haley's youth. The development of the public school system of Chicago, described as "the greatest triumph of the municipality," was, on a grander scale, yet another demonstration of the American commitment to learning.[4]

As the leader of the organized teachers of Chicago, Haley modified and extended the ideology of the common school movement. She defined democracy as "freedom of activity directed by freed intelligence." Alarmed by the increasing concentration of wealth and the related dangers which the machine civilization posed to an open and democratic society, Haley presented her book as the story of the war of privilege against the people. In her last chapter, "The Darkling Plain," she described Chicago as "the proving ground of democracy." Despite the gloomy chapter title, which reflected the severe blows the teachers and the schools had suffered during the depression years, Haley remained optimistic and retained her faith in the public school system. She called upon other teachers to "take up the knapsack of service." Using a description, the Fifth Estate, which the progressive reformer from Wisconsin, Robert LaFollette, had bestowed upon the organized teachers, she urged her followers to comprehend and to teach the political and economic lessons which she had learned. To Haley the survival of democracy in America rested with the Fifth Estate.

While Haley's allegiance to democracy, opportunity, and education may be viewed as a legacy from her agrarian past, her method of achieving goals was distinctly modern. The approach was organizational activity which she described as "combined effort for mutual aid." Urban life demanded structure and representation; interest groups and organizations were the vehicles for active participation in civic affairs. The Chicago Teachers' Federation was established in 1897, during the major depression of the 1890s. It was formed to defend the recently enacted pension system which had been established two years earlier to help provide a modicum of security to urban teachers in a period of economic stress.[5] The Chicago Teachers' Federation differed from state and national associations whose major activities were annual meetings and from local literary discussion societies to which teachers politely belonged. Administrators were excluded; women grade school teachers constituted the membership. The federation was a purposive organization which recognized the material needs of its members. A secure pension system, tenure, and improved salaries were the necessary

[4]Charles Merriam, *Chicago: A More Intimate View of Urban Politics* (New York: Macmillan, 1929), p. 85 (hereafter cited as Merriam, *Chicago*).

[5]David P. Thelen suggests that the depression experience aroused universal emotions of fear and anger and united the fragmentary reform movements around the issues of tax dodging and corporate arrogance. "Social Tensions and the Origins of Progressivism," *Journal of American History*, 56 (Sept., 1969), pp. 336-41.

conditions to meet the organization's primary objective: "to raise the standard of the teaching profession."[6]

Margaret Haley became active in 1898 and helped to elect Catherine Goggin to the presidency of the CTF. Goggin and Haley then teamed up to defeat a school centralization bill in the Illinois legislature. From this initial exposure, Haley would attend every legislative session through 1935 and become the veteran member of Illinois lobbyists. The CTF grew rapidly and had 3,000 members, almost exclusively women, by the turn of the century. Further, the organization had developed aggressive female leaders whose fight against the proposed school legislation "laid the foundations of a political power that would be the 'Marvel of Chicago.'"[7] The participation of the CTF in the urban affairs of the city is a major theme of Haley's autobiography.

The CTF's next crusade in Chicago grew out of the teachers' concern about revenue for the rapidly growing public school system. In leading this fight Margaret Haley made her most significant contribution to urban political reform. Faced with the school board's inability to pay promised salary increases, she discovered that major corporations in the city were successfully evading taxes on their franchises. Armed with evidence, the CTF took five major utility and street railway companies through city and state review bodies and then to the courts before winning the case. The resulting reassessment secured approximately $600,000 in back taxes and increased the annual tax income of the city by $250,000. Haley's victory blended with the insurgent reform movement emerging in the cities and brought her national recognition from the progressive coalition of consumer, taxpayer, and citizen interest groups. Her method of gathering sound factual information reflected a scientific, rational approach to reform; her solicitation of the public in the interests of democracy was identified with the approach of reformers such as Samuel "Golden Rule" Jones of Toledo, Tom L. Johnson of Cleveland, and Robert LaFollette of Wisconsin. The teachers' crusade coincided with similar movements across the nation as Americans became increasingly alert to two broadly based issues: tax reform and corporate arrogance. An editorial comment from the national monthly *Review of Reviews* illustrated the outlook of this early phase of progressive reform when it reported that "a very great lesson

---

[6]*Constitution and By-laws of the Chicago Teachers' Federation,* pamphlet in the Chicago Teachers' Federation Files, Chicago Historical Society (hereafter cited as CTF Files). The objectives were "to raise the standard of the teaching profession by securing for teachers conditions essential to the best professional service, and to this end to obtain for them all the rights and benefits to which they are entitled; the consideration and support of the Pension Law; the study of parliamentary law."

[7]William Hard, "Margaret Haley, Rebel," *The Times Magazine,* 1 (Jan., 1907), p. 233.

lies in the fact that this splendid triumph over hideous fraud and corruption has now been carried through by energetic women school teachers."[8]

While the teachers' tax fight eventually secured higher salaries, more significantly it initiated Haley and her organization in municipal affairs. As a former teacher and disenfranchised female, she performed as an educator, bringing the concerns of the teachers to civic organizations, church groups, labor unions, and women's clubs. She became familiar with the organizational structure of the city and with the major social issues confronting the people of Chicago. Her knowledge and fame were shared with the members of the CTF and her skills as a public speaker were sharpened. In both word and deed, Haley conveyed the theme of citizen participation. Her identification with this egalitarian or "democratic" side of the progressive movement stood in marked contrast to the centralist tendencies of the business interests and upper-strata groups which have been identified with reform in the first decades of the twentieth century. Through the years, the theme of adequate tax revenues for an urban school system, including the issue of school land leases, remained one of Haley's strongest concerns.

Following the tax fight, the CTF made another critical decision in 1902, when the members voted to affiliate with the Chicago Federation of Labor. Haley led the way, successfully refuting criticisms regarding the unruly and turbulent class represented by the labor movement. Together with John Fitzpatrick, the organizer and later president of the CFL, Haley spoke for the unity of different classes of workers against the holders of corporate privilege. The labor movement would be enlightened and extended through the affiliation with the CTF; the elementary teachers, 97 percent of whom were women, would gain male allies who possessed the weapon of the ballot. Thus the CTF introduced female white-collar unionism into American life. This affiliation of women teachers with hod carriers, teamsters, carpenters, and horseshoers set the CTF apart from other teacher associations; the poet Carl Sandburg, while a newspaper reporter for a small Chicago daily, described it as a "purple patch on the pedagogical field."[9] Over the years this radical departure encountered mounting opposition which brought eventual retaliation from those opposed to organized labor.

The formation of the CTF corresponded with the general pattern of response to industrial-urban America which historians have described

[8]David P. Thelen, *Robert M. LaFollette and the Insurgent Spirit* (Boston: Little, Brown and Co., 1976), p. 25; "Chicago's Franchise Taxes—and New York's," *American Monthly Review of Reviews*, 24 (Dec., 1901), pp. 656-57.

[9]Carl Sandburg, "Margaret Haley," *Reedy's Mirror*, 24 (Dec., 1915), p. 445 (hereafter cited as Sandburg, "Margaret Haley").

as an organizational revolution. The tax fight placed Haley and her organization in the mainstream of insurgent reform. But the decision to join the Federation of Labor was of such consequence that "radical departure" was an appropriate description. Although grade teachers in a number of large cities formed associations at this time, none of these took a similar step. The CTF was the first and only large body of teachers to affiliate with labor prior to 1916. While other urban teacher associations sometimes participated in civic affairs as part of the loose, shifting coalitions which worked for local and state reforms, they did so without making permanent alliances. From another perspective on the history of organized labor, the relationship between the teachers and the CFL reinforced the strong commitment which labor made to public education in Chicago. This long record of support is at odds with revisionist interpretations which consider schools to be instruments for social control imposed upon workers.[10]

Studies of urban progressivism suggest that reform efforts were often led by local businessmen and aspiring professionals who sought to integrate and centralize municipal decision making. As historian Samuel Hays has stated it, "The source of support for reform in municipal government did not come from the lower or middle classes, but from the upper class. . . ." Elitist leaders attempted to exclude lower status groups from political power and office. Recent accounts of school reform in Philadelphia and St. Louis, of political power in Birmingham, and of civic participation by university professors in Chicago support this concept of leadership from the top down.[11]

Writing some fifty years earlier, a University of Chicago professor, Charles E. Merriam, expressed similar understandings about his city. Merriam was a distinguished political scientist who experienced politics firsthand as city councilman for three terms and as a candidate for mayor on several occasions. He wrote that the business elements were the "most effectively organized" of the economic groupings of the city.

---

[10]"A Radical Departure in Unionism," *Scribner's Magazine*, 33 (June, 1903), p. 763; "The Chicago Teachers and Life and Labor," *Life and Labor*, 3 (May, 1913), p. 146; Alice Henry, *Women and the Labor Movement* (New York: George H. Doran, 1923), p. 86. For a discussion of revisionist interpretations see Diane Ravitch, *The Revisionists Revised: A Critique of the Radical Attack on the Schools* (New York: Basic Books, 1978).

[11]Samuel P. Hays, "The Politics of Reform in Municipal Government in the Progressive Era," *Pacific Northwest Quarterly*, 55 (Oct., 1964), pp. 157-69; William H. Issel, "Modernization in Philadelphia School Reform, 1882-1905," *Pennsylvania Magazine of History and Biography*, 94 (July, 1970), pp. 358-83; Selwyn K. Troen, *The Public and the Schools: Shaping the St. Louis System, 1838-1920* (Columbia, Mo.: University of Missouri Press, 1975); Carl V. Harris, *Political Power in Birmingham, 1871-1921* (Knoxville: University of Tennessee Press, 1977); Steven J. Diner, *A City and Its Universities: Public Policy in Chicago, 1892-1919* (Chapel Hill: University of North Carolina Press, 1980). See also David C. Hammack, "Problems in the Cities and Towns of the United States, 1800-1960," *American Historical Review*, 83 (Apr., 1978), pp. 323-49.

When they wished to act in unison, the business groups were "the real masters" of Chicago. Business leaders dominated such organizations as the Civic Federation, the City Club, the Union League Club, the Commercial Club, and the Association of Commerce. Merriam noted that there were numerous cases where business interests did not coincide with the interests of the majority of the community, causing "bitter and deplorable struggles with the mass of the people on the question of franchises, public ownership, strikes, schools or other similar problems involving the respective rights of the many and the few."[12]

Haley and Merriam were active participants and frequently allies in these struggles over public issues. Each understood the role of interest groups and the power of the business community. They knew that "the great drama of urban life," as Merriam described it, was being played by organizations. The grade teachers of Chicago defied the business elite and established a long-term identity with one particular organized interest when they voted to affiliate with the Chicago Federation of Labor. Applying lessons learned in the tax fight and aware of the importance of voting power, Haley hoped to create a partnership of working-class interests bringing together the factory, the home, and the school. She placed her faith in this alliance as the means to further democratic reform including the ballot for women. Merriam had great respect for the CTF version of urban liberalism. In reviewing the record of the organization, he wrote that as "a well organized and aggressively led group the Federation has had no superior among all the groupings of the City, even among the professionally political organizations."[13]

The success of the CTF in civic life surprised even Haley. In a 1903 letter responding to an inquiry about teacher organizations from another city, she wrote:

> The work of our organization has grown to such an extent that we now have an office which is open every day of the week during business hours. We have a stenographer, and we are continually adding to our office equipment.
> The funny thing about all this is that the business world with which we are daily coming in contact takes the whole thing for granted as if there was nothing unusual about it. The office of the Teachers' Federation and the Federation itself is as much an accepted fact and as essential a part of the business of Chicago now as the Board of Trade, the City Hall, or even the Board of Education itself. The part which the Teachers' Federation will take in the civic question as well as the educational problems is a

[12]Merriam, *Chicago*, pp. 108-10.

[13]J. Joseph Huthmacher, "Urban Liberalism and the Age of Reform," *Mississippi Valley Historical Review*, 49 (Sept., 1962), pp. 231-41; Merriam, *Chicago*, p. 126.

matter of as much interest and inquiry as is the attitude of the Federation of Labor, the Civic Federation or the Municipal Voters' League, or even the newspapers on these questions.

That the Teachers' Federation will take a position is never questioned; we have got beyond that point.[14]

From this established position, the CTF moved next into politics.

Political activity in Chicago was regulated by mayoral elections held every two years until 1907 and every four years thereafter. The great ethnic diversity and pattern of settlement created a feudal system of factional politics described by Merriam as "an intricate tangled skein virtually impossible to disentangle." Leaders of the factions within the two major parties sought the office of mayor as a source of patronage and control. Those who succeeded in building the necessary political coalitions included three career politicians: two Democrats, Edward F. Dunne (1905-1907) and William Dever (1923-1927), and a Republican, Fred Busse (1907-1911). Two others who have been described as upper-class notables were able to combine party support and broad electoral appeal: a Democrat, Carter Harrison II (1897-1905 and 1911-1915), and a Republican, William Hale Thompson (1915-1923 and 1927-1931). The era of shifting party strength from 1897 to 1931 ended with the election of a Democrat, Anton Cermak, which introduced the long domination of the Cermak-Kelly-Nash machine.[15]

The election of Mayor Dunne in 1905 was a victory for the CTF. Dunne was an Irish Catholic who built an effective coalition which brought together ethnic machine politicians and progressive reformers. The organized teachers had campaigned vigorously for causes which he endorsed and had been particularly effective in securing signatures on petitions supporting such issues as municipal ownership of the street railways and legislation for an elected school board. Since Illinois law enabled women to vote for school elections, the latter issue would help the CTF in its efforts to protect salaries and to bring democracy to the school system. Haley remembered the high value her Irish immigrant mother had placed on education and knew that in a city where approximately three-fourths of the population were either first or second generation, the school issue was of vital importance.

With Haley as a member of his "Kitchen Cabinet" and his "silent" advisor on school affairs, Dunne's appointments to the Board of Education were unprecedented. Persons who supported the democratic aspirations of the CTF were appointed; three of his first seven

[14]Margaret A. Haley to Franklin S. Edmonds, June 2, 1903, CTF Files. Unfortunately, there are very few letters of such richness preserved in the CTF collection.

[15]Merriam, *Chicago*, pp. 97-98; Donald S. Bradley and Mayer N. Zald, "From Commercial Elite to Political Administrator: The Recruitment of Mayors in Chicago," *American Journal of Sociology*, 71 (Sept., 1965), pp. 160-64.

appointees were women. As a result, the Dunne school board, unlike previous boards, was not dominated by businessmen. From Haley's perspective, businessmen had very clear interests, primarily associated with keeping taxes low, which usually conflicted with the needs of either the children or the teachers.

From the beginning, the Dunne Board was surrounded by controversy. This experience offered "Gentle Jane," as Haley derisively called Jane Addams, a lesson in practical politics which Addams painfully recorded in her book, *Twenty Years at Hull House*. The board considered such controversial issues as school land leases, the pension system, the promotional system, and teacher councils. On each of these issues, Addams sought agreement which would satisfy the various factions concerned with evolving school policy. Her failure to follow the recommendations of the CTF distressed Haley, whose disappointment with Addams is evident in both women's versions of this episode. The controversies which surrounded the school board helped Busse defeat Dunne in 1907.

School tensions were eased in 1909, when a new board appointed Ella Flagg Young to the superintendency. Young, a long-time Chicago school administrator who advocated advisory teachers' councils, was greatly admired by Haley. She was the first woman to hold such a position in a city school system. Significantly, Young was able to effectively blend the workings of an efficient administrative bureaucracy with the participatory aspirations of the teachers during her almost six years of service.

When former Mayor Dunne was elected governor in 1912, the CTF and the Federation of Labor stepped up lobbying activity in the state legislature and campaigned hard for enactment of such progressive reforms as the initiative and referendum and for defeat of a vocational bill which would create a dual system of schools. Governor Dunne, who derived major support from the Irish Catholic community of Chicago, supported these reform measures. His administration reflected the workings of urban liberalism at the state level.[16] In general, the issues supported by Chicago's business community, including the Cooley vocational bill, were those opposed by the CTF and the CFL.

[16]John D. Buenker, *Urban Liberalism and Progressive Reform* (New York: Charles Scribner's Sons, 1973), pp. 10-11, 37 (hereafter cited as Buenker, *Urban Liberalism*). A recent article which reviews the literature on the role of Irish Americans is Robert Sean Wilentz, "Industrializing America and the Irish: Towards a New Departure," *Labor History*, 20 (Fall, 1979), pp. 579-98. The civic activism of Haley and the women teachers does not support the conclusions of a recent study which analyzed the capsule biographies found in the first edition of *Woman's Who's Who* (1941). The author contends that women educators had "a lower political consciousness than women in the professions" and that they "did not feel the need to reform society." Barbara Kuhn Campbell, *The "Liberated" Woman of 1914: Prominent Women of the Progressive Era* (Ann Arbor, Mich.: UMI Research Press, 1979), p. 179.

On the local level, the period of calm which had seemed to prevail under Mrs. Young's superintendency collapsed in 1915 when a new school board, under the administration of Mayor Thompson, mounted a direct attack on Haley and her organization. William ("Big Bill") Thompson introduced a new order of urban politics to Chicago. In the campaign for mayor, his advisors cut out Progressive reformers and party professionals. Using techniques perfected by both, the campaign played upon ethnic prejudices and hostilities. The "little red schoolhouse" was a major issue as the Thompson forces deliberately cultivated the newly enfranchised women voters. Dark hints and allegations were directed at the CTF, suggesting that the Catholic church had undue influence in the public schools and that Irish Catholics controlled the teachers' organization. Since Catholics were the only major group sufficiently alienated from the common school movement to create their own alternative school system, these suggestions had a strong nativist appeal, despite the lack of evidence to support them. Confirming the fears of his opponents, once in office Thompson proved to be a spoilsman. He used his position to gain control and patronage over the administrative agencies which the reformers had established to manage such services as health care, public utilities, and transportation.[17] Given the magnitude of the Board of Education's budget and the public interest in school issues, the CTF was a likely target for the Thompson forces.

The attack from the Board of Education came by way of a resolution which denied teachers the right to belong to any organization affiliated with trade unions or employing business agents. When this rule, named for its sponsor, Jacob M. Loeb, was applied in 1916, sixty-eight teachers were ousted.[18] Thirty-eight of them were members of the CTF, including all eight of the officers. The board majority portrayed Haley and her associates as "lady labor sluggers," and in so doing conveyed the image that these foes of entrenched privilege themselves served a "special interest" detrimental to the public good. Whether the special interest was interpreted to be organized labor, the Democratic party, or the Catholic church, business leaders, angered by Haley's political activities, supported this move. The CTF once again sought redress through the city and state governmental system including the courts. This astounding affair was eventually resolved with the teachers re-

[17]Barry D. Karl, *Charles E. Merriam and the Study of Politics* (Chicago: University of Chicago Press, 1974), p. 79 (hereafter cited as Karl, *Merriam*); Reid, "Professionalization," pp. 161-63. See also the *Day Book* (a small Chicago daily newspaper), Feb. - Apr. 5, 1915.

[18]Jacob M. Loeb, the president of a fire insurance company, was appointed as a Jewish representative on the board by Mayor Harrison. His action in leading the board attack on the organized teachers led Carl Sandburg to write a poem dedicated to Loeb. This was published in the *Day Book*, Sept. 8, 1915, during Sandburg's years as a reporter for that publication. It is reprinted in Appendix A.

stored one year later, a secure tenure law enacted, and the school administrative structure and board reorganized. Unfortunately, in the process the CTF affiliation with organized labor was abandoned and Haley's grand design for urban reform using the combined support of the working class and enfranchised women was aborted.

While the Loeb rule struggle did not destroy the CTF, it sowed seeds of internal decay. Formal affiliation with the Chicago Federation of Labor was ended as the teachers were forced to compromise with both Thompson and the hated board president, Jacob M. Loeb, to secure the return of their members. The reelection of Thompson in 1919 kept one of the nation's most corrupt administrations in power. Extensive graft and abuse of the large educational budget served only to weaken the public school system.

Yet another turbulent political episode was introduced with the election of William Dever as a reform mayor in 1923. The school board brought a new superintendent, William McAndrew, from New York to head the school system. Within a few weeks, Haley considered him to be simply a tool of the business interests. McAndrew raised a storm of controversy by abolishing the advisory teachers' councils, establishing a system of junior high schools, and implementing a platoon form of scheduling. Once again, a battle over the schools took place with Haley and the CTF leading the opposition, aided by organized labor.[19] In Haley's words, McAndrew "played the devil in the schools." Eventually, she succeeded in ousting him from Chicago. But all of this provided the Republican, "Big Bill" Thompson, with still another opportunity to exploit the school issue and he was returned to the office of mayor for a third term in 1927.

The problems of keeping pace with a system which found more children not only attending schools, but staying in the schools for more years of education, were compounded by the fiscal abuses of the corrupt Thompson board. Well before the Great Crash of 1929, the public schools of Chicago were in serious financial difficulty. As this crisis deepened, Haley took an active role in the movement to secure more revenue. She placed her faith in a reassessment of all property in the city. Meanwhile, the schools kept in operation by borrowing against anticipated tax revenues. Thus when the depression struck the public schools were already in financial trouble and the teachers experienced repeated payless paydays. The plight of the Chicago teachers became known across the nation.

Haley reviews the fiscal situation during the period from 1927 to 1935 in chapters 10 and 11, "Nero Fiddles" and "Rome Burns." Given

---

[19]The McAndrew years provided the sociologist and educator, George S. Counts, with material for an excellent sociological study, *School and Society in Chicago* (New York: Harcourt, Brace and Co., 1928) (hereafter cited as Counts, *School and Society*).

the enormity of the crisis and the immediacy of her perspective, these are the weakest sections of the autobiography. However, the chapters provide insights on the impact of the Great Depression on public education. Haley's keen understanding of taxation was of particular value in this crisis, and her judgment was confirmed by the elaborate survey of the Chicago schools, conducted by George Strayer of Columbia University. It shared Haley's conclusion that the city's tax system was obsolete. A classic note of irony can be found in Haley's last lobbying effort before the Illinois legislature. At the 1935 session she worked to secure a reduction of the emeritus pension, which had been passed during the McAndrew years as an addition to that perquisite which had inspired the formation of the CTF in 1897. This reduction seemed necessary to prevent the closing of the Chicago schools and under those circumstances Haley supported it.

The themes of bureaucratization, feminism, and professionalism were inextricably linked to the active role the CTF played in urban affairs. The shift from village to urban life brought changes in school organization. Large, complex school systems could not be administered by local three-member boards such as Haley had experienced in Grundy County. In the 1890s, city school systems developed bureaucratic structures organized in hierarchical fashion and supported by rules and procedures aimed at efficient and orderly operation. School administrators and university presidents such as Andrew Draper in Cleveland and Nicholas Murray Butler in New York encouraged these reforms, which often paralleled developments in the business community. One administrator expressed this as follows: "Every business of large magnitude in the country recognizes the importance of placing the responsibility for any particular part of that business in the hands of one man or one woman. A railroad or bank in which each member of the board of directors was more or less a superintendent would be laughed to scorn, and its management would have but one outcome—utter failure. The same is true in schools."[20] In Chicago the principal advocate of administrative centralization was William Rainey Harper, president of the University of Chicago. With support from the business leaders of the community, described by one reformer as the "self-respecting comfortable class," Harper became chairman of a committee appointed by Mayor Harrison to study the public school system.[21]

The Harper Commission Report was hailed as "the most exhaustive and most authoritative contribution that has been made to the litera-

---

[20]Orville T. Bright, "Changes—Wise and Unwise—in Grammar and High School," *Addresses and Proceedings of the National Education Association*, 1895, p. 277 (hereafter cited as *Proceedings, NEA*). See also Tyack, *One Best System*, pp. 126-76.

[21]Andrew S. Draper, "The Crucial Test of the Public School System," *Journal of Education*, 47 (Jan., 1898), p. 19.

ture of city school administration." Essentially, it recommended a
shift of executive authority from the school board to professional
administrators. The board was to approve policy and to hire trained
managers to run the system. Responsibility for the curriculum, textbook selection, and the teaching staff, including appointment, promotion, and supervision, was to belong to the superintendent. A business
manager was to have similar stature in fiscal matters. Both officers
were to have a measure of security in the form of six-year terms. A
smaller board of education was to confine its concerns to educational
policy; old abuses such as political "pull" affecting teacher appointments and promotions and the manipulation of purchases, building
contracts, and land acquisitions were evils which the Harper plan
intended to correct. The recommendations of this 1898 commission set
the agenda for proponents of school centralization, termed administrative progressives by historian David Tyack, for the next thirty years.[22]

While the legislative proposals which resulted were being discussed,
Harper was quoted as saying that the tax structure could not support
an anticipated fifty-dollar-per-year salary increase for the teachers. To
bring more men into teaching as recommended in the report, Harper
suggested that any increases be paid to the small number of men
teaching in the system. The leaders of the CTF were enraged. As Haley
dramatized it, "the cause of women suffrage advanced further that day
than it had gone in fifty years in Illinois." Haley linked Harper with
John D. Rockefeller, the major benefactor of the new university, and
attacked the bill as an attempt to introduce the "one man power
system" of Standard Oil into the schools. In testimony before a legislative committee in Springfield, Haley said the Harper plan "provided
for a superintendent who would need to be omnipotent as well as
omnipresent in all parts of the system at all times, and capable of
perfect justice, and that the only instance in history where there had
been such a visitor to the earth was nineteen hundred years ago and
that he was crucified. . . . the teachers of Chicago did not believe that if
he returned to earth that he would come to Chicago by way of the
Midway Plaisance (University of Chicago)."[23] The bill was defeated.
Repeated attempts to secure similar legislation in subsequent sessions
were opposed successfully by the teachers and their labor allies.

In 1917, after twenty years of conflict, the issues of school bureaucri-
tization were finally resolved by the legislative act which also ended the
crisis surrounding the Loeb rule and the ouster of the sixty-eight

[22]Nicholas Murray Butler, "Educational Progress of the Year," *Educational Review*,
18 (Sept., 1899), p. 174; *Report of the Educational Commission of the City of Chicago*
(Chicago: Lakeside Press, 1899) (hereafter cited as *Report of the Educational Commission*).

[23]Margaret Haley, "Autobiography," Seattle transcript, 17th installment, Feb. 6, 1912,
CTF Files.

teachers. The Otis bill not only provided a secure tenure system for urban teachers but also reduced the school board to eleven members and gave statutory authority to the superintendent.

Those who worked for clearer definitions of administrative responsibility rarely gave attention to the role of teachers. In Chicago, however, educators such as Francis W. Parker of the Cook County Normal School and John Dewey at the University of Chicago made this issue a topic of concern. Identified with the education of teachers, they recognized the need for a professional role for this group. Autonomy in the classroom was one necessity and tenure and pension laws were valuable in this regard. But to prevent isolation in the schools and to promote professional identity, a system of representation through teachers' councils from building to district to central system was recommended. The leading theorist for this was a Chicago district superintendent, Ella Flagg Young, who wrote her doctoral dissertation on the subject under Dewey's supervision. She argued for advisory roles on such important educational matters as the course of study and the selection of textbooks. She warned that the efficiency movement tended to develop a system which would be viewed as "a great machine" for the processing of children into educated citizens.[24]

With the support of the school board, Superintendent Edwin G. Cooley worked to strengthen executive authority during his term of office from 1900 to 1909. Cooley established a merit plan based on administrative review, abandoned the de facto teachers' council system, and failed to support the teachers in their salary fight. This enabled Haley to argue that school reform as advocated by centralizers such as Cooley and his business supporters denied principles of democracy within the schools and thereby deprived both teachers and the people of their rights. The theme of democracy in the schools reflected the same participatory philosophy within the system as did local and state crusades, endorsed by Haley, for such legislation as the initiative, referendum, direct election of senators, and woman suffrage.

The issue of how the schools were to be managed received major attention from the short-lived Dunne school board. Lengthy reports on the merit system and the teachers' councils were written and debated.[25]

[24]Ella Flagg Young, *Isolation in the Schools* (Chicago: University of Chicago Press, 1901), pp. 12, 17.

[25]Jane Addams described the movement toward administrative centralization in *Twenty Years at Hull House*. As she reviewed her service on the Board of Education, she wrote that the "one cure for 'pull' and corruption was the authority of the 'expert'." She then warned of the dangers of a system which relied too heavily on administrative authority at the expense of those teaching within the system. Addams concluded that the struggle between the superintendent and the teachers had become "an epitome of the struggle between efficiency and democracy." Jane Addams, *Twenty Years at Hull House* (New York: Macmillan, 1911), pp. 333-35 (hereafter cited as Addams, *Hull House*).

the system in the years 1909 to 1915; she restored the teachers' councils and maintained a close working relationship with Haley and Catherine Goggin. Following the reorganization of the schools after the passage of the Otis Law, the board acted to recognize the councils officially. This recognition included released time from the school day for the council meetings. When Superintendent McAndrew moved to discard the advisory system, he precipitated a four-year losing battle with Haley and her followers. To Margaret Haley bureaucratization had a direct relationship to the increasing concentration of wealth. She viewed both developments as evils. School centralization, particularly as represented by men such as Cooley and McAndrew, were manifestations of the efforts by business interests to control schools at the expense of the people.

Haley gave recognition to her own role in the women's movement when she wrote that the suffrage campaign advanced more in one day than it had in fifty years as the result of William Rainey Harper's call for salary increases for men teachers only. The concern regarding the low numbers of males in the grade school classrooms was real; Chicago reflected the feminization of the schools which took place in the last half of the nineteenth century. The percentage of women teachers in the United States increased from 59 percent in 1870 to 70 percent in 1900; in urban centers such as Chicago, approximately 2 percent of the elementary teachers were men at the turn of the century.[26] Significantly higher percentages of men were found in the high school classrooms and the administrative ranks. The result of this pattern of staffing was that a disproportionate number of men held those jobs which provided both higher pay and higher status. Women in the schools were expected to play a subordinate role, similar to that found in the society at large outside the schools.

The 1898 Harper Report had said the Chicago schools needed teachers who possessed broad culture and sound professional training. In describing why many teachers fell short of this standard, the report cited political influence in appointment and promotion and concluded that, as a result, "there is sure to be a large number of incompetents within the force." The inference seemed clear: given the large numbers of women teachers and the recommendation that men be paid higher salaries, the incompetents were primarily located in the ranks of the women grade teachers.[27]

The members of the Chicago Teachers' Federation were understandably sensitive to such allegations from an eleven-member commission

[26]Tyack, *One Best System*, p. 61.
[27]*Report of the Educational Commission*, p. 64.

composed exclusively of males. The CTF had been formed to defend a pension system which favored women teachers by enabling them to retire after twenty years of service while requiring twenty-five years for men. Further, the fixed pension of $600 for life was paid to all regardless of the larger contributions made by the higher-paid male teachers and administrators. When the men principals' organization sought to change this system in 1897, the women teachers organized. The successes gained in defending the pension law and in defeating the Harper bill provided important lessons in political activity for Haley and her colleagues. This experience, in turn, enabled the women teachers to support the tax fight, the affiliation with organized labor, and participation in civic reform. Harper's sexist remarks helped to stimulate the awakening conscience of women.

Chicago was well served by women activists during the Progressive Era. Among these were the four other "maiden aunts" who looked after the city. Identified by William Hard, a *Chicago Tribune* reporter, they were Jane Addams and Julia Lathrop of Hull House, Mary McDowell of the University of Chicago Settlement, and Dr. Cornelia DeBey, a close friend of Haley and a Dunne appointee to the school board. Other prominent women reformers included Margaret Dreier Robins, Florence Kelley, Alice Hamilton, Grace and Edith Abbott, and Sophonisba Breckinridge. These Progressives were primarily associated with social work and their political activism was not as intense or direct as that of Margaret Haley. This led Hard to write of her work, "It is a political career unparalleled in the history of the women of America."[28]

Women's awareness found expression in Haley's efforts to broaden and reform the National Education Association. The movement culminated in 1910 with the Chicago teachers electing Ella Flagg Young to the presidency. Thus Young was the first woman to serve as the administrative head of a large city school system and the first woman president of the NEA. Haley was credited as the master hand who guided the election campaign; the press celebrated the result as a "triumph without parallel in the history of women's organization." From that point on, the NEA gave much greater attention to the needs and concerns of the classroom teacher.[29]

A recent study of the woman suffrage movement by Ellen Dubois concludes that participation in the suffrage campaign did far more than the eventual vote to create "the basis for new social relationships between men and women." Activity in the movement demonstrated

[28]William Hard, "The Fight for the Schools," *The Times Magazine*, 1 (Feb., 1907), p. 367.

[29]Reid, "Professionalization," p. 229.

what the leaders had expected—"that self government and democratic participation in the life of the society was the key to women's emancipation."[30] Governor Edward F. Dunne of Illinois held a similar view on women's struggle for the ballot in his state. When the former Democratic mayor signed the suffrage law in 1913, the political leaders of the campaign, Mrs. Grace Wilbur Trout, Mrs. Antoinnette Funk, and Mrs. Sherman Booth, were present at the ceremony. So was Haley, who listened as Dunne said it was the work of Haley and the CTF for good government in the city and state which had converted him to the cause of woman suffrage.[31]

In an early draft of her autobiography written in 1912, Haley listed enfranchisement of women first in a series of political reforms which she thought were necessary to democratize the public school system. Speaking at an annual meeting of the NEA in 1914, she told her audience, "Men politicians care only for the fate of those who have the ballot in their hands."[32] Yet in the final version of her book she failed to mention her role in the 1913 suffrage campaign while giving detailed consideration to the defeat of the initiative and referendum in that session of the Illinois legislature. In her last chapter Haley wrote that her story is that of her organization. She used a rather common disclaimer when she stated that she wrote "with no intention" of extending her personality—the normal "desire of all autobiographers." This may explain her failure to discuss the personal recognition she received in the suffrage victory. But a more likely explanation rests with the results of enfranchisement. Certainly from the vantage point of the 1930s, there was little to cheer in terms of the impact women had on American political campaigns. On the municipal level Thompson exploited the "little red schoolhouse" issue, usually to advantage, in each election beginning with the mayoral campaign of 1915. On the national scene reformers were unable to find evidence that women voters had changed significantly either the quality or the results of the political process. Had Haley been able to write her story in the 1970s, no doubt she would have addressed the women's movement in greater detail. Whatever the explanation, however, Haley chose to ignore her role in the passage of the suffrage law. Nevertheless her example of

[30]Ellen Carol DuBois, *Feminism and Suffrage: The Emergence of an Independent Women's Movement in America, 1848-1869* (Ithaca, N.Y.: Cornell University Press, 1978), pp. 201-2.

[31]Illinois was the first state east of the Mississippi River to grant women the right to vote. Carrie Chapmen Catt called the victory in Illinois a "turning point" in the national suffrage campaign. Catt and Nettie Rogers Shuler, *Women Suffrage and Politics: The Inner Story of the Suffrage Movement* (New York: Charles Scribner's Sons, 1923); *Chicago Record Herald*, June 27, 1913; *Margaret A. Haley Memorial Booklet* (Chicago: n.p., 1939), pp. 17-18, CTF Files (hereafter cited as *Haley Memorial Booklet*).

[32]*Journal of Education*, 80 (July 13, 1914), p. 91.

organizational skill and political effectiveness made a significant contribution to the feminist cause; for that she deserves greater recognition.

The theme of professionalization represented another front in Haley's story of conflict. Major differences in perspective on the subject of professionalizing the field of education existed between school administrators, who were primarily males, and women grade teachers. Both groups shared a common concern regarding the low status of the occupation of teaching, however. Writing in 1903, William McAndrew described teaching as the "rag-tag and bobtail" of the professions; Margaret Haley once portrayed teaching as a procession rather than a profession. Such characterizations, including that of Professor Charles Judd of the University of Chicago—"a mobile mob of women meditating matrimony"—were indicative of the transitory nature and low public regard for the field.[33] In an era of consolidation, the CTF provided a structural mechanism for moving from procession to profession. Through its vigorous participation in civic affairs, the formal organization acted both as a vehicle for change and as a referent group for its members. Improved salaries and pensions, job security, more adequate tax revenue, and a greater voice in school policy were specific items in Haley's agenda. These improvements were intended to enhance professional attitudes of self-respect and autonomy. The success of the CTF inspired other groups. Women grade teachers in urban areas throughout the country, from Boston to Los Angeles and St. Paul to Atlanta, modeled their organizations along its lines, but without labor affiliation. As an invited speaker and by correspondence, Haley helped to bring the story of the CTF to the women teachers of the nation.[34]

[33]McAndrew's description is found in "The Present Status of the Professions—Public School Teaching," *World's Work*, 5 (March, 1903), pp. 3187-93. Haley made this reference in her 1935 dictation, p. 748. She provides Judd's characterization in chapter 9, p. 222, of this volume.

Teachers' salaries and their relationship to professionalism were a subject of continuing concern. Haley's salary of $35 per month in 1880 compared with estimated averages of $124 for men and $48 for women in city schools as presented by David Tyack, *One Best System*, p. 62. Following World War I, salaries received considerable attention. The NEA reported that beginning teachers in Washington, D.C., would earn $500 per year while government clerks would start at $1200. A popular monthly published an article which stated that the average annual teacher's wage of $630.64 was $243 less than the average wage paid to scrubwomen in the U.S. Naval Yard in 1918. In the following year the U.S. Commissioner of Education, P. P. Claxton, stated that "teachers are now paid less for their work than any other class of workers. . . ." *NEA Proceedings, 1918*, pp. 724-40; *McCall's Magazine*, 46 (Sept., 1919), p. 2; "NEA Field Secretary to Superintendents and Boards of Education on the Subject of Teachers Salaries, February 24, 1919," leaflet in CTF Files.

[34]Haley was the invited speaker at meetings of teacher groups in Milwaukee, St. Paul, Philadelphia, and Boston. As evidence of her popularity, A. E. Winship reported that she often spoke five evenings per week during the initial stages of the tax fight. See correspondence in the CTF Files; *Journal of Education*, 51 (May 3, 1900), p. 285.

Other participants on the educational scene did not share Haley's priorities. The area of administration was emerging as a distinct class within the occupation, and the developing supervisory positions were held almost exclusively by schoolmen whose approach to the myriad problems of the city school system was administrative centralization. The bureaucratic hierarchical model sought by Chicago superintendents, including E. Benjamin Andrews, Edwin Cooley, and William McAndrew, clashed with the democratic aspirations of Haley and the organized teachers. As Haley made apparent, school politics were not limited to struggles between educators and representatives of the public, whether board members, councilmen, or legislators; they also involved internal conflict between different understandings of professionalism by teachers and administrators. This struggle, in turn, was marked by sex differentiation in that the grade teachers were almost exclusively women, while the superintendents and principals, with rare exceptions, were men.

On the national scene these discrepancies were also evident. The National Education Association was founded in 1857. Forty years later there were less than two thousand members, almost all of whom were city and state administrators, professors of education, and college presidents. Key leaders of the organization, such as Nicholas Murray Butler of Columbia University, endeavored to make the association a forum for this method of bureaucratic top-down authority. To Butler these philosopher-kings were the elite leaders responsible for the profession. The teachers were to follow their lead.[35] Instead, Haley recognized that the annual meetings of the NEA were a potential forum for addressing the problems of city school systems and of the teaching force. In 1901, Haley attended the meeting in Detroit and had the audacity to challenge the U.S. Commissioner of Education, William Torrey Harris, from the floor of the convention. Two years later in Boston she led a successful fight against a move by Presidents Butler of Columbia and Eliot of Harvard to give the NEA's president, rather than the state delegations, the power to appoint the nominating committee. She was also successful in establishing a committee to investigate the economic status of teachers. The next year Haley was given a place on the program, speaking on the topic, "Why Teachers Should Organize." Curiously, Haley did not refer to this speech in her autobiography. As a valuable historical document summarizing her agenda for the profession, it is included in the appendix to this volume.

Through the first two decades of the twentieth century, two forces

---

[35]On this subject see Richard F. Whittemore, *Nicholas Murray Butler and Public Education* (New York: Teachers College Press, 1970).

struggled for power within the NEA. Characterized as "insurgents" and "the Old Guard," the groups possessed certain identifiable features. The insurgents or progressives tended to be midwestern in geographic orientation and feminine in gender. Colorfully depicted as the "Great Unwashed" by Haley, this group included practitioners, a majority of whom were classroom teachers, and spokespersons for the normal school movement. The Old Guard or conservative element, in contrast, represented an eastern orientation and was composed primarily of established schoolmen who acted in administrative and university teaching roles. The intense and sometimes bitter conflict between these groups was to last until the 1920s.[36] By successfully exploiting the opportunity to enroll large numbers of local teachers while taking advantage of special convention rates from the railroads, the Chicago teachers were able to use their contacts in other cities to secure results. The most notable of these was the election of Ella Flagg Young to the presidency in 1910 at the Boston meeting. The grade teachers then created a federation of teacher organizations. This National League of Teacher Associations was formed by twenty-two organizations including the CTF in 1912. The following year the NEA responded with a new section, the Department of Classroom Teachers, another reflection of the growing sensitivity to the needs of the "Great Unwashed." Haley ended her chapter on the NEA with the Chicago meeting held in 1912. Her neglect of later developments is difficult to explain; it may simply show her general satisfaction with the accomplishments to 1912 and her preoccupation with local affairs after that year. But it illustrates as well her strong identification with her own organization and her disenchantment with the national teacher movement in the 1920s and '30s.

Following World War I the NEA conducted a vigorous membership campaign which emphasized the unity of the profession. The goal of 100,000 members was reached in 1922. As enrollment grew, the town meeting approach became outmoded and a committee on reorganization was appointed in 1915. Margaret Haley attended the 1920 meeting in Salt Lake City and noted sardonically that the site was chosen to prevent "packing" of the convention by the masses of city teachers. She had successfully used this tactic the previous year in Milwaukee. At Salt Lake City the plan for a representative assembly of six hundred delegates was adopted and local domination of the annual meetings came to an end.

Haley's ambivalent reaction to the reorganization is found in chapter 8. It contains both triumph and defeat. The increasing membership of

[36]Reid, "Professionalization," pp. 201-46.

the NEA reflected the CTF goal of teacher participation, albeit often this came as the result of the urgings of the local administrators. By 1920, the patterns of alternating presidents of the NEA by gender was operational, giving evidence of the success of the feminist campaign. On the other hand, as the pioneer of the organized teacher movement, the CTF, through Haley's adroit political tactics, had been an influential force in the earlier reform of the association. The new structure with its representative assembly, based on state organizations and led by state and local administrators, seemed to reinforce the hierarchical nature of the public schools of the nation. The ability of Haley and the CTF to secure future changes was limited effectively by this new structure.

A similar experience occurred on the local level. In 1900, elementary teachers constituted 94 percent of Chicago's teachers. This percentage declined steadily with the success of the public school movement. The shaping of the high schools brought increasing numbers of high school teachers. In 1912, a small group of men teachers led by Herbert Miller, a charter member of the CTF, organized the Chicago Federation of Men Teachers. Two years later a Federation of Women High School Teachers was formed. Both federations secured charters from the American Federation of Labor as did the CTF. When the Loeb rule was passed in 1915, the teachers responded with a show of unity by creating a national teachers' union. Eight groups, including four from the Chicago area, established the American Federation of Teachers on May 9, 1916. The aims of the AFT, as stated in its constitution, closely followed those of the CTF. These vowed to raise the standard of the teaching profession, to obtain all rights to which [teachers] are entitled, to bring associations of teachers into relations of mutual assistance and cooperation, and to promote democratization of schools. The CTF, by far the largest organization, was chartered as Local Number One. Haley was designated national organizer. A man, Charles Stillman, was elected president since the high school federations were "well aware that Miss Haley believed that the Chicago Teachers' Federation must do its own fighting, that any strength in the new setup would necessarily be remote, that she believed in local and independent organizations."[37] As this passage from one of the first officers indicates, the local situation, centering on the school board's ouster of thirty-eight members of the CTF, demanded Haley's attention.

Giving evidence of the parochialism of her interests, Haley referred only to the withdrawal of the CTF from the AFT, which she described

---

[37] The statement was made by Freeland G. Stecker, a Chicago teacher and financial secretary of the AFT, in a mimeographed history of the organization, "The First Ten Years." *Ibid.*, pp. 248-49.

as a "recently organized fledgling." Further, she obscured the reasons for withdrawal from the ranks of organized labor in May, 1917. That action was necessary to gain the return of the ousted thirty-eight CTF members and to secure passage of a sound tenure system through the Otis Law. Haley lamely explained the capitulation as a response to America's entry into World War I. She wrote that the support of Samuel Gompers and other labor leaders for intervention "alienated the great body of teachers in the Chicago public schools from the American Federation of Labor." Her strong Irish heritage with its hatred of Great Britain is evident in this account. However, in retrospect it seems the immediate concern for protecting the teachers from future reprisals made political accommodation with Mayor Thompson and board president Loeb a matter of the highest priority.

The two small high school federations were of little consequence in the struggle between the board and the CTF. Thus, they were not forced to withdraw from the AFT. Haley's personal friendship with John Fitzpatrick, president of the Chicago Federation of Labor, who recommended the withdrawal, continued through the rest of her life. She served as an officer of the Women's Trade Union League and on the executive committee of the Labor party which ran Fitzpatrick for mayor in 1919. It was expected that some day the CTF would return formally to the ranks of organized labor.

This did not occur. Instead, tensions grew between the high school federations and Haley's organization. As one veteran of this period noted, younger teachers were not impressed with Haley's "continued reference to past triumphs" nor her "unwillingness to cooperate in any activity she could not control."[38] There were also issues of substance. Haley favored a single salary schedule for all teachers in the system regardless of grade level or sex. Since high school salaries were substantially higher, little support was found outside the grade schools for such a concept. The high school teachers did not support Haley's strong opposition to McAndrew's junior high school system. As the financial crisis deepened in the late 1920s, the high school federations and the CTF split over tactics. The former wished to press for tax rate increases and to follow the old CTF strategy of legal action against tax dodgers. Haley placed her faith in the reassessment of all property in the city. Neither approach proved successful when the schools of Chicago, which had been partially financed by borrowing against anticipated tax revenue, were hit severely by the Great Depression.

By the mid 1930s, Haley devoted much of her limited energy to the completion of her autobiography. Apparently the CTF hoped that the

---

[38]Herrick, *Chicago Schools*, p. 238.

recounting of her story would help inspire confidence in the pioneer organization of the nation's teacher movement. However, as Haley's health worsened, the two high school federations encouraged the formation of new units including a direct rival, the Elementary Teachers Union. These groups combined in 1937 to create a new entity, the Chicago Teachers' Union, which was granted the old CTF position of Local Number One by the American Federation of Teachers. Haley bitterly opposed these developments and the CTF refused offers to become part of the new union. A victim of heart disease, Margaret Haley died in January, 1939, at the age of seventy-seven. Her organization, beset with factionalism following her death, lingered on until 1968, when it officially closed its doors.

In retrospect, both within the school system and on the national scene, the teachers of Chicago challenged the approach to professional advancement conveyed by the administrative class and rejected the corporate model of school goals and governance. Further, Haley and her followers set in motion a radical alternative to unity from the top down in the form of unionization. In the enthusiasm of insurgent reform, the CTF found that respectability and autonomy could be achieved best through affiliation with the working class. Viewing themselves as under-represented, underpaid, and overworked, the teachers joined the ranks of organized labor to advance their understandings of professionalism.

With the withdrawal from the American Federation of Teachers in 1917 and the reorganization of the National Education Association in 1920, the members of the CTF were estranged from the two national organizations which they had helped to shape. The NEA, spurred by an effective membership campaign, would become a large organization which reflected the hierarchical school systems of the nation. The AFT also experienced a strong burst of union activity after World War I before going into precipitous decline during the 1920s. AFT locals in large cities survived, however, to become the centers for a new phase of organizational activity some forty years later when both the NEA and the AFT came to accept the CTF model of professional organization for teachers only.

Margaret Haley was a remarkable woman whose life story presents the response of a particular individual to the forces of modernization. Her crusading spirit, shaped by the depression experience of the 1890s and emboldened by her successes in the insurgent progressive movement in Chicago, retained a vibrant consistency throughout her career. To the end Haley considered reform as a fight of "the people" versus "privilege" or "the public interests" versus "the selfish interests" in true progressive fashion. Given this outlook and her determined, aggressive personality, Haley, in contrast to Jane Addams, publically challenged the stereotype of women as gentle, intuitive, and submissive. Even her choice of titles for her autobiography—"Battleground" or "Forty Fighting Years"—were evidence of Haley's personal identification with "unladylike" qualities.

As a personality Haley evoked strong responses from others. Described as anathema to her opponents, she was portrayed as a militant, a radical, a lady labor slugger, a character assassin, and an advocate of mob rule. Frequently these descriptions came from those who used such slogans as "take the schools out of politics" to maintain their own positions. But the intensity of the labels also reflects the reaction of others to Haley's tendency to dramatize and even to exaggerate situations and personalities. To her admirers and friends Haley was a skilled organizer and master of political tactics. Called tireless, brilliant, courageous, warm, and witty, most frequently she was described as dynamic. Through the years she was depicted as "a modern Joan of Arc in civic affairs," one of the "Five Maiden Aunts" who made things happen in Chicago, an orator in the tradition of John Altgeld and Robert LaFollette, and the Patrick Henry of the classroom teacher movement.[39]

Two observers of the Chicago scene provided insightful commentaries on the personality of Haley. Carl Sandburg, while a reporter for the *Day Book*, a small Chicago daily, described her as a pervasive force in the community, who figured from day to day in events that held city-wide attention. In 1915, he wrote: "for fifteen years this one little woman has flung her clenched fist into the faces of contractors, school land lease holders, tax-dodgers and their politicians, fixers, go-betweens and stool pigeons. . . . Over the years the Tribune, the News and the ramified gang of manipulators who hate Margaret Haley have not been able to smutch her once in the eyes of decent men and women of this town who do their own thinking." In an article in *Reedy's Mirror*, Sandburg concluded: "A little woman, but a dynamic living force now. A little woman, but she will be a rare memory of the labor world and of politics at a later time when the biographers, the portrait painters of Clio, do their calm work."[40]

At the time of her death, Richard Finnegan was the editor of the *Chicago Times*. His long career as a Chicago reporter had closely paralleled Haley's public life. As is evident in the autobiography,

---

[39]Merriam, *Chicago*, p. 216; A. E. Winship, "A Woman's Victory for Schools," *Everybody's Magazine*, 7 (Oct., 1902), p. 393; William Hard, "Chicago's Five Maiden Aunts," *American Magazine*, 62 (Sept., 1906), pp. 481-89; Sandburg, "Margaret Haley," p. 445; R. R. Smith, "The Changing National Education Association," *National League of Teachers Associations Bulletin*, 13 (Apr., 1930), pp. 29-37.

[40]*Day Book*, Sept. 24, 1915; Sandburg, "Margaret Haley," p. 445.

Haley recognized the importance of the news media and she established many effective relationships with members of the press. Finnegan recalled his own association with her and gave this description: "a little woman with a pleasant smile and charming manner, a friendly voice, rich eyes that understood much and saw a lot—saw realities and humors of life—eyes that were anxious to twinkle with an inherited Irish gaiety but eyes that were looking mostly for the answers to challenging questions, questions that gave her voice, her whole personality a vibrancy and aliveness." Reporting Margaret Haley, Finnegan said, "a newspaperman was privileged to observe and to write one of the greatest stories of Chicago."[41]

Sandburg and Finnegan were newsmen who identified with Haley's civic activism. Among her most constant foes were two of the city's major newspapers, the *Tribune* and the *Daily News*. This was the result of her unrelenting opposition to the favorable long-term leases of school lands held by the publishing firms. Despite this record of conflict, the *Daily News* paid strong tribute to her in its editorial pages. Calling her "the embodiment of informed and fearless citizenry in action," the editorial offered an eloquent eulogy: "Now Margaret Haley is dead. She fought a good fight. By her example she charted for all of us the method by which well-administered government is to be gained and kept."[42]

Margaret Haley possessed a keen sense of history and carefully preserved those records which provided documentation for her speeches and writings, such as the CTF periodicals which included the *CTF Bulletin* published from 1901 to 1908 and *Margaret Haley's Bulletin*, 1915-1916 and 1925-1930, complete stenographic reports of mass meetings and legal cases, and detailed minute books. These tools, which she called upon regularly, are valuable historical documents.

On four separate occasions Haley prepared material for her autobiography. In 1910, following Ella Flagg Young's election at the Boston meeting of the NEA, she dictated an account of the tax fight while vacationing at a lodge in Allenton, Massachusetts. She resumed work on this in December, 1911, following her suffrage campaign work on the west coast. This Seattle manuscript included events through 1911. In June, 1929, she prepared a lengthy account of the reassessment story. Then, in the late summer and fall of 1935, following a long period of rest at Palos Verdes, California, she dictated an

---

[41]*Haley Memorial Booklet*, p. 17. Finnegan (1884-1955) covered nearly every beat in the city prior to assuming the position of editor of the *Times* in 1929. His last five years were spent as consulting editor for the *Sun Times*.

[42]*Chicago Daily News*, Jan. 10, 1939.

846-page narrative which is rambling, disorganized, and sometimes overstated.

These materials were reviewed and edited by a former newspaper reporter and writer, Mary Synon, who had assisted Haley in preparing speeches and position papers for several years. With her help Haley wrote a final version which she intended to call either "Battleground" or "Forty Fighting Years." The CTF initiated a campaign to sell advance copies to members in 1936. The publicity release reviewed her significant achievements in local and state affairs and concluded: "For forty years she has been showing by deeds the part the teacher can play in the body politic. Now by words she shows how the war waged by a small group of teachers may be continued and enlarged to insure ultimate freedom for the schools. Her chronicle is a new beacon in the long and struggling history of real American democracy. No one, in or out of the schools, who has an interest in the freedom of educators and education, can afford to miss this dynamic story of a splendid fight in this cause."[43]

The book project was an effort to strengthen the CTF in its struggle with the rival teacher organizations moving to establish a unified Chicago Teachers' Union. When no publisher was found, the net effect was a further drain on the finances of Haley's organization. Failing health kept her from renewing the effort and the publication was abandoned.

The final version of the autobiography is a reflection of the period in which it was written. Haley shaped her story around themes which she considered to be of continuing relevance. By her selection, as has been suggested earlier in this introduction, Haley neglected to amplify certain other topics. The most important of these were the CTF's participation in the ranks of organized labor and the movement to gain the vote for women. Key elements in her agenda during the progressive years, each of these topics had lost considerable significance after World War I and she either ignored or distorted certain episodes related to them. From today's perspective more attention to them would enhance the narrative. But it should also be noted that Haley's response to the machine civilization as written in her last chapter retained the old progressive concerns regarding the forces of privilege. Her appeals for more democracy and better understanding of

---

[43]Mary Synon was a former public school teacher, a reporter for the *Chicago Journal*, and the author of numerous short stories, several novels, and a biography of William McAdoo. References to her work with the CTF are found in the CTF Files. A brief biography is located in Matthew Hoehn, ed., *Catholic Authors: Contemporary Biographical Sketches* (Newark: St. Mary's Abbey, 1948), pp. 723-24. In describing her own contribution, Synon indicated that she was "only the aid and in no way the author." Synon to Paul R. Reynolds, December 3, 1936, CTF Files.

the workings of the economic and political system continue to be essential for American civilization. Her recognition that effective participation by the people in making those decisions that directly affect them is the precondition for economic, political, and individual freedom in a democratic society is remarkably contemporary.[44]

Haley's narrative is a unique contribution to our understanding of the history of such major topics as urbanization, education, women, and labor. In his study of the urban reform movement, John Buenker deplores the fact that "so few of the practitioners of urban liberalism left any account of their activities in the form of memoirs or papers." The educational historian David Tyack reminds us that much of the written history of the schools "has revealed the perspective of those at the top of the educational and social system."[45] Haley brings the perspective of a woman, a labor organizer, a grade school teacher, and a member of the new stock to her story of Chicago. While she called the editorials in her *Bulletin* the "View from the Masthead," a more appropriate title would have been the "View from Beneath the Deck." Without Haley's story women grade teachers seem as unlikely a group as one might find in terms of effective organizational activity, but this volume contains important insights into the role of women, urban progressive reform, the development of the bureaucratic urban school system, and the beginnings of white collar unionism. Margaret Haley gives us a most unusual and significant account of America in the process of modernization.

My interest in Margaret Haley and the Chicago Teachers' Federation goes back to the summer of 1963, when I began research on the organization. Through the kindness of Grace Manton, CTF president, and Francis Kenney, who succeeded Haley as business representative, I was given permission to use the CTF collection. On my recommendation these records were donated to the Chicago Historical Society when the federation office was closed. The final version of the Haley manuscript, which was in the possession of Miss Kenney, was given to me prior to her death in 1968; it has been deposited in the collection at the Chicago Historical Society.

In preparing the manuscript I have retained the text of the Haley account in its entirety, including the few errors in spelling and grammar which she overlooked. As editor, I have expanded the text by adding footnotes which are intended to clarify Haley's statements and provide further information and identification. All of the footnotes are

---

[44]On the subject of self-portraits by women, see Estelle C. Jelinek, ed., *Women's Autobiographies: Essays in Criticism* (Bloomington: Indiana University Press, 1980).
[45]Buenker, *Urban Liberalism*, p. 208; Tyack, *One Best System*, p. 4.

the editor's modifications to the original narrative. Biographical information is taken from standard reference works such as *Who's Who in Chicago* and newspaper obituaries. Additions and corrections within the text are denoted with brackets. The appendices, illustrations, and index complete the editor's contributions.

Many people have contributed to this book. I am indebted to members of the Haley family—in particular, Gerald J. Haley, Jr., and his sister, Margaret, who are descendents of Margaret A. Haley's brother, Dennis—for their cooperation and endorsement of this project. John H. Keiser, Ronald Shaw, Sherry Darrell, Lorman Ratner, Richard Clokey, and Bette Walden read the introduction and offered helpful criticism and suggestions. Frederic C. Jaher of the University of Illinois provided a careful analysis of the entire manuscript. University support, including a research grant from the Indiana State University Evansville Foundation, has my special appreciation. Rebecca A. Clark typed the manuscript skillfully and the staff of the University of Illinois Press helped to guide the project to completion. Archie Motley, Curator of Manuscripts at the Chicago Historical Society, recognized the importance of the CTF materials and has been a continuing source of support and encouragement. From the beginning, Robert H. Wiebe of Northwestern University has been associated with my study of Haley and the CTF. I have benefitted immeasurably from his exemplary skills as both teacher and scholar, his insightful commentary on my writings, and his warm friendship. Finally, I am grateful for the patience and understanding of my wife, Joanne, and our children, Erik and Kristin.

Battleground:
The Autobiography of Margaret A. Haley

❧ I ❧

I Grow Up

1

I never wanted to fight.

When I look back over my seventy-five years of life, forty of them spent on hectic battle-fronts of the unending war, I realize that, like all crusaders, I have stormed in where kings and courtiers feared to tread. I have beaten my fists, and sometimes my head, against stone walls of power and privilege. I have railed at mayors, at governors, at legislators, at presidents of great universities. I have banged machine-guns in defense of certain basic principles in which I believed and continue to believe. For them I have fought without fear and without favor; but within my own soul I know that I have never sought a battle for its own sake, although I have never evaded one when it was forced upon me.

Now that my fighting days must be nearly over I say, as did Richelieu, that I have had no enemies save those of the state; and I add that, if I could have won the same results in any other way, I should never have fought at all.

It was my lot, however, to come into maturity just when women were struggling for political, economic, and social independence. It was the time of the Olive Schreiners, the Ellen Keys, the Susan B. Anthonys, the Lucy Stone Blackwells.[1] To win rudimentary justice, women had to battle with brain, with wit, and sometimes even with force. If you happened to be born wanting freedom for yourself, for

---

[1]Olive Schreiner (1855-1920) was a radical feminist who argued that women were superior to men. Her books included *The Story of an African Farm* (New York: H. M. Caldwell, 1883), *Women and Labor* (New York: Stokes, 1911), and *From Man to Man* (New York and London: Harper and Bros., 1927). Ellen Key (1849-1926) was a Swedish-born writer who held similar views and stressed the social importance of motherhood. Her best-known work was *Love and Marriage* (New York: G. P. Putnam and Sons, 1911). Susan B. Anthony (1820-1906) and Lucy Stone (1818-1893) were prominent leaders of the women's movement in the United States.

your group, for people at large, you had to fight for it—and you had to fight hard. Those of us who were flung on the frontier of the war for human rights had little choice of weapons or of battlegrounds. We had to make our own slings and arrows. If we have won with them anything of lasting value—and, in a way, I think that we have—it was because we knew that we were never fighting for ourselves alone. Always with us marched the army of the silent, the poor, the oppressed, the shackled. If we faltered, we had to remember them and keep on fighting.

I was born in war-time.

All through my childhood and my youth, the echoes of that war sang like bugles. Illinois had been not only the home of Abraham Lincoln but also the scene of Elijah Lovejoy's murder by the mob in defense of his Abolitionist printing presses. Joliet, the town of my birth, was fairly distant from Springfield and from Alton, but no child upon the Illinois prairies in the twenty years that followed Appomattox could grow up without consciousness that men lived in causes and for causes.

Freedom!

The thrill of it was in the air. Perhaps the vast dome of the midland sky and the great sweep of the midland prairies gave to us a stirring sense of the freedom of life. My first memory is of the sky, the vivid blueness of it above the bright gold of wheat fields. We had moved in my infancy from the town of Joliet to a farm three miles from Joliet. There we were to remain for ten years. There I was to receive those impressions which I realize now to have been the motivating purposes of long years spent in a great and growing city. On the farm I came into such consciousness of the beauty of the world that in later years I longed to make the loveliness of nature available to all children. If I have had a threading purpose through battling for a cause, it has been that desire. Always, as I looked at the wistful children of the city streets, I have remembered the happiness in which my own childhood was spent and ached in the wish that they might find something, at least, of such joy.

As families ran then, ours was small. My mother [Elizabeth Tyrrell? Haley], who had been born in Dublin, was one of thirteen children. According to tradition, I as the eldest daughter should have been weighted heavily with responsibility for my younger brothers and sisters. On the contrary, they took, even in childhood, the attitude to which they have held through life. Always they seemed to be trying to shield me from cares and burdens, to make no difficulties for me, to help me when I might need their help. Perhaps it was because I was very small, and often ill. At any rate, I have no recollection of ever having been responsible for the care of the younger Haleys. We all seemed to be growing up together, with no one of us imposed upon or imposing upon another.

There were eight of us Haley children, but only six of us grew into manhood and womanhood. My elder brother, Thomas, the only one older than myself, drowned when he was twelve years old. Strangely enough, there is a tradition in my father's family that the eldest son is always drowned. His eldest brother had lost his life by drowning, as had his father's eldest brother. Another one of us, a younger sister, died in her babyhood.

I was the second oldest, Jenny and Eliza came after me, then the three boys, James, Edward, and Dennis.

I was so tiny that once, when my mother took me to see my grandmother, the old lady, remembering the Irish superstition about the proper way to treat changelings whom the fairies had brought, said that they ought to put me out on a shovel. I did not know then the implication of her remark, but I did realize that there was something disparaging in it and I went outside the house to cry.

Except for a greater number of books and a more direct association with the world of events outside the farm, we lived, I think, after the fashion of most farm families of that time and place. We had reasonable security and comfort, but little luxury. Our interests and amusements were those of all farm children, riding on the horses that weren't being worked in the fields, driving to town for market day or church, playing with each other in old-fashioned games, I-spy, pom-pom-pull-away, King William-was-King George's-son, Farmer-in-the-dell, and What's-your-trade.

We had another game, not named, probably a relic of the destructiveness of war, and played by us only on Christmas Day. Then we stood in two lines and flung at each other the gifts we have received. If they broke, they broke. Once, when I had been given a little book illustrated by colored pictures of delectable ladies, I hesitated to enter the game lest I wreck the gift, for already I was treasuring it. The mob spirit of childhood took me into the fray, however, and I threw the book at the opposing line. But how gently I threw it, and how I prayed, as I threw, that it remain intact!

Sometimes even now I can see the look of the road on our way to school. In winter it was only a dark streak through the snow, but in summer it was a path of loveliness. Wild roses grew in hedges at either side. We children going to school walked in our bare feet through the cool dust. On the way between our farm and the schoolhouse we passed the place of a neighbor, a woman who watched for us every day to give us cookies and apples.

On our first day in school, we children had our own tragedy. We had left our lunch in the wagon of the man who drove us there and had to go hungry until he returned from town and left our lunch with the teachers.

My recollection of the school is that all of us there were very young, too young to work in the fields. I can't recall any particular interest which the school awakened in me. My mother taught us to read at home. Even then I could read from our big family Bible and from a pictorial history of Ireland, but the teacher never seemed to find out that I could read at all.

In the winter we couldn't go to school. The roads were impassable in the heavy snows. In the summer, however, we went to the little school nearest to the farm. It was a one-room structure, the ordinary country schoolhouse of its time. There was a seat across the back, and benches in front of it. The little children sat in the back. I don't remember that any one paid the least attention to us. We weren't asked to read, to write, to recite. I remember that I wanted to look into the geography that some of the older pupils used, but I never had the chance. The teacher asked me where I'd secured the pencil, the pen and ink, and the copy-book which my father had bought for me. I can't recall that she asked me any other questions. Certainly I asked her none. Children didn't question their elders then.

That silence, standing as a barrier between youth and age, seems to me now the essential and greatest difference between education then and education today. Parents and teachers in that time had an attitude toward children vastly different from the present-day idea. It wasn't exactly repression. It was simply a failure to include a child's mentality in adult consideration. Children asked no questions about a world which was supposed to be beyond their comprehension.

I remember that one winter afternoon I stood beside my mother and stared through the window at the falling snow. She was sewing on some little garment, perhaps for one of us, perhaps for the child who was coming. After awhile I saw that she was crying, although she was singing a hymn. I asked her no questions. She said nothing to me, but I understood perfectly the reason for her tears. My father was away from the farm, and she was fearful lest he be lost in the rising storm before he could reach home. It never occurred to me to ask her anything about the situation.

I always picked up information at home without direct conversation. Children didn't talk about events with their parents then. Nevertheless, they knew what was happening. There's an atmosphere in such a relationship that's different from the one established by question and answer. We'd hear my father and mother talking about things that were much bigger than the happenings in our family circle, and in a vague way I'd realize that beyond our way of life was another kind of existence; but I never asked them about it.

Although we lived for ten years on the farm our interests, even at that time, were not entirely of the soil. My father [Michael J. Haley] was not a farmer, and had to leave the running of the farm to hired help. He himself was never on the farm for any long span of continuous time. He was a builder of bridges, a worker in steel and stone, and I had the impression that he was far away from home for great periods of time.

Looking back at him now, I realize that he must have been far more remarkable than we, his children, understood then. He was born in Canada, and had come into the United States as a child. He had seen— he told me this after I had watched the glow in the sky from the Chicago fire—a convent burned by Know-Nothings in the east, and had decided, although he was but a boy then, to come westward.[2] He had found a job on the building of the Illinois and Michigan Canal. The job must have had other tasks, but he always referred to it as "jigger-carrying." Each man employed in the building of the canal was allowed a jigger of whisky a day. The jigger boy took it to them. Perhaps the experience influenced him to a sobriety that was rare in his time and group. For, although he was no prohibitionist, he never drank liquor.

From the canal work he had gone into structural contracting, but he continued his interest in waterways. He had a line of boats on the canal, carrying stone from the quarry near Channahon up to Chicago.

[2]It is likely that this was the burning of the Ursuline Convent in Charlestown, Mass., on the night of Aug. 11, 1834. The mob which participated in this episode was motivated by anti-Catholic and anti-Irish feelings. Later, such nativist sentiments led to the formation of the short-lived American or Know-Nothing party of the 1850s. Ray A. Billington, *The Protestant Crusade, 1800-1860: A Study of the Origins of American Nativism* (New York: Macmillan, 1938), pp. 68-76.

Michael J. Haley (1827-1905) was a delegate from the Joliet Knights of Labor to the Seamen's Hall Convention in March, 1884. At this meeting held in Chicago, the Illinois State Federation of Labor was formed and Michael J. Haley from Joliet was elected state treasurer. The historian of the ISFL noted that several ardent followers of Henry George attended the convention; among them was Haley who "described simply but effectively how he had seen the poor people of Ireland die of hunger while the land was monopolized by the rich." This passage does not square with Margaret Haley's statement that her father was born in Canada; perhaps he was describing experiences of his wife, who had come from Ireland. *Joliet Daily News*, Mar. 27, 1884; Eugene Staley, *History of the Illinois State Federation of Labor* (Chicago: University of Chicago Press, 1930), pp. 29-30, Appendix D; *Chicago Tribune*, May 6, 1905.

Haley was active in Joliet politics as both a Greenbacker and a member of the Trades and Labor Council. In the civic election of 1884, he was a leader of a "peoples" movement which brought victory to the Democratic ticket. *Joliet Daily News*, Mar. 25, 30, 31, Apr. 2, 1884.

He and his partner, F. T. Sherman, owned the quarry. Chicago was their market and place of business, but my father held, as long as he could, to the countryside.[3]

It was, I think, not merely love of the land which held him. It was some vision of the country itself. He knew every stone along the canal. They had been laid like keystones, accurately measured, marking the right-of-way. Later all record of them was lost, but he remembered them, for it had been part of his work to set them down when he rose to the rank of surveyor. He knew, too, the fundamental purpose of that waterway and of all the western waterways. He was one of their first advocates, seeing them as media for transportation of heavy materials like coal and iron and stone, and secondarily, as curbs on the railroads, that were, even then, throttling over transportation development. I can see him now, dynamic with energy, bent over maps of the Mississippi Valley, explaining to some caller methods and routes, seepage and drainage, boats and bridges.

He was, too, a student of economics. Of course, the aspect that intrigued him was the political. His work—the sale of stone for public buildings and the contracts for erection of these and bridges—naturally brought him into direct contact with politicians; but he remained, to the end of his life, an idealist and a theorist.

Afterward I was to come into understanding of the reasons for the sharp differentiation between the two types of Irish in American politics. I was to learn that the same cause—the oppression of their race in Ireland—had reacted differently on two divisions of the Irish people. Persecution had crushed one group of Irish into submission to an established authority and a correlative intention of getting from it, by fair means or foul, whatever might be grasped. It had roused the other group to continuing struggle against any and all injustice. The fighting Irish. The Tones and the Emmetts and the Parnells. In spirit my father was one of them. On the American midlands he thrilled to the war-pipes of Home Rule and Land League; but he also hearkened to

[3]The Illinois and Michigan Canal was built between 1838 and 1848. The canal linked Chicago on Lake Michigan with the Mississippi River and the Gulf of Mexico via the Des Plaines and Illinois rivers. Irish laborers from eastern cities were attracted to Illinois by the contractors to provide cheap labor for the project. Financial problems led to the issuance of scrip, which the state accepted as payment for land. Many of the workers turned to farming to support their families. William V. Pooley, *The Settlement of Illinois, 1830-1850*, Bulletin of the University of Wisconsin, no. 220, History Series (Madison: University of Wisconsin, 1908), pp. 390-91; James W. Putnam, *The Illinois and Michigan Canal* (Chicago: University of Chicago Press, 1918), pp. 70-71.

The quarry business was an auxiliary enterprise which developed to provide building materials for both the canal and the emerging city of Chicago.

the trumpets of the awakening political causes in our own United States.[4]

Looking back now to that time, I can see that it must have been one not unlike the present in economic difficulties and in the disturbance of people's minds because of them. I cannot recall the gist of the political discussions which I heard—for my mother never sent us children from the room where my father would be talking with his callers—but I remember the quality of excited tension which marked them. The Grange movement was rising then.[5] Men must have been talking matters of public finance, for I know that my father campaigned for Alexander Campbell when he went to Congress from our district on a greenback platform [1878]. Agrarian troubles surged around us. We even had our own experience in them.

I remember standing by the window in our kitchen on the farm and watching bailiffs and their helpers drive into the barnyard and take out a thousand dollars' worth of corn that had been husked and put in for us there by our neighbors.

My father had an oral agreement with [Horatio] Seymour, the [former] governor of New York, for the rental of that eighty acres of land on which the corn was planted. My father had three hundred and twenty acres of good land and he rented this eighty acres from Seymour of New York. A man in Joliet who posed as the agent of Governor Seymour apparently had the right, or professed to have the right, to rent that land. My father had taken no paper of any kind to substantiate the rental. To him, the word of Governor Seymour was good, and it was the order of the day at that time that men's words were good.

What happened then should not have happened. The man who held the lease had the documentary proof of having rented it. He was stubborn. I don't think he was dishonest. He offered to sell his lease. My father wouldn't pay a penny. He had an old kicking horse; and Kier, the claimant, would have taken that horse for the lease. It was the stubbornness in the man that wouldn't let him admit he was wrong.

[4]Haley cites the three heroic figures of the Irish rebellion. Theobald Wolfe Tone (1763-1798) founded the Society of United Irishmen in 1791, Robert Emmett (1778-1803) died on the gallows in 1803, a martyr to the cause of Irish independence, and Charles Stewart Parnell (1846-1891) was the political leader, identified with such issues as land reform and home rule, during the 1880s.

[5]The Grange or Patrons of Husbandry represented an attempt by rural Americans to improve their cultural and economic lives. The movement flourished in the 1870s in the Midwest and the South. State legislation which established regulatory commissions and attempted to prevent rate discrimination by the railroads and elevator operators was referred to as Granger laws. Ernest L. Bogart and Charles Manfred Thompson, *The Industrial State, 1870-1893, Centennial History of Illinois*, vol. IV (Chicago: Illinois Centennial Commission, 1922), pp. 82-90.

My father, too, had a stubbornness in his nature that often stood him in good stead, but sometimes I think he went wrong on it.

My father ordered the corn planted. The neighbors husked it and put it in the corn crib. My father went to Chicago, and Kier sent for the corn. My mother was afraid of violence. She'd rather every friend we had in the neighborhood would have taken the stuff out and not leave it to those people with coal wagons and carts.

After the storm was over, my father was calm. I think he was thinking it over to himself. People then didn't air what they had in their minds.

It taught me a tremendous lesson. All through my life I have remembered not only the terror of legal seizure of something I held, but also the danger of stubbornness. I've often hesitated in action to ask myself if I were merely stubborn or if I were holding to something essential.

If there was one thing that differentiated my experiences, my way of doing things, from the way of other children it lay in the fact that I did capitalize my experience. Perhaps it was because I got some awfully hard knocks.

When I was about three years old—and it must be one of the first things I remember—I was going to be taken to Joliet. That was something! I was going to get a ride behind the horses! I was going away! and I had on a white dress, but I chased a hen under the house in the dirt, and came out all dirty. They were going to leave me home!

That awakened me to a consciousness of the relation of cause and effect. I had done something I shouldn't have done, and I was going to pay for it. They must have let me go. I know perfectly well I didn't stay, for I can't remember the misery of staying; but I had learned one lesson.

It's the ability to remember your experiences and build on them that educates you.

I was ten years old when we left the farm. Looking back, I realize the best gift of those years. It has been an inner peace.

That's what the country does for you. There's no such thing as rush in the country. The seasons determine when men shall work. They get up early in the morning when it's delightful, go off to the fields, and, when it gets hot, rest under the trees a while, except in harvest time. Then all hands turn in.

The laborers come to each farm to get in the hay, and they have to work together. It's a joyous time. The men want to avoid the rains and get in the grain. Everybody's watching the weather.

It's the seasons that determine for them—you can't hurry the seasons. All this life where we have the clock and the rushing and tearing isn't the normal and the natural life. In the country you have the whole sky and the out-of-doors and all these things that are life itself.

That was what the farm gave me.

2

We moved to Channahon to be near the quarry.[6] The town was tiny, with only three hundred residents, but it was, as all villages are, a world in miniature. To us children it was immensely interesting, endlessly diverting.

Our principal amusement was Mrs. Harrington. She came to wash for us. All of us clustered around the washtub. Mrs. Harrington talked all the time. She rubbed, and she scrubbed, and she talked, and if those that were nearest crowded and the rest couldn't hear, there was a pushing and a scrambling. You'd hear us all laughing. I don't know what she talked about because she just talked.

The poor little village of Channahon was hit by fever and ague. Everybody had to be taking medicine, especially quinine. My God! anything in the world but quinine! When you felt a shake come on, you'd go off and lie under a hedge rather than take your quinine. The village was dying with malaria. You can remember the scars all your life that come from that.

At one time the only two people who were able to move around in the village were a young girl and my father. He was strong and healthy and lived on fresh air, and he cured himself. Physically he was a normal healthy man, and he had the kind of sense that rabbits have; he knew what to do. My little sister died. That was a heartbreak for me. After all these years I can remember the pangs of that first grief.

The quarry was full of interest. It was a joy and a delight to be taken down there. We went through a beautiful drive on the Illinois River and heard the birds, yellow warblers and goldfinches, when we'd go early in the morning.

The quarry was within a two-mile ride or less if my father went down the towpath, but he had to pay one cent fine and costs each time

[6]The villages of Channahon and Minooka are located between Joliet and Morris, Illinois. Michael Haley is listed as the proprietor of Sherman's Stone Quarries in the Business Directory of the *Combination Atlas Map of Will County, Illinois* (Elgin, Ill.,: Thompson Brothers and Burr, 1873). According to the Patron's Directory of this publication, he was born in Canada and came to Will County in 1837. Haley's place and date of birth are confirmed in the U.S. Census Records of 1850 for Will County. There he is listed as twenty-three years of age, a laborer, and a member of the household of James Tyrrell.

to the justice of the peace. My father said to him, "Why don't you fine me in bulk, and not stop me each time?"

There was a canal lock at Channahon, and we used to watch its working.[7] We rode sometimes through the locks on the stone boats, always setting out with a grand sense of adventure. I was just starting to read novels—*Children of the Abbey* was the first—and I dramatized our journeyings.

When I was about eleven or twelve years old, I had typhoid fever. I was away from home, and only twice during a month was I conscious. Once was when a house near us took fire. The sparks came over and terrified the family with whom I was staying. I was on the second floor and the house had an outside stairway. I was rolled up in a quilt and taken downstairs. The sparks fell on my face and I woke up.

At the end of that illness I came on something which has had a tremendous effect upon my point of view. Although we children were silent, we were never kept out from hearing the discussions of our elders. We never joined in them but we listened eagerly to their talk. There was constant talk then of the money question. My father received from Alexander Campbell a pamphlet on Finance. I cannot remember its arguments now, but I read it then with tense interest. That, I think, was the beginning of my recognition of the association between a governmental currency system and the daily lives of the people of the country.[8]

I think that one of the great things in my life was the little school in Channahon. We had a very remarkable teacher there, Cyrus W. Brown. Richard Barr, dean of the Illinois senate, once said that Brown was the only lawyer he was ever afraid of. Afterwards, when I knew more about teachers and teaching, I knew Mr. Brown was unique. He didn't use textbooks. We never saw him with a book in his hand. We weren't chained to books.

It was a three-room school, a room each for the little children and the intermediate and the top. I can't remember being in the intermediate room. I was so small I had to stand on a box to write on the board. I was the only child in the room who couldn't reach up high enough. I was very much disturbed because I had to have the box.

We had a piano, although I never played it. Others did, however, and I listened entranced, wistful before a world I could not enter. Even

[7]The section of the Illinois and Michigan Canal containing this lock has been preserved in Channahon State Park and is designated a National Historic Landmark.

[8]Alexander Campbell (1814-1898) was a former mayor of LaSalle, a state representative (1859-1860), and a member of the U.S. House of Representatives (1875-1877). His address, printed as a sixteen-page pamphlet, was *The True American System of Finance, A Lecture Delivered Before the Mercantile Association of Chicago, October 1, 1862* (n.p., 1862). A copy is found in the CTF Files.

now one of my sharpest memories of the village is the sound of music in the twilight.

3

The vein of the Channahon quarry gave out. My father had another quarry at Aux Sable, and to be nearer to it we moved to Morris.

There weren't many amusements for children in that time, outside those which we created for ourselves. I remember how thrilled we were when my father told us that he was taking us to a lecture by a phrenologist. We hadn't the least idea what a phrenologist was. He had to explain to us the science and the art of reading heads from the outside in.

We trudged through the snow that crunched sharply under our arctics until we came to the hall where the lecture was to be given. We were early enough to find seats directly under the lecture platform.

We listened breathlessly to the man as he explained how different human traits could be determined by the look of a person's head. In the course of his talk he spoke sneeringly of Susan B. Anthony.

Instantly my father marshalled us all up from our seats and led us out from the hall. As we faced the rest of the audience, Jenny and Eliza and I were horribly conscious of the unconventional nature of my father's command.

When we had come just outside the hall, he stood us in a line and said, "I don't know Susan B. Anthony and I suppose that I never shall, but she's a woman who is working for a cause, a just cause, and I will not allow my children to continue to listen to any half-baked nincompoop who sneers at her."

It was long years afterward before I met the leader of the cause of woman suffrage, but in that cold winter night in Morris I had learned the lesson of respect for the women who lead causes for the ultimate benefit of humankind.

Morris was, in a way, the least interesting of our places of residence; but it had its points. For it was in Morris that I first came into realization of the need and the value and the joy of work.

I was catapulted into teaching. We had been in a very comfortable position all through my life up to and including that summer. Then came an experience in the business world where the partners of my father were perfectly willing to give a bribe to get a contract. He was unwilling to do it and they told him if he didn't do it they couldn't get the contract and would stop the work from going on.

The firm was Reed, McMeachin, Haley, and Reed. The first Reed was the elder man, the last was his nephew, and the elder controlled the younger. The elder was buyer for the Joliet Penitentiary. A later investigation was made of his peculations and he left the state and never came back to it, dodging the grand jury indictment.

The partners closed the quarry up by an injunction. Of course, it was eventually lifted, but it spoiled the chance of a contract; it left the firm not a responsible bidder. My father's partners didn't believe my father would go that far. But he did—that was his type of mentality—with the result that everything for us folded up like a concertina.

I saw my father come into the auditorium where we were having our closing exercises in June of that year.[9] When he entered, I saw his pale face. I knew it meant I must begin to dig for myself and for the rest of the family. I had been singing. I didn't sing any more.

If I live a hundred years, I'll never forget my father's look and all it conveyed of defeat and the consequences. It meant for me the end of school and I had to prepare to do something else.

I discovered a little Normal school, where I could learn something about teaching. There I got my intellectual stimulus for teaching, the sense of responsibility to do it—from a man who was destined to be an important factor in my life on later occasions when he had become Judge Orrin N. Carter.

The influence of that little school was potent. It would have awakened in any one a sense of responsibility toward children. The teachers of the school, both Mr. Carter and Mr. Cook, who was afterward at the Illinois State Normal, were uplifting and inspiring.[10]

I took very seriously everything that I heard. My mother had always insisted that we children follow through to its end anything that we started. She valued education as only the Irish, who had been denied the full measure of education they desired, could value it. She knew by experience the truth of the old Irish maxim, "Educate in order that your children may be free."

The Irish, however, in order to hold their souls, had been forced to give up even education. They had to send their sons to France or Spain or Belgium to secure education at all. Those who were unable to do that had to give up educational opportunities in order to keep their religion. They developed that tenacity of purpose and integrity that refused to give up whatever they considered most important.

[9]The school was St. Angela Academy in Morris. A boarding school for girls, it was owned and operated by the Sisters of the Holy Cross from 1857 until 1958, when it closed. Archive Narratives of St. Angela Academy, Archives, St. Mary's College, Notre Dame, Indiana.

[10]John W. Cook (1844-1922) was on the faculty of Illinois State Normal at this time. It seems likely that the Cook and Carter Normal School was a private institution offering Saturday extension classes for teachers in the Morris area. Later, Cook served terms as president of both Illinois State and Northern Illinois State Normal Schools. He was a leading advocate for the normal school movement.

The children in Ireland, under the Penal Code of England, could denounce their father's religion and get title to his property. The entire Penal Code system was disruptive of education, but it could not take away, even from the common people, the desire and intention and ability to secure some sort of education for their children. It was that background which was responsible for my mother's insistence upon our educational training.

I was still attending the little Cook and Carter Normal school when I started to teach. My first teaching job was in a little country school about a mile from Dresden Heights.[11] It was a nice little school, with nice children. Country children are simple.

From the first day I went into the school, I loved the work. I liked the children and I think they liked me. I never in the world could have taught them if it hadn't been for their own characters. I had forty children to teach except in the winter. The youngest child in the school was my first educational experiment.

When I started out to teach, I didn't know anything about any educational movement. I was too young and too isolated. I had not been in an atmosphere where I would be likely to learn what the world outside was doing in education. I was getting my own work done and I had plenty to do. At the little Normal school I got what I needed for the work in the school when I went back on Saturdays and reported to Cook and Carter. They checked up against my experience, against what I was doing, and made suggestions about what I might do. It was a very practical way of getting the Normal school idea.

The county superintendent of schools of that county was a forward looking man, Higbee [John Higby] by name, who believed in training for teachers—and that belief was almost revolutionary in that time. Under him we didn't learn how to teach merely by growing up and growing older. He put the feeling into us that we must be trained and that we must go on with our training.

Fortunately for me, he was not as political minded as most modern superintendents of schools. He was a dear old man, a minister with a conscience, a profound student, human and helpful.

Mr. Higbee [Higby] must have been an educational experimenter, for at a teachers' meeting he brought in the first phonograph I ever saw. It was a recording instrument as well, for it repeated a speech that he had made into it on a previous occasion. "The next generation," it wheezed in a poor but startling imitation of his voice, "will be what this generation makes it." The statement impressed me even more than the mechanical miracle.

I began teaching with the dawning of the new education. I got a

[11]The year was 1878-79, and Haley was sixteen years old.

school in which there was only one child who hadn't been in school before, little Jimmy Murphy. He was a white-haired little boy not more than five years old, and it wasn't very long before Jimmy was the best reader in the school. They didn't know what to make of it. I got training in phonics from Allan Carter's father in the Normal school and I took it up religiously. Jimmy was the only one I could try it on. He was a wonderful little pupil.

The rest of them sat with their eyes and mouths open, for Jimmy had an uncle who was only nine years old and Jimmy would read better than his uncle. They could understand that Jimmy was really reading, while they were deciphering, "The—cow—saw—a—calf." You wouldn't give them a picture of a cow in sections and expect them to piece it together. When you put a child at something like that, he doesn't dream it's a cow.

But when you show the cow and the word "cow," he makes the connection himself. And if you put "sow" next, he has no trouble. Between the phonetic system and the word method, he could read through the reader in a few weeks. The others had to spell every word and then the next word.

Any old dub was good enough for a teacher then. They hadn't any idea forty-five or fifty years ago of training a teacher.

The first school I taught had on the school board a man who couldn't read or write. I never had seen him. There were three directors and the two who made a majority had chosen me. I wasn't there very long when an encyclopedia was stolen. This man had been responsible for buying it. The other two made him go out and find the encyclopedia.

He came up to the step of the school—it was an old log step—on his horse and whacked at the door with a whip. He scared the wits out of me. I wouldn't go to the door, but sent one of the children. He said, "It's Mr. Devoy."

I said, "What does he want?"

"He wants to talk to you."

I went to see what he wanted. He said, "I come to see about them damn velocipedes that was stole."

It was my first meeting with a member of a Board of Education.

The children in my first school seemed older than those of the country school I had attended in my early childhood. Perhaps it was only because I was more conscious of the fact that children were required to work. Day after day the boys would go out from the school to drive home the cows and help milk them. In the summer seasons they had to work in the fields. There was compensation other than financial in their labor. But the tasks were, nevertheless, heavy on such young shoulders. Possibly, though, they gloried as I did in the ability to assume responsibility.

I boarded at a nearby farm with the Clennon family. During the time I was there, I saw the older children, one after another, leaving the place to go to a Colorado ranch. Their departure was, I realized, a result of economic pressure and I felt vaguely but regretfully that there was something wrong in a system which caused a mother to grieve in silence as Mrs. Clennon did.

I used to go home to Morris every Friday night. One of the Clennons went to the Normal school in Morris. His mother used to call for him on Friday nights and so she drove me in to town as long as the roads were passable.

Later in the year, though, when the roads got bad, I used to go on horseback to take a train at Minooka. Willie Clennon would go with me to take back my horse. We had to have a lantern to flag the train. Once, as I tried to get down from the horse, I was caught in the pommel of the saddle. I was hanging with my head down and my clothes pulled up and I had to roar to tell Willie to keep away with his lantern. He had to put the lantern down and come and help me. I can remember yet my fear that the train would come before he could extricate me from the pommel.

I must have been a tremendous conformist in those days. As a child, I am sure that I never had a thought of any kind of revolution. Whatever was the thing people did, I did that. I followed the manners and the customs.

My mother was always waiting for me when I went home on Friday nights. It never occurred to me that she might have had other duties or interests that would keep her away from the front door as I came toward it. I cannot remember ever returning home from that little country school without finding her in the doorway.

On Christmas Eve, I was terribly delayed by an awful storm that swept over the prairies between Minooka and Morris. The train crawled along more and more slowly, until I began to wonder if I should be home even for Christmas Day. I could picture all the rest of the family gathering around the Christmas candle, which my mother always lighted at six o'clock on Christmas Eve, while my father said the grace for light.

I was growing desperately sorry for myself, snow-bound in a day coach that was growing colder every moment, but finally the train steamed into Morris. All my little brothers were at the station waiting for me. One of them carried a lantern and by its light they led me through high banks of snow to the joy of home.

4

We moved to Joliet in the spring of 1879. I would have reached the town in time to have a week or so before I had my school there, my second school. On the Saturday before the Monday when we were to move, however, my uncle, Tom Tyrrell, came into Morris. My sister Jenny was at his house. She was teaching too. He told my mother that Jenny was very, very ill and he was afraid of diphtheria and thought my mother should go to her. Mother sent a telegram to my father in Chicago to meet her there and bring a doctor from Joliet with him.

It was sad for us to see her go away that Sunday night. We were left alone to move. All the furniture that would be moved first was packed. Everything was packed except breakfast dishes and beds to sleep in.

We were up far too early in the morning and over at the station on the Rock Island Railroad. All our goods and chattels were in the freight car. There were myself and my sister Eliza and my three brothers. The youngest was a little fellow. He had the family cat in a pillowcase. The other family idol we had was a piece of waxwork. It had water lilies and some toads. The water was a looking glass. It was big and round and had a bell glass over it. That couldn't be put in anything. One of the older boys had that.

We sat in the station, poor youngsters, scared stiff. The train was being switched back and forth. Every time the train would start to go forth we'd start to get on it, and then it would back up.

After a while, the train pulled out and left us. We had to run after it and get on and crawl up on the steps. We all got on and then, when we got on the back of the caboose, we found the door locked. We had to sit outside until somebody at a wayside station saw us and wired ahead to let us in. We were scared within an inch of our lives, but the cat and the waxworks landed safely.

When we got to Joliet, we got to the house and got the furniture in. On Wednesday morning we were to meet at the train the doctor who had gone with my father to Jenny; but on Tuesday night I came down with diphtheria. We knew it was that. Eliza got some medicine from the doctor and he left and told her to use that to swab my throat. She used it the first night. She swabbed it every time she thought of it. She had my throat raw. Poor Eliza had to go back and report to the doctor. That poor man didn't know where to go, with the two patients, miles apart.

A friend of my father's, a man with the same economic beliefs, lived near us. Eliza went down there and told his wife of my illness. She fixed up her own house and told her children she wasn't coming back until I was well. I had never seen the woman before, but she was an angel of mercy to me. She stayed with us until my mother could come when Jenny recovered.

It was certainly an inauspicious entrance to a new life.

We had a house at the edge of the town nearly at the city limits. The house was large, and set in a ten-acre tract, not a farm, but with an orchard and berry bushes. It was in the Joliet house that I grew acutely conscious of the movements of the time, both political and educational. My father was working then as an inspector of material on the construction of the City Hall in Chicago, but he was at home for weekends, and his coming always brought men in to talk over the events and tendencies of the period. How they talked! Of the merits of the Hayes-Tilden controversy, of the results of the Panic of '73, of the personality of James G. Blaine, of the Molly Maguires, of the railway strike of '77, with its all-day battle in Chicago when nineteen persons had been killed, of cabbages and kings and of the Irish land question. I heard as much of Parnell in my girlhood in Joliet as James Joyce ever did from his Aunt Fanny in Dublin. I heard, too, from friends of my own age of changing methods of education.

I taught a little country school just outside the town.[12] Many of the people who lived out there and whose children attended that school were people working in Joliet. They were not all farmers. It was a very delightful little school and I have very good co-operation from the people who were responsible. One was a lawyer in Chicago who lived there, and who had great appreciation of any effort made by the teachers.

The work I had been doing in connection with my school with the Cook and Carter school couldn't be carried on, but I got into a circle in Joliet where a study of educational methods was being made through a group of teachers who were following movements that were then very lively ones in America. My touch with them gave me an opportunity to do better than I could even have done at the Normal school, for I had already caught the spirit of the system.

That educational interest which was vaguely in the air took me to the summer session of the Illinois Normal School near Bloomington.[13] Its concrete application there kept me in that school for a longer session. For the principal of the high school department of the Bloomington Normal was Edwin Janes [Edmund J.] James. He also had a

[12]Haley taught at this school for two years, 1879-80 and 1880-81.

[13]It is likely that Haley attended Illinois Normal during 1881-82 as a student in the high school department. She was admitted to the normal school itself in the fall, 1882, but there are no records of her completing the semester. This information was obtained from the Office of Admissions and Records at Illinois State University.

class in economics. That was the year after Henry George's *Progress and Poverty* came out and a group of us—I don't remember, five or six or seven or ten—read *Progress and Poverty* with Professor James. James was afterwards at the University of Chicago and then president of the University of Illinois.[14]

During the war he went to Washington, at a time when every official was opposed to the Irish revolutionists and John MacNeill had been thrown in prison in England for his part in Easter week. He had decided that Easter week was not the time for that rebellion, but at the same time he was associated with the Sinn Fein movement, and James came down to Washington to beg Wilson to make a protest for the government to get MacNeill out of the British prison. He was risking unpopularity in doing it, but he did it out of a belief that no one like MacNeill should be held prisoner.

He went to Europe that year. He married the daughter of a professor in Berlin. We gave him the money to buy a set of books on economics because he could get them cheaper in Germany. They say that when his first child was born, he used to walk the floor and recite his stuff to the baby.

I don't know how much value the baby received from the recitation, but I do know that Professor James took me into a wide world when he introduced me to Henry George. Now, long years afterward, I see that the value of the Single Tax theory was less in its essence than in its by-product of arousing people to interest in the relation between taxation and fundamental human justice. *Progress and Poverty* was the bible of the few who followed Henry George all the way through his theory; but the prophet was more potent than his prophecy.

I went back to Joliet with a greatly increased idea of my own importance. After I had taught for some months in the school just outside the town, I told the superintendent that I was worth five dollars a month more to the community. I was getting thirty-five. After some hesitation, he agreed that I was, but he kept putting off making the actual arrangement. Finally I issued an ultimatum. If he didn't sign the contract to pay me the higher salary by noon of the first day of

---

[14]Edmund J. James (1855-1925) was a distinguished American educator. He was the principal of the Model High School at Normal, Illinois, from 1879 to 1882. He taught at the University of Chicago from 1897 to 1901 and served as president of Northwestern University from 1902 to 1904, prior to his presidency of the University of Illinois from 1904 until 1920.

Progress and Poverty, published in 1879, became one of the ten best selling nonfiction works in the history of American publishing. George blamed the increasing gap between the wealthy and poor on monopoly and proposed a "single tax" on the unassessed increment in land values as the remedy. Haley's father was also impressed by the writings of Henry George. See note 2.

the fall term, I was not going back to the school. He didn't send me the contract, and I left the job.

The year was 1880. I was nineteen years old. The world stretched before me. I packed a bag—we called it a valise—and took the train to Chicago.[15]

[15]Haley may have visited Chicago in 1880; she did not begin teaching in the Chicago area until the school year 1882-83. See notes 1, 3, and 4 in the following chapter.

⊶⟦ II ⟧⊷

I Find the Battleground

1

Chicago in the Eighties was still a frontier town. I had known it intermittently through my childhood, for my mother's people had come into it before it had been incorporated, although they had later left it. I had seen it growing out of its ruins after its great fire, but it had, strangely enough, failed to impress me then. Jenny and I had, a little while before, gone with my father over the framework of the city hall, walking on perilous beams in unladylike adventuring. Even then Chicago must have been the lodestar for the ambitious girls of the Middle West. I must have come into it with some thrill of the spirit of Dick Whittington; but I was even less introspective then than I am now, and my impression is that my one thought was to find another teaching job.

Although such finding was comparatively easy to what it would be now I didn't get the job at once. The city proper had its limits at Pershing Road, then 39th Street, on the south, Ashland Avenue on the west, and probably at North Avenue on the north. I found a home with a cousin, Mrs. McDonald, who lived in Englewood. Her proximity to the Normal School and the coming of Colonel Francis W. Parker to that institution set my course. I'd study under him while I was waiting for a teaching job of which I had a promise.[1]

[1]According to official records, Haley began teaching in the Cook County school system in 1882. Her assignment for eighty days of the school year was at the Lemont School south of Chicago. It seems likely that she taught as a substitute during the remainder of the year. Her salary was $40 per month. Cook County, Ill., *Biennial Report of the County Superintendent of Schools, July 1, 1882 to June 30, 1884* (Chicago: J. M. W. Jones Stationery and Printing Co., 1885), p. 46.

The chronology of her teaching career presented in notes 11-13 and 15 of chapter 1 conforms to the description prepared by her sister Jennie in *Margaret A. Haley Memorial Booklet*. This source says she taught at the Lewis Champlin School during the fall semester of 1883 and then left teaching for a term to study at the Cook County Normal School with Colonel Parker. *Haley Memorial Booklet*, pp. 66-69.

Parker (1837-1902) came to Chicago in January, 1883, from Quincy, Mass., where he had promoted a series of public school reforms which shifted the emphasis from subject

John W. Cook of the Normal School in Bloomington had told me of Parker. He was, Cook had said, a great light shining on the barren fields of education in the United States. Already he had won a following for his theories and practices, and I knew that I was fortunate to have a chance to study under him. Later I was to know that not only Colonel Parker but the people whom he attracted into his following were to be the inspirational force of American education for a long, long time: Josephine Locke, a bubbling fountain of joy, who came from St. Louis to teach the art of life as well as of technic; W. W. Speer, out of Iowa and worth a dozen of the Cooleys whom the state of the Tall Corn afterward sent in; Ella Flagg Young, endowed with the keenest intellect I have ever met in man or in woman; [William Lawrence] Tomlins, a magician in the teaching of music, a man who could do with classes, both of teachers and of children, what no other instructor could, leading them from a wilderness of ignorance by the force of his own desire to enlighten. That group was to leaven the lump of a city's school system, to project the golden age of a city's educational processes.

Even then Chicago was less restricted than were the eastern cities. We never had to get rid of the king from our books as did New York and Boston and Philadelphia. We never had the melancholy attitude of Puritanism entirely overwhelming us, but whatever grayness lingered in schoolrooms was dispelled by the Parker leadership of that time. Parker and Josephine Locke stood for color in education, Tomlins for the harmony of life, Mrs. Young for a deep contentment of the spirit that was by no means static. As the world grew she grew, comprehending and adapting herself to its changes.[2] Tomlins still heard the angels. Even after the schools had been regimented and the golden age was over, he listened to the music of the spheres.

In review I can see that I had been born and raised among people who had, in one way or another, always insisted upon independence of mind. My father's and my mother's people had left Ireland in order that they might have it. The schools I had attended had, as far as the time allowed, permitted it. Some of them had fostered it. I did not

matter to self-discovery. Called the "father of progressive education," Parker was the principal of the Cook County Normal School, which in 1896 became the Chicago Normal School, until his death. See Jack K. Campbell, *Colonel Francis W. Parker, The Children's Crusader* (New York: Teachers College Press, 1967).

[2]The key person in this list of educators was Ella Flagg Young (1845-1918). Her assignments in the public schools of Chicago included those of teacher, principal, district superintendent, principal of the Chicago Normal School, and finally, superintendent from 1909 to 1915. She was the first woman to achieve such an office in an urban school system and was also the first woman elected to the presidency of the NEA (1910). Young's important role in Chicago school affairs is evident in the pages of Haley's manuscript. A recent biography is Joan K. Smith, *Ella Flagg Young, Portrait of a Leader* (Ames, Iowa: Educational Studies Press, 1979).

identify, however, or value the meaning of academic freedom until that year. Colonel Parker was breaking away from old traditions of education which, like long clothes, "habiliments of the grave," had to be stripped from women before they could move in mental as well as in physical ease. Thanks to him and to [John] Dewey, [William H.] Kilpatrick, and [George S.] Counts, who followed him, children today are less hampered by the old reserves, less prisoned by the old mental barriers.

The Normal School rose then among fields of clover and of daisies, but already its bucolic peace was being threatened. The ground on which it stood had been the gift to the county of a man named [Edward S.] Beck with the provision that it must always be used for normal school purposes. His heirs, fighting his will, were erecting opposite the school a block of apartments, later known as the Sunshine Flats, in the supposed hope of driving out the school, a consummation which not even the spreading of the city around the place has effected. In that time, however, there was a freshness in the school itself which marched in harmony with the prairies we could see from every window.

Colonel Parker was by no means pacific in his quest for sweetness and light. He roared, he growled, he stormed, he banged—even more than had old [Edwin C.] Hewitt down at the Illinois Normal. He shook dry bones in things and in people. He scared the wits out of students, and he terrified teachers. He sent for parents and shamed them into aiding their children. He was Reform Rampant—and I watched him with unterrified glee. Never in all my life have I feared anything or anyone, least of all established authority; and in him I somehow sensed the fundamental justice of his attitude and saw the need of his method. More surely than anyone else he taught me that a straight line is the shortest distance between two points. I was to remember that twenty years later.

I got a job teaching at the Hendricks School in the Town of Lake.[3] That was the district of the Union Stockyards, then a sprawling, malodorous neighborhood, but not the heterogeneous district it is now. Eastern Europe had not yet inundated its dreary streets. Most of the children at the Hendricks School were those of English, Irish, and German parentage. They were, for the most part, alert, eager to learn; but the school itself was almost hopeless.

I had been on my own in teaching at Minooka and Joliet. Here for the first time I came under the supervision of a principal—and what a principal! She had never gone further than third or fourth grade in

---

[3]Cook County, Ill., *Biennial Reports of the County Superintendent of Schools, July 1, 1884 to June 30, 1886,* and *July 1, 1886 to June 30, 1888.*

school, and she had not, as some others had done with notable success, trained herself into any equivalent of the schooling she had missed. Unfortunately for her, the school had but four rooms, and the children of the district were sharp of perception of human frailties, particularly the frailties of their supervisors. They knew that she was a fraud. They couldn't help knowing it. Once, in my room, she told the youngsters that codfish was salty because it came out of salt water. You couldn't put her sort of ignorance over the children of the Stockyards pioneers. All we teachers could do was to keep her as dark as possible. The only advantage of her lack of pedagogical training was that it left me free to practice what I had learned at Normal.

I taught in the Hendricks School for twenty years.[4] In the course of that time I saw Chicago change from the units of neighborhoods, the Town of Lake, Hyde Park, Englewood to the south of the original city, into the wide area that it was at the turn of the century. I saw, too, the beginnings of movements that have not yet ended, movements which were to stir the minds and hearts of men and women. The part I have had in some of them is the reason for the writing of my story. For men and women die, but the war for social and economic justice must go on if there is to be freedom to humankind. Since the time when I came to Chicago I have seen great causes wax and wane. I have seen the world pass through phases of idealism and of selfishness. I have seen men ready to die for causes, and I have seen the same men grow hard and indifferent to the sufferings of others. I have seen right triumph for a little while, only to be overwhelmed again by evil. I have seen the wide swing of time's circle and vast changes on the face of the earth; but I have also seen that always some one waits to take up the torch that the wearied drop from tired hands. That knowledge is the ultimate reward of the long war for academic freedom in which I have been a soldier in the ranks.

The Eighties were years of great national expansion, of railroad building, of industrial development, but they were also years of growing unrest. In Chicago we had a railroad strike which affected me only in a threatened inconvenience about going home to Joliet for a weekend. The anarchist riot, however, came closer to my political consciousness. My father knew old Carter Harrison, then the mayor of the city, very well. He also knew police officials and methods, and he believed, as John Peter Altgeld believed when, as governor of Illinois,

[4]Haley taught at the Hendricks School from 1884 to January 1900. The school was located in the township of Lake and became part of the city school system in 1890, when this area south of the stockyards was annexed. *Proceedings of the Board of Education, City of Chicago,* 1889-1890, pp. 250-251 (hereafter cited as *Proceedings, Board of Education*). The Haley family resided in the Township of Lake.

he issued the anarchist pardons, that the police had captured and the courts had condemned the convicted men on insufficient evidence.[5] We Haleys, living then in Englewood, quiet citizens of a quiet neighborhood, did not know from our Chicago newspapers that such men and women as William Dean Howells, Robert G. Ingersoll, Henry Demarest Lloyd, Charles Francis Train, William Morris, Stopford Brooke, and the Besants, Sir Walter and Annie, were rising to protest Judge [Joseph E.] Gary's condemnation to death of men whose crime was not proven murder but the charge that their words, spoken or written, in protest against the existing order, had incited some one unknown to commit murder. We knew, though, that we Haleys, particularly my father and I, did not approve of that decision; and time after time we put down our evening reading of Dickens, our singing of "Genevieve" and "Marguerite" and "I Dreamt that I Dwelt in Marble Halls" to argue the pros and cons of the controversy.

In spite of extraneous causes life itself was simple then. We lived in an unpretentious, pleasant house that had plenty of room around it. We had but two neighbors in our block. One of the families, the Browns, had a pony and basket cart in which we often went picnicking down to Jackson Park, afterward the site of the old World's Fair. Mrs. Brown was an artist who used to point out to us the beauties of the rambling road through the woods and the loveliness of the lake. I can remember her regret at the encroachments of the growing city. "They'll live to be sorry," she said when the towns to the south voted to be annexed to Chicago.

For my own part I liked the growth. It was change, development, opportunity. The World's Fair was magic.[6] The theaters and concert halls were sheer joy. My brother Dennis and I used to go to the top gallery of the Auditorium to see the great actors, to hear the great

---

[5]Since Haley was not teaching in Chicago during the railroad strike of 1877, she may be referring to either the streetcar strike of 1885 or the Pullman strike of 1894.

Carter H. Harrison (1825-1893) was elected to five terms as mayor of Chicago. A Yale graduate, a native of Kentucky, and a Democrat, Harrison became wealthy in real estate. His terms of office included the years from 1879 to 1887 and 1893. He was assassinated by a disappointed office seeker.

John Peter Altgeld (1847-1902) was elected governor in 1892 and was the first resident of Chicago to hold this office. A former lawyer and judge, Altgeld reviewed the records of three men convicted for the 1884 tragedy when seven police officers were killed by a bomb in Haymarket Square. Finding no connection between the anarchists and the bombing, Altgeld pardoned the three in June, 1893, and a public uproar ensued. The governor also clashed with fellow Democrat, President Grover Cleveland, in 1894 over the dispatching of federal troops to Chicago during the Pullman strike. Harry Barnard, *Eagle Forgotten: The Life of John Peter Altgeld* (Indianapolis: Bobbs-Merrill, 1958).

[6]The World's Fair refers to the Columbian Exposition of 1893, marking the 400th anniversary of Columbus's voyage. It was held in a newly erected "White City" on Chicago's lake front five miles south of the business district.

singers. He could mimic the whole performance the next night for the benefit of those of the family who hadn't seen it. As all families were then, we were intensely dependent on ourselves and each other for entertainment. There was, besides, a strong bond between us. All of us, particularly Eliza and Dennis, seemed to know when anything was happening to any one of the rest of us. Recollection of some of the instances of that curious telepathy seems to bear out the tales of explorers concerning the strange telepathic knowledge of African tribes. Just last year, not knowing of Eliza's illness, I started back from California to Chicago, impelled by a certainty that she needed me. I was just boarding the train when I learned that she was dead.

The Homestead strike raised issues not yet solved. The Pullman strike raged almost across our dooryard. Federal troops, sent by President Cleveland over the protest of Governor Altgeld, marched from the Englewood station. Depression weighed down upon the city as it did upon the nation. Later I was to learn how all these events were even then affecting the lives of all us common folk, but in the early Nineties I was less interested in economic and political issues than in educational.[7] I had found a new world through the group at the Chicago Normal, and I was going to keep myself in it even though I had long since left the portals of that institution.

Some one at Normal—either John or Sarah Byrne—told me of the Buffalo School of Pedagogy. In 1896 I set off for it. Nicholas Murray Butler, speaking with the voice of God, was already holding forth there, but William James was the indicating numeral which determined the value of the school. Everyone else there was a cipher. James was a mighty wind whirling through dark corridors, clearing out cluttered corners of the mind. I no longer recall what he taught me in that session; but I can never forget the inspiring force of his personality. Because of him I came away from Buffalo thrilled with the pride of my profession.[8]

[7]The Homestead strike occurred in a suburb of Pittsburgh in 1892. The strike, which ended in defeat for the steelworkers' union, retarded the growth of organized labor for several decades. The depression of 1893 was one of the most severe the nation had encountered.

[8]The Buffalo School of Pedagogy, affiliated with the University of Buffalo, was founded in 1895 for advanced students of teaching. Financial considerations forced its closing in 1898. In the summer of 1896, following the annual meeting of the National Education Association held in Buffalo, the school held a two-week summer institute. *Educational Review*, 10 (June, 1895), p. 104, 12 (Sept., 1896), p. 194; Charles R. J. Collins, "The University of Buffalo School of Pedagogy, 1895-1898," *Niagara Frontier*, 19 (Summer, 1972), pp. 30-41.

William James (1842-1910), one of America's foremost thinkers, presented a series of lectures which were later published as *Talks to Teachers on Psychology* (New York: Henry Holt, 1899). Henry James, ed., *The Letters of William James*, 2 vols. (Boston:

I went from there to the Catholic summer school at Lake Champlain, but it was another Catholic summer school, the one at Madison, Wisconsin, which gave me another widening view. There, in 1898, for the first time I came into knowledge of the fundamental issue in the unending war for academic freedom: the right of the teacher to call his soul his own.

[Thomas Edward] Shields, a doctor of divinity in the St. Paul Seminary for the training of boys for the Catholic priesthood, was one of the most powerful and influential educators of his day.[9] Working on a farm in his boyhood—he said the neighbors used to call him *omadhaun*—he had developed a naturally scientific mind. He had already invented from spun glass the first machine for registering emotions, the precursor of the lie detector. He had already outlined and was putting into effect an educational method destined for marvelous results. His laboratory was the schools conducted by the Third Order of Saint Dominic, a Catholic sisterhood with a mother house at Sinsinawa, Wisconsin, having for Superior Mother Mary Emily Power, one of the farthest-visioned pioneers of the Mississippi Valley. The Dominicans, inspired and directed by Dr. Shields, established a system which is still years ahead of the public school system of the United States because it was conceived and fostered in independence. The Sisters flocked to the Shields' lectures. The summer school on the shores of Lake Mendota was a flutter of white robes and black bonnets, a dovecote apparently untroubled by knowledge of hawks; but the birds of prey were in the high sky above it.

Dr. Shields came from the archdiocese of St. Paul, the most mentally active and the most politically disturbed of any Catholic unit in the country. John Ireland, its archbishop, was a mighty man. He had fought a great battle for the Americanization of the people he shepherded. There was a movement on foot to recognize the linguistic and racial divisions of the Catholic populations of the United States. German bishops were to be sent to German-speaking congregations, Italians to Italian. Archbishop Ireland, seeing the dangers of the system, battled this buttressing of foreign thought.[10]

Atlantic Monthly Press, 1920), II, p. 40. The topic of Butler and his role in the NEA is discussed in chapter 6.

[9]Thomas Edward Shields (1862-1921) has been described as "perhaps the leading Catholic educator in the United States during the first quarter of the twentieth century." *New Catholic Encyclopedia*, 15 vols. (Washington, D.C.: McGraw Hill, 1967), XIII, p. 176.

[10]John Ireland (1838-1918) was the first archbishop of St. Paul, Minnesota. The rural colonization movement which he organized and directed was considered the most successful such endeavor in the United States. Yet Haley informs us that it was not without its critics even within the church. Ireland was a strong advocate of the Americanization of immigrants, the rights of labor to organize, and racial equality. See James H. Moynihan, *The Life of Archbishop John Ireland* (New York: Harper, 1953).

One of his methods of combat was the colonization of the Northwest by Irish settlers. In the colonization scheme, however, he ran athwart Jim Hill. Jim Hill was the Great Northern Railroad. He claimed title to some of the land which Ireland had taken for his colonists. He clouded title by getting the cases into court but keeping them from being heard. Ireland was called to Rome to explain his failure in a financial scheme. It took the Republican party—William McKinley and Mark Hanna—to save him from Hill's attacks and machinations. He returned to St. Paul uncensured but beaten, a mouthpiece for "the full dinner pail," an apparent friend to Hill.

Dr. Shields, with others of the archbishop's friends, deprecated his surrender. If he had stood out against Hill, if he had fought the cause to its end, even though he had lost it, he would have remained a great man. Many of them thought it, but Dr. Shields said it to Ireland. Ireland didn't like his candour. He was taking it out on Shields at that time. With McKinley in the White House he was in high power, but he could not intimidate his subordinate. Shields went right on telling his world that Ireland was wrong in his political and financial affiliations. No one ever stopped Shields from voicing his opinions. Even when he was a professor at the Catholic University in Washington and we went into the Great War, he was one of the most vociferous of a tiny minority that opposed American intervention in Europe. Thomas Acquinas swinging the sword of Don Quixote!

2

Some one has said that the fraternal beneficiary insurance organizations of women did more to pave the way for women toward public life than did the actual enactment of the Nineteenth Amendment. Possibly it's true. I made my own entrance into the courts and the newspapers through membership in one of these organizations, the Women's Catholic Order of Foresters.[11]

I was a dimly obscure and entirely uninterested member of one of its units, called courts, when the returned delegate from one of its conventions told me that the High Chief Ranger, a Mrs. Elizabeth Rogers, had secured her own election for life, "merely as a compliment." I announced at the meeting that I was against anything of the sort. I'd

[11]The Women's Catholic Order of Foresters was a fraternal insurance society established in Chicago in 1891. Eight years earlier, a men's Catholic Order of Foresters was formed for the purpose of providing death benefits to the families of deceased members. The women's organization had a similar mission and was founded by thirty-seven members of Holy Family parish. In 1894, it was chartered as a nonprofit society by the state of Illinois. The name of the women's organization was changed to the National Catholic Society of Foresters in 1966.

never seen Mrs. Rogers, I didn't know much about the organization, I knew nothing of its politics, but I knew the principle of election for life was wrong, un-American, autocratic. I said so whenever the topic arose during the year, and the women of the court elected me delegate to the next convention.

With a group of women—Annie Daley, Mary Downes, Mary Finan, and a score of others—who were also opposed to the idea I studied parliamentary law. "What you should have taken," Father Ed Kelly said to us afterward, "was not a manual but a shotgun." I don't know why I was chosen to lead the fight. I'd never before attended a convention. I knew nothing whatever of insurance law. I knew something of the theory of politics, but nothing of its practice. I weighed less than a hundred pounds. I was far more interested in a new blue silk dress than I was in any cause. The only qualification I had for the doubtful honor was my willingness to tell Elizabeth Rogers herself that she was all wrong.

She was presiding at the Handel Hall convention when I arose, as the manual directed, "on a question of information."

She said, "No questions of information will be answered today."

I bobbed up again. "On a point of order."

"No points of order."

Time and again I rose on points of personal privilege.

Each time she denied me.

Then I got mad. I said, "You're an autocrat. Your rule is gag rule. Your convention is a mob. I've never been part of a mob before, and I won't be one now."

I walked out of the hall, went over to a hotel room I had taken, and went to sleep. After awhile Mary Downes, who had taught before me in the little school down in the country and who'd been the bane of my life there because of her reputation for superiority, came in. I said, "What are they doing over there?"

She said, "What's it to you? You quit. You deserted us."

"But I couldn't stand it."

"The rest of us are trying to stand it."

I got up, and went back. A woman outside said to me, "They're voting to expel you."

I thought she meant expulsion from the convention. I knew that it required a two-thirds vote, and that Mrs. Rogers couldn't muster that. I went to the door. The guards tried to stop me, but I passed them. I had already been expelled not merely from the convention but from the order, although by a bare majority vote, but I didn't know it. I was still in my own mind a delegate. I walked to my seat. Then hell broke loose.

Never have I seen more terrible passions than those which raged around me, against me that day. Women stormed, sobbed, shouted. Through it all Mrs. Rogers pounded the gavel. Women came rushing toward me, hands upraised, eyes gleaming with hatred. Other women tried to stand between to save me. I don't know what would have happened had not Mrs. Squire, the building manager, gone to the platform. "If you don't get quiet at once I shall call the police," she threatened. The Rogers crowd knew she meant it, and fell quiet. She said to me, "Come up here, and say what you have to say." Another storm broke, but she quieted that, too. I went to the platform.

If I had known I'd been expelled from the order I'd have said more, but perhaps I said enough. I was looking down on faces twisted with hatred, faces of women who were under other circumstances good wives and mothers and sisters and daughters and friends and neighbors. But I had touched the raw nerve of their pocketbooks, and they were going to punish me! That was the base of the battle. Mrs. Rogers had permitted women beyond the age limit to enter the order. In a little while the policy would wreck it, but their heirs would have the amounts of their policies before that time. That was the secret of her power. For that they would have dragged me limb from limb. Once more their roar arose. "Come out," Mrs. Squire bade me, and led me away through the stage door. "You can't be here when they vote."

When they voted they threw out the life clause. The officers, however, wrote to my court official notice of my expulsion. Father John Dennison, chaplain of the court, took it from the secretary, who resigned in fear rather than read it. "This is libelous, slanderous, and untruthful," he told the members. "If you insist upon hearing it, I shall refuse to remain as your spiritual adviser." They made no motion to hear it, but they elected me secretary.

I took my case to Francis Walker, one of the most able lawyers who ever faced a judge or jury. We could never have afforded his ordinary fee, but he laughed so hard at the whole affair that he said he was repaid in something better than money. "Why did they expel you?" he demanded.

"An old Irish woman there said I'd called Mrs. Rogers an acrobat."

He shouted. "We'll get an injunction," he said.

It was the first time I met those processes of law with which I was to become so achingly familiar during the next forty years.

Francis Walker was short, stout, careless sometimes of personal appearance, but he had a wit which was as nimble as he was weighty. James Hamilton Lewis, later senator from Illinois, won a wider national reputation but old lawyers in Chicago remember yet how Walker worsted him in a jury trial. Lewis, always dapper, used to come into court every morning, and, while he removed his yellow chamois gloves

with elegant gestures, would address the court, the clerk, the bailiff, the
jury, and finally the opposing attorney, Walker, with suave courtesy.
The mannerly advance was beginning to impress the jurors. Then, on
the final day of the trial, Walker came into court wearing a huge pair
of white gloves, undertaker's delights. Moving forward ponderously,
he chanted, "Good morning, Your Honor. Good morning, Mr. Clerk.
Good morning, Mr. Bailiff. Good morning, Gentlemen of the Jury."
Then, shoving up to his meticulous adversary, he roared, "Kiss me,
Ham!" He won the case.

Mrs. Rogers expelled a whole court from the order, and Walker took
me before Judge [Edward F.] Dunne to apply for [an] injunction. It
was the first time I'd ever met him, the first time I'd appeared before a
judge. I was fearfully impressed by the approach to a judiciary, but I
knew I was right, and when Judge Dunne asked me about what had
happened I told him. Like Walker, he laughed till he shook. My first
impression of him was his sense of humor. Afterward I was to know
him well, his keen scholarship (he was a graduate of Trinity in
Dublin), his kindly humanitarianism, his finely balanced judicial
sense, his occasional political weaknesses, but what I best remember of
him is his twinkling love of a joke. He granted the injunction, and the
Appellate Court and the Supreme Court sustained him.

The case was still pending in the upper courts when the next
convention was called. By that time the majority of the delegates was
willing to reinstate me and have the case dismissed, but Mrs. Rogers
held out. Father Dan Riordan, Father Dennison, and Father Ed Kelly—
the Father Kelly of the Dooley papers—spoke to the convention, advising the women to put me back before I had the legal right to sue them
for libel.[12] The delegates wanted my assurance that I wouldn't sue, and
they sent for me. I went back to Handel Hall, entering as I had left it,
by the rear entrance, this time to avoid the reporters. Father Riordan, a
grand gentleman of the old school, tall, thin, aristocratic, a just man if
ever one lived, said to me, "Do nothing to arouse them."

I stepped out to the stage. Below me I saw women whom I'd known
for years, but I'd hardly have known them then. They were weeping,
distraught, frantic. Others shouted to me, "Apologize! Apologize to
Mrs. Rogers!"

[12]The Dooley papers refer to the political articles written by the Chicago humorist
Finley Peter Dunne. Characters, including Martin Dooley, Mr. Hennessey, Jawn McKenna,
and Father Kelly, commented on the world around them. Dunne's dialect pieces written
during his Chicago years were published in the *Chicago Evening Post* between the years
1892 and 1898. Two studies which examine these writings and help illuminate the
subject of Irish assimilation in urban America are Barbara C. Schaaf, *Mr. Dooley's
Chicago* (New York: Doubleday, 1977) (hereafter cited as Schaaf, *Mr. Dooley's Chicago*)
and Charles Fanning, *Finley Peter Dunne and Mr. Dooley: The Chicago Years* (Lexing-
ton, Ken.: University Press of Kentucky, 1978).

I said, "I can't apologize. When I left this hall I said that she had a mob. She still has."

Mrs. Rogers went down on her knees, and began to pray. The shouting started again, but the three priests managed to quell it. I didn't apologize, but I was reinstated. I had justification, but that wasn't what I wanted by that time. So many other events had occurred in the time between my two appearances on the stage of the Forester conventions that my one anxiety was to clear off that slate.

3

The Chicago Teachers' Federation was organized in March of 1897. Some of the principals of the grade schools were attacking the pension law which had been enacted in 1895. The rank and file of the teachers in those schools held a mass meeting in the assembly hall of the Franklin School. The meeting appointed a committee of three, Elizabeth Root, Minnie Stafford, and Catharine Goggin, to do whatever in its judgment might become necessary for the defeat of the law which was being pushed to oust the law then in force.

The legislation of 1895, granting a pension to teachers, had been the direct result of Catharine Goggin's interest in other teachers and foresight for them.[13] I did not know her then, but I came to know her a little later. For nearly twenty years she and I were to work together in a struggle that was to try souls and bodies. Throughout that time I saw her sometimes defeated and sometimes triumphant, praised, blamed, calumniated, oppressed; but I never saw her lose her temper or her sense of justice. Even when I protested against her opinions I was always afraid that she was right. Usually she was. A thin, spare woman who wore white shirt waists which remained miraculously clean and hats which she could twist to grotesque angles when she saw the need for comedy for relief in troubled gatherings, she won leadership through sheer honesty and held it through sheer integrity.

Far better than I did, she knew the political situation in Chicago and the political aspects of the Board of Education. Her cousin, Judge [James] Goggin, had been a member of the board.[14] He was an eccentric, kindly man who always listened to tales of injustice or of woe. Teachers in need of money—and the pay was so small that most teachers who

[13]Catherine Goggin (1855-1916) began teaching in the Chicago schools in 1872, following her graduation from Central High School. She taught in the Jones School and, as Haley indicates, was a leader in teacher organizational activity prior to the formation of the CTF. *Chicago Tribune,* Jan. 5, 1916.

[14]James Goggin (1842-1898) was a Superior Court judge. He served on the first Chicago Board of Education in 1871 and later acted as an attorney for the board. *Chicago Daily News,* March 29, 1898.

had any responsibilities needed money all the time—went to him. He
sent them to his cousin Catharine, who was not only thrifty but who
had some money outside her salary. She would lend them money
without interest. She told me that no one had ever defaulted from her
promise to pay. The stories she heard gave her knowledge of the need
of pensions for the teachers, and she took up the subject with Governor
Altgeld. He not only favored the idea of the pension and secured its
passage through the legislature but he put in that bill a tenure clause
which was to do more than any other measure in securing for Illinois
teachers freedom of action.

It was his idea then that teachers who contributed to a pension fund
on the assumption that they would remain units in the school system
should be assured of benefit from their contributions. He realized also
that teachers, even more than industrial workers, required some certainty of continuous employment in order that they might be able to
do better work in the system. The children attending the schools would
be, he saw, the ultimate beneficiaries of this protection for the teachers;
but, being a lawyer and a judge before he was a governor, he based his
action not upon a remote ideal but upon a present emergency. The
result of the clause, however, reached further than the immediate need.
Had it not been for the tenure clause, the Teachers' Federation would
probably have died a-borning. As it was, it defeated the pending
substitute pension bill, which would have taken out the tenure clause
among other benefits, and remained a potential fighting force for the
raise in salary which the teachers so badly needed. The maximum
salary at the time, a salary which had remained stationary for twenty
years in spite of mounting costs of living, was $800 a year, the average
one about $600.

The Federation was not, however, as was often supposed by its later
enemies, merely an organization for financial profit. From its inception it contended that a living wage and economic surety for the
teachers was an essential base for any successful school system. There
could be, its organizers knew, little real improvement in the schools
unless proper material conditions protected the teacher. Its organizers
did not know, however, how soon they were to be forced into their first
big battle in the long and still unwon war for academic freedom.

In April, 1897, Carter Henry Harrison II was elected mayor of
Chicago on a platform of liberal democracy. Had he been a liberal
democrat, he might have rewritten the history of his party and become
President of the United States. It was, however, his misfortune and his
city's misfortune that he was not. We did not know him, though, in
1897, and we took at face valuation his promise to help the teachers get
a raise. Later he told Ella Flagg Young that a mistake had been made

in not killing the Federation then and there before it had attained prestige. From the point of view of political power and entrenched financial privilege, it certainly had![15]

Harrison had already appointed William Rainey Harper, president of the University of Chicago, to a place on the school board. The appointment was to fill an unexpired term, but Harper didn't know that. Harper, not knowing then either that the board had not enough money to pay the proposed raise to the teachers—Harrison knew it, but kept the information to himself—fought against the increase, which averaged less than $50 a year. Fifty dollars! It wouldn't buy cigarettes for a smoking woman of today, but it meant books, and lectures, and a little music, and perhaps a new dress to us then. To some of us it meant a little better food for our families. A committee of teachers protested to Harper. He told them that they were getting as much as his wife's maid. And that to women who were expected to train children to be the future citizenry of the country!

Indignant, the Federation—I was one of its board of managers by that time—sent a delegation to Harrison to protest against Harper's reappointment. Harrison didn't reappoint him. He did something much better for him. He made him chairman of a commission on education. Its report came out in December, 1898, with a recommendation for passage by the Illinois legislature of a long, involved educational bill.[16]

You can still stir up controversy in Chicago by mention of that report or the subsequent Harper Bill. The commission, almost literally composed of butchers and bakers and candlestick makers, was nothing but a mouthpiece for Harper. Harper, head of the Rockefeller-endowed institution on the Midway, was an educational mossback. Trained in Germany, he scorned women. He held down salaries at the university, and even defied that Sanhedrin, the university senate, when it came to trying to hold down salaries and privileges of teachers in the public schools. Dr. Emil W. [G.] Hirsch, who was always sympathetic with the teachers, told me, a long time afterward, that Harper had told him that he could get all the teachers he wanted for $600 a year, and that he

[15]Carter H. Harrison II (1860-1953) served five terms as mayor of Chicago (1897-1905 and 1911-1915). Both of the Harrisons received broad support from the electorate; unlike many of the Democratic political leaders, they were not identified with any particular ethnic group. Harrison's previous experience included law, real estate, and newspaper publishing. He wrote two autobiographical accounts, *Stormy Years* (Indianapolis: Bobbs-Merrill, 1935) and *Growing Up with Chicago* (Chicago: R. F. Seymour, [1944]).

[16]The Harper Report was published as the *Report of the Educational Commission of the City of Chicago* in 1899. Based on research of city school systems throughout the nation, the 248-page report is a valuable document which presents the problems of urban school administration at the turn of the century.

couldn't see why public school teachers should get even as much.[17] He tried to put his theory of suppression into practice with the report.

If we'd only known then some of the things we found out later, through years of disillusioning association with politics and politicians, we'd have found the core of the Harper report, and shown it in all its rottenness to the public. For its pivotal point—although we were not to discover it for a long time—was its clause concerning school land leases. School land leases! The theme of forty fighting years! The reason why great corporations and great newspapers and great political parties have striven, year after year, to maintain the indefensible privileges that corrupt boards of education have given them. School land leases. The Africans in the woodpile. The Harper report recommended that the Board of Education have power to enact without revaluation ninety-nine years leases upon the most valuable land in the world. Because of that clause it won the support of the great interests who stood to profit from this flagrant raid upon money intended by the government of the United States for the benefit of the school children of the community. We had no notion what we were fighting when we took up arms. We thought we were defending our own rights. We found, in time, that we were defending all the people.[18]

A copy of the report, a massive volume, was delivered to each school in Chicago late in December. John McCarthy, principal of the Hendricks, brought me his copy. "This Harper Bill is a bad bill," he told me. "It's dangerous, revolutionary. The Chicago Teachers' Federation has the machinery to fight it, and it should make the fight."

I took it in to the Federation. Elizabeth Burdick, then its president, who could by no stretch of imagination be considered forward-looking, said that the report meant nothing. The Harper Bill would not even be presented to the legislature.

The newspapers—those not profiting by the ninety-nine year lease clause—didn't agree with Miss Burdick. Their editors thought the Harper Bill a very live issue, and sent reporters to interview Dr. Harper. He told them that something had to be done as the existing tax levy could not meet the salary schedule which had just been voted us by the Board of Education, giving us the fifty dollar a year increase. He proposed that the increase of salary be left to the men but cut off from the women. The schools flamed into protest. I think that the cause of woman suffrage advanced further that day that it had gone in fifty years in Illinois. Sometimes the enemies of a cause do it far more good

[17]Emil G. Hirsch (1851-1923) was a rabbi, scholar, and civic leader. On the faculty of the University of Chicago as well as rabbi of the Chicago Sinai Congregation, he was considered a leading spokesman for the radical wing of reform.

[18]See also pp. 94-95, pp. 114-20, pp. 195-97, and pp. 260-63.

than do its friends. Voting women today owe more than they know to William Rainey Harper.

4

The meetings on the Harper bill gave to the members of the Teachers' Federation a consciousness of power and of responsibility. Those of us on the firing lines realized, however, that before we could do anything constructive we'd have to clean house.

We'd felt that the 1898 elections of the Chicago Teachers' Federation had not been honestly conducted. We suspected some of our officers of catering to the Board of Education rather than representing the teachers. Three officers of the Federation had lobbied for the Harper bill. One of them read to us at an executive meeting a letter from the superintendent of schools praising her for sagacity and wisdom because she'd declared that the teaching of drawing and music in the schools was a nuisance that should be eliminated. The fight against drawing was a fight by the drawing book publishers against the woman who could find no value in their books. The superintendent, E. Benjamin Andrews, former president of Brown University, who had presumably been foisted on Chicago because he'd been a supporter of Bryan in the free silver fight, was backing the book interests. Josephine Locke, the drawing supervisor, was representing the advanced and advancing educational methods of Col. Parker and W. W. Speer and Mrs. Young. The lines were being pretty tightly drawn, and we had to make decision where we'd stand.

Catharine Goggin was nominated for the presidency of the organization. She won the office after a struggle which brought in as much dirty politics as any precinct brawl. Anonymous letters, attacks on her race and religion, scurrilous attacks flooded the schools. Elizabeth Rogers was no more dictatorial over the Fighting Foresters than Mrs. Bratton, the presiding officer of the Federation, on the day of the nominations. It was her purpose to keep Miss Goggin from being nominated, but through the advice and aid of Ella Flagg Young we won that point.[19]

The opposition to Miss Goggin engaged for the election a hall so small that it could not have accommodated half the teachers who were coming to vote. They declared, too, that they had the authority to appoint judges and clerks of election. Without proper instruction Mrs. Bratton went to Judge Orrin N. Carter, the county judge, quoting him

[19]This election was held March 25, 1899. Goggin received 1,701 votes, and her opponent, 542. *Chicago Tribune*, March 26, 1899. See also "Minutes of the Chicago Teachers' Federation, Book no. 1, May 28, 1898-June 24, 1899," CTF Files.

as authority then for all her statements. When I protested against something she said she asked me if I wouldn't take his opinion. I said I wouldn't take the opinion of the Supreme Court on a matter that had not gone before it in due form of law. I told no one that I'd once gone to school to Judge Carter. I discovered, too, that one member of their majority on the board was not entirely in sympathy with them. I worked on her until she voted against them on procedure about printing the ballots.

On the morning of the day they were going to Judge Carter an insidious letter of attack against Miss Goggin was sent to the schools. I took it to her, and we went together to the *Daily News.* Its editor—Fay [Charles M. Faye], I think—said it was a dastardly trick and advised us to get out an answer. I was so busy with it I almost forgot to go to Carter's court. When I got there he looked down from the bench, and said, "How do you do, Maggie? I haven't seen you for a good many years. Whom are you representing?"

"Catharine Goggin," I said, although another teacher had expected to be her spokesman. I had more confidence in myself, though, than I had in her, and I seized opportunity by the tail.

Judge Carter suggested that the presidential candidates each select two clerks and two tellers for each district and, as there were fourteen districts, one presidential candidate should select seven judges and the other select another seven judges, taking alternate districts. He advised each candidate to select the judges in the other's stronghold, after the manner of the two dominant political parties.

On the question of the ticket, the opposition declared that I had taken unfair advantage of them by putting Miss Goggin's ticket first. Judge Carter said that if the ballot had been printed and circulated, it could not be changed. He agreed that if I ordered the official ballots sent to his office when they were printed, he would send all the election machinery over to the place of election, and ridiculed the idea of attempting to vote thirty-five hundred people in a tiny auditorium in a limited space of time.

At ten o'clock the next Saturday morning, the polls were opened in the drill hall of the old Masonic Temple. All day long, teachers poured into the building, filling not only the drill hall but all the other rooms of the seventeenth floor. All along the hall stood policemen to keep order, but by that time their presence was not necessary. When the polls closed, the counting showed that Miss Goggin had received almost four times as many votes as her opponent.

I brought out of the Federation fight something far more important than a sense of victory. It was the memory of a statement that Mrs. Young had made when Miss Goggin told her why she had become a candidate for the presidency of the Federation. The trouble, she declared, was that the officers of the Federation wanted to impose their will on the membership instead of making themselves the means of giving expression to the will of the teachers. Mrs. Young paced the floor with her hands behind her back. She stopped in a turn of her walking and said, "I understand. There are two hostile principles struggling for supremacy and one or the other must prevail. There is no such thing as a third party or a peace party under such conditions."

Another statement which she made at about the same time remained in my memory to help me make decisions in other crises. The election of Miss Goggin had restored peace to the Federation, but a difficulty arose in regard to the right of the retiring officers to call a meeting. This special meeting had been scheduled without proper official action. When we reached the hall, we found copies of what purported to be a protest against the Harper bill. The paper, however, failed to contain any of the vital objections of the teachers to the bill. All the matters considered in it were of minor importance. In order to secure proper consideration by the body of the real question at issue, we had to take the rule away from the presiding officer, one of the relics of the old order. Ransom E. Walker took an appeal from a decision which she made against a point which I raised. She refused to put the appeal. Walker arose and put the appeal himself to the house. The house sustained him. The meeting was declared to be a mass meeting and not a meeting of the Federation. I said that since the body was a mass meeting, it should select its own presiding officer, and nominated Walker for the chairmanship. The presiding officer left the chair and Walker took the gavel.

I told Mrs. Young with great glee of how we had managed the situation. She said, "Why did you women, when you selected a chairman, select a man? Why did you advertise to the world that women were not competent to fill that position?"

It was a lesson I never forgot.

Andrews, the superintendent—already known as "Bulletin Ben"— brought in to a meeting of the school management committee of the Board of Education a list of teachers whom he intended to drop from the schools. Tom Brenan, who had followed Judge Goggin as a member of the board and who was, as long as he lived, the friend of the teachers in the grade schools, asked if these teachers had been notified of the action. Andrews said that such notification was not necessary. I don't know whether he was ignorant of or contemptuous of the law which insured our tenure of office. He certainly had the Harper attitude of making the teachers "hands" and the superintendent Almighty God. The tenure clause was too firmly set in the pension law, however,

for him to ignore, when it was waved in his face. Tom Brenan, his long
hair shaking in fury, did the waving with a flourish. Then he seized
Andrews' list, flung it on the floor, and ground it with his heel. That
ended Bulletin Ben's attempt to break that law.[20]

Naturally, those of us who were fighting now in the forefront of
battle rejoiced.

We had tasted blood and we liked the taste.

5

The Nineties went out in trailing glory. They had been hard years,
crowded with industrial outbreaks at home, with war in Cuba and the
Philippines, with economic disturbances, with political revolts; but
they had also been glamorous years. I was still young enough to see the
world not as a darkling plain but as the splendid field of the cloth of
gold; but I was old enough to have learned that there was something in
life higher, finer than personal happiness, something that gave all
even though it demanded all. Without conscious intention I had, I can
see now, been moving toward what must have been my vocation: a
fighting future.

I did not know it, however, as in one of the last weeks of the century I
looked out on a snowy street. My widowed sister's only child, a little
girl who had been given my name, was ill. We feared for her life, and I
was praying that she might be spared to us. "Oh, God," I pleaded, "do
not take her from us. Not so soon." Then, out of that strange sense of
bargaining which some of us have toward the Almighty, I made
promise. "If only You'll leave her to us, I'll give all the rest of my life
to doing something for other children, for all children."

I hadn't the least idea what that work was to be. Only when, on the
last day of the century, I had to decide if I should take the risk of service
in a cause did I remember my promise. In that remembrance I saw not
the scope but the true significance of the work I might do. It would be
labor for the teachers of the city, but it would be, far more truly, work
for the children of the city. Only through the freedom of their teachers
could the children remain free. In the light of that visioning I had no
choice to make. It had been made for me.

The New Year came to Chicago with joyous revelry. Bells rang, and

---

[20]E. Benjamin Andrews (1844-1917) came to Chicago in 1898 and replaced a popular
superintendent of schools, Albert G. Lane. Andrews was the former president of Brown
University and a former mentor of William Rainey Harper of the University of Chicago.
Rumors of a binding together of the public schools and the private university flourished.
The autocratic Andrews resigned his position before his two-year term ended.

whistles blew, welcoming the new century. In a party as gay as any I laughed and sang and shouted with the best of them, but just as the first gun of Nineteen Hundred roared into the night I looked backward for a moment, and said goodbye to youth.

∘⟦ III ⟧∘

The Tax Fight

1

Isaiah T. Greenacre, for thirty-five years guide, philosopher, friend, and lawyer to the Chicago Teachers' Federation, once said that the tax fight had been "conceived in iniquity, born in sin, and adopted by two virtuous old maids."[1]

William Rainey Harper had been right when he had said that the tax levy would be insufficient to pay the teachers the increase which the Board of Education had granted in 1898. This increase was to have been paid in three installments. The first had been paid. The second, one of fifty dollars, had been due in January, 1899. The board, for lack of funds, had been unable to pay it. The third installment was due in January of 1900. Toward the end of 1899, the teachers realized that this installment would not be paid and that the raise given in 1898 would be taken away and the schools closed for two weeks.

Not only the teachers in the schools but the parents of children who would be kept out of school by this arbitrary ruling of the board began to ask why this course was necessary. No one seemed to know the answer. The only one given by the Board of Education was an indirect statement that it might have to close the schools for a couple of months in addition to the regular vacation.

The Teachers' Federation was seeking a solution as anxiously as the members of the board; but at that turn of the century we were babes in the woods in knowledge of the relation between the effect of closed schools and the cause of public official incompetency and dishonesty. Individually and a little vaguely, we all knew that city and county and state politics were honeycombed by what we called "boodle." As a

---

[1]Greenacre's relationship with the CTF lasted from 1900 until his death in 1944 at the age of eighty-one. He was a graduate of the Union Law School, which later merged with the Northwestern School of Law. As a member of the City Council from 1895 to 1897, he gave special attention to the tax system. His experiences as a tax lawyer led the board president to recommend him to Haley and Goggin. See p. 57.

body, however, we teachers had no information then of how it was affecting our daily lives and the lives of the children whom we were teaching.

2

On a day in the Christmas holidays of 1899, I came downtown to my dentist. He was not in to keep his appointment with me, but he had left word for me to wait as he would return within an hour. I went over to the office of the Chicago Teachers' Federation in the Unity Building to kill that hour of time. In the little office, John O'Neill, then a grade teacher in the Seward School, was talking to Catharine Goggin. He was telling her about a newspaper article which he had recently seen in a paper whose name he could not remember. The article had stated that the Illinois State Board of Equalization was allowing large Chicago corporations to escape taxes on property valued at millions of dollars. The article had mentioned the fact that the Pullman Company had one hundred million dollars' worth of property escaping taxation; the Union Traction Company, seventy-five millions; the Peoples Gas Company, over fifty millions; the street railways, telephone, electric light, and public utilities companies, almost as much again unlisted by the taxing body.[2]

I don't know why I should have seized upon the information with avidity; but it suddenly seemed to me that in this circumstance was the answer to our desperate questionings. It looked as simple to me in that moment as it does now after thirty-five years of sighting the range. If the great corporations paid their legal taxes, there would be plenty of money to operate the schools. Why, then, didn't the great corporations pay them?

I tried to make O'Neill remember in what paper he had read it. He couldn't recall the name or the date. He couldn't remember whether it was a morning or an afternoon paper. I asked him to find it for me and bring it down to the office the next day. He said he would, but on the

---

[2]The State Board of Equalization, created in 1867, was responsible for raising or lowering the total assessed value of property of any county to make property in that county bear a just relation to the assessed values of property in other counties in the state. *Laws of the State of Illinois, 1867*, p. 105. In 1872, the board's authority was extended to cover the property of railroad and telegraph companies and the capital stock of all companies or associations incorporated under the laws of Illinois. *Laws, 1871*, p. 1. The board was abolished in 1919 and its powers and duties were transferred to the newly created State Tax Commission. *Laws, 1919*, p. 718. The *Proceedings of Annual Meetings of the State Board of Equalization*, 1867-1873, 1877-1908, and the *Record of Assessments and Equalizations of Corporations*, 1888-89, 1894-1904, are available in the archives of the state of Illinois, Springfield.

next day he came back without it. After a long search of newspaper offices, we abandoned effort to get the story. Not until nearly a year afterward, however, did we discover the truth, not only in the newspaper article, but back of it.

Its publication had happened in this way, according to the story afterward told us by a racketeering lawyer who had been one of the principals in the set-up and who gave the tale in great detail and with a showing of damnatory evidence, in an apparent effort to insure immunity from public blame for himself.

This lawyer, as he told us, chanced to have a client corporation that was legally exempt from a tax levied against it by the State Board of Equalization. Instead of informing this client of its legal exemption, he said that he would take up the case with "the boys in Springfield." He then took it up with a member of the State Board of Equalization, who advised him to ask five hundred dollars for his services and split it with himself. The lawyer got his five hundred dollars from his client for services which should have cost no more than twenty-five or fifty dollars, but he did not divide with the member of the State Board. The member kept peppering him with inquiries about his share in the fee. The lawyer had already spent it and in some trepidation made appeal to a friend of his own who was a reporter on the *Chicago Daily Journal*.

The reporter, who knew his way around, promised to aid his friend. He ran a story, apparently written with great care, which revealed to those who knew the methods of the "tin cup boys" of Springfield that the State Board of Equalization members were blackmailing the corporations into individual payments to them. The lawyer sent a marked copy of this paper to the Board member and the latter immediately dropped his threats.

The reason why we hadn't been able to find the story was because it had appeared in a first edition, which had small local circulation and which was not kept on file in the offices. Its publication, however, had evidently brought both the lawyer and his reporter friend into realization that they had an interesting lead. There followed other short articles on the same topic, among them opinions of leading Chicago lawyers concerning methods which might be used to force the State Board of Equalization into performance of their legal duty in taxing the big corporations. Only two hundred and fifty dollars, actual cash, was involved in the transaction between the racketeering lawyer and the member of the State Board of Equalization, but it led through devious ways toward the final justice of exposing the methods of the State Board of Equalization and forcing the great corporations to pay a more equitable share of taxation. The *Journal* reporter had put together the information which he had about what would be the just and right valuation of the intangible properties of the great utilities and other corporations of the state (incidentally, it is interesting to note that these valuations were almost exactly the same as those which were finally and legally set by long court litigation).

One of the lawyers who had been asked for an opinion as to the proper method of forcing the State Board to do its duty had been Isaiah T. Greenacre. Greenacre had told the reporter who interviewed him that it would be possible to take a short cut by mandamus proceedings to the supreme court of the state. We laughed afterward when we realized that the man who was to become our attorney and who, by his valiant, unflagging efforts, won for us such notable success had been inadvertently the agent of a Machiavellian plot, to throw the fear of public disclosure into the quaking hearts of the statehouse boys.

One of the other comic sidelights on the situation came when John O'Neill, the man who had called our attention to the story, later came to me with a request to "lay off the Board of Equalization" because his friend, Roger C. Sullivan, by that time Democratic boss of the Illinois State Legislature, wanted our "activities against the Board to stop." I told O'Neill that Sullivan was no friend of mine, and he said that we were all Irish Catholics and ought to stand together. I told him I'd be damned if I'd stand with any Catholic, Irish or Dutch or anything else, who'd defend procedure like that of the State Board. I'm putting that down now not only because it's always been my creed, but because it's the creed of so many others of my faith and race.[3]

The corporations might have read the *Journal* story with interest but, by one of those strange twists of fate which make accident the

---

[3]Roger C. Sullivan (1861-1920) was considered the boss of the Democratic party in Illinois. Starting as an apprentice in the railroad shops in 1879 earning $1.75 per day, Sullivan became a multi-millionaire through various business enterprises, particularly those in the gas utility realm. He rose to political power following the assassination of Carter Harrison in 1893. For the next quarter century, he was a dominant force in local, state, and even national politics. For much of this period, Sullivan controlled the party machinery while another faction, that led by Carter Harrison II, controlled City Hall. Charles Merriam, *Chicago*, pp. 96-97, 113.

The success of Irish Catholics in Chicago politics has been explained by Martin Myerson and Edward C. Banfield. They contend that in both the city council and the party hierarchy, the Irish dominated due to (1) their religious affinity with other important ethnic groups and (2) the fact that no single ethnic group had a clear majority in Chicago. Thus, Irish Catholics were the most acceptable and logical candidates for office. They cite a politician's quote: "A Lithuanian won't vote for a Pole and a Pole won't vote for a Lithuanian. A German won't vote for either of them, but all three will vote for a 'Turkey' (Irishman)." Edward C. Banfield, *Political Influence* (Glencoe, Ill.: Free Press, 1961), p. 136.

agent of destiny, the Chicago Teachers' Federation had also found the
rat hole.

I began searching for information about the State Board of Equalization and its duties. John O'Neill didn't know whether it was appointed
or elected or why he had voted, if he had, for its members. I went
upstairs in the Unity Building to the office of John Feeley, a young
lawyer who, a little while later [November, 1900], defeated William
Lorimer, the "blond boss of Illinois," for a seat in Congress.[4] From
Feeley I borrowed a copy of the Illinois statutes and sought in the book
some facts about the State Board of Equalization. Most of what I read
about assessing "the capital stock and franchises over and above the
tangible property as assessed by the local assessors" was Greek to me,
but I did get out of it knowledge that the State Board of Equalization
was elected by the people, one member from each Congressional district, and that the election was held at the same time as the presidential
election, the term of office being for four years. I also found that it was
the duty of the State Auditor to preside at its meetings and to send a
report to the County Clerk of each county showing the amount which
the Board had assessed each corporation on its capital stock and
franchises over and above the assessment made by the local assessors on
the tangible value of the property.

I did not know then what capital stock and franchises meant, but I
did know that, whatever it was, the law called it intangible property
and that the State Board of Equalization should assess it and that the
amount of this assessment should be indicated in this report. Here was
something I could see and touch, a report. Where should I find one?

I asked John O'Neill if he'd come down at ten o'clock the next
morning, the last day of our vacation, to go with me to the County

[4]William Lorimer (1861-1934) was a Republican. Like the Democrats, the Republican
party was composed of several factions. Three of these were identified by Charles
Merriam, who was both a participant in Chicago politics and a distinguished political
scientist. These factions were centered on the leadership of Charles Deneen, William
Lorimer, and Fred Busse and corresponded to geographical areas of the city—the
southwest, the west, and the north side, respectively, of Chicago.

The two parties, together with various interest groups, constituted a political system
which Merriam described as "an intricate tangled skein which I should not undertake to
disentangle, even if I could." Merriam, *Chicago*, pp. 94-97. Despite the loss in 1900,
Lorimer was elected eight times to the House of Representatives. Following his 1909
election to the U.S. Senate, he was ousted from his seat by his colleagues in 1911 after an
investigation of bribery and corruption related to the election. This case helped split the
Republican party nationally prior to the 1912 presidential election. Joel A. Tarr, *A
Study in Boss Politics: William Lorimer of Chicago* (Urbana: University of Illinois
Press, 1971). At the local level, Tarr sees both the Republican Lorimer and the Democrat
Sullivan as political leaders who attempted to rationalize the chaos and instability of
urban affairs. The political machine provided a mechanism of control through a series
of accommodations between representatives of the political and economic systems, with
particular attention to such municipal services as utilities and transportation.

Clerk's office. He didn't come, but while I was waiting for him I asked Catharine Goggin to appoint me to a vacancy then existing on the finance committee of the Federation. Armed with this authority, I seized the chairman of the finance committee, and dragged her with me over Washington Street and up Clark to the old County Building. I knew that the County Clerk of Cook County was certain to be a politician who wouldn't know much about the organization of his office and that some "chief clerk" would be the real authority in the giving of information. I knew, though, that if I asked in the County Clerk's office, no one would tell me the truth, and so I went into the County Treasurer's office and inquired the name of the assistant to the County Clerk who would have the State Auditor's report of the assessment made by the State Board of Equalization on the capital stock of the corporations of Cook County.

The man I questioned gave me a queer look, grinned, and said, "Archie Cameron is your man, but I doubt if you can find him by yourself." He called a boy, whom he told to take us to Archie. We followed the boy through circuitous passages. We wound in and out among book racks, long tables, from which men seated on high stools peered curiously at us from under green eye shades, on through gateways, locked on the inside, but opening to the touch of our guide. He finally pointed a cautious finger and said in low tones, "That's Mr. Cameron, the man with the pen over his ear."

The boy disappeared and we went up to Cameron. He told us he was very busy and had no time to give us. I told him we were in no hurry and could wait. A clerk gave us two high stools, on which we climbed. Inadvertently I caught enough of Cameron's conversation with the two men with whom he was talking to realize that it was about taxes. I climbed down from my stool and, telling Cameron that I too was interested in taxes, asked if I might listen if the gentlemen were willing. Cameron grunted. Not knowing whether he meant assent or dissent, I drew nearer to listen. The three men moved their chairs closer together so that I could catch only the falling crumbs.

I heard enough, however, to learn that Cameron was explaining how, in accordance with the recent amendment to the revenue law, he was spreading the taxes. The two men were attorneys for one of the numerous public bodies which had obtained temporary injunctions on the ground that the method was illegal and unfair. After they had gone, Cameron turned to me and curtly asked what I wanted. I told him I wanted to see the report which the State Auditor had sent to the County Clerk showing the assessment made by the State Board of Equalization on the capital stock of the corporations of Cook County. He asked me who wanted the report. I told him the six thousand teachers of Chicago wanted it, and I thought of Ethan Allen demanding the surrender of Fort Ticonderoga in the name of the Great Jehovah and the Continental Congress, which at that time had never met.

He asked me why the teachers wanted the report. I said that we wanted to find out if it were true that the State Board of Equalization was allowing the Chicago corporations to evade their taxes. "Why do you think they are?" he asked us. When I explained, he snorted, "A newspaper report, and you don't even know the name of the paper! Go back and tell the teachers from me, a thousand to one it isn't correct."

"No," I said, "I will not take any man's word for it. I want to see that report myself. It's a public document, isn't it? And I have a right to see it, haven't I?"

He did not answer me. Like Bluebeard's wife looking for her rescuer, he stared appealingly toward the circuitous passage, through which, at that opportune moment, his rescuers appeared in the persons of four representatives from the offices of the Corporation Counsel and the City Comptroller. They too had come to find out how the County Clerk was spreading the taxes in order to determine whether or not the city was getting its fair share and, if not, to recommend an injunction suit. Cameron moved his class in tax spreading over to a window. Uninvited, I followed. The men were so much taller than I and their faces were so close together that I was almost entirely shut out of the session, until Denis Sullivan turned to me and said, "Do you really want to hear this?"

I said, "I certainly do." He stepped aside and let me take his place.

Cameron's explanation of his tax spreading was so simple and clear that I was satisfied that he was apportioning the taxes according to the law and that if the Board of Education or any of the other boards were expecting relief from their financial stringency through court proceedings instituted for the purpose of compelling the County Clerk's office to spread the taxes differently from what Cameron was doing, they would fail. Then and there, I came to the conclusion that the teachers must look to remedies other than injunction proceedings against the County Clerk.

After the representatives from the city hall had gone, Cameron turned to me and almost angrily demanded, "*What* do you want?"

I answered, "The same thing that I wanted when I first came in two hours ago."

"What's that?"

He made me repeat my lesson, which he had shrewdly guessed I had so recently learned. He probably hoped that by that time I had exhausted my store of tax knowledge. Realizing I could still put it together, he looked at me, thrust his hands in his pockets, whistled, looked at me again, and then glanced over in the corner at a young man whom I was to learn was a reporter for the city press. He had been present from the time I had gone into the office and was watching the whole performance with evident interest. Cameron then walked slowly to the files and, returning, placed in my hands the report of the State Auditor, subscribed and sworn to and bearing the seal of the great State of Illinois.

I glanced eagerly down the alphabetical list, which contained the names of 136 corporations in the city of Chicago. I looked for the Union Traction Company, for the Chicago City Railway Company— not there. I tried to find the other street railways, the Peoples Gas, the Pullman Company. I looked in vain for these and other corporations. "Is this a complete list?" I asked Cameron.

"Yes."

"Where's the Pullman Company? Where are the others?"

"Aren't they there?"

"Didn't you know they are not here? What does it mean, that they are not here?"

"It means," he said, "that they are not taxed."

I smiled at him and said, "I'm glad, Mr. Cameron, that I did not go back and tell the teachers of Chicago that the newspaper report was not true." I said, "We'll copy this." At his release his whole office rushed to give us help, papers, pencils, pens. We copied the entire list, not daring to stop for a moment until we had finished it.

Cameron let us do it, but when we were through and asked him to verify it, he told us he would give us a certified list, properly made out by his office. It would be ready, he said, by the following Tuesday. I told him I could not call on Tuesday as I would be back in school. I asked him to mail it to the office of the Teacher's Federation.

He said, "No; you call for it." He looked at me then and said, in a gentle, kindly voice, "What are you going to do with that report?" I told him I was going to take it to the teachers to show them that their salaries were to be cut because a public body had been remiss in its duty in not forcing sufficient legal taxes from those corporations to pay them. Then he said, "If the teachers are going to take up this matter and go into it seriously and fully, they can do a great deal of good."

He went to the files and took down reports of the State Auditor for ten years back. He showed me how, ten years previously, the State Board of Equalization had made some pretense of assessing these corporations on the value of their privileges in using the Chicago streets for their own benefit, but how the assessments had grown less and less each year until in that year, 1899, not one dollar of franchise tax had been assessed against those public utilities corporations whose names I had looked for in vain on the official list.

On Tuesday, the 2nd of January, 1900, I went back to the Hendricks School. I taught all day and closed my desk in the afternoon with the full intention of reopening it the next morning. I have not been in a schoolroom since.

3

I picked up the official list at Cameron's office and took it to Catharine Goggin. I asked her if she, as President of the Chicago Teachers' Federation and a tax payer, would institute mandamus proceedings to compel the State Board of Equalization to do its duties and assess these corporations. She said that she would if she were so advised by some one who was competent to advise, but that she did not consider me competent. I told her that I knew I was not, but that I did know that mandamus was the proceeding by which the officers of the Foresters had been compelled to do their duty when they had failed. The thought flashed through my mind, "I'll ask John P. Altgeld if mandamus is the proper proceeding. He knows and he'll tell me and it won't cost the teachers anything." I asked Catharine Goggin if she would accept Judge Altgeld's opinion and act on his advice. She said she would.

For years I had known Judge Altgeld. My father had been his loyal friend and supporter. The Federation office was in his Unity Building. In his office on the sixteenth floor was one of the few telephones of the time in Chicago. When we needed one, we used it. Sometimes when I had gone into the outer office, I had seen him bent over his desk studying masses of papers, struggling to carry on his work, while his faithful associates, Joe Martin and George Schilling, stood guard between him and a too demanding world. He was then a defeated, sick, tired man; but to the end of his life, he remained the Eagle.[5]

He had been for a few years the head of his party in Illinois, but he was to remain for many the inspiration of the liberal democracy of the nation. Altgeld had been and was being pilloried, misrepresented, misunderstood. He was unquestionably the greatest governor Illinois has ever had and one of its two greatest citizens. Like Lincoln, he saw with and felt with the common people. Like Lincoln, he endured in his lifetime the martyrdom of human loneliness. Like Lincoln, he must have known, as Vachel Lindsay saw him, that

"To live in mankind is far more than to live in a name."

[5]Altgeld was immortalized in verse by Vachel Lindsay in "The Eagle That Is Forgotten," *Collected Poems* (New York: Macmillan, 1925), p. 95.

Altgeld had been born in Germany, reared in grinding poverty on a farm in Ohio, and understood the needs and rights of the people. In a time honeycombed with the dishonesty of public officials and rotted by the sycophantic attitude of others toward power and privilege, Altgeld remained steadfast to his principles. The charge has been made against him that he used for himself money from Ogden Gas inherited from his nephew, John W. Lanehart. [Waldo R.] Browne, Altgeld's official biographer, has said that Altgeld used this money to replace Lanehart's own losses and that he sold the Ogden Gas stock for exactly what Lanehart had paid for it, while shrewder politicians held it a few months longer until it soared to the price which made them million-aires and which would have enriched Altgeld as well. He knew this possibility, but he refused to profit by it.

Forrest Crissey who made a study of Altgeld's public life and who was not influenced by any sympathetic association with him, tells the story of how Altgeld turned down a half-million-dollar bribe to sign a traction bill which his successor in the governorship afterward signed.[6] The story stated that on the day before the traction bills known as the Eternal Monopoly Bills, which had been passed by a corrupted Legis-lature in the interest of the traction companies of Chicago, went to Governor Altgeld for action, Mike Boylan, [John W. Lanehart] the governor's business partner and general handy man, came into the Unity Building vaults with a stranger. Boylan introduced him to the clerk and stood by while the man took from two telescopes packages of money, which he placed in one of the big wall boxes. They went out together, but Boylan came back alone in a few moments. "Guard that box," he told the clerk, "There's a half-million dollars in it."

Afterward—when the man who had engaged the box had come back and taken out his money—Boylan told that after their departure from the vault, the other man had flung the keys to the deposit drawer before him and said, "You know what to do with these." He had then wheeled out of the door of Boylan's office and disappeared before Boylan came out of a daze to overtake him. Boylan realized then in what a terrible position he had placed Governor Altgeld and dreaded the necessity of telling him of his innocent complicity in the attempted bribery.

Altgeld came back from Springfield the next day to face the fact that he was about to lose all financial control of the Unity Building, into

[6]This story, first told in an article in the *Chicago Tribune*, was reprinted in 1904 in a book by Crissey entitled *Tattling Tales of a Retired Politician* (Chicago: Thompson and Thomas, 1904). Fictional names were used with Altgeld called "Cal Peavey," the Unity Building was "the Empire Building" and John W. Lanehart was "Mike Boylan." Haley uses this episode to illustrate her high regard for Altgeld.

which he had put years of work and effort and all the savings of a lifetime. Boylan regretfully added to his burden by telling him the story. Altgeld rose to his feet, pointed his long, bony finger at Mike, and shouted in a rasping voice, "Young man! I'd advise you to take better care of that damn scoundrel's money than you ever did of any money in your life."

That night, he wrote a veto message on the traction bill that almost burned up the pages on which he set it. Then he called in his real scrappers and began a fight against foregone defeat. He almost had to kidnap three weak-kneed members of the opposition and he threatened two others with the penitentiary, but he won support of his veto by three votes. He celebrated the triumph by surrendering to his creditors all the property he had accumulated in fifty years of back-breaking labor.

That was John Peter Altgeld.

I found Judge Altgeld in his office. He was staring out of the window on gray skies. He turned to me as I flung at him, "Is mandamus the proper legal proceeding to institute to compel a public body to do its duty when that body fails to do it?"

One of those rare smiles that his friends knew passed over his face. "What are you up to now?" he asked me. I told him that I wanted him to answer the question for me. He said, "What public body are you after?"

I answered, "The State Board of Equalization. It is letting the corporations escape their taxes."

A bitter, cynical look crept over his worn, pale face. More to himself than to me, he repeated sarcastically, "The State Board of Equalization. Do you know that when I was governor of this state, I tried to get before that board to show the sworn statements I had received from the State Auditors of practically every state in the Union, showing that the Pullman Company evaded its taxes in every state, on the plea that it paid in all the others? I could not even get a hearing before that board to present my demand that the Pullman Company be taxed in this state. What can you expect to do?"

"You have not answered my question," I said, and repeated it.

Judge Altgeld said, "Mandamus is the proper proceeding, but you will not find a court in Christendom that will give a decision against that State Board of Equalization and those powerful public utilities corporations."

I told him I had to go back to Miss Goggin and tell her what he said, and that I was afraid she would not be willing to begin mandamus proceedings if he said we could not win; besides that, I did not see why we should not win if we were right.

Judge Altgeld shook his head sadly. With that strange, far-away look which always seemed to be in his eyes, he stared at me. In a voice of infinite pathos that I have never forgotten, he said, "No; you are right, but you will not win." Then, arousing himself, he threw back his head, his eyes flashed suddenly, and he added, oh, so kindly, "But go ahead! You will not win, but you will wake up the people of Chicago."

I hurried down to Catharine Goggin and told her just what he had said. "Maybe we won't win," I thought it my duty to add.

Without a moment's hesitation, she calmly said, "I don't care whether we win or lose if we are right. I shall go ahead at once."

Mary E. Lynch, a member of the Federation, insisted upon taking me to Graham H. Harris, President of the Board of Education.[7] I, myself, could see no good reason for going to him. We did not need his approval and his disapproval might add to our initial difficulties. Miss Lynch, however, dragged me over and told him that I had come to inform him what Miss Goggin intended to do on the next Tuesday morning.

"What does Miss Goggin intend to do on Tuesday morning?" he asked. I told him of the mandamus proceedings and he literally fell back against the door of the room. I did not know then that his father-in-law, Jesse Spalding, was at that time president of the Chicago Union Traction Company, one of the worst offenders. It was paying taxes on a physical valuation of $12,000,000 when it should also have been paying on at least $75,000,000 of intangibles—the use of the city streets—the amount it was assessed in the following year.

Harris asked me if we had competent legal advice. Just then, Catharine Goggin came in and confirmed my statement that we had the best in the city. Without mentioning Judge Altgeld's name, I told him what the Judge had said. He said that he would not like to see the Chicago Teachers' Federation go into anything in which they could not win; that the Corporation Counsel and the attorney for the Board

[7]Graham H. Harris (1857-1933) was a lawyer whose board experience lasted from 1897 to 1906. As president for all but the first year of his service, he gave support to the teachers as evidenced in the following passage from a letter he sent to Governor Richard Yates: "Good schools cannot exist without good teachers and good employees. The safer we make them feel in respect to their tenure of office, the more contented they are financially, and the more they can be assured that in their declining years they will have some compensation, the better the work they will give us, and hence the schools will be better and the public through its children will profit thereby." May 7, 1901, CTF Files.

The Chicago Board of Education was established in 1857 and replaced the system of control by seven inspectors which had prevailed during the first twenty years of public education in the city. Members of the board, which had grown from fifteen to twenty-one by 1900 through annexations, were appointed by the mayor for terms of three years. Herrick, *Chicago Schools*, pp. 24, 45, 83. This is the most detailed study of the history of the public school system of Chicago.

of Education were trying to get more revenue for the schools in the city; and that he would like to have us consult with them before we did anything.

I told him of my experience in the County Clerk's office and added that I thought that anyone who depended upon the Corporation Counsel's method of securing financial relief was doomed to disappointment. He asked us to come to his office at nine o'clock the next Tuesday morning. I told him that I had to be in school. He said, rather testily, "You don't have to be in school if I ask you to come here," and dictated letters to our principals asking them to excuse us from school on that day.

When we returned to his office, he said, in a tone of decision and command, "I have seen the Corporation Counsel and I am tired of expedience and temporizing. You people are right. Go ahead, in the name of the children of Chicago, and I am with you."

It was my turn to gasp. As soon as I could recover, I said, "You need not tell us we are right. We know we are right and we are going ahead, but I wish you would say that to the people who need to hear it."

He asked, "Whom do you mean?"

I replied, "The teachers."

He said, "I will. How do you want me to tell them?"

"Write them a letter."

"I will," he said. He turned to Miss Goggin. "Will you," he asked her, "as President of the Federation, write me a letter and ask me what I, as President of the Board of Education, think of the teachers taking up this work?"

Miss Goggin wrote the letter. He approved it. Then I asked him if Miss Goggin and I might have a leave of absence for a year with pay. He caught his breath and gave me a sharp look. "You don't want much, do you?"

I said, "I don't think that it is asking much, to ask for your bread and butter while you are doing such work as this for the city, and to have your whole time to do it in. If this work is worth anything to the schools in the city, it should be worth the price of our bread and butter while we are doing it."

He said, slowly and thoughtfully, "I believe you are right." Then he added, "I can give you the leave of absence myself and I will, but I shall have to ask the Board of Education for your salary and I shall do it."

Eight hundred dollars, the yearly salary paid the primary teacher in Chicago in 1900—Catharine Goggin was a primary teacher—and $825, the salary paid the grammar grade teacher—I was a grammar grade teacher—was the investment he asked of the City of Chicago in two women who started out to buck the line of subsidized taxing bodies, of corrupted legislators and corrupting corporations. We didn't take it, however. Our salaries from the Board of Education ceased with the beginning of our larger public service. The teachers themselves—from that day to this—paid us and all the consequent bills.

We started with leaves of absence for the next week.

The next week was hectic. Graham Harris sent us to John S. Miller, one of the best lawyers in Chicago, and a recognized authority on taxation. Miller was unwilling to undertake the case but, out of friendship for Harris, gave us the benefit of his advice. He told us not to select such corporations as the Pullman Company, for, he said, they would move out of the state rather than pay their taxes, and public sentiment would not be with us if we were responsible for that loss to the community. He advised us to select public utility corporations like the gas, street railway, telephone, and electric light companies, which have the use of the public streets and which could not move out. He said that these companies' privileges in the streets were immensely valuable and that the law provided that they should be taxed in proportion to their value. He said that he believed the public school teachers should be the natural advisers of the public on the important subject of taxation, but he would not advise us to go into the courts. If we insisted, however, upon going in, mandamus was the proper proceeding.

A year later, while that mandamus suit was on hearing in Springfield, I was called as a witness against the State Board of Equalization. After I had been on the stand the greater part of two days, John S. Miller, then one of the attorneys for the State Board of Equalization, started to cross-examine me. Why, he asked me, giving me a list of thousands of corporations, had I selected certain corporations and omitted others in instituting the suit? Had I seen that list? Yes, I had. Why did I choose what I had chosen for attack? By that time I had forgotten just why I had chosen them; but he drove me back against the wall, flinging the question at me for the tenth time before I suddenly remembered the source of my inspiration. "I selected those corporations," I flung out, "because John S. Miller told me to."

The look that came into his face, as it changed from red to gray and back to red again, indicated only too plainly how entirely he too had forgotten the friendly advice which he, as a good citizen, a former member of the Board of Education and a former Corporation Counsel of the City of Chicago, had given in the previous year to two public school teachers.

4

Graham Harris had given me a copy of a red book called "Chicago Securities," which listed the intangible as well as the tangible values of all important Chicago corporations.[8] I found in John Feeley's copy of the statutes of Illinois an item which stated that it was the duty of the assessors of each county to send certain prescribed printed schedules to the corporations in the county, and to list these information schedules when they should be filled out by the corporation officers in statement of the amount of capital stocks and bonds and market value of the shares of stock. The assessors should then write in the assessment made by them on these tangible properties and send these schedules to the county clerk who, in turn, should send them to the State Auditor at Springfield. That officer should bring them before the State Board of Equalization.

I found, too, that the State Board of Equalization was charged with the duty of ascertaining the value of the capital stock and franchises of the corporations, over and above the assessment made by the local assessors on the tangible property, and assessing this intangible property according to its value. The law also gave the board the power to make rules to determine the value of franchises and especially made these rules binding as law. The State Auditor should report to the county clerk of each county the names of the corporations and the capital stock assessment made against each of them by the State Board of Equalization on their franchise values. The law was simple and specific—once it was brought into the open. So was the rule where it could be dug out of the dark where it had lain since 1875.

Archie Cameron had ready for me, when I went back, the copy he had promised me of this report. I asked him to let me see the corporations' capital stock schedules sent to his office by the assessors, as required by law. He said the assessors had not sent any.

I went directly to the assessors' office and asked the chief clerk, [William] Kingsley, to let me see the copies of the schedules filled out by the corporations. He told me they had been sent over to the County Clerk's office. I told him they had not been sent there. He finally admitted—after many exits and entrances—that the corporations never filled out the schedules. I read aloud to him the section of the law concerning them, stating that in the event that corporations failed or refused to fill out the schedules, it should be the duty of the local assessors to fill them out, from the best information they could obtain.

---

[8]*Chicago Securities* was an annual publication prepared by the Chicago Directory Company. Its full title was *Chicago Securities: A Digest of Information Relative to Stocks, Bonds, Banks and Financial Institutions of Chicago.* The 1899 publication was the ninth edition.

I asked Kingsley to let me see the schedules which the assessors had filled out from the best information they could obtain. He disappeared and, returning, said that the assessors had not filled out any schedules. "In the thirteen years I have been in this office, those schedules have never been filled out," he said, "by either the corporations or the assessors."

I said, "I am glad I have at least found out for the teachers, whose salaries are to be cut, why the school funds are short."

Kingsley said, "I do not think it will happen again."

I said, "I do not think it will, either. The teachers will see that it does not."

They did.

Kingsley protested that the fault was not with the assessors, but with the County Recorder. I went over to the County Recorder. He said the fault was with the Secretary of State who had never forwarded him a list, and dictated a letter to the Secretary at Springfield, asking him to forward the list at once. Two days later, when I returned, the Recorder read to me the Secretary's answer. The list, he wrote, had never been compiled in his office. He thought some other office in the state—he wasn't sure which one—had that responsibility.

Eighteen hundred and ninety-nine was the first year in which public utilities corporations had completely escaped taxation on intangible values. In other years, the State Board of Equalization had set *something*.

Meanwhile, Catharine Goggin and I had gone to Isaiah T. Greenacre. Graham H. Harris, in speaking of lawyers, had said that Greenacre was one of the cleverest and best tax lawyers in the city. He added that he had gone in the Chicago City Council and had come out poor. We decided that he was the man for us. In the thirty-five years which have elapsed since he took over the destiny of counsellor to the Chicago Teachers' Federation, I have never had occasion to regret for a moment that choice. No lawyer could have given to any client a larger measure of knowledge of the law, understanding of human nature, and unswerving loyalty than Greenacre has devoted to the cause. From the experience of other men who cast their lots with us, I am certain that, at any time during those years, he might have left us with great financial profit to himself. Never once has he faltered in advising us and presenting our cases. Sometimes I've scrapped with him all over his office, all the way through corridors and down in elevators, across streets, and up into courtrooms; but I've always discovered that he'd been right and that I'd been wrong in the argument. That doesn't mean, though, that I wouldn't argue it all out with him again tomorrow. That's another day.

He told us that the proper method for us to pursue was a mandamus proceeding in the Supreme Court of Illinois against the State Board of Equalization. As a public emergency measure, it would take precedence of other cases on the calendar and come to trial at once. I felt then and knew afterward that it was the proper procedure, but the counsel of others overrode Greenacre and myself and we took the long road around Robin Hood's barn instead of the short cut.

At that time, the city and the county and all the taxing bodies had started suit against the County Clerk to make him spread the taxes in a different manner. If we could have taken our case into the Supreme Court during the next seven or eight days, before the County Clerk started to spread the taxes, we might have forced the corporation taxes to be put on the books. That would have lowered everybody's taxes. If we could have added $600,000,000 of escaping tax valuation to the record, we would have materially decreased the general taxation. The tax which every small home owner had to pay would have been immediately reduced. It was as true then as it is now that the ability of great corporations to escape just taxation was the reason for the increasing burdens upon the small tax payer.

What we wanted to do was to show the public that the failure to produce enough money to give the teachers the salary the board had promised them was due to the fact that the most valuable property in Illinois—the privilege given corporations to capitalize the people's gift to them of the use of public streets for their own exclusive uses—was not put on the tax rolls. If it had been, the board would have had money to pay without placing any additional burden upon the people.

In 1900, twenty-eight years after the taxation machinery for the determination of corporation values had been set in operation, the City of Chicago was getting less from corporate taxes than it had in the year after Mrs. O'Leary's cow had kicked over the lamp and started the great Chicago fire in 1871.

The Grange Movement of the early Seventies had been responsible for the law of 1872, which gave to the State Board of Equalization power to assess the intangible element in corporation values. Before that, the tax setting bodies would tax only what they could see. They couldn't get at the taxable values of the railroads, and the farmers, who were even then suffering from the political and financial power of the railroads, tried to put in law a method of getting at these values. The law made the Board of Equalization judge of the rule it should make to determine intangible values, but provided that when that rule was adopted it became a law and binding on the board.[9]

[9]See note 2, p. 43.

I began work on the last published report of the State Board of Equalization and went backward to the report of 1872. I should have started at the beginning, for it was in the first report that I found the right legal method. The rule then adopted by the board had provided that the board should ascertain the number of shares of capital stock of a corporation, the value per share as quoted on the 1st day of April of any year, then multiply the number of shares by the valuation of the stock quotation, to determine the value of the capital stock. It was to use the same method with the bonds, then add the two values, and deduct the assessed valuation of the tangible, physical property, including real estate and personal property. Application of that rule to the public utility corporations of Chicago in the year 1899 would have set $264,000,000 as the value of the capital stock, including franchises. Deducting the assessed valuation of real estate and personal property, it left $230,000,000 of franchise values in the five public utilities then operative in Chicago. For every dollar of actual value of these corporations there was six dollars of franchise value—and the franchises were public gifts!

There were two street railways, the Chicago City Railway, which was under its own charter and could not combine with any other street railway in Chicago; and the Union Traction Company, which had all the street railways on the north and west sides. The value of the Union Traction Company was $87,000,000, of which $12,000,000 was what the tangible property had been assessed by the assessors. That left $75,000,000 representing the value of the franchises. The Chicago City Railway, whose franchise would be nullified if it ever combined with any other company, had stock at a market value of between thirty-three and thirty-eight million dollars, although it was set down for nothing at all. Altogether, the valuations of the five corporations—the Peoples Gas Light and Coke Company, the Chicago Edison Company, and the Chicago Telephone Company were the other three—were $35,000,000. According to the little red book, "Chicago Securities," which Graham H. Harris had given to me, the total valuations should have been nearly seven times that amount.

The Board of Education is itself without power to levy taxes in Chicago. Throughout the State of Illinois, the boards of education, with few exceptions, levy their own taxes. These, however, are elective boards; the Chicago board is appointive. It is a fundamental principle of law in the United States that, even when elected officers create an appointed board, they do not give them the power to levy taxes. Fortunately for the community, that much of our fundamental Americanism has remained a motivating power in the American mind. The City Council of Chicago, prior to 1917, passed ordinances in connection with the tax levy for the Board of Education. In February, 1900, a little while after we had taken up the fight, the Council passed an ordinance providing that the Board of Education should use as much of the amount appropriated to it by the Council as was necessary to restore to the teachers the cut that had been made in their salaries. Through that door, the Honorable "Jawn" [John] McKenna—the Misther Hennessy of Finley Peter Dunne's Misther Dooley papers—came into our lives.[10]

5

From the first day of the fight, the grade school teachers of Chicago had risen as a phalanx against the vague but apparently overwhelming power which we had almost inadvertently attacked. This was, remember, in the year of Our Lord nineteen hundred. Chicago, in spite of sporadic reform movements, knew practically nothing of the close and hidden relationships between public taxing bodies and great commercial and industrial interests. Women in Illinois had the privilege of voting for trustees of the University of Illinois once in every four years.[11] Only a few far western states had complete woman suffrage. There were, it is true, a few women in Illinois who had been fighting valiantly for votes for women, Dr. Frances Dickinson, head of the Harvey Medical School and cousin of Susan B. Anthony, Dr. Julia Holmes Smith, Dr. Sarah Hackett Stevenson, Dr. Mary Thompson, Antoinette Van Housen Wakeman, Katherine Leckie—dear Katherine Leckie, the warmest hearted, reckless souled idealist who ever turned copy in at a newspaper desk!—Catherine Waugh McCullough, Margaret Sullivan—one of the greatest editorial writers in the United States—had all championed the cause of women.

There was, however, no concerted movement at that time toward women's active participation in political life. We were stumbling along in the dark. The grade school teachers of Chicago had to take on

[10]John McKenna was an anomaly in that he was an Irish Republican politician from the stronghold of Irish Democratic politics on the south side, the neighborhoods of Bridgeport and Brighton Park. He held a number of posts including membership on the State Board of Equalization. Later, he was chief inspector of private employment agencies for the state of Illinois. McKenna served as the straight man for Mr. Dooley in Finley Peter Dunne's columns. In 1918, he wrote his own book entitled *Stories by the Original Jawn McKenna from Archy Road of the Sunworshippers Club of McKinley Park* (Chicago: J. F. Higgins, printer, 1918). Schaaf, *Mr. Dooley's Chicago*, pp. 50-51.

[11]In 1891, the Illinois General Assembly passed an act which gave women the right to vote at elections for any officer of schools under the general or special laws of the state. To qualify, women had to possess all qualifications applying to men voting in such elections including age, residence, citizenship, and registration. *Laws of Illinois, 1891*, p. 135.

trust the decisions of the Board of Managers of the Chicago Teachers' Federation. The board arrived at these decisions, not by the arbitrary rule of any one individual, but by the counsel and advice of large numbers of the teachers. Day after day, scores of women used to come into the offices of the Federation, bringing information they had acquired here, there, and everywhere, from brothers and fathers and sometimes from sweethearts, about methods of procedure and information which might be secured. Without the active interest of these women, the board of managers could not have made those decisions, which Catharine Goggin and I carried out. Without the splendid loyalty, the quick understanding, the unswerving fealty to right of the thirty-five hundred grade teachers of Chicago, the tax fight could never have been continued and won. Not for a day did Catharine Goggin or I fail to realize that we were not only merely the instruments of a purpose but that we were the representatives of women who believed in us as well as in their cause. Equally well we realized that our ability to do our work depended upon their cooperation. For thirty-five years that cooperation, which brought us in contact with every phase of life in the city, has never failed.

Through their own efforts, the teachers secured neighborhood audiences for the hearing of the evidence we were unearthing about assessments and the lack of assessments, mostly the latter. At these meetings, they distributed leaflets showing the values of the big corporations and what they had escaped in taxes by the failure of either assessors or State Board of Equalization. By graphs and charts we showed how the public paid, both by franchise gifts, and by payment of streetcar fares and other unnecessarily high public utilities rates. A remarkable fact is that not a printed sheet was ever found on the floor or on the seats of any of the halls after the meetings had adjourned. The audiences always took them home. Occasionally, collections were taken up at the meetings to help defray expenses, but nearly all the money was raised by voluntary contributions from the teachers themselves. They passed out pamphlets at church doors, tacked signs on telegraph poles, and left our so-called literature in barber shops, drug stores, meat markets, and saloons. Sometimes newsboys put them in newspapers and distributed them. Sometimes merchants rolled them up in bundles which they were sending out from little stores. We piled up interest in the smaller meetings by having such speakers as Jane Addams, Kate Starr Kellogg, Dr. Rufus A. White, the Reverend Thomas Cox, and even Bishop John Lancaster Spalding. In February, 1900, we decided to hold a mass meeting in Central Music Hall.

Dr. Hiram Thomas was to have been a speaker at the meeting, but he was ill and his wife, Vandalia Thomas, came in his stead. Mrs. Thomas made a fine speech with only one slight mistake, charging the Board of Equalization with one of the shortcomings of the Board of Assessors. A man in the audience leaped to his feet and roared out a challenge to her. He was brought to the stage and forced to listen to her explanation. Then someone recognized him as Jawn McKenna, member of the State Board of Equalization. All the aroused emotion of the teachers against that board burst in flares over Jawn's head. He went out through the wings so fast that he left his hat on the table.

Two days later, however, he came into our office in the Unity Building, not for his hat, but on a more important mission. He told us—Anna Norris Kendall; Catharine Goggin; George Schilling; and a reporter from the *Herald*; and myself—that we were on the wrong track in attacking the State Board of Equalization. He said that the teachers' cut came from a blunder of the Board of Education and that the City Council could fix it up if we would go and ask them. He said that the Council had failed to appropriate enough money for the teachers' salaries. There was plenty of money, he declared, if the City Council would appropriate it. He would, he added, talk business for us.

When Jawn said that, I looked at him. "Now, Mr. McKenna, if you're here to talk business—but that isn't business. You know perfectly well that the State Board of Equalization has not done its duty. You know I see through you."

He said, "I believe you do. We'll talk." He talked plenty, telling us how to go about getting the money from the City Council. We realized that he was only trying to draw our fire away from his State Board of Equalization, but we utilized his information, and secured from the City a provision in the tax-levy ordinance that so much of that levy as was needed to restore any cut in the teachers' salaries for 1900 should be used to restore that cut.

After McKenna had left our office, he must have realized that he had made a fool of himself. He had been there for four hours, talking all the time. Perhaps when he went back to the city hall, somebody might have told him what was likely to happen. At any rate, he went over to the *Chicago Journal* and gave them a story in complete contradiction of everything that he had said to us. The *Journal* called us up, and never published the story that McKenna had given them, but our story of what he had told us in the course of his four hours' visit appeared.

Another aftermath of the Central Music Hall meeting concerned Jane Addams. She had made a speech at the meeting, a very fair but in no way inflamatory [sic] one, which was reported in the newspapers of the following day. C. K. G. Billings, then the President of the gas company, which was escaping taxes on $50,000,000, had been one of the large contributors to Hull House. In spite of that Jane Addams spoke against what she had been told by her co-workers were his financial interests. Mr. Billings later stopped his contributions to Hull House.

I went before the Board of Review to ascertain from that body if it would put in its schedules the property of the corporations omitted in 1899. Through its attorney, the board announced that the inclusion was not its duty.[12] We went to the Board of Assessors, to the Corporation Counsel, to the County Attorney, to the Town Collectors, to the County Collector, and finally, to the County Board. We asked the County Board to publish a list of delinquent taxes. For the first time, we secured immediate action from any public officials. The County Board printed the list just before the aldermanic campaign of 1900. Our tax committee sent a pledge to every candidate for alderman, requesting that it be signed. These pledges demanded that no renewal or extension of franchises be granted the street railways of Chicago until they paid the taxes then owing, through the failure of the State Board of Equalization to assess these corporations on their capital stock. The Chicago Teachers' Federation sent a letter to the City Council asking the Council to grant no further extensions until these delinquent taxes were paid. We selected the Union Traction Company for horrible example because it was asking at that time for an extension of franchise. The Council referred the letter to a special commission. The commission promised us that we would be invited to appear at any hearing, but we were never invited and no action was ever taken. The alderman I interviewed, one of the Gray Wolves, told me he'd vote for the ordinance even if he had to seek a more salubrious climate later.[13]

[12]Haley reveals her frustration with the complex legal and governmental structure which characterized urban affairs at the turn of the century. The public schools were a part of city government governed by an appointed board but dependent on fiscal appropriations from the elected city council. Yet the unit of tax assessment was the county of Cook. Assessment administration, by act of the 1898 legislature, was the responsibility of thirty local assessors, a five-member Board of Assessors, and a three-member Board of Review. Each of the officials was elected and each body, including the State Board of Equalization, was virtually independent of the others. One authority described it as a system "characterized by absence of scientific method, duplication of function, diffusion of responsibility, and secrecy of operation" which specifically fostered inefficiency and irresponsibility. As a result, the tax system became simply an adjunct to the political organization in power. Herbert D. Simpson, "The Chicago Complex," *Atlantic Monthly*, 146 (Oct., 1930), pp. 539-40.

[13]The Gray Wolves were members of the City Council who were considered to be "boodlers." Their political manuevers to exploit the city's finances are described in Lloyd Wendt and Herman Kogan, *Lords of the Levee* (Indianapolis: Bobbs-Merrill, 1943). Two reform organizations, the Civic Federation and the Municipal Voters' League, were formed in the 1890s to respond to the problem of political corruption. Michael ("Hinky Dink") Kenna, John ("Bathhouse") Coughlin, Ed Cullerton, and John Powers were prominent Gray Wolves who were targets of the MVL and the press.

For six weeks through the early autumn of that year, I went every day but Sunday, and sometimes twice a day, to the offices of the County Clerk, of the Board of Review, and of the Board of Assessors, to find out whether the assessors would keep their promise that they would make public statement showing the capital stock of assessed corporations. Our Federation had presented them with the necessary data with which to make these statements, but when we realized from the report of the Board of Review that we were getting nowhere with the public officers of Cook County, we decided upon legal action and proceeded to prepare a petition for mandamus to compel the Assessors to make out these schedules. On Monday, October 8, that petition was filed in the name of Catharine Goggin, a tax payer of the County of Cook, State of Illinois. A second petition, in the name of the people of the state, on the relation of Miss Goggin, was also prepared. It was necessary to have the State's Attorney of Cook County sign this petition before it was presented to the court.

"King Charlie" Deneen, later governor of and senator from the Commonwealth of Illinois, was State's Attorney.[14] Outside an iceberg, he was the coldest proposition the city ever had as a public official. I had known him for years in my own neighborhood of Englewood, and I had an idea that, if he knew what I was doing and what I wanted him to do in it, he'd slide out from either refusal or acceptance of the obligation. I got over to his house about seven o'clock in the morning. If he'd been up and dressed, he might have got out the back door. But he came down before breakfast to see me.

He read the petition over carefully and saw that it meant that he was asked to sign it on behalf of the tax payers of Cook County against the Board of Assessors. He called to my attention the political facts that the members of the board were running for re-election on the same ticket that he was, and that election day was less than a month away. He sidestepped, as all politicians do, telling me to see the assessors and get them to come to his office.

I said, "They'll run a mile from me. How can I get close to them?"

He said, "I want to give them a chance, anyhow. They're on the same ticket with me, but serve it on the clerk."

The first man I met in the County Building was James Gray, the only Democrat on the Board of Assessors. I told him what Deneen had said to me. He laughed uproariously. "I'll be there," he said, "but I'll bet you a dollar you don't get the other lads in."

[14]Charles S. Deneen (1863-1940) was one of the leaders of the Republican party. His power base was the Scandinavian wards of Chicago's southwest side. He was state's attorney for Cook County from 1896 to 1904 and later served as governor (1905-1913) and U.S. senator (1925-1931).

He was wrong, though, for although they didn't appear in Deneen's office an hour later, they sent John C. Richberg, their attorney to represent them. Gray said he didn't represent anybody but himself and that he was only there to hear whatever was said. Richberg brought in law books, piling them from floor to ceiling, and trying to argue with Deneen about the law in the case. He also declared the assessors were filling out the schedules. At Deneen's request he agreed we could see the schedules before they were filed with the County Clerk. He was, I think, embarrassed by the necessity for his appearance, for his wife had been one of Catharine Goggin's closest friends and he had always assumed to be a leader in liberal thought.

Deneen was also on a spot. He was a candidate for re-election and had to stand by the other candidates of his party. If he didn't sign the petition, however, he knew that Greenacre who was with Catharine Goggin and myself in Deneen's office, and who had notified him that he had another petition ready, would put in the other petition, on Catharine Goggin's behalf, not signed by him. His only chance was to lose time so that the assessors could put in fraudulent schedules and so he sent us back to the assessors. From Charlie's attitude, Greenacre saw how he was delaying. Before noon, Greenacre had the second petition, signed by Catharine Goggin alone, filed in the court. While Deneen and Richberg sweated all afternoon in consideration of Deneen's signature to the other petition, Greenacre beat them to the gun. He knew that, having made all other legal attempts, this was the only feasible action.

God must have been with us teachers in our tax fight, for on the Fourth of July, 1900, Hearst's *Chicago American* went on the news stands for the first time. Before that time, we'd had only desultory support from the Chicago newspapers, which were, for the most part, so involved in their own political associations that they couldn't continuously support any fight against the existing order. The *Tribune* and the *News* had their plants on land leased at more than favorable terms from the Board of Education. The *Journal* was owned by the Wilson family, who held similar favored leases. The *Chronicle* was owned by John R. Walsh, whip for Chicago's great and growing financial interests over the Republican party in Illinois. The *Inter-Ocean* was an agent of the same party. The *Post* was too consciously social to advocate our cause; only its star reporters, like William L. Chenery, who came to it a few years later, dared uphold us. The *Herald*, because of its independent editor, "Pa" McAuliffe, gave us an opportunity to state our case to the public; but until the advent of the Hearst papers—the *American* and its younger sister, the *Examiner*—we had on our side no definite organ of opinion.

The Hearst papers did not always go full distance with us. Andy Lawrence played his own game too shrewdly to jeopardize it always, even for those causes in the public weal which Hearst advocated. California and New York were farther away from Chicago in those days, and it was safer to take a chance that the chief wouldn't catch up with local issues; but, in the main, the *American,* the *Examiner,* and the later *Herald Examiner* have maintained, as their own policy, support of our struggle against unjust levying and spreading of taxes under the pretense of needing the money for the maintenance of the public schools.

Through the years, a long parade of Hearst men, editors and reporters, marched through the story of the teachers' struggles, giving us aid and advice as often as we gave them news: James Pegler, James Bickett, William Curley, Hilding Johnson, Sloan, Westlake, Straube, Florence McCarthy, Victor Watson, and a score of others. Without them and without the independent reporters and editors on other Chicago newspapers, men who sometimes risked their own jobs to tell the truth, "Billy" Williamson, Richard Burritt, Richard Finnegan, Anthony Czarnecki, we would not have advanced as far as we have. To the gentlemen of the press, we have owed a debt that we could repay only by breaking in their cub reporters—and I suspect that for a long time the cubs have been set on us to cut their teeth.

To the hard-working women reporters of those days who did so much to establish traditions of yeoman service in the newspapers—we gave even greater gratitude. They were our sisters in the struggle, and to them we gave and still give the laurel of achievement for a pioneering that kept pace with our own.[15]

The Hearst papers had advertised the teachers' meeting which had been called for the afternoon of that day in Central Music Hall. The teachers' salaries had been cut, and they were receiving that day their lowered checks. I was to be one of the speakers there and so, in the late afternoon, I told Richberg and Deneen that I had to leave them to go to the meeting. I would tell the teachers, I said, who had been responsible for everything, for the salary cut, for the withheld taxes, for the lack of money in the schools, for the "run around" that we'd been given from the time we started to work on the problem.

Before Catharine Goggin's petition could be filed we had to see the schedules made by the Board of Assessors and know that they were

---

[15]Persons referred to were Anne Forsyth, Katherine Leckie, and Mary Synon; the names were removed from the final draft by Haley. See also pp. xxxiii, note 43, and p. 60. The muckraking journalist Lincoln Steffens found the Chicago press "the best in any of our large cities. There are several newspapers in Chicago which have always served the public interest and their advice is taken by their readers." *The Shame of the Cities* (1904; reprint edition, New York: Hill and Wang, 1957), p. 192.

fraudulent, insufficient and inadequate. The assessors were making the schedules unwillingly but, between the devil of a pending case against them and the deep sea of an election in the next week, they knew they had to make a front of doing something. Richberg went over from Deneen's office and helped the assessors work on the schedules. We argued with the board for the right to see the schedules before they were taken to the County Clerk. We knew that we had to see them to make our petition stick. The members of the board were working in their shirt sleeves, cursing like a crowd of hoboes and damning the school teachers. Finally, however, they showed us the schedules. All of them were wrong. We finally forced them into letting us go over the schedules with Richberg.

"What do you want?" he asked us.

We said, "The correct schedules."

"If you get that, will you withdraw the suit?"

"We'll act on our lawyer's advice."

Next day Greenacre told us that the Board of Assessors might file their own schedules with the County Clerk. We went down to the County Clerk's office and found Richberg there, looking over the schedules which the assessors had sent down. He also had the correct schedules, which we made out showing $264,000,000 as the correct taxable valuation of the utilities corporations. He was crossing off the items on the assessors' schedules with red ink and setting in the figures which stood on our schedules. He saw us and realized that we had him in a tight corner. He made a place for us at his table and submitted each schedule to us as he finished it. We compared it with our own and verified it. Knowing that we had won as much by this method as we could have done in court, we, after consultation with Greenacre, withdrew the case against the Board of Assessors after the schedules had been sent, according to law, for file in Springfield with the state auditor.

Then, the schedules disappeared from sight. No one in any public office could find them. We had, however, made schedules exactly like Richberg's, drawing ink lines through items wherever he had. The *Chicago American* somehow obtained copies of the schedules and ran the reproductions and a story about them the next day. On the day after that, the original schedules reappeared in the office of the Board of Assessors.

That night, I went to Springfield.

6

Springfield, the capital of Illinois, was then as now a legislative camp, torn between two bitterly contrasting forces of American political life.

Located in the middle of the state, it has been surrounded by the atmosphere of the southern and rural division of the commonwealth. Into its low bowl, however, had already come those politicians from a growing Chicago who were, even then, projecting their policies of urban domination. In other parts of the United States and in other times since the beginning of the century, the struggle between these two forces may have become battles of essential ideals. In Springfield then, as in Springfield now, the battle was not for any ideal, but for the spoils of war.

Looking back upon the Springfield of thirty-five years ago and considering the Springfield of today, I can see that the one marked difference in these two periods is one of method rather than of goal in politics. The capital of Illinois today is dominated by a great political machine operated by a few men, none of them in the Legislature. Most of the legislators, including the administration leaders in both houses, are mere puppets of this machine. In 1900, although the machine existed, individuals stood out sharply against an equally murky background: "Fire Escape Gus" Nohe, "Tobacco Hank" Evans, "Billy-goat" Cadwallader, "Cap" McKnight, "Benny" Mitchell, our friend "Jawn" McKenna, and a score of others, probably no more venal, but certainly more picturesque than their successors. They were the outposts of a condition which was then, even more than now, characteristic of American public life, the alliance between entrenched capital and purchasable politicians.[16]

We met Springfield in the Chicago Union Station when a group of politicians boarded the same train. Perhaps I should qualify on saying that they boarded it, for one of them, big "Ed" Cullerton, one of the "gray wolves" of the Chicago City Council, was almost killed in trying to get on the train. The porter and the brakeman dragged him through the coach where I sat; all the time, he yelled at the top of his voice curses against "those damned school teachers." The train crew deposited him in the baggage car, flinging him on the floor, while he still yelled at the women who were threatening the old-line political power which he represented and for which he was going down to lobby.

The next day we attended a meeting of the State Board of Equalization or its capital stock committee, where the schedules were presented. The men, very civil, polite, sticky with sweetness, gave us a hearing.

---

[16]Haley identifies Henry H. Evans, a Republican member of the senate, who represented Kane County from 1881 to 1908, and two members of the house elected to the Forty-Second General Assembly (1901) from Cook County: Augustus W. Nohe (R) and Benjamin M. Mitchell (D). McKnight, Cadwallader, and McKenna were members of the State Board of Equalization.

The woman with whom I was rooming in Springfield, while I was alone there later, told me I did not realize the kind of people I was dealing with. She said that she had had some of the state board members as her roomers and advised me to send to Chicago for Miss Goggin. I didn't, of course, but I watched the proceedings until Greenacre, to whom I reported every day, was satisfied that the board had evaded its duty so flagrantly that we were justified in presenting a petition for mandamus against its members. Then it adjourned and didn't meet again till after election. Then it met again, with only one of its seven Chicago members re-elected. All of them just as dilatory as before. And transacting all business behind closed doors. Their game was to give us no chance to go into court, but under the law had to get their work done in time for tax-spreading.

On the evening when I took the draft of the petition, with Catharine Goggin as relator, down to Springfield to Elbridge S. Smith, State's Attorney of Sangamon County, the *Chicago Journal* ran this bit of doggerel:

"Mandamus proceedings were brought by the teachers
Against the incorporate tax-dodging creatures;
'No, no,' say the ladies, 'you cannot flimflam us,'
We will keep up the fight though every man damn us."

Judge Murray F. Tuley, the chancellor of the Cook County bench, who had decided that our petition should be brought against the State Board of Equalization at its place of meeting, came down in the elevator of the County Building with me on the day of his decision. He evidently felt that his decision might have discouraged us, for he said to me, "Don't give up; don't be discouraged. Take this petition to Springfield. Go on with the good work. You are right."[17]

On the 16th of November, the State's Attorney of Sangamon County filed the petition at the last possible moment before five o'clock. At the hearing on November 21st, John S. Miller, who had guided us so much better than he had intended, represented the State Board of Equalization in a demurrer to our petition, arguing that the courts had no authority over the board. James Graham, his associate in the case, made a powerful plea to the court not to tear down the pillars of the Republic by disturbing the equilibrium guaranteed by the Constitution in its provisions for balances and checks.

[17]Murray Tuley (1827-1905) was a highly respected jurist who was elected judge of the circuit court continuously from 1879 until his death. A liberal Democrat, he was called the "father of the municipal ownership movement in Chicago." His open letter to Edward F. Dunne helped bring about Dunne's candidacy for mayor in 1905. The letter was printed in the *Public*, Jan. 21, 1905. See the following two chapters and Ray Ginger, *Altgeld's America* (New York: Funk and Wagnalls, 1958).

Judge [James A.] Creighton presided in an uncomfortable, badly ventilated room, heated only by a big stove like the one in the school where I had taught near Dresden Heights. Those near it were roasting, while those at the other end of the room were freezing. The cold spread further than the room, however, when Judge Creighton gave decision, "This petition shall be heard." When the State Board of Equalization, then in session, heard the verdict, surprise, consternation, and fear gripped every man in that body. They adjourned precipitately and scurried out like rats.

In the hall of the Statehouse, I met old "Cap" McKnight, carrying his usual satchel. I heard that there would be a meeting of the capital stock committee of the board the next day to hear some of the representatives of Chicago corporations. The situation was so tense that I came back to Chicago to secure an official stenographer, rather than trust either telephone or telegraph wires. I was in Chicago just two hours, then with the stenographer took the ten o'clock train back to Springfield.

On the next morning, the board held a meeting in the senate chamber. One of its members presented a new rule for determining the value of franchises—which assessed the corporations involved on a full value of twelve and a half millions instead of the more than two hundred millions we had demanded as their proper valuation according to the law. Without explanation or discussion and without one dissenting vote, the board adopted the resolution and adjourned.

On that afternoon, the board held a hearing in one of the committee rooms of the senate, apparently to give them justification for an act already accomplished, the making of a new and illegal rule. Nearly two score attorneys, representing the great corporations of Chicago, had come down to Springfield. There, for the first time, we saw lined together the generals and the sergeants major of the Unholy Alliance. The State Board of Equalization—Louis Hershimer, the secretary, Cap McKnight, old Cadwallader, Captain Rogers, who with the Burlington Railroad owned most of Downer's Grove, Richard Cadle, a fat roly-poly of a man, long-faced Crittenden, who had introduced the new rule, Works of Rockford, who was seldom heard or seen until the word "railroad" came up in meeting, Martin, who always looked as if he were about to say grace, Jawn McKenna, and Barnes, the smoothest, most explanatory special pleader of them all—represented the people of the sovereign State of Illinois. McKenna had told us that his job on the board wasn't worth very much to a Chicago man, because the railroads could buy half a dozen downstate men for what they would have to pay for one Cook County member. Watching the assembled membership, I wondered if anyone might be able to solve by algebra the complete cost of the board to the people willing to pay for it.

Before them stood the counsel for the great corporations who could and had paid the purchase price: Bliss, attorney for the Chicago City Railway Company; W. S. Beale, of the Edison Company; James Meagher, of the Peoples Gas Light and Coke Company: W. W. Gurley, of the Union Traction Company; and a score of other lesser lights. Of them all, Gurley was the only one decently courteous to the teachers. The rest of them bared fangs at us. Old Major Blodgett, purchasing agent for Union Traction, who always sat in with the State Board of Equalization and who received his mail at a desk in the senate chamber, shouted that Miss Goggin and I—taxeaters! he called us—should be thrown out of the window. Blodgett asked the board members what they would do if we were men instead of women and added, to their laughter, "If they were policemen or firemen, you *would* throw them out of the window." We had had a verbatim report made of everything that was said at the hearing and, when Bliss discovered that we had a full record, he tried to buy the notes from our stenographer.

No decision was made at this meeting but, a little while later, the capital stock committee of the board met in secret session and made a new rule and a pretended assessment, afterward declared illegal by the courts, on the five public utility corporations of Chicago, fixing the full value of the capital stock and franchises over and above the tangible property at $12,500,000, a mere fraction of their real value.

The State's Attorney of Sangamon County had been injured by a fall and our case was necessarily postponed. The State Board tried to prevent hearing of our mandamus proceedings on the ground that the board went out of existence with its election of new members. The court overruled this objection and again ordered the petition to be heard.

The time for hearing the suit was postponed until the March of the following year, 1901. In January, 1901, the Legislature assembled. Because of the balloting for United States Senator, no business except the introduction of bills was being done. Three bills aimed to destroy the Chicago teachers' pension were introduced, one which would have repealed the law entirely, and the others, more cleverly camouflaged, but to the same purpose.[18]

Bernard F. Mullaney, then a Chicago newspaper reporter, afterward secretary to Mayor Busse, and after that one of the officials of the huge Insull interests, came to me at the Leland Hotel. He asked me if the Teachers' Federation was interested in the Chicago teachers' pension law. I explained that one of the reasons for the existence of the

[18]This was the Forty-Second General Assembly, which convened on January 9 and adjourned on May 4.

Federation was the pension law. A committee of the Federation was, even then, preparing amendments to the law which would strengthen the pension fund, and I told Mullaney that any law to create a permanent fund must provide, as did the original act, for the compulsory contribution by the teachers to the fund. I realized, while I was talking with him, that he was uneasy about his errand and that he evidently did not enjoy his interview. I do not know to whom he reported it, but the bill which was introduced in the Legislature destroyed this feature of the pension, letting contributors slip in and slip out as they pleased.[19]

Because of the Sangamon County suit, I had to be in Springfield the greater part of the time, and so I was authorized by the Federation to work against the passage of these pension bills. David Shanahan was then, as he was to be for many years, the authorized leader of the Republicans in the house of representatives.[20] I had a number of letters from teachers in his district, asking him to use his influence against the passage of the bills. Shanahan read the letters in deep disturbance, then he said, "When you teachers stayed in your schoolrooms, we men took care of you; but when you go out of your schoolrooms, as you have done, and attack these great, powerful corporations, you must expect that they will hit back."

"Then am I to understand, Mr. Shanahan, that this bill in the Legislature to destroy the teachers' pension fund is the corporation comeback at the teachers for making them pay their legal taxes?"

Shanahan said, "Yes," turned on his heel, walked back to his seat in the house, and sat down.

One bill was defeated, but the more drastic of the other two bills was sent into a committee that paid us little heed. We explained to the committee that, if this bill became law, any teacher might withdraw at any time from contributing to the fund and yet might return after nineteen years, contribute for one year, and then retire on full pension. This would, of course, destroy the fund. I saw every member of the committee, and won their promises to put this pernicious option out of the bill.

[19]*Proceedings of the Board of Trustees of the Public School Teachers' Pension and Retirement Fund of the City of Chicago* (July 10, 1901), p. 2. CTF Files.

[20]David Edward Shanahan (1862-1936), who represented the Bridgeport section of Chicago, was considered the "dean" of the Illinois House of Representatives. Elected in 1894 as a Republican, he held that seat until his death. He was speaker of the house for six sessions. *Illinois Blue Book, 1935-36* (Springfield: State of Illinois, 1936). Fifteen days before the 1936 election, Shanahan died. The Democrats capitalized on this by using the vacancy on the ballot to elect a person who had been defeated previously in the primary. Under the state's cumulative voting system, Richard J. Daley was elected through a successful write-in campaign. Mike Royko, *Boss: Richard J. Daley of Chicago* (New York: Dutton, 1971), p. 40.

Donahue [Francis E. Donoghue], the representative who said he had written the bill, told me that he had not spent fifteen minutes upon it. I told him a butcher or a blacksmith would have done it better. I was angry and he was angry, and our voices grew so loud that the speaker had to call us to order. Before he ordered me off the floor of the house, I yelled at Donahue that he would not have dared to draw up such a bill against the policemen's or the firemen's fund.

In spite of all our efforts, including the presentation to representatives, senators, and governor, of communications from thousands of teachers who would be affected by the measure, the bill was passed, but with a provision that if the teachers went out from the pension they had to stay out. One of the reasons for its passage was, I am sure, the fact that many Chicago principals had acted in conformity with orders from the superintendent of schools and lobbied for the bill. The Governor, Richard Yates, showed me letters from Chicago school principals which convinced me of their intention to aid that pernicious legislation. Thanks to them, that pension bill was passed by the senate on the very day, the very hour—the stroke of noon—that Judge Thompson's decision against the State Board of Equalization was rendered in our favor. That failure and that victory were characteristic of most of our later failures and victories. We lost in the legislatures and won in the courts.

To the same legislature came Banquo's ghost, the rehabilitated Harper bill. We knew that it had to be fought, just as the pension legislation had to be fought. But we also knew that, at that particular time, they were dead herrings dragged across the trail. We realized that the cards were stacked against us in the legislature and we knew that, unless we won the tax fight, we would be completely sunk. From the distance of more than a third of a century, I can see now how apallingly ignorant both Catharine Goggin and I were then of the kind of politics that was being played in Springfield. If God were always on the side of the strongest legions, we certainly couldn't have won even a skirmish. Nothing but the sublime ignorance of two women who didn't even know the depth of the quagmire they were traversing brought us through.

At the beginning of this year, Catharine Goggin's and my own leaves of absence from the Board of Education had expired. We had to make decision between staying in our profession and continuing the fight into which we had been drawn. Continuation in the schools would have been easier for us but, by that time, we both realized that unless we stayed on our new jobs, there wouldn't be much of a job for anybody in the schools. The Federation, understanding the importance of our labors, voted to make us its representatives, at a pay equal to what we would be earning in our schoolrooms. We were, therefore, direct representatives of the Federation, endowed with a freedom which made it possible for us to accomplish results which could not have been won by teachers or principals under the direct domination of superintendents or boards of education which might be opposed to the measures the teachers advocated.

7

Judge Creighton, who had sustained our petition for mandamus, had gone to another circuit and Judge Owen P. Thompson, of Jacksonville, came to Springfield. We knew nothing of him except Elbridge Smith's declaration that he was an honest man, from whom we had nothing to fear. The Sangamon County Court subpoenaed from Chicago delinquent witnesses, officers of big corporations, to appear in court. We had to furnish warrant-servers. The trial proceeded in a courtroom just as cold as the one where Creighton had presided. Judge Thompson sat with his overcoat collar turned up and sneezed most of the time. I had burned my arms on an alcohol curling apparatus, which had tipped over and set fire to the carpet. I dared not go near the stove, and I could not endure the weight of my coat sleeves, so that I had to shiver in a brilliant red blouse with gold bands that gave it a military effect. I looked militant, but I felt miserable.

Greenacre kept his valuable papers in a small satchel. He asked me to take care of it. I guarded it carefully every day in the courtroom and carried it with me to the hotel every noon and every night. After I had been carrying it for several days, I opened it to find a paper for which he asked me. Instead of papers, I found it filled with pink silk underwear. I had sent home to Chicago for some lingerie. My sister had sent it to me by express, in a satchel that was an exact duplicate of the one which Greenacre had given to me. It had been put in my room at the hotel and, without noticing, I had taken it instead of the other satchel, which had been put away, out of sight in a closet. For days, I had been asking at the hotel office for the express package which the records showed had been delivered there. I had a bad moment when I opened the satchel, for my imagination projected itself into the possible scene when I might have opened the satchel in court and dragged out the lingerie instead of a legal document.

We had other trouble with the Greenacre papers. He had asked me to separate them, as they were badly mixed. I was working over them when a call came to go to court. As there was no table in the room big enough to spread them on, I had put them on the floor. When I went back, I found that the maid had put them all in the garbage can. The proprietor of the hotel helped me fish them out of it. There was not one missing, but in ten minutes more they would have all been destroyed by fire.

Every time I had gone back to Chicago during these months, I received a message from a woman who was a friend of my own and of the racketeering lawyer whose alleged failure to divide the spoils had started the newspaper publications about the State Board. She wanted me to meet him. I didn't, of course, have the least idea of why she wanted me to meet him, for, at that time, we had no knowledge whatever of his association with the racket. She told me, however, that he had some valuable information regarding the Board of Equalization. We had so many people telling us that they knew people who had information that it was impossible to run them all down. But we finally decided that, because of this man's political and personal connections, he might possibly have information of value to us; and so Greenacre went to him.

For some reason all his own, one which none of us ever fathomed, this lawyer gave out a story. He said that if he were subpoenaed, he would come to Springfield as a witness to tell a story of his own service as money-passer between a Chicago lawyer and certain members of the State Board of Equalization.

We decided to subpoena the member he mentioned. I went to his home town to see that the summons was served. I found the sheriff glad to have the chance. He actually went at the job with avidity. The member came to Springfield the next day. He begged Greenacre not to put him on the stand. He wept like a child, telling how respectable his family had always been, what a respectable father and mother he had, and how it would break their hearts if he should be disgraced.

Next day, Greenacre put Bliss, the attorney for the Chicago City Railway Company, on the witness stand. He asked him about envelopes passed in the Union League Club, and said to contain definite amounts of money apparently designed for members of the State Board of Equalization. Bliss's face grew crimson as he frantically appealed to the court to protect him against what he called the unjust and unwarranted insult of Greenacre's questioning. He threatened to sue Greenacre in the Chicago courts, but he never brought the suit. Greenacre decided against putting the member of the Board on the stand and the attorneys for the State Board did not, of course, dare to put him there. The racketeering lawyer fell down on us. He left Chicago for the wide west. The only time I ever saw him again was while I was watching this same case in the United States Supreme Court in the Capitol at Washington. I ran into him. He was one of a large group representing Indian Territory in its appeal for statehood.

I had to go on the witness stand to tell what Jawn McKenna had said, in the Federation offices and at our Central Music Hall meeting, about the methods and purchasability of the board. The attorneys for the board and the corporations struggled to keep the substance of those statements out of the record, but Judge Thompson overruled them. It was at that point that John S. Miller asked me why I had chosen certain corporations and I replied that he himself had told me to do it.

On the 1st of May, 1901, Judge Thompson declared that the Board's assessment on the corporations involved was fraudulent and that its new rule was illegal, null, and void. He ordered the board to reconvene and reassess the companies according to the law and the old rule which, he said, the board had set aside illegally.

The peremptory writ of mandamus was awarded.[21]

After Judge Thompson had awarded this writ, the attorneys for the board and the public utility corporations involved secured a temporary injunction from Judge [J. Otis] Humphrey in the Federal Court of the Southern District of Illinois. This injunction prohibited the State Board of Equalization from making the contemplated assessment which had been ordered by Judge Thompson's writ.

The attorneys also appealed the Thompson decision to the Illinois Supreme Court but, toward the end of October, that body affirmed the Thompson decision and ordered the peremptory writ to issue. Judge Thompson was still on the Sangamon County circuit and it would become his duty to issue the writ. I believe that no judge ever enjoyed his duty more, for in the meantime he had come into personal knowledge of the methods of that gang.

Years afterward he told me that, shortly after the federal injunction had been granted, he had been sitting out in front of the old St. Nicholas Hotel in Springfield when a man whom he knew well came to sit beside him. He pulled back his coat and revealed a great wad of bills, as he suggested to Judge Thompson that he postpone the execution of that mandamus writ. Judge Thompson knew that the man was down and out; he knew that he had undertaken the attempted bribery only because of his terrible need of money. He felt that the choice of this man as an agent was an insult added to the injury of the attempted bribe. His old friendship for the unfortunate agent of the would-be bribers kept him from statement at the time, but no one could have heard him deny those attorneys a delay in the execution of that mandamus writ without realizing that there was something back of his indignant refusal. On the 21st of November [1901], he ordered the State Board of Equalization to return its assessment to his court without

[21]*Chicago Tribune,* May 2, 1901.

delay. The attorneys asked him to postpone execution until after the hearing of the federal court's temporary injunction. He said in effect, "Not one day. Not one minute. The State Board of Equalization will make a return on that mandamus writ to this court on the morning of November 22 when this court opens or its members will take the consequences."

On the night of November 21, the members of the board decided that the jig was up. Federal court or no federal court, they knew that if they did not bring in the assessment to Judge Thompson, they would be in contempt of his court and liable to go to jail. On the other hand, they feared that if they made the assessment, they would be in contempt of the federal court and that Judge Humphrey might send them to jail. They were between the devil and the deep sea, but they evidently feared Judge Thompson the more, for at midnight they came to Greenacre, awakening him from sleep at the Leland Hotel, and asking him to go to the Statehouse with them. They said that they didn't know how to make the assessment and they wanted his help. He thought that they might be trying to kidnap him in order to get him out of the way of the court session the next morning, but he took a chance and accompanied them to a scene which was, he said afterward, the best show of the year.

The members of the board were huddled in one of the Statehouse rooms. Crittenden, who had once been a teacher, seemed to be the only one able or willing to do any work. He sat at the head of a table, while some of the others slumped in chairs around it. Louis Hershimer slouched in a window seat. Roly-poly Cadle was lying on the floor. "Can't you get rid of these two damned women nuisances?" he demanded of Greenacre. "I'm a bachelor and Louis Hershimer here is a widower. I'll let Louis have his choice of these two teachers and I'll take what's left." Hershimer put up an objection but Cadle said, "My God, Louis, anything to get rid of them!"

He was still trying to make a horse trade, when the jailer of Sangamon County came in. "For your comfort, gentlemen," he said, "I have just come in to tell you that I've cleared out one tier of cells in the jail so that you may be all together tomorrow."

Roly-poly said, "If it is any satisfaction to you, Greenacre, to know that we are scared, I'll tell you that we're damned scared, and this is no joking matter."

Greenacre told the board that he could not make the assessment for them, but that he could give them any information they desired as the law gave them authority to seek information from any source. They, however, must do the actual work. They struggled over it all night and brought it into court in the morning.

That same morning, before Judge Thompson's court convened,

Judge Humphrey discreetly dissolved his temporary injunction. Had he let it stand, the question would have gone at once before the United States Supreme Court because it was a clash between state and federal authority. If the members of the board had been sent to jail, the corporations could not have permitted them to stay there. A writ of habeas corpus might have been issued immediately, and that would have brought the question to the United States Supreme Court. The federal judges knew, possibly, that they would lose in such a proceeding, and they must have known, too, that no body can be enjoined for a threatened act. It was the height of absurdity to assume that a body was going to do an illegal act. The dissolution of the federal injunction cleared the case in Springfield. We had, we thought, won complete victory. We didn't know then how devious were the ways of big business or how it could influence other decisions.

The corporations then appealed to Judge [Peter S.] Grosscup in the Federal Court of the Northern District of Illinois for an injunction to restrain the collection of the tax under the new assessment claiming they had paid their taxes once for the year 1900. We knew that the federal Circuit Court should not have taken jurisdiction on the case at this point, but we feared years of delay would result if we made protest and that we would lose the public interest we had evoked. Judge Grosscup granted the injunction. He held with the Supreme Court of Illinois that the first assessment, of twelve and a half million dollars, was too low, but he also declared that the second assessment, made by the State Board under the order of the Supreme Court, was too high, not because the board had not obeyed the law, but because the claim was made that other property in the state was not assessed on a basis of full cash value and that their property should not be so assessed. He failed utterly to give recognition to the fact that the public utilities corporations were in a class all to themselves and could not be measured by the ordinary constitutional or statutory rules. Judge Grosscup then appointed a master in chancery to make a third assessment according to his idea of what the assessment should be, and gave the companies forty days from the date of his decision to pay the taxes under this new assessment. By this action, Judge Grosscup set aside the rules of the State Board of Equalization, which had been made law in 1873, sustained in the Supreme Court of Illinois, and later in the United States Supreme Court.[22]

Our next difficulty was to get a hearing before Grosscup's master in

[22]Peter S. Grosscup (1852-1921) was judge of the U.S. Circuit Court of Appeals, Seventh District, from 1899 to 1911. His decision was reported in the *Chicago Tribune*, Nov. 20, 1901. He was one of two judges who issued the injunction against Eugene Debs and the American Railway Union in 1894. Described as a man of "impeccable conservatism" by Richard Hofstadter, Grosscup's attitudes toward corporations were ex-

chancery. We knew now that we were playing against an opposition which sought postponement and delay. Elbridge S. Smith, of Springfield, who was now in the Attorney General's office and who had been assigned to the duty of defending the State of Illinois against Judge Grosscup's injunction, would come upstate only to find that the attorneys for the corporations did not appear. I remember how James F. Meagher would come to the door of the room where Master in Chancery Bishop was presiding, stick in his head, look around, see either Smith or myself, then stride out in a manner of seething indignation. Between Meagher and Smith, there arose a feud which was probably one of temperament as much as of opposition in work. Meagher, representing the Peoples Gas Company, had an idea of the divine right of corporations, even going so far as to say in Springfield, "A perpetual franchise is our Heaven-born privilege." If Meagher snarled like a tiger, baring his teeth as he spoke, Smith fought like a lion. He knew that there was no use in appealing from the vacillating decisions of Bishop to the equally pulpy decisions of Grosscup, but he kept on fighting at every step. I know positively that, during that time, he was offered $250,000 by one of the attorneys of the fighting corporations just to stay away from those hearings.

When the master in chancery sent his recommendation on assessments to Judge Grosscup, Grosscup cut down the intangible element value from $230 million to $138 million. Had it not been for his interference, the actual amount of taxes to be collected would have been $1,800,000 instead of a little more than $598,000. The attorneys for the corporations continued to fight, even against that payment, but the Hearst papers were making things so hot for Judge Grosscup that he could no longer postpone action. He ordered the money to be paid. Some of it was being paid in his court when Smith served notice that he would take an appeal from Grosscup's calculations to higher federal courts. It was arranged, however, that the City and the Board of Education should receive the money ordered paid by Judge Thompson.[23]

8

Immediately upon the payment of this money in 1902 to the City Treasurer of Chicago, Mayor Harrison sent a communication to the

pressed in "How to Save the Corporations," *McClures*, 23 (February, 1905). See Richard Hofstadter, *The Age of Reform: From Bryan to F.D.R.* (New York: Knopf, 1965), pp. 221-22.

[23]In his decision, which was reached in April, 1902, Grosscup noted that the State Board of Equalization had acted under duress in reaching its assessment. *Chicago Tribune*, Apr. 5, 1902.

City Council urging that body to restore to the firemen and policemen their loss of pay, from the money turned in through the efforts of the teachers. He made no such recommendation, however, for the teachers who had also been cut, although the City Council had by provision in the tax levy of 1900, declared the money of the cut should be restored to the teachers by the Board of Education. The firemen and policemen received the salary which had been lost to them.

When the Board of Education got the money through the Grosscup decision, its finance committee prepared a report recommending that the board's share of this money should be used to pay coal bills and bills for the cleaning of the schools during vacations. It did not vote one dollar of this money for teachers' salaries! On Greenacre's advice, we served notice on the members of the board that, if the report of the finance committee were adopted, injunction proceedings against the City Treasurer would be started by the teachers to prevent the money from being paid for any purpose other than to return our loss in salary for the year 1900. A copy of this notice was put on the desk of each member of the board at the meeting of July 9, 1902; but the notice was destroyed and the board adopted the report of the finance committee. There was nothing we could do but proceed into other legal measures.[24]

It is significant that at the same meeting the Board voted for the first time, a bonus system for teachers who would take and pass certain examinations under a secret marking system.

The President of the Teachers' Federation, Ella A. Rowe, headed the list of those teachers who wished to become parties to a suit demanding from the Board of Education the money owed them. Judge Tuley would not grant an injunction against the board, declaring that the courts did not assume that a legislative body would do illegal acts, but he would grant an injunction against the City Treasurer restraining that officer from paying out warrants issued by the Board of Education against this back tax money for any purpose except the payment of teachers' salaries. As diligent creditors, we had taken precedence over all other creditors. We had secured the money and the City Council had already appropriated it. We had triple claim. Furthermore, teachers' contracts ran from September to June and their salaries could not be cut on any mid-year. On thirteen occasions he fixed the time for final hearing of the case, and on thirteen occasions postponement was asked. Judge Tuley finally announced that he would refuse further delay and set a date for a final hearing.

A few days before that date, James Meagher and Roy Shannon,

[24]In July, 1902, the Board of Education received approximately $250,000 from the total of $598,000 which Judge Grosscup had ordered paid. *Proceedings, Board of Education,* 1902-3, p. 20; *Chicago Record Herald,* July 10, 1902.

representing the Board of Education, appeared before Judge Tuley in his chambers and told him that they wanted the case sent to another court. I shall never forget how the old man, Nestor of the Chicago bar, looked as he asked them, "The case will be appealed to the Supreme Court, no matter which side loses, will it not? The questions to be determined are questions in law, are they not? Do you mean to insinuate that you think I would not be fair?"

At this point, Graham Harris, President of the Board, stepped forward and admitted that it was the Board of Education who was unwilling to have Judge Tuley hear the case. He gave as reason a statement that Judge Tuley had already expressed himself on the case. Judge Tuley said that he had no knowledge of any expression in regard to the issues involved and added, "I'll say now that I consider the Board of Education morally bound to give this money to the teachers if they can do it legally. I do not want to hear this case now. You have no right to demand that I shall not hear it, and I have no right to refuse, but I would prefer to have it sent to another judge." The old man sat back in his chair, seeming to shrink from the blow that these lesser men had dealt to his honor. I believe that he never got over the insult they offered him, but his eyes flashed fire and, as they suggested a judge, he said, "No. You have no jurisdiction of a judge. I will send the case to another judge."

Clarence Darrow, who had become Greenacre's associate in the case, answered, apparently without much consideration, that he had no objection to the judge whom the representatives of the Board of Education had named. I pulled his coat tails and told him, as quickly as I could before the deed should be done, that we wanted no judge they selected. Then, Judge Tuley sent the case to Judge [Edward F.] Dunne.[25]

Stripped of the verbiage of jurisprudence, the questions of the suit were these: Did the Board of Education owe the teachers a debt for the year 1900? Had the Council of the City of Chicago appropriated money for the purpose of paying that debt? To determine the first question, the whole matter of contract between the Board of Education and the teachers had to be considered. To decide the second, the purpose and intent of the Council, in making the appropriation for education purposes in the year 1900, had to be determined and the powers of the Council in the matter defined.

In the proceedings of the City Council under consideration, the

[25]Edward F. Dunne (1853-1937) was judge of the circuit court of Cook County from 1892 to 1905. An Irish Catholic with a family of thirteen children, Dunne accepted the requests of friends to run for mayor on the Democratic ticket in 1905. As the following chapters relate, Dunne was a close friend of Haley and the teachers. His children attended the public schools of Chicago.

report of the meeting at which both the appropriation and the levying ordinance were passed showed that the appropriation for education purposes in 1900 was $7,125,000. An asterisk had been placed after this figure, calling attention to a footnote at the bottom of the page which stated that a sufficient sum of this money should be used to restore the salaries of the experienced teachers for 1900. The entire amount appropriated and levied by the Council was not collected in 1900, as it exceeded the 2½ per cent limit on the assessed valuation of property allowed by law for educational purposes. By our tax suit, however, we had made up this shortage.

Our attorneys based their claim on the fact that the Council had specifically appropriated the money to pay this debt. The Board of Education denied the right of the City Council, an elective body, to dictate how it (the Board), an appointive body, should spend any amount of the money appropriated for educational purposes.

The determination of whether or not a debt to the teachers really existed brought in the question of tenure. The attorneys for the Board of Education argued that the teachers accepted their election in June with the knowledge that the Board's rules provided for fixing salaries at the beginning or soon after the beginning of the fiscal year in January. They contended that by a retroactive process, which they outlined, the teachers could be forced to work for whatever the Board set in January, no matter what the salary stood when the teachers were hired in June. According to this reasoning, the teachers might have worked for nothing for several months and been actually in debt to the Board at the end of the year. They acknowledged that it was a unilateral contract, but argued that, as the teachers had accepted payment under it without protest, they had forfeited any right under the law to complain. They contended that the schedule of 1898 had no binding force after the year 1898. They outlined the position of the Board of Education that it had the right to dismiss any teacher at any time, with or without cause. Our attorneys claimed that the civil service clause of the pension law, which provided for a trial on charges before dismissal, nullified these rules.

In order to support its case, the Board of Education called to the witness stand Graham H. Harris, President of the Board, and Mayor Carter H. Harrison. At that time, as far as I knew, Judge Dunne was neither considering nor being considered for any candidacy for mayor of Chicago. Because the essential issue involved—the right of public school teachers to assured salary and assured tenure of office under the law—was one of the vital differences between the two men in political viewpoint, their meeting in this trial was, I think, fraught with a deeper drama than we knew then.

Clarence Darrow asked Mayor Harrison if Graham Harris had not told him that he hoped that the Board of Education would be able to restore the teachers' salaries to the old schedule. The mayor said that, from a rereading of his own letter of March 22, 1900, to the Chicago Teachers' Federation, he believed that he had been under the impression that Harris would be able to restore the salaries.

"And the finance committee so believed?" Darrow asked him.

The question was objected to and Judge Dunne, peering over his glasses, said, "He cannot testify to the mental processes of those gentlemen. If anything was said by the other members of the committee, Mr. Harrison, you may state it."

"I cannot recall anything of that sort," Harrison said. "Judge, this is four years back."

In 1904, [August 22] Judge Dunne rendered his decision in favor of the teachers, holding that as diligent creditors under the law they had won it.[26] The Board of Education took an appeal from his decision to the Appellate Court, wasting all the time that was possible. Herrick, Allen, Boysen, and Martin, hired by the board, secured thirteen continuances. While that appeal was still pending, he was elected mayor of Chicago [in 1905], and had the power to appoint his own Board of Education. The Board didn't wait, however, until his complete board to pay the money to the teachers, but the Dunne Board stopped the case from going to higher courts [and the teachers who were parties to the suit were paid.]

The appeal on the State Board of Equalization case which E. S. Smith took over Judge Grosscup's ruling in the federal court did not reach the United States Supreme Court until the spring of 1907. James Hamilton Lewis, Corporation Counsel under Dunne, represented the City of Chicago before that tribunal. He had just gone through a hard campaign and was probably exhausted, for three times the judges stopped him to ask him what he was talking about. I thought I might be able to give him some information which he lacked and so I went over to the hotel where I thought he'd be. I asked the clerk if Colonel Lewis had come. He said, "No; but he's expected here. I know he is because Judge Grosscup has been here asking for him and is expecting him!"

The next morning, when I went into the dining room of the same hotel for breakfast, Grosscup and Lewis were sitting together. Lewis, who was facing me, happened to look up after a while. His reaction was purely automatic. He bounded out of that seat and went to another table, where he sat alone for the rest of the meal.

[26]The full text of Dunne's decision was printed in the *CTF Bulletin*, 3 (Sept. 9, 1904), pp. 1-3, 5-6. Twenty-three hundred teachers were awarded amounts ranging from $14 to $150. *Chicago Tribune*, Aug. 23, 1904.

We lost the case, but Justice Oliver Wendell Holmes [Jr.] was one of the three [two] who signed a dissenting opinion.[27] Holmes said that it was the first time in his experience upon the Supreme Court bench that the court had ever declared that a tax that was clearly evaded (the amount was clearly fraudulent) could be excused on the ground that all the other evaders hadn't been caught. Holmes said, further, that the Supreme Court never should have taken the case at all. The case should have been left in the jurisdiction of the Supreme Court of the State of Illinois. He said it was the first time in the history of the United States Supreme Court that jurisdiction was taken on appeal from a non-judicial body—the State Board of Equalization—and not from the Supreme Court of the State.

9

We had won for those teachers of Chicago who had been parties to the suit a comparatively small amount of money. We had, however, established in law the moral principle of the teacher's right to be safeguarded in her contract with a Board of Education. We had found out that we could win something for ourselves by our own efforts. We had defeated the despotism which Boards of Education and great financial interests had tried to use against us. We had freed ourselves from fear. We had been given blows, but we had given back blow for blow. We had, too, established, quite without conscious intention, another principle. We had made the grade school teachers of Chicago the spokesmen for the common people. In fighting our own fight against the tax-dodging corporations and the tax-eating politicians, we had called the attention of the people not only of Illinois but of the entire nation to the fact that the small tax payer was paying the major part of the cost of government.[28] Without conscious intention, we had fallen into step

---

[27]This decision was delivered on Oct. 21, 1907; the text was published in the *CTF Bulletin* 6 (Nov. 1, 1907), pp. 3, 7-8, together with a history of the case by Haley. The case was numbered 115 and was officially titled: Samuel B. Raymond, County Treasurer of Cook County, Illinois, and ex-officio County Collector of Cook County, Illinois; John J. Hanberg, his successor as such County Treasurer and County Collector, et al., Appellants vs. Chicago Union Traction Company. The other corporations for whom the decision also applied were: The Peoples Gas, Light, and Coke Company, Chicago City Railway, Chicago Telephone Company, and the Chicago Edison Company. Together, they represented the major utility and transportation system of the city.

[28]The tax fight brought national fame to Haley and the CTF. The *Journal of Education*, the nation's most influential school periodical, lauded Haley and Goggin as "heroic woman investigators." (Aug. 5, 1901), and the Illinois Supreme Court decision was applauded in *World's Work*, the *Outlook*, and the *American Review of Reviews*. See Reid, "Professionalization," pp. 64-65.

with the great marching movement of midwestern liberalism in the United States.

In those early years of the century, the middle west was home to that group of men and women whose ideals were to wax and wane and wax again as determining factors in American political life. Altgeld, stricken as he spoke of the Boers, was dead. [William Jennings] Bryan, who had sat at the head of his coffin while care-worn, toil-stained men and women trudged in out of the rain to look upon the dead face of the man who had borne their troubles in his heart, never entirely caught the spirit of the sad little man for whom he mourned; but he was an evangelist of the creed of public weal as against private privilege and, in spite of political defeats, was arousing a people to knowledge of their inherent rights. "Old Bob" LaFollette, in Wisconsin, was carrying on his tremendous work. Henry Demarest Lloyd was preaching his doctrine of what he called "the religion of labor," whose mission it should be "to advance the Kingdom of God into the unevangelized territory of trade, commerce, and industry." Brand Whitlock and Vachel Lindsay were holding high the torch. "Golden Rule" Jones practiced his theory in Toledo, and Tom Johnson spread light from Cleveland. Louis F. Post cannonaded through the columns of the *Public*. Jane Addams, tortured though she sometimes was by consciousness of some of the financial contributors to Hull House, nevertheless would at times stand valiantly and nobly. John Dewey was preaching democracy in education and the right of the teacher to academic freedom. Thorsten Veblen was thundering his demand for educational and economic independence. It was a time of awakening consciousness of human brotherhood.

For weal or for woe, we joined the ranks.

⚬❘ IV ❘⚬

The Battle Front Widens

1

The end of the nineteenth century had brought a great educational awakening. Its result had been to demand democratic methods in education, but this awakening had extended only to the methods of teaching. We had lost on the administrative side. There we had grown less democratic. That was due largely to our industrial, economic, and political system. To such an extent had our industrial ideal, which is essentially monarchical and military, vitiated the public mind of that period that it had been easy to carry over this industrial ideal into the administration of the schools.

Great educators, John Dewey, Colonel Parker, Mrs. Young among them, had recognized that democracy in education, either in methods of teaching or administration, could not be secured while the public mind was vitiated by the ideal of the industrial factory system, which made the man at the top the only possessor of directing brain, and the thousands below him the mere tools to carry out his directions. They realized that educators could not stand alone and that if the ideal of democracy were to be secured in one field, it must be secured in all. That ideal meant freedom to the human mind.

Step by step, we had won a fight against a political condition that cramped the schools by withholding from them the money legally and justly due them. We realized, however, that this was only one salient of a long line of battle. At other points we were losing rather than gaining ground. The number of teachers in the Chicago schools had been decreased by 654, while the number of children in the schools had increased more than 6,000. This meant that the teachers retained had to take over the care of the additional pupils. At the same time their schedule had been abolished and their salaries set back.

To this burden was added the so-called "promotional" examination, based on a secret marking system, which the teachers knew from its inception to be unjust and unfair. Any candidate who was unsuccessful in this "promotional" examination and whose average was seventy had the privilege of attending a public revision of his papers; but no candidate whose paper was below seventy was permitted to attend the revision or allowed to see the papers. After the day of revision, all papers were destroyed.[1]

The school system was an autocracy in method. "Bulletin Ben" Andrews, unable to administer it to the satisfaction of his superiors, was pushed back on Bryan's hands and taken by him out to Nebraska. Edwin G. Cooley, who had been brought from Strawberry Point, Iowa, to LaGrange, Illinois, by Will Mack, one of the leading salesmen of the Prang Book Company, was appointed Superintendent of Schools. Many years later, in the course of a quarrel between Cooley and Mack, Richard Finnegan of the *Journal* asked Cooley if Mack had brought him to Chicago. Cooley said, "Mack could not keep his own position in the Prang Company except for me." When Finnegan told Mack what Cooley had said, Mack, with many oaths, retorted that Cooley could not have kept his job except for Mack.[2]

The Prang Company had been particularly obtrusive in insisting that Chicago Public School drawing teachers should force the use of their drawing books upon their pupils. There had been a bitter fight when W. W. Speer and Josephine Locke, backed by the Chicago Art Institute method of teaching students without the aid of set textbook models, had refused to foist any drawing books upon the school pupils, particularly as at that time the children themselves had to pay for the books and could, in many cases, ill afford them. Josephine Locke was driven out of the school system, and Speer was slated to go in the early part of 1902.

Up to that time, I had never met Carter Henry Harrison, II, Mayor of Chicago. As a last resort, on the day when Cooley was to recommend his selected list of district superintendents, which left out Speer, I went to see "O.K." Bob Burke.[3] I told him curtly and briefly what I'd come for. "I have a right to expect you, as a politician, to know better than to

[1] This "merit system" was introduced in July, 1902; this was the same month that the Board of Education refused to allocate the $250,000 obtained from the CTF tax suit to the teachers. *Proceedings, Board of Education*, 1902-3, pp. 21-22.

[2] Edwin G. Cooley (1857-1923) was superintendent from 1900 to 1909. In 1911 the Commercial Club sent him to Europe for a two-year study of vocational education. The Cooley vocational plan was a controversial issue in Illinois politics through three legislative sessions (1913, 1915, 1917).

[3] Robert E. Burke, a high ranking member of the Cook County Democratic organization, was a close ally and campaign manager for Harrison. Wendt and Kogan, *Lords of the Levee*, pp. 206-7.

continue to do things that irritate the teaching body of Chicago. You must know that, in the end, this policy must react against any administration responsible for it. Unless something is done to stop it, W. W. Speer is to be dropped by the Board of Education tonight. He is the last educator left in the system. It seems to be the policy of this administration to drive out of the system every man or woman who has any contribution to make by which the work of teaching is a delight instead of a drudgery to both children and teachers, and who will stand up and make a fight for the right of the teachers to do their teaching. He is paying the penalty tonight. The Board is going to fire him."

Burke, short, fat, heavy lipped, shrewd eyed, said to me, "Have you seen the mayor?"

I said, "I have come now to see the mayor."

He said, "Have you seen Mr. Harrison?"

I said, "No; I have no intention of seeing Mr. Harrison. I have come to see the mayor of Chicago."

Burke picked up the phone, called Ed Lahiff, the mayor's private secretary, and ordered, "Come over, Ed."

It was evident that Ed demurred, for Burke said, "Put on your hat and come over." He sat silent for the few minutes until Lahiff came, then he commanded, "Take Miss Haley over to see Mr. Harrison."

Harrison heard my story and said, "Why did you not come to me before?"

"I wouldn't have come to you now," I said, "if I had known of anything else to do."

Harrison said, "I will undertake to stop that from going through tonight."

He did; but two weeks from that day Speer was dropped as district superintendent.

As early as 1898, Ella Flagg Young, who soon afterward resigned from the schools because of the autocracy of Andrews, proposed what seemed to be a reasonable restraint on the objectionable "one-man power" which dominated the schools. Recognizing the fact that all wisdom is not centered in one head, however great, realizing that the experience gained by teachers in the actual work of teaching should not be ignored, and knowing that there must be a certain unity of action in a large school system, Mrs. Young suggested the plan of a council of teachers in each school. From these councils, representatives should be chosen to form a central council, of which the Superintendent should be a member. On the surface, the plan seemed to be merely a co-operative measure to promote understanding and good will. In reality, it was the declaration of independence in the war for academic freedom.[4]

Chicago was not unlike other cities of that time in the restriction and subserviency of its teachers. John Dewey declared:

> If there is a single public school system in the United States where there is official and constitutional provision made for submitting questions of methods, of discipline and teaching, and the questions of the curriculum, textbooks, and so forth, to the discussion and decision of those actually engaged in the work of teaching, that fact has escaped my notice. Indeed, the opposite situation is so common that it seems, as a rule, to be absolutely taken for granted as the normal and final condition of affairs. The number of people to whom any other course has occurred as desirable or even possible—to say nothing of necessary—is apparently very limited. But until the public school system is organized in such a way that every teacher has some regular and representative way in which he or she can register judgment upon matters of educational importance, with the assurance that this judgment will somehow affect the school system, the assertion that the present system is not, from the internal standpoint, democratic seems to be justified. Either we come here upon some fixed and inherent limitation upon the democratic principle, or else we find in this fact an obvious discrepancy between the conduct of the school and the conduct of social life—a discrepancy so great as to demand immediate and persistent effort at reform.
>
> What does democracy mean save that the individual is to have a share in determining the conditions and the aims of his own work; and that, upon the whole, through the free and mutual harmonizing of different individuals, the work of the world is better done than when planned, arranged, and directed by a few, no matter how wise or of how good intent that few? How can we justify our belief in the democratic principle elsewhere, and then go back entirely upon it when we come to education?[5]

As a body, we teachers had not—nor have we yet—even approximate control over members of or entrants into our profession. Doctors and lawyers have taken the right road in establishing organizations and methods which give them some check over their fellows. Teachers, however, are admitted into our profession by arbitrary and usually by

[4]This plan for a system of teachers' councils was the subject of Young's dissertation, "Isolation in School Systems," which was completed in 1900 at the University of Chicago under the direction of John Dewey. It was published as the first volume in the Contributions to Education series under a revised title, *Isolation in the Schools*.

[5]As found in the *Elementary School Teacher*, 4 (Dec., 1903), and reprinted in the *CTF Bulletin*, 2 (Feb. 26, 1904), pp. 1-3, 5-6. As head of the Department of Philosophy and Education of the University of Chicago from 1894 to 1904, Dewey (1859-1952) was familiar with the educational scene in Chicago.

political rule. The miracle is that the moral and educational standards of teachers in general are as high as they remain. We are, however, saddled with the responsibility for the weaker members of our profession, just as are the doctors and the lawyers, but we lack any self-determination concerning whom those fellows shall be. The teachers' councils, established later, and utilized for a little while, would have gone far toward minimizing this evil, as well as toward founding a real democracy in the public schools. At that time, however, such a consummation looked as far away as the stars.

2

By that time, the Chicago teachers had come to know the oppressiveness of political domination. We had learned the greed and the ruthlessness of corporate power. We had seen how entrenched, organized human avarice, working through the machinery of the law, had secured not only the resources of nature, oil wells, coal fields, and iron mines, but the machinery of production and distribution, and privileges of transportation, communication, intelligence, and the medium of exchange. Behind these law given privileges, it had reached out for further power until it had grown so great that it needed only to recognize in any institution an enemy, to annihilate it or to demand and secure it as one more added to its list of tools. The school, alone, was powerless against organized wealth.

The law is the machinery for the adjustment of social relations and the restoration of social equilibrium. The law, however, can be put in motion only by those having voting power. Except in a few western states, the women of the nation had practically no voting power. We realized that we had to fight the devil with fire and, if we were to preserve not only our own self-respect but the basic independence of the public schools, we must make powerful political alliance. We made it, naturally, with the social group which had the same elemental interest as our own—the welfare of the great body of public school children. That organization was the Chicago Federation of Labor.[6]

All the tendencies of the time, as well as our own experience, had been swinging us toward active participation in the great and growing labor movement of the world. It was not easy, however, to convince all

[6]The CFL was formed in 1895 as both the political vehicle for the city's unions and the city central organization affiliated with the American Federation of Labor. As an affiliate, its purposes were to promote organizational activity and to regulate relations between the trade unions of Chicago. John H. Keiser, *Building for the Centuries: Illinois, 1865 to 1898, Sesquicentennial History of Illinois*, 6 vols. (Urbana: University of Illinois Press, 1977), IV, p. 252.

our own members that this was our next step. One of the few compensations of teaching in that time seemed to be a teacher's consciousness of a certain social superiority over her non-teaching neighbors. Some of the teachers thought they would lose this if they should join any organization like the Federation of Labor. The Chicago Federation of Labor, through John Fitzpatrick, organizer of the American Federation of Labor, invited the Chicago Teachers' Federation to affiliate with organized labor and join a body which already counted 200,000 working men, voters of Chicago.

After five weeks' deliberation, we finally came into a general meeting of our own Federation for consideration of the subject. Jane Addams came to that meeting [November 8, 1902] and electrified our members by telling them that they were already a union. The only question now before them, she said, was whether they should avail themselves of the help they could get from other unions. Some of the women were horrified by her words, and they had to look up to see that it was Jane Addams talking. But the Gentle Jane was so respectable and aristocratic that they had to swallow their prejudice and join the parade. We openly, without fear, and with so much publicity that I marvel that the mayor of Chicago of that time, Carter Henry Harrison II, fails to recall the event, joined the Chicago Federation of Labor in November, 1902.[7]

Our first actual association with the Chicago Federation of Labor was exactly what our Victorian associates had forecast. Only a limited number of us, however, knew just how riotous was that occasion; these were the delegates who attended the next annual election of officers of the Federation of Labor, an event which occurred in January, 1903.

We were beginning to think that the labors of Hercules had been wished upon us, but we didn't know until we got into it that we'd been elected to clean the Augean stables. Just after we'd elected our own delegates to the Federation of Labor's election, a committee of the delegates from other organizations came to Catharine Goggin and myself. They told us that they were volunteers trying to oust from control "Skinny" Madden, whom they characterized as a corrupt tool of the large contractors, who were now warring on the small contractors, and who had for some time controlled the elections of the Chicago Federation of Labor by sharp and dishonest practices. We

[7]CTF Minute Book no. 3, Nov. 8, 1902, CTF Files. The affiliation was reported in the major newspapers including the *Tribune*, the *Daily News* and the *Record-Herald*. The comment regarding Harrison refers to the passage in his autobiography where the former mayor wrote: "No publicly acknowledged unionizing was accomplished during my terms of office; what was secretly effected I had no means of learning. After Dunne's election the Teachers' Federation openly affiliated with the Federation of Labor." Harrison, *Stormy Years*, p. 333. See also note 15, p. 35.

passed on their information to our delegates, who decided to vote with the anti-Madden faction.[8]

Catharine Goggin and I had been placed in charge of a small anteroom outside the main hall of a building on Adams Street, where the voting took place. The day was Sunday. Balloting began at ten o'clock in the morning, and the polls were to close at five o'clock in the afternoon. Many of our delegates came in to talk with us before or after they cast their ballots. Two or three times during the day, we heard what we thought might be scuffling, but we didn't know until we saw in the newspapers the next day, that it had been the throwing downstairs of some of Skinny Madden's repeaters.

About a half hour before closing time, Catharine Goggin, Anna Murphy, and I went with some of the women from other labor organizations out in the room where the balloting was being done. At five o'clock, the judges announced that everyone except the judges and clerks should leave the room. Many did. Catharine and I did not. The announcement was repeated several times, but we remained. One of the clerks came over and told us we were to go. But with many other delegates, who were protesting in loud, angry voices, we sat tight. Finally, the protestations grew so violent that our friends among the delegates, who had previously asked us to stay, came over to warn us to go. I walked up to the table upon which stood the ballot box.

"There's going to be trouble," men shouted at me.

"If there's going to be trouble, I shall be right here." I could see dozens of guns and I could see, too, the looks on the faces of some of those men. I thought that the next moment would bring bloodshed and so I attempted to speak. Someone in the crowd shouted, "Hats off!" Men took off their hats. Someone gave me a chair to stand upon, for otherwise I could not have been seen or heard. I begged those men to think of the organizations which they represented and the thousands of men, women, and children for whom they were acting. I appealed to them on behalf of the teachers, who had come to them for protection for themselves and for the children of the public schools. I asked the protesting delegates to step aside and appoint a chairman, with authority to speak for them. The Madden forces withdrew to one side of the room, the anti-Madden to the other. Each one selected a spokesman. The spokesman for the Madden opposition demanded that the ballot box be left and the votes counted in that hall, and not be taken to the Sherman House, as the judges and clerks had announced they intended. It had been the custom to take the ballot box through the

---

[8]Martin B. ("Skinny") Madden was president of the Junior Steamfitters Union whose "sluggers" were featured prominently in the newspaper accounts of the 1900 building trades strike. Lloyd Lewis and Henry Justin Smith, *Chicago: The History of Its Reputation* (New York: Harcourt, Brace, 1929), p. 266-67.

streets under police guard, but the police were subservient to Madden, and on the way these boxes were always exchanged for other boxes which contained ballots showing the result that Madden wanted. That was how he had kept control; in the language of Misther Dooley, "Let anyone vote, but let me count the ballots," had been his slogan.

The spokesman for the Madden judges said it would be impossible to remain in the hall, as it was only rented until six o'clock. The spokesman for the belligerent delegates drew out of his pocket a receipt for the payment of the hall up to twelve o'clock that night. The judges agreed to remain until midnight. I was appointed to select a representative to watch the count. I selected Catharine Goggin, but the men of the anti-Madden group insisted that, since she would be the only woman present, I must be permitted to name another woman to stay with her, and so I chose Anna Murphy to remain. Everyone but the judges, clerks, and watchers left the hall.

As I went downstairs, I noticed that policemen were standing so close through the corridors and out upon the sidewalks that they could almost touch each other's hands. The line went all the way from Adams Street to the Sherman House. I went with some of the other delegates to the owner of the building and rented the hall until noon the next day, as we knew that the Madden judges would delay the count of the ballots so that they could not be finished at twelve o'clock that night. He told us that the electric lights would go off at twelve o'clock and, after that, they would have to use the gas lights in the building. In the interim between changing the electric light to gas, there would be a moment or two of darkness. We bought a pound of candles and sent them up to Catharine Goggin, with instructions for her to light several of them about ten minutes before twelve o'clock.

A few minutes before twelve o'clock, Skinny Madden and his gang walked into the voting room. Catharine Goggin said that the look in Madden's face when he caught her eye and saw the lighted candles was worth all the trouble that had preceded the moment. He could not conceal his disappointed rage. She said that the judges and clerks, in one glance, told Madden plainer than by any language that the jig was up. Madden and the gang left, and the count proceeded quietly until five o'clock the next evening. When the result was announced, not one of the Skinny Madden gang had been elected. He was ousted from control of the Chicago Federation of Labor.[9]

[9]John Fitzpatrick (1870-1946) and Edward L. Nockels (1869-1937) were leaders of the reform movement. They secured control and Fitzpatrick, who was an Irish immigrant, went on to serve as president from 1906 until 1946. Nockels was secretary from 1903 to 1937. Haley was a successful candidate for a position on the legislative committee in this election. *CTF Bulletin*, 2 (Jan. 23, 1903), pp. 6-8. She served as a lobbyist for the Chicago Federation of Labor for the next fourteen years. Haley to Henry R. Linville, Mar. 15, 1920, CTF Files.

3

The Harper bill, which had been rehabilitated in 1901 by the Civic Federation and brought before the Legislature in that year, bobbed up again in the Legislature of 1903. By that time, we realized that there was something in that educational bill which the big business of Chicago wanted very badly. The objections made to the bill by the Federation of Labor were based largely on the fact that the bill fortified the autocracy already in the Chicago schools. The Federation of Labor did not know then, any more than we did, that the milk in the cocoanut [sic] was a carefully hidden provision authorizing the Board of Education to extend leases of the school land for ninety-nine years without revaluation. Even without that knowledge, however, the Federation of Labor and our own Teachers' Federation were pounding against the bill.

Senator Richard Barr, one of the finest men ever in the Illinois Senate, told me that this educational bill would not come out of the committee on education in the senate, of which he was the chairman, without notification to me.[10] I was working for the initiative and referendum bill, for a child labor law, and against a vicious vocational bill which Cooley had sent down from Chicago. I knew that I could rely upon Barr's word, but I had to watch the educational committee in the house. "Fire Escape Gus" Nohe was its chairman. One day he walked into the committee room with the educational bill in his pocket, took it out, then, still holding it in his hand, walked back to the floor of the house, and announced that the committee, which hadn't met at all, reported his bill favorably. Most of its twenty-five members were in the house, but they were so accustomed to that kind of procedure that they didn't even challenge it. I tried to make some of them protest, but they said it would be useless, as that was the way the Legislature did business. I told Senator Barr what Nohe had done, and he assured me that, if there were to be any hearing of that bill in his committee because of the house action, he would notify me. I had to return to Chicago and I was there when I received a telegram from Senator Barr. I went back to Springfield at once.

When I registered at the Leland Hotel the next morning, I saw on the book before me the names of seventeen people from Chicago; among them were Clayton Mark, chairman of the finance committee of the Board of Education, the man who had recommended the striking out of the revaluation clause in the lease of the school lands at the corner of State and Madison Streets and who had given a lease of that

[10]Richard Barr (1866-1951) was a former mayor of Joliet and a good friend of Haley. He served in the Illinois senate from 1902 to 1950.

land for ninety-nine years to the bank of which he was vice president. Another man on the register was Donald Morrill, who had been an attorney for the *Chicago Tribune.* Another was Frank Loesch, an attorney for the Pennsylvania Railroad.

Senator Barr was ill and about to return to his home in Joliet. He told me that he could not preside at the meeting because of that illness and that old "Tobacco Hank" Evans, who had won his name as a representative of the tobacco trust, was to preside in his stead. I told him that it looked to me as if everything had been all arranged.

He said, "Yes; I think they are. I do not know what has happened and I do not know what interests are back of that bill, but I believe it will be recommended out of the committee today."

I remembered then that a man named Thiele, who had been representing groups of people who were opposing the Harper bill, had told me that Dan Campbell, who with Fred Busse controlled the senate, had assured him that the educational bill would not pass. I went to Campbell just as the educational committee of the senate gathered and told him that he was not acting in accordance with the promises he had made to certain people in Chicago. Campbell gave me one look, then started for the committee room. He went to the head of the table, where old Tobacco Hank Evans was already sitting, whispered something to him, walked around the table, and came out.

The hearing continued, although no one mentioned the ninety-nine year lease clause. Then Tobacco Hank announced that, in the absence of the chairman of that committee, Senator Barr, no action could be taken by the committee. The men from Chicago looked at one another and at the chairman, not seeming to understand what had happened. The bill was not recommended that day, and failed of passage altogether.

4

Long before the tax fight had been finished, we teachers had realized that for our own preservation we needed to effect certain reforms in the governmental machinery of our city and our state. The counter attacks on us drove us into support of the measures which would have given us as well as the rest of the public greater freedom: the Initiative and Referendum, Direct Primary, Municipal Ownership of Public Utilities, and election of the Board of Education by popular vote.[11]

When the Supreme Court of Illinois had ordered the State Board of

[11]Illinois law gave women the right to vote in school elections as early as 1891. See note 11, page 60. Haley saw this as a critical step in moving forward the cause of woman suffrage.

Equalization to assess public utility corporations and the federal courts, through Judge Grosscup, had stopped the collection of that tax, we realized that the corporations, especially the street railways of Chicago, were fighting for time. We found out that their franchises had expired—the United States Supreme Court had announced this in 1903—and that they were operating their railways in the streets of Chicago merely on sufferance. Their attorney told the Board of Equalization that their franchises were not worth a dollar.

We realized, however, that if the street railways were using the federal courts to tie up the payment of their just and legal taxes, they must be fairly certain that they were going to secure an extension of their old privileges. We therefore prepared a petition to the City Council, asking that body to grant no more franchises to these street railways until they had paid the taxes which they owed the City. We then made ready petitions to be circulated by the school teachers, with the intention of presenting them to the Council. There were five thousand of these petitions in circulation.

When two school principals came into our office with another petition, they explained that their petition had been drawn up in compliance with a law which has come to be designated as the Public Policy Law. Daniel Cruice, of the Referendum League, who accompanied them, asked me to substitute their petition for ours. Their petition had three questions on it:

1) Are you in favor of municipal ownership of street railways?

2) Are you in favor of municipal ownership of electric light and gas companies?

3) Are you in favor of the direct primary?

All three of these questions were matters of deep concern to us. We therefore called the teachers together and suggested that they either substitute this petition for the one we had already given them or that they take both petitions and secure signatures for them.

Through the efforts of the teachers, the Referendum League petition was signed and, at the election of April, 1902, the people of Chicago voted on these three questions. The vote was five to one in favor of municipal ownership of street railways, gas and electric light utilities, and of direct nomination. The victory was the more notable because every newspaper in Chicago, with the exception of Hearst's *Chicago American*, opposed the adoption of these liberal measures.[12]

The advocates of municipal ownership were troubled by the question of the city's right to undertake the ownership and operation of

[12]As reported in the *CTF Bulletin*, 1 (June 6, 1902), pp. 1-3. See also Warren M. Persons, "The Chicago Teachers' Federation," *The Commons*, 10 (Aug., 1905), p. 444, and Reid, "Professionalization," pp. 66-69.

street railways without authority from the State Legislature. In order to settle that question, a bill was introduced into the Legislature. This bill, later to become the Mueller Law [1903], provided that the City of Chicago should have the power to take over the street railway lines before any franchise was granted. The Chicago City Railway Company seemed to be in favor of the bill and the Union Traction Company against it. The fight in the Legislature grew so hot that the Speaker was dragged from his chair and might have been killed had it not been for the interference of some women on the platform. The members tore up desks and cuspidors and flung them at the Speaker. He had aroused their anger because he had permitted a motion to be made striking out the enacting clause from the Mueller bill and had refused a demand for a roll call. On a show-down, the motion to strike out the enacting clause was lost. When a roll call was taken, the Mueller Law was passed. It was afterwards adopted by the senate and signed by the governor. It gave to the cities of Illinois the power to own, construct, and operate their street railways, but it required that the law should be submitted by the city council of the city to the people of any city before it would become operative.

The next step was the necessity of getting the City Council of Chicago to submit the Mueller Law to the vote of the people. On the recommendation of Henry Demarest Lloyd, whose book, *Wealth Versus Commonwealth*, had established him as one of the leading liberals of the United States, and who took charge of the campaign, a petition to the City Council was immediately prepared, asking that body to submit the Mueller Law to the people. The petition was one of the largest ever drawn up in an American municipality. Lloyd was selected to present it to the City Council, but on the very night when it was to be taken in, he died [September 28, 1903]. It was a sorrowful procession that hauled that huge petition into the Council chamber. Its leaders knew that Lloyd had literally sacrificed his life to the cause he had been advocating. The City Council, moved not by his sacrifice but by the tremendous number of names on the petition, voted to submit the Mueller Law to the people of Chicago. In April, 1904, the law was submitted and ratified. By it, the people were enabled to construct, own, and operate their own street railways and to issue street railway certificates for their purchase and construction. It is because of this law that the finances of the City of Chicago are not in a worse state.[13]

The Council had in preparation an ordinance for giving franchises to the street railways. In 1903, Mayor Harrison had been re-elected on a

---

[13]Reid, "Professionalization," pp. 90-95. See also Caro Lloyd, *Henry Demarest Lloyd, 1847-1903*, 2 vols. (New York: G. P. Putnam and Sons, 1912).

solemn pledge to the people that he would not sign any franchise until it had been submitted to and approved by them. In August, 1904, however, Mayor Harrison in his official proclamation to the people of Chicago announced his intention of signing the pending franchise ordinance unless, within the next two weeks, a petition signed by one hundred thousand people asking to have the ordinance submitted was presented to him. In the absence of such a petition, he would consider, he said, that the people had taken a silent referendum and had approved of the ordinance.

The time limit of two weeks was absolutely unreasonable. There was already in circulation a petition under the Public Policy Law which had almost the required number of signatures and which would have been filed within a few days with the Secretary of State. This petition contained three questions: (1) Direct Primary, (2) election of United States Senators by direct vote of the people, (3) home rule and taxation for the counties of Illinois. The law permitted only three questions to be submitted to the electorate at any one time. If the petition which Mayor Harrison suggested were to be circulated and signed, the other petition would have to be withdrawn. The Referendum League refused to withdraw its petition and flung back its challenge at the mayor. So hot was the fight brought against him that he was obliged to recede from the position which he had taken in his proclamation.

By this time, we teachers had become thoroughly convinced that until there was a Board of Education administering the schools in the interest of the people instead of in the interests of the tax-dodging corporations, it was useless for the teachers to attempt to carry on a successful campaign. It was like a nation trying to carry on a civil and a foreign war at the same time. I felt that we should end the civil war. In other words, I realized that we must get a board of education that would co-operate with the teachers in getting the revenue for the schools. The Municipal Ownership, Initiative and Referendum movements offered the only hope through which we might expect to secure such a majority. It seemed to me then that any majority who would believe in municipal ownership of the street railways ought also to believe in public ownership and control of the schools. We threw our forces into the Municipal Ownership movement, in the hope that it might result in the election of a mayor who would restore the schools, as well as the streets, to the people.[14]

There had been circulated in 1903 another Public Policy petition.

[14]Haley and the organized teachers, together with school children, circulated large numbers of petitions for each of the referendum campaigns. Louis Post, the editor of the *Public*, wrote "the victories won in Chicago for municipalization of public utilities are directly traceable to its (CTF) work." *Public*, May 5, 1906, p. 101.

One of the questions on it was: Shall the Board of Education of the City of Chicago be elected by the people? At the spring election of 1904, the people had voted in favor of the elective board by a majority of two to one; but when a bill was presented to the Legislature for such an elective board, the Legislature had failed to pass it.

In the autumn of 1902, the people of Illinois, voting under the Public Policy Law, had registered their desire for an amendment to the State Constitution providing for the Initiative and Referendum. In 1903, a resolution providing for that amendment, authorizing the people to initiate legislation and to have legislation referred to them, was introduced at Springfield. That resolution, also, was defeated by the Legislature.

This refusal to enact the will of the people into law forced the teachers of Chicago to fall back on the election of a mayor whom they believed would be fair and just as their only hope of securing a board of education in sympathy with their aims and hopes in the tax crusade. Had the Legislature of Illinois seen fit to obey the expressed will of the people of Chicago, the women of the City, particularly the women teachers, would not have been forced into the indirect method of campaigning for any particular mayoral candidate. It would have been much more satisfactory to have had an elective board of education than to have taken the roundabout way of electing a mayor in the hope of securing appointments of fair-minded men and women upon the Board of Education.

The Legislature of Illinois!

⚬⟦ V ⟧⚬

The Dunne Board

1

Some day a bright young man—or, possibly, a bright young woman—
in Congress will bring into that body the question of Chicago school
land leases, and awake to find himself more famous than old Cap'n
Streeter of Streeterville. For the school land leases are not only the
major theme of the long and unended difficulties within the Chicago
public school system but also a major theme in American political life.
In few places has the exploitation of public interest by private greed
been shown as clearly as in the instance of the Chicago school land
question.

The Ordinance of 1787, that wise and far seeing document, which
also forbade the extension of slavery into the Northwest Territory,
decreed that one square mile in every thirty-six within the borders of
that Territory should be set aside for the use of public education. Had
this land been retained—and some of the best constitutional lawyers in
the nation have stated that, in their private opinion, no body but the
Congress of the United States has ever had power to allow its use for
any other purpose—there would now be far more than enough money
in school treasuries to give every child in Illinois a first-class grammar
school education without one cent of taxation on the people of the city
or state.

The admission to statehood of those states, including Illinois, within the Territory ratified rather than abrogated this provision of the
Ordinance. The state Legislatures passed on to local boards of education whatever control they had over the exactly designated lands. In the
case of Chicago, boards of education have sold or leased so much of
this land under terms unfavorable to the public weal that the question
of the school lands has become one of the major political issues of this,
our time. Sometimes the issue has been clouded deliberately by those
whose duty it was to keep it clear. The interests involved in the sale or
leasing of these lands have been so influential and powerful that men

and women who have been good citizens in other public relationships have absolutely failed in their duty in this particular phase of their public lives. Only once in the history of the City of Chicago has any board of education made genuine effort to secure public justice through proper valuation of school lands. This board was the so-called Dunne Board; and to its struggle for readjustment of school land lease values may be traced the continuing, determined, and vicious opposition which beset its path through the period of its existence.

2

Through the early years of the century Chicago, the city, was awake to the need of public action upon questions affecting the common weal: Initiative and Referendum, public ownership of utilities, elective boards of education, and the general rights of Labor. The City of Chicago, official representative of its people, had failed, however, to take action consonant with the voiced desires of its citizens. Time and again, Carter Henry Harrison II had been elected upon a platform promising settlement of the turbulent traction question; but time and again that settlement had been delayed. By 1905, the advocates of Municipal Ownership had grown weary of these protracted promises and in a burst of enthusiasm at a meeting in the Sherman House, named Judge Edward F. Dunne as candidate for mayor on the Democratic ticket.[1]

The naming of Judge Dunne by this organization was nothing but the expression of a hope. The publication of the story, however, aroused a great many more people to the same hope. Among them, Judge Tuley and Clarence Darrow became leaders of the large but scattered Dunne cohorts. They overcame Judge Dunne's reluctance, however, only an hour before the nominating convention went into session.

Before the nominating convention could meet, the City Council was speeding its work of preparing the ordinance which granted to the city railway companies extension of their franchises. The *Chicago Examiner* took up the work of securing petitions under the Public Policy Law. Ordinances were to be submitted to the people at the April

[1]Mayor Harrison announced that he would not be a candidate for reelection in the fall of 1904. The campaign between Dunne and the Republican candidate, John M. Harlan, focused on the issue of municipal ownership with the Democrat pledged to immediate municipal ownership and his opponent pledged to a gradual approach following the settlement of all legal issues. As an Irish Catholic, Dunne was able to enlist broad ethnic support while keeping the party loyalty of the Harrison faction. See note 3, page 45 and note 25, page 81.

election. Final action by the Council was therefore deferred until after the vote. Public sentiment was so strong against granting any extension of the franchises that the Council did not dare to pass the ordinances.

Judge Dunne was elected as an expression of the awakened liberalism of Chicago. No mayor of his city went into office, I am convinced, with a clearer, surer intention of restoring to the people of his municipality their essential right to recognition in public affairs. It was his misfortune that he held office for only two years and that he could not in that time, hampered as he was by political opposition in his own party as well as by the enemies of that party, effect the full measure of his intentions. He was hampered too by his own judicial temperament, always seeing both sides of every argument before he would make any decision; but his decisions were, in the main, on the side of the angels.

One of his first decisions concerned the Board of Education. Because of my belief that he would be the best man for the interest of the public schools, I had campaigned for his nomination and election. After his election, I asked him to consider Jane Addams as a type of citizen for appointment upon the Board. He told me that he viewed very favorably the making of this appointment and asked me if I would talk to her about it. For several years, Jane Addams had been peculiarly trusted by the teachers of Chicago. On two momentous occasions, she had proved herself the true friend and the wise counsellor of the Teachers' Federation, once when she had advised us to join the Federation of Labor, and again when she had, at a public meeting in February, 1905, assailed the existing and so-called "promotional" scheme which had been established in the schools by Edwin G. Cooley, the Superintendent.

When I went as Mayor Dunne's emissary, I found Hull House up in arms against the idea of their head resident going on the school board. Miss Addams herself felt that she should not assume this additional responsibility but, with assurance that Mayor Dunne would not appoint anyone on the Board not satisfactory to her, thus making it possible for her to put into effect her policy for the schools, she consented to accept the appointment, provided that Mrs. Emmons Blaine, who was one of the Harvester McCormicks by birth and a daughter-in-law of the Plumed Knight, should serve with her.[2]

[2]The Plumed Knight was James G. Blaine (1830-93), who served as speaker of the U.S. House of Representatives from 1869 to 1875. He was the unsuccessful Republican candidate for the presidency in 1884. His daughter-in-law, Anita McCormick Blaine, is the subject of a recent biography by Gilbert H. Harrison. In a letter to President Harper of the University of Chicago, dated June 15, 1905, Blaine indicated that she had been assured that Mayor Dunne intended to do something for the ten thousand children in elementary schools who were being taught in warehouses, converted garages, and store

Miss Addams made no opposition to the appointment of Dr. Cornelia DeBey, although Dr. DeBey was probably then, as she was afterward, a thorn in the Gentle Jane's side.[3] She had an uncanny ability in finding Jane's fallacies and of prodding her with the consciousness of them, even though she shielded them wherever she could from public discovery. The doctor, tall, thin almost to the point of emaciation, wearing clothes almost as mannish as Dr. Mary Walker's, knew what we were to find out later: that Jane Addams was a social rather than a moral leader. Years afterward, Anna Garland [Garlin] Spencer told me that we had done Jane Addams a serious injustice in expecting her to be a William Lloyd Garrison instead of what she really was, a sensitive plate reflecting the feelings of others and having unusual power of putting herself in the other fellow's place. With the public, however, we believed at the time that Jane Addams was a great moral leader, and our disappointment was bitter when she failed, as time went on, to live up to our expectations of that leadership.[4]

The first act of the Dunne Board was the beginning of negotiations to have the teachers' suit for back salary against the Board of Education dismissed. It was almost a year later, however, when the money was paid.[5] The amount for each one of the 1,653 teachers who filed into

buildings rented by the city. Harrison devotes five pages to a discussion of the Dunne Board without mentioning Margaret Haley or the Chicago Teachers' Federation. Presented in this fashion, the story seems simply one of internal conflict between board members wherein wirepulling, cliques, and conspiracies are the main features. Gilbert H. Harrison, *A Timeless Affair* (Chicago: University of Chicago Press, 1979), pp. 123-27.

[3]Cornelia DeBey was an osteopathic physician and former teacher who gained fame when she helped mediate the stockyards strike in 1904. She was a proponent of kindergartens in the public schools and a close personal friend of Haley. *Chicago Record-Herald*, Sept. 11, 1904.

[4]Anna Garlin Spencer (1851-1931) was a minister, lecturer, and writer on social issues. For three years, 1908-11, she was a lecturer at the University of Wisconsin; Haley spoke with her during the summer of 1909 in Madison. Edward T. James, ed., *Notable American Women*, 3 vols. (Cambridge, Mass.: Belknap Press, Harvard University Press, 1971), III, pp. 331-33; Haley, "Autobiography," Seattle Transcript, 17th installment, Feb. 6, 1912, CTF Files.

Addams' version of her experiences on the Dunne Board is found in *Hull House*, pp. 327-39. See also Allen F. Davis, *American Heroine: The Life and Legend of Jane Addams* (New York: Oxford University Press, 1973), pp. 131-34.

The other members appointed by Dunne were John C. Harding of the Typographical Union, Emil Ritter, a former teacher and former CTF member, Dr. Wladyslaw A. Kuflewski, a reappointment who represented the Polish community, and Modie J. Spiegel, a businessman who was identified with the Jewish community.

According to Louis Post, a later Dunne appointee, these persons were unique in that they represented a broader philosophical and social outlook. A business orientation, both in board composition and outlook, had characterized earlier boards. In addition, most of these members were either suggested or approved by Haley. Post, "Living a Long Life Over Again," p. 303, Louis F. Post Papers, Library of Congress, Washington, D.C. (hereafter cited as Post, "Living a Long Life").

[5]*Proceedings, Board of Education*, 1905-6, pp. 762-71.

Isaiah T. Greenacre's office to receive a check for the back salary was not large, only $45, to cover the cut for the six months from January to June, 1900; but the moral effect was beyond reckoning. What these teachers had endured as a result of their courage and daring in this attack upon vested wrongs will never be known. No individual or group of individuals can attack entrenched privilege in its stronghold without arousing cruel counter attack. The teachers of Chicago had been paying that penalty. The so-called promotional examination scheme of salary advances was the method used against them. They had suffered, too, from an attack on their pension laws, from the secret marking system, which was entwined with the promotional examination scheme, and from the overcrowding in the schoolrooms which had come from the reduction of the number of teachers in the system. Dave Shanahan had been right when he had told me that the corporations would strike back at us.

Under the method then in vogue, the mayor appointed seven new members yearly to replace those whose terms had expired, upon a Board of Education numbering twenty-one members. This method kept a majority of the previous board until the second year of any mayor's administration, so that it was July, 1906, more than a year after his election, when Mayor Dunne was able to secure a working majority on the Board. Before that time, however, Jane Addams had been made chairman of the school management committee. To that committee, Cooley, the Superintendent of Schools, then recommended a modification of his so-called promotional scheme.[6]

This scheme, which later was shown to be nothing but a method of keeping a long list of teachers on the short side of the payroll, pretended to be one of academic advancement. The teachers were given their choice between taking an examination at the end of their seventh year of service, or of presenting five courses of study of thirty-six hours each. These courses could be taken in institutions accredited by the superintendent and the principal of the Chicago Normal School or the work could be taken entirely in the normal school. Only two courses of study could be taken in any one year at Normal, or rather in the extension department of the normal school, but there was no limit in the rules to the number of courses of study that a teacher could take in any school year in the accredited institutions. Teachers who had taken such courses of study since the time of their appointment as teachers in Chicago and whose efficiency marks were satisfactory were permitted to apply at once for a salary advance. At least one course of

[6]The Cooley promotional plan was introduced in 1902; teachers at the seventh year or more of experience received salary increments upon successful passage of examinations. *Proceedings, Board of Education*, 1902-3, p. 21.

study had to be taken within the previous two years before application for the advance could be made.[7]

When Cooley brought his money-shaving and teacher-punishing plan to the school management committee, Jane Addams invited me to come to Hull House for a conference with herself, Dr. DeBey, and Ella Flagg Young. At the conference, I took the position that I could not presume to speak for the teachers in the Chicago Teachers' Federation, and certainly not for all the teaching body of Chicago not included in the Federation, on any such matter. The scheme had not been considered by the teachers. I insisted that the teaching body, as a whole, could be trusted to discuss such a scheme and that any assumption that they were not both competent to discuss it and fair-minded enough to do the right thing in it was an insult to the whole educational corps. All of them agreed with me, but Miss Addams said that she feared Mr. Cooley would not favor our plan. I told her that I thought the duty rested upon her if the superintendent refused to do it. Before we left the conference, Jane had agreed that she would take up the matter with Cooley.

Two days later, Mrs. Young sent for me. We met on the Englewood station platform and between trains talked out what was on our minds. Mrs. Young said that Jane Addams was wholly unable to cope with Cooley and that she ought not to go alone or be sent alone on such matters to him. She told me that Miss Addams had told her that Cooley had said that he had consulted with his friends, the editors of the Chicago newspapers, and they had told him that he did not need to yield to the teachers, that Carter Harrison was going to be nominated again, that Mayor Dunne would be down and out, and that he, Cooley, would only need to hold on to assure his own victory. I went immediately to the telephone and asked Miss Addams which newspaper editors had told Cooley that he would not need to submit his promotion scheme to the teachers for ratification. Jane said she did not feel at liberty to tell me. On the following Wednesday, the report was submitted to the Board of Education without having been submitted to the teachers. John Harding, one of the Dunne members, protested that he had not had time to read the report submitted to him. There were, however, eleven votes to suspend the rules. Jane Addams' was one of them. The report was adopted.[8]

---

[7]As Haley describes, Cooley's modification was the substitution of academic course work for the exams. His letter to the school management committee containing the details of this substitution was dated April 27, 1906, and reprinted in the *CTF Bulletin*, 5 (May 11, 1906), pp. 1-4. To be eligible for either the exams or the course work, teachers had to receive high efficiency ratings from their principals. This was described as a "secret marking system" by the members of the CTF.

[8]*Proceedings, Board of Education*, 1905-6, pp. 773-76; 813-15.

The scheme was in operation when Mayor Dunne appointed his
second batch of seven members to the board.[9] On the first meeting after
these appointments, an investigation of the scheme was ordered. Wiley
W. Mills, one of the new appointees, asked for the records of teachers'
efficiency and the salary payrolls. He picked twenty-five schools at
random, copied the efficiency marks of the teachers, took the payrolls
of those teachers and copied the record of the salaries. He found
teachers with efficiency marks as high as 95 or even 100 who were
drawing the low salary of $850 or $875. He found teachers whose
records of efficiency were as low as 60 drawing the highest salary, of
$1,000. These teachers were all in the same grade and of the same
number of years of experience. He decided that the so-called merit
system of reward by salary advances, on the face of the record, was a
misnomer. Dr. DeBey asked that investigation be made in the 245
schools of the system to ascertain if the same condition existed everywhere.

Louis F. Post, afterward Assistant Secretary of Labor in the Wilson
cabinet and one of Chicago's most valuable and far sighted citizens, was
made chairman of the investigating committee. His committee found
that the Cooley system was practically disrupting education in the
Chicago public schools. By that system, teachers were being tested on
their loyalty to immediate authority rather than on their loyalty to
ethical and educational principle. On December 5, 1906, the Board of
Education adopted the report of the Post committee, which recommended the abolition of the secret marking system and marking in
percentages, provided that all principals should report inefficient
teachers, and that all inefficient teachers after reasonable probation
should be dismissed if they did not improve. It abolished also the
promotional examination and study credit system for salary advances,
thereby providing that the salary advances should be automatic from
the first year to the maximum. The report also provided for bringing
the rules of the Board of Education into harmony with the state law as
embodied in the teachers' pension law, which provided that no teacher
should be dismissed without trial on charges. In other words, the Post
report merely reasserted the constitutional rights of the citizen.[10]

[9]Addams, DeBey, Harding, Ritter, Haley, and Louis Post met at Dunne's home to
select this group. A vacancy enabled the mayor to appoint eight. The key appointment
was Louis F. Post (1849-1928), an advisor to Dunne during the mayoral campaign and
the editor of the *Public*, the most influential single tax progressive weekly in the
Midwest. Others were Wiley W. Mills, a lawyer who had been an aldermanic candidate
on the single tax platform; Philip W. Angsten, an advocate of municipal ownership; Dr.
John Guerin, an Irish Catholic friend of the mayor; John J. Sonsteby, secretary of the
garment workers' local; and Raymond Robins, a social worker from the Northwestern
University Settlement House. Two conservatives, Rev. Rufus A. White and P. Shelly
O'Ryan, were reappointed.
[10]*Proceedings, Board of Education*, 1906-7, p. 490-534.

On the night when the Board of Education adopted this report, Modie Spiegel, chairman of the finance committee, let the cat out of the bag by announcing that it would bankrupt the board to pay the teachers these proposed salaries. Spiegel was asked if the board rules did not provide for paying the teachers when they had complied with the requirements and how he could defend the board from failure to keep its contract with the teachers. He said, "The Board of Education is dishonest in telling the teachers that it will pay them these salaries if they do the work. What the Board of Education should do is to notify the teachers that, even if they do this work, we cannot pay them and that we therefore withdraw these conditions."

In spite, however, of Spiegel's assertion, the board adopted the Post report and as a result 2,600 teachers had their salaries advanced in February, 1907. They never drew the advance, however, for in April, 1907, Fred Busse was elected mayor of Chicago.[11] By the end of May, he had thrown out the Dunne Board—with the exception of Jane Addams and Mrs. Emmons Blaine and one or two others—illegally, although that board was to return later by due process of law. His board, installed in June, 1907, repealed the Post report and put back the 2,600 teachers to the low salary. It also re-enacted the secret marking system and the Cooley promotional scheme.

The teachers returned to their schools that autumn in confusion and discouragement. The future of justice looked dark for them. There was, however, a gleam of light already glowing on the horizon, although it was then no bigger than a pin point. Among the schools approved by Superintendent Cooley for courses to be taken by the teachers for promotional credit was the Chicago Art Institute. In the autumn of 1907, fifteen teachers went to the Institute for classes. Among them were two women of enormous political influence, who told me that they were to get credit from the Board of Education for five courses which they were taking concurrently. They would complete these in January, would get the credit and be advanced in salary. I asked them to go ahead and establish the precedent. On the 15th of January, 1908, they received credit for these five courses, which they had taken in a period of less than four months, although it was supposed to take two years and a half.

I then secured copies of the Board of Education rules and gave them

[11]Fred Busse (1866-1914) was the postmaster of Chicago with business interests in hardware and coal. During the campaign, which was for a four-year term of office, the Republican Busse promised to appoint a nonpartisan school board and slow the movement for municipal ownership. Harold Ickes, who had managed John Harlan's campaign for mayor in 1905, described Busse as a "near-hoodlum." Harold Ickes, *Autobiography of a Curmudgeon* (New York: Reynal and Hitchcock, 1943), p. 108. See also note 4, p. 46.

to Ralph Holmes, Registrar of the Art Institute. I asked him if he could take care of a large number of teachers in classes. He said that he could, and I passed the word to the teachers. Thirteen hundred of them went into classes at the Institute. By the 1st of May, they had completed the five courses; then they filed application for credit with the Board of Education.[12] Cooley, who had been in Europe, returned to find that he had been hoisted on his own petard. One man said that Cooley had set a trap for the teachers and that the teachers had walked off with the trap. Cooley removed the Art Institute from the list of accredited institutions, without taking into account the fact that the directors of that institution were exactly the people whom he had tried for years to please. The Institute did not stay long off the list of accredited institutions. The Dunne Board, returned in December, 1907, by a decision of the Illinois Supreme Court, rallied enough force within the next year to clip Cooley in his czardom of the superintendency and to put Ella Flagg Young in the Normal School. One of her first acts as superintendent, when she was appointed by a later Board, was the reinstatement of the Chicago Art Institute in the list of accredited schools.

3

When Mayor Busse removed Louis F. Post, Raymond Robins, Wiley W. Mills, John J. Sonsteby, and Dr. DeBey from the Board of Education, he left Jane Addams, Anita McCormick Blaine and a few others in office. The removal was ordered at the City Council meeting on Monday night, May 20, 1907.[13] Immediately afterward, a meeting of some of the hold-over members, P. Shelly O'Ryan, one of the Harrison appointees who had been reappointed by Mayor Dunne and who had not been removed by Busse, John C. Harding, a Dunne Board member who had not been removed at that date, Rufus A. White, another Harrison member reappointed by Dunne, Mrs. Blaine, and Jane Addams, was held at Mrs. Blaine's home. At this meeting, it was arranged to call off the meeting of the school management committee in order that its chairman, Miss Addams, would not be obliged to take any position on the question of the removal of the Dunne Board members.

I knew nothing of this meeting until the next morning when, at Miss Addams' own request, I met her in Dr. DeBey's office. She talked

[12]*Proceedings, Board of Education,* 1907-8, pp. 814-28; 883-85; 957-58.

[13]The order came from Mayor Busse, who had sent letters on May 17 to twelve members requesting their letters of resignation. Reid, "Professionalization," pp. 132-33.

to me for some time about the meeting of the previous night, but I did not get it through my brain that she had intended to call off the regular, scheduled meeting of the school management committee for that afternoon. I was not, I think, more than ordinarily stupid. It was probably because the whole idea was so preposterous and my trust in her still great enough that I could not understand that she could hold any such intention. The three of us went out on the street to go over to the old Union Restaurant. As we went along, Jane said to me, in her usual sweet and gentle manner, "Do you know that I'm not at all ashamed to be seen walking along the street with you?" I thought for an instant that she was joking and started to retort in kind; then I saw the glint in Dr. DeBey's eyes and the quirk of Dr. DeBey's mouth. I knew then that Jane had meant exactly what she had said.

Evidently she didn't want to be seen too long in public with me, though, for she left the doctor and myself, to take a car back to Hull House. We'd been in the restaurant a little while when Dr. DeBey said something that made me understand that Jane had been calling off the school management committee meeting that should have been held that afternoon. I went to the telephone and told her that I didn't want her to think I had understood her when she had talked with me in the morning, and that I wanted her to know that I would have expressed myself very differently if I'd realized what she had been talking about. She didn't even combat me when I accused her of having abided by Busse's decision instead of fighting against it. Had she held the meeting of the school management committee, it would have put Busse up against the necessity of removing her or of showing that he lacked the courage to remove her. By staying away from the committee meeting, she let him out of a perplexing situation. I didn't say then all I might have said to her, but I know I said enough to let her know that I knew where she stood.

In the same month, the Legislature of Illinois passed an amendment to the existing pension law for teachers. This amendment provided that the board of trustees for the administration of the pension fund should consist of nine members, six to be elected by the contributors to the fund, two to be chosen by the Board of Education from its own membership, and the ninth to be the secretary of the Board of Education. This law went into effect in July of that year, but the election of the new board did not take place until the following October. Instead of waiting, however, until the teachers had elected their six members, Otto C. Schneider, President of the Busse Board, appointed a temporary pension board in July. The Board selected Schneider and Jane

Addams for its members on this temporary body and authorized Schneider to choose the six representatives from the teaching force. There was no authority in the law for this procedure, but the Busse Board calmly ignored the law that was to go into force.[14]

I had a talk with Jane Addams about the situation. She told me that she had already told Schneider that he had made a grave mistake in his appointments of the teachers on the pension board. Schneider had told her, she said, that the teachers' union would have no representative on that pension board while he was able to keep her off.

The temporary pension board made arrangements for the nomination and election of teachers' representatives to be held in October. A pension delegate convention was held in September. One delegate was sent from every school. The teachers were trying to secure the use of an Australian ballot, as against the post-card system, which made it possible to ascertain how any teacher had voted. Some of the members of the Board of Education were trying to have Cooley's name placed on the ballot, and the teachers did not want to have to vote on an open ballot for or against the superintendent. The question was raging when Jane asked me what I thought of Cooley as a candidate. I said that if there were one thing irritating to the teachers of Chicago, it would be to be forced into a position on an open ballot concerning Mr. Cooley.

Practically all the contributors to the pension fund signed a petition addressed to Miss Addams as chairman of the temporary pension board, requesting that board to provide for a secret ballot and offering to defray the additional expense by voluntary contributions. This petition was received at a meeting of the temporary pension board. Catharine Goggin was in attendance there, as she had been at every meeting of the pension board from its first in 1895. When the time arrived to call the meeting to order, Jane Addams arose, left the room, held a conference in the hall outside with Otto C. Schneider, then returned to the committee room, and announced that the meeting would be an executive session. The newspaper reporters left. Catharine Goggin said, "Does that mean, Miss Addams, that I must go?"

Jane said, "Well, it means an executive session."

Catharine Goggin left.

There have been conflicting reports about that executive session, but I do know that the temporary pension board refused to comply with the request of the delegate convention and the petition for the secret ballot. The postal-card vote was ordered. I believed then and I still

---

[14]The bill passed the legislature on May 11. The new law was reprinted in *CTF Bulletin*, 6 (May 24, 1907), pp. 1-3.

believe that the Busse Board wanted to dominate the nomination and election of that pension board because of the money accruing to it by the law which the State Legislature had just passed. This money, appropriating to the pension fund the interest on the bank balances of the educational fund in the City Treasurer's office, amounted to fifty thousand dollars a year. The City Treasurer, on the advice of Busse's Corporation Counsel, refused to turn this money over to the teachers' pension fund for the reason, he said, that he was advised that the law was unconstitutional. At the same time, he was turning over every month public money to the firemen's and policemen's pension funds, and no Corporation Counsel had ever advised that the payment of such pensions was the use of public money for private purposes. The teachers knew that it would be necessary for the new pension board, once it was elected, to go into the courts and fight for that money. By chance, again, I had discovered that one of the members of the temporary pension board wanted as attorney for that body the very man in the office of the Corporation Counsel who had written the opinion declaring the law unconstitutional.

When the teachers learned that the unanimous request of their representatives had been refused and that they had been denied the right to a secret ballot, they believed that the denial meant that people whom they distrusted but against whom they would not dare to vote would be forced on the ballot. There was only one way to circumvent the plot. That was by flinging it out into the open; by letters, by voice, by meetings, and by every means in our power, we told the town what was being done.

The fourteen district conventions for the nomination of members of the permanent pension board were held on the morning of September 20. There were six vacancies to be filled, two for the three-year term, two for the two-year term, and two for the one-year term. In each one of the fourteen conventions the same two people were nominated for the three-year term, another two for the two-year term, and a third two for the one-year. That is, there were six nominations to be made, and only six names appeared on the ballots. The temporary pension board could have an open ballot or a secret ballot or any kind of a ballot that it pleased. The teachers of the pension fund had gone on strike and named their own ticket. These nominating conventions were a joke with the politicians, but no one understood better than the machine politicians of Chicago that they meant organization. The Busse Board was a little slower on the up-take than the others, but it finally accepted its defeat.

When the newly elected pension board organized, the secretary— who was *ex officio* the secretary of the Board of Education—nominated

Jane Addams for president of the board; then moved that the nominations be closed, and that she be elected unanimously. The six representatives of the teachers said nothing. They just sat there and stared at her. She ruled the motion made by the secretary out of order, and asked that another name be put in nomination. It was. The new name was that of the representative of the Teachers' Federation, whom Schneider had said he would not allow on the pension board. She was elected and the secretary of the Board of Education, who had been secretary of the pension board for twelve years, refused to act as secretary any longer. The six teachers nominated and elected their own secretary.[15]

Shortly after the reorganization of the pension board, I spoke at Hull House at a meeting of the Women's Trade Union League. John R. Commons, of the University of Wisconsin, was the principal speaker. The subject of the meeting was the organization of municipal employees into labor unions. There was supposed to be a discussion from the floor after the speaking but, although the hall was filled with public school teachers, no discussion arose. Corinne Brown was so impressed by the silence of the audience that she asked Jane Addams what it portended. Jane asked me. I said, "The time has come and gone in Chicago for discussion of these questions. The time has come for action, and the people in Chicago who should have acted have fallen down. How can you ask why a body consisting as largely as that body did today of public school teachers should not get up and discuss such a question as the organization of municipal employees into labor unions, after what has occurred in this city recently against the organization of municipal employees? We have Russia in Chicago. We have it right in our public school system. We had evidences of it in the recent occurrences in the Chicago teachers' pension board. When a woman in your position, sitting as president of the teachers' pension board, will order an executive session without vote of the board and in that executive session will destroy the written request unanimously made by the elected representatives of the contributors to the teachers' fund, backed up by petition of the teachers, practically all of them the contributors to that fund, for a secret ballot, have you any reason to expect those teachers to discuss freely at a meeting at Hull House the questions that you had before the body this afternoon?"

Miss Addams said that I did not state the question fairly.

I said, "I do not know what occurred in that executive session, but I do know that John T. Ray, principal of the Crerar School, who was

---

[15]According to Haley's successor as business representative, Francis Kenney, the CTF retained control of the pension board until 1955. See also Herrick, *Chicago Schools*, p. 99.

one of the members of the temporary pension board, had stated in a public meeting in Fullerton Hall that Miss Addams, the president of that board, had ordered the petition of the teachers thrown into the waste basket. You have not seen fit to say what did occur at that meeting, but others have stated publicly. If they do you an injustice, you owe it to yourself and the teachers to correct it."

Miss Addams said that she did not say she would throw the petition in the waste basket, but objection had been made to the petition on the ground that it was anonymous or, rather, that the communication which accompanied the petition was anonymous and that she had said, "Let us not consider the petition, but let us consider the resolution adopted by the convention." The board had refused, she told me, to accede to the request in the resolution.

"Will you make a statement if what I have said is wrong?"

She began by saying that I did not understand how she had to work, that she wanted to get forty playgrounds.

I said, "Jane Addams, you pay too dear for your forty playgrounds, or forty times forty playgrounds, when you trade them off for the fundamental rights that the teachers have, namely, the right to petition and the right to a secret ballot on their own business, and when you lose what is scarcely less vital, the confidence that the teachers had in your faith in your ideals of democracy and your willingness to live up to them. The faith and the confidence that the teachers have had in you, at a time when there was general lack of faith in the leaders, was a possession of which you have robbed the teachers. No number of playgrounds, or any other material gain, can ever compensate for what you have caused the teachers of Chicago to lose when they lost their faith in you."

4

To Frances Temple, teacher in the old South Division High School, belongs the credit for the idea of establishing teachers' councils in the Chicago public schools.

Ella Flagg Young had already advocated the measure and had insisted upon basing her work at the University of Chicago, where she went after her resignation from the public schools had been forced by "Bulletin Ben," upon this thesis; but the idea would have remained academic had it not been for Mrs. Temple's insistence upon it. In season and out of season, she would take the floor at Federation meetings in order to hammer upon the right of the teachers to express themselves upon textbooks, courses of study, and everything on both educational and administrative sides of the schools. The tendency toward centralization in education was sweeping over the country, and would probably have engulfed us hopelessly if it had not been for her determination that we would see its dangers.

She pointed out that the teachers must leave to boards of education the business side of administration, but that they must hold out against exercise of the educational function by one superintendent who would keep thousands of teachers merely takers of orders instead of educators. She compiled the first collection of the utterances of famous educators on the question. She showed the Civic Federation educational committee that the great educators of the United States and Europe were on record in favor of tenure of office for school teachers and in favor of school councils. The committee favored her assumption, but the Civic Federation as a whole did not and prepared a bill for the Legislature which failed to embody any such wise provision as teachers' councils or trial for teachers before dismissal. Because of her insistence on such a provision, she lost her position in the schools. Her work went on.

As the idea developed, the teachers established a quasi-official system of school councils. The teachers of each school elected two delegates, one primary and one grammar grade teacher, who represented the school in the district council. The delegates in the district councils elected representatives to the central council. The teachers in each school constituted the school council. Each of the councils, the school, the district, and the central council, had power to initiate any subject for discussion and to present the subject to other councils.

These voluntary organizations remained in force until 1903, when Superintendent Cooley destroyed them. The Dunne Board undertook to create a system of educational councils, and would have put it into force had it not been for Mayor Busse's action in removing so many of its members. Ella Flagg Young had aided in preparation of a report to the school management committee in favor of the school councils, and had called attention to the fact that the only body of professional people who had no choice in the selection of their tools was the teaching body.

5

In 1818, when Illinois was admitted to the Union, the government of the United States, acting under the provisions of the Ordinance of 1787, gave—among other property—the square mile between State, Madison, Halsted, and Twelfth Streets to the state to be held in trust for the support of the public schools and the education of the children of the district.

Through the incorporation of the City of Chicago, the administration of this property came under the jurisdiction of the Chicago Board of Education. Little by little, this inheritance of the children of the community was squandered by these boards until, by the end of the last century, only a small portion was left. One of the first acts of city government in Chicago was the sale, about 1836, of the entire square mile, with the exception of one block—that bounded by Madison, Dearborn, State, and Monroe Streets—for less than forty thousand dollars. Fifteen years later, ten years before the beginning of the Civil War, this square mile was worth six million dollars. By 1900, its value, irrespective of improvements, was hundreds of millions of dollars. With the exception of a few squares in New York City, it was one of the most valuable square miles on the western continent. The rent from this square mile of land would have been sufficient to support for all this time the entire school system of the whole state of Illinois.

At the end of the Civil War, the *Chicago Tribune* Company leased from the Board of Education property for the establishment of its plant, with the stipulation that at the expiration of its lease about thirteen years later, it could buy the land if so inclined or the Board of Education would buy the improvements which the *Tribune* Company would have set upon it.

In 1880, when the time came to exercise the option, the agreement was repudiated by the City Council, on the ground that the school board had had no authority to make it. The *Tribune* was unable to buy the land, and the board would not buy the building. The *Tribune* was therefore forced to remain a tenant of the school board. At that time, all school lands were being leased by the Board of Education to various tenants for a long term, but with the provision that there should be a revaluation every five years, and that the rent should be 6 per cent per annum upon this valuation. The purpose of this was to enable the school fund to get the benefit of the advance in the value of the lands as the city grew larger. Under this arrangement, the lessees erected buildings which were similar to other buildings of the vicinity that were not on leased ground. Revaluations were made from time to time, each much higher than the former, but the lessees, many of them prominent citizens, had been able to exert such influence that the rent produced by this ground had always been far below that paid for ground belonging to private individuals, in the same locality and no more desirable, so that these school land leases had become very valuable over and above the value of the buildings. Some of them had been sold for large sums, and others were being held at prices that could not have been secured if fair rentals were being paid.

By 1895, the owners of four great daily newspapers held leases of school lands. Three of these papers were being actually published on school lands. When certain men made strong efforts to compel the payment of a fair rent on this land, they had been made targets of abuse by at least one of these newspapers. The original leases made between the Board of Education and their lessees provided that the board alone should select three appraisers for determination of revaluation. The theory on which the contract was made was that the tenant should pay all that the ground was worth and that, as the members of the board were not personally interested, they would not ask more.

Sometime in the late Eighties, the Board of Education waived its right and entered into a contract whereby, in the future, it was to select only one appraiser, leaving the other two to be selected by two different judges of Chicago. It was the supposition that judges were both able and honest, but as Governor Altgeld pointed out a few years later, "Experience had shown that, as a rule, judges are as sensitive to newspaper influence as other men."

In the course of the passing years, the Board of Education had done plenty of horse trading in the way of swapping lands so that, in addition to the square block which was all that was left of the square mile, the board had also given out on lease other downtown property. The *Daily News*, then on Madison near Wells Street, occupied one section of it. The First National Bank of Chicago occupied another. These sections were under the same legal restrictions that covered the original square mile; that is, they were school lands not subject to taxation but presumed to be in use for the benefit of the schools.

In 1880, a group of leases was executed by the so-called "Business Board" of that time. These leases were to run until 1985. They covered what was then the most valuable property in Chicago and what was to become, within the next half century, infinitely more valuable. Among the lessees were Jacob L. Kesner, Rosalie Cavana, the McVicker Theater Company, James K. Sebree, Chambers Farwell, D. F. Crilly, Stumer, Rosenthal, and Eckstein, G. B. Jenkinson, Bishop and Company, the estate of J. E. Otis, Mary H. Otis, the Metropolitan Building Company, the *Tribune* Company, and Caroline F. Wilson. The Otises—Ralph F. Otis, one of the principal heirs to this estate, was afterward a member of the Board of Education which changed the basic school laws of Chicago—leased the most important corner of the strip, the southwest corner of State and Madison Streets. Caroline F. Wilson was one of the owners of the *Chicago Daily Journal*. The Otises, the Metropolitan Building Company, the *Tribune* Company, and Caroline F. Wilson secured in 1895 a privilege not then granted to the other lessees. Through A. S. Trude, then attorney for the *Chicago Tribune* Company who had become a member of the Board of Education, action was taken to strike out from the school land leases the revaluation clauses. The rentals were fixed for ninety-nine years without revaluation.[16]

At that time, the entire square block was paying only $166,521 a year rental. The corresponding piece of ground on the opposite side of the street was paying more than twice that sum in addition to its taxes, since the school grounds are exempt from taxation. The law had contemplated that, because of the lack of taxation, the rentals should be higher. Instead of that, they were kept lower. In 1895, the Otis lot at the corner of State and Madison Streets, a piece of property 48 by 80 feet, was paying $15,120 a year rental on the ground and no taxes. It was an old building of little value, but Otis, its tenant, sublet it at a rental which, after paying the ground rental and all expenses, netted him over $40,000 a year.

From that time onward, every educational measure introduced in Springfield with the sanction of the Chicago City government held a joker regarding this revaluation clause. The Harper bill had it, although we did not know of that fact until years later. Only in the light of that later knowledge could we realize why the struggle to put it over had been so bitter. The three teachers who had gone to Springfield to lobby against the bill before the committee which was hearing it had to invoke their constitutional rights before they could be heard. Buried in the heart of that bill was a provision for giving all lease holders of school fund lands ninety-nine year leases without revaluation. Every dollar of rent that had been lost to the school fund by selling the school land or by changing the school land leases had to be made up by the tax payers of Chicago. The burden fell then, as now, upon the small tax payers. It has been the burden of every cry raised against the Chicago Teachers' Federation since the beginning of the tax fight that we, as a body, forced additional expenditures in the schools and, consequently, heavier taxation upon the poor of the city. There never was a charge more untrue and less sustainable by evidence. The Federation, from the first day of the tax fight until this present, has definitely stood for the raising of public money by the equitable spreading of taxes. With the knowledge we have gained of public officials and public methods and of the alliance between great wealth and purchasable politicians, we have known that the only way in which equalization of taxes could be secured was by forcing rich and powerful tax dodgers into payment of their just taxes and by trying to

[16]Alfred Samuel Trude (1847-1933) was a prominent Democrat who was board president in 1895, when the agreement to drop the ten-year renegotiation provision was reached. See also *Proceedings, Board of Education*, 1906-7, pp. 560-67; 1038-46.

win back at least some measure of the enormous amounts of money literally given away by the Board of Education to the lessees of school lands.

The Supreme Court of the State of Illinois had repeatedly held that a ninety-nine year lease was a sale. It had also held that the Board of Education was not authorized by law to sell school lands. Competent lawyers were holding the opinion that the changes made in the school land leases were illegal, but at that very time the Commercial Club of Chicago took to Springfield a bill designed to make it lawful to change the remaining school land leases so that the lessees would have the same advantages enjoyed by the *Tribune*, the Wilsons, and the Otises.

When Mayor Dunne came to the appointment of his Board of Education, he had a particular desire to have Louis F. Post not only one of its members but its leading light. Post was at that time editor of the *Public*, which was being financed by Tom Johnson of Cleveland.[17] Post hesitated to accept appointment because of his moral obligation to Johnson to keep the paper going. I had to go to Cleveland to find out from Johnson if he would release Post from the more onerous duties of his editorship. Johnson did this gladly, and Post was able to devote full time to the work of the Board of Education.

He was hardly in office before a systematic campaign of abuse and misrepresentation against what they called "the Dunne School Board" was begun by certain Chicago newspapers.[18] The reason for the campaign lay, of course, in the pending question of the school land leases. Fearing that the "Dunne Board" would try to stop the plundering of the schools through blocking of the methods theretofore used, the beneficiaries of these fraudulent lease alterations began their attacks. Post went carefully into the entire matter of the school land leases. He found so much ground for action that in 1907 the Chicago Board of Education brought suit against the *Chicago Tribune* Company for the purpose of invalidating the one-hundred year ground lease held by the *Tribune* from the board. Clarence N. Goodwin, representing the board, made claim that the revaluation clause in this lease, requiring readjustments of rentals every ten years, had been struck out in 1895 through collusion and fraud. In consequence of that act, he alleged, the *Tribune* was paying only $47,500 a year for land worth $95,000 a year, according to the valuations of neighboring properties. For the

[17]Tom Johnson (1854-1911) was a wealthy street railway entrepreneur who was converted to the single tax cause. Cleveland was looked upon as a model of efficient city government under Johnson's four terms as mayor. Two associate editors were added to the staff of the *Public*. The offices of the *Public* were in the Unity Building, where the CTF offices were located. Post, "Living a Long Life," pp. 293-95.

[18]The most vitriolic attack came from the *Tribune*, which described the Dunne appointees in an Oct. 10, 1906, editorial as "freaks, cranks, monomaniacs and boodlers."

use of three of the seventeen floors operated by the *Tribune*, the Board of Education paid $32,000 a year rental.[19]

Goodwin did a good job on the case. He wasn't stampeded by the tremendous forces which arose to intimidate him. The case was heard in the courts of Cook County and was on its way to the Supreme Court of Illinois, in the intention that it would eventually reach the United States Supreme Court, when Dunne was defeated for re-election and Fred Busse became mayor of Chicago.

In the gallery of portraits of the mayors of Chicago, Fred Busse's should have special distinction, not for any good deeds performed in office, but because he was by all odds the absolutely perfect personification of a political machine. Fred was "One of the Boys." He came into office with the declared and fixed intention of making the world safe for the other boys. True to form, he raided the Dunne Board. In May, he sent letters to six members of the school board asking for their resignations. When they didn't give them, Busse announced to the City Council their removal and the appointment of their successors. Among those whom he left on the board were Jane Addams and Anita McCormick Blaine. He left also a few of the Harrison appointees whose terms had not yet expired, among them P. Shelly O'Ryan. O'Ryan had not been a pillar of strength in any liberal movement on the board, but he came to bat when Busse ordered the board to call off Goodwin from continuance of the suit against the *Tribune*. O'Ryan took the stand that Goodwin had been engaged by a board which Busse had dissolved and that the subsequent board could do nothing whatever to him. Goodwin, of course, refused to withdraw the case.

Judge Windes, before whom the case was called, denied the motion of Angus Roy Shannon, who appeared for the Busse Board, and asked for a postponement of the case. At the insistence of Goodwin, who claimed that the removal of the Dunne Board members by Busse was illegal and that he still represented the legal board, the case was held in the courts. It went through Judge Charles N. Walker of the Circuit Court of Cook County, Master in Chancery Roswell B. Mason, and up to the Supreme Court of Illinois. There in 1910 it was decided in favor of the defendant, the *Chicago Tribune*.[20]

Mr. Justice Cartwright, giving the decision, said that leases granted until 1985 did not constitute sales. He also pointed out that A. S.

---

[19]*Proceedings, Board of Education*, 1906-7, pp. 1038-46, 1050-51.

[20]Extensive background on the school land issue is found in the pages of the *CTF Bulletin* and the *Public*. Of particular value is the Dec. 7, 1906, issue of the *CTF Bulletin*. The board vote to press the suit against the *Tribune* was taken May 8, 1907. *Proceedings, Board of Education*, 1906-7, p. 1087. The circuit court decision is reported in *Ibid.*, 1910-11, p. 15.

Trude, the *Tribune* lawyer, had not been a member of the board at the time of the agreement of 1899. (It was the earlier, not the 1899, agreement that was the basis of litigation.) He stated that, although there had been great advance in price in Chicago downtown real estate, all future valuations were "guesswork and speculation," and so—by some mental process he did not explain—the valuations of 1905 should hold for 80 years. The decision further stated that, although constitutional provision put it beyond the power of the Legislature to divert school lands to any purpose other than the support of the schools, there had been no diversion of the property in question to any other purpose. There was no connection, he said, with the Fourteenth Amendment, which Goodwin had invoked on the contention that the procedure had deprived the school children of Chicago of property without due process of law.

"Words used in the statute," said Mr. Justice Cartwright, "are not to be taken in their ordinary acceptation."

And that was that.

The removed members of the Dunne Board, Post, Mills, Sonsteby, Robins, Dr. DeBey, and Harding, took into court proceedings to secure their return. The case went through the lower courts and finally on December 17, 1907, the Supreme Court of Illinois decided that Mayor Busse had no power to remove members of the Board of Education whose terms had not expired and ordered their return to their positions. Their return to power made possible a little later one of the greatest benefits the Chicago school system ever had—the appointment of Ella Flagg Young as Superintendent of Schools.[21]

6

Edward F. Dunne had gone into office on a liberal program. Looking back upon the years of my acquaintanceship with Chicago, I should say that he was the one real liberal mayor the city has ever had. His

[21]The decision is printed in *CTF Bulletin*, 7 (Dec. 20, 1907), pp. 2-4. The replacements named by Mayor Busse were in keeping with his campaign against the policies of the Dunne Board. The new members included: Theodore W. Robinson, first vice-president of Illinois Steel Company; Otto C. Schneider, a retired manufacturer; Chester M. Dawes, a railroad attorney; Daniel R. Cameron, a printing executive; Severt T. Gunderson, a building contractor and real estate broker; John R. Morron, the president of a glue company; Francis C. Waller, a coal company and insurance executive; George B. Limbert, a steamfitting supplier; George T. Trumbull, president of a vault and safe company; Dr. Alfred D. Kohn, a physician; and Dr. Alexander L. Blackwood, a professor of clinical medicine. *Chicago Chronicle*, May 28, 1907. The reaction against the Dunne members was illustrated by the absence of women and the strong business orientation of this group of eleven. The *Tribune* applauded the demise of the "radical talkfast element" and the end of Haley's domination. May 16, 1907.

term of office was, however, for only two years; and it was not possible to accomplish in that time the reforms which he advocated and which he sought to effect.

The most important issue of his time was Initiative and Referendum. It was the voiced desire of the people of Chicago that this measure should become law. There were, however, tremendous legal difficulties in the way which would have required more time than Dunne's mayoralty term to overcome. The vested interests of the town were, of course, against the measure. It might have been put across, however, as a national rather than as a local issue, a little later, if William Jennings Bryan had possessed the fortitude to hold out for it in the Democratic National Convention in Denver in 1908. Tom Johnson told me, on his way back from Denver, that Bryan had traded his ideal of an Initiative and Referendum plank for the nomination. Years later, Bryan himself was to express his regret that he had not put through the plank. For, if that plank had been put in the platform of 1908, repeated in the platforms of 1912 and 1916, and carried out to execution by the Democratic party in the way it put through the Federal Reserve Act, the United States would probably have kept out of war in 1917.

There were so many local issues requiring readjustment that the Dunne administrative forces decided that the best way of clearing them all was a new charter for the City of Chicago. To that end, legislative action was secured and in 1907 the proposal for a new charter was submitted to the voters of the city. The proposed charter had first been prepared by a charter convention. Later, the Legislature ripped the work of that convention to pieces. The charter offered for vote was a third and final draft, resulting from the joint labors of the Chicago charter convention and the State Legislature. It had been so emasculated that any person who had voted in good faith for the draft of the charter convention could do nothing else but vote against the mutilated remains which were presented to the people.

The constitution of the State of Illinois is probably one of the worst instruments of its kind in any commonwealth of the American union. It is clumsy; it is obsolete; it is an iron band around any attempted spirit of expansion. It makes progress almost impossible. One of the few methods by which anything beyond its stated provisions can be accomplished is through a constitutional convention, but that method is so complicated and cumbersome that those who seek release from the iron bands of constitutional constriction have to seek other methods. Under the existing constitution, it was possible to invoke the power of amendment; and an amendment was drafted designed to permit the Legislature to pass special laws for the local municipal government of

Chicago, with the salutary limitation that all such laws should be submitted to the people of Chicago and stand or fall upon their yea or nay by popular vote. This amendment, known as the Charter Amendment to the constitution, was passed by the Legislature and adopted by the people of Illinois. It was one of the few times when we approached anything like actual Initiative and Referendum. Its final result showed the value, both immediate and lasting, of that method.

Soon after the amendment had been approved by the people, a convention assembled, not of popular representatives, but composed of members appointed by certain self-selected clubs, societies, associations, and governing bodies. It was not the beginning of the regime of misrepresentative government in Chicago, but it was one of its outstanding examples. The curse of our city has been less the gangsters, less the Al Capones, the Gennas, and the Dillingers, than it has been the men who have constituted themselves, without benefit of popular election or even of administrative appointment, the guardians of the public weal. Once—years later—we even had Samuel Insull heading a Citizens' Committee to tell us how to run the town honestly![22] His predecessors in 1905 drafted what they called a new charter. During this time, there was a demand for a charter convention whose members should be elected by the people of the city. This demand was steadily disregarded by the City Council and by the Legislature, and systematically stifled by powerful special interests and their allied newspapers. Finally, the City Council and the Legislature adopted a resolution providing that a convention should be called composed of delegates appointed by the City Council, the mayor, the governor, the Legislature, the County, the library, sanitary, education, and park boards, seventy-four in all. This convention assembled on December 12, 1905.

For years the City of Chicago had struggled against an inadequate charter and incompetent and corrupt officials. A few people had worked valiantly to win freedom for the city. What happened? They had won a convention where every person in it had been chosen by some official or officials whose places and power were being jeopardized by the projected change. The very persons and interests whom the new order sought to control were themselves controlling the convention. There were, however, in it a few delegates of independent mind. They forced the convention to take some halting steps toward intel-

[22]Samuel Insull (1859-1938) was a public utilities magnate whose organization, Commonwealth Edison Company, supplied the electric power for Chicago. By 1930, Insull's empire had extended to thirty-two states with assets in excess of two billion dollars. With the depression, Insull's company fell into receivership and he became a target of public bitterness and resentment. Forrest MacDonald, *Insull* (Chicago: University of Chicago Press, 1962).

ligent municipal government. The people of the city were aroused to such an extent that the convention had to accept their measures. The compromise effected by them was adopted by the convention without a dissenting vote and sent to the Legislature.

The original draft of the charter had some progressive measures. The charter which came back for popular approval from the Legislature had none. The Legislature had substituted the old gang primary system in place of the genuine direct primary provided by the charter convention. The city had been gerrymandered for thirteen years in order to keep some of the old gang in office. Civil service was practically abolished. The spoils system was re-established. Protection for tenement homes was eliminated. Sub-sidewalk space was given away, thereby providing additional space for department stores which should have cost them hundreds of thousands of dollars every year in rentals. The public schools were practically turned over to any City Hall machine which wanted to make use of them. When the new charter had been sent to the Legislature, it contained no mention of ninety-nine year leases on school lands. The Legislature inserted the words, "for a term not longer than ninety-nine years from the date of granting the lease." Banquo's ghost had come back again. The Legislature also established one-man power over the public schools and increased taxation one-third. It also provided for special school bonds to be sold to banks and other financial institutions and to be resold by them at a profit to tax eaters for investment purposes. All the interest on these bonds and all the bankers' profits were to be paid by the tax payers of Chicago, a system as improvident to a community as if a private citizen were borrowing money for living expenses in order to increase his cost of living for the following year without any increase in capital. The provisions for the granting of ninety-nine year leases and for the power of removal of the Board of Education by the mayor were copied verbatim from the old Harper bill. With a few unimportant changes in minor details, the educational chapter of the charter, which had been prepared by a committee of the Merchants' Club, was the one-man power Harper bill, which had been defeated in the Legislature in 1899, rehabilitated by the Civic Federation in 1901 and again defeated in the Legislature, and under the direction of the Chicago Board of Education again presented to the Legislature in 1903 as the Mark-Cooley bill and again defeated.

By a vote of 122,054 against it to 59,446 for it, the new Chicago charter was defeated at the polls on September 17, 1907.[23]

---

[23]*Chicago Record-Herald*, Sept. 18, 1907.

Its defeat was victory for the progressive forces of Chicago; but the fact that it had been so deadened in purpose that it had to be defeated was a set-back to the entire progressive movement. It was a long time before we ever again came as close to victory as we had in the beginning of the movement for a new charter; and not since that time in Illinois has there been such a spontaneous demand for real democracy in public government as there was in the first year of Dunne's administration.

Thirty years have gone by since that time of high idealism, and it is only now that any forces in the city are reawakening to consideration of the vital issues of public ownership of utilities and other methods of control of privileged wealth which animated the crusaders of the early years of the century.

7

With Busse's election, we teachers were apparently cut off from all association with the City Hall. It's a long lane, though, that has no turning. By one of those dispensations of Providence which have kept us alive all these years, we found the turn.

Nano Hickey was one of the most alert and valuable members of the Federation. She was keen, tireless, shrewd; but she was also vitally sympathetic and so humanly kindly that even the people whom she opposed out of principle liked and trusted her. She used to go down to Springfield with Catharine Goggin and myself, and was one of the best lobbyists who ever went to that normal school of lobbying. Nano never bothered about the bill at stake. If the members of the Legislature wanted it explained, she'd tell them to talk to somebody else. She never went into any intricacies of explanation. She didn't have time. Always, though, she's get the idea across of the way in which she wanted the man to whom she was talking to vote. Men who wouldn't even talk to Catharine and myself would tell Nano the truth. She called it "giving her the low-down." Perhaps they felt that they might just as well have the credit for truth telling to her, as she'd find it out anyhow.

She had a basic understanding of the kind of men in the Legislature. She seemed to know the weaknesses of men and to appreciate that there were forces pushing them into positions which they themselves did not seek. She had, I think, for all men the same feeling of desire for helpfulness that she had for her own brothers.

One night we were just going into the St. Nicholas Hotel, the stronghold of the Democrats in Springfield, when Nano saw a big man, a member of the Legislature, reeling drunkenly toward a cab at the curb. The cabman was trying to inveigle him into the vehicle. In a flash, she knew what was likely to be the result for the drunken man; he would be taken by the cabman to one of the Springfield resorts, and wake up next morning not only robbed but an easy victim for blackmail. Nano gave the cabman a push which put him off, then she took hold of the legislator's arm and marched him back into the hotel, where she put him in care of some of his more sober companions, telling them to take care of him. That man was her friend through all the time he held office in Springfield.

In Chicago, Nano's best friends were the Kings. There have been other restaurants of fame in Chicago, Billy Boyle's old chophouse; Schlogl's, where John Eastman, publisher of the *Chicago Journal*, was wont to hurl catsup bottles at both his friends and his enemies when he went into his berserk rages; Vogelsang's, where the Harrison regime gathered in informal session; Henrici's, where there was no orchestral din, but an awful clatter of dishes, while the town's leading lawyers tried their cases with each other over the square tables; but no restaurant ever became as important a political, newspaper institution as did King's on Wells Street. At noon for six days in the week, King's was the "hang-out" for County Building and City Hall politicians and reporters of the afternoon newspapers. At night, it was the meeting place for morning paper reporters, for press men, and for leaders of labor groups.

There were six King girls and one King boy. Their mother was a widow, who had started the business because of the popularity of the sandwiches which she used to make for her son. He worked in the mechanical division of the *Herald* and sometimes shared the lunch which he brought from home with other men there. They liked it so well that they insisted on paying for the sandwiches which he gave to them. That took his mother into the business of supplying them with sandwiches. After a while, they said, "Why don't you start a restaurant?" That's how King's came to be a newspaper restaurant.

Nearly all the six King girls married newspaper men. Jenny King married Barney Mullaney. Barney was Busse's secretary. If we had any difficulty which had to go to the mayor for action, we'd have Nano take it to Barney. Almost invariably she brought home the bacon. As a matter of fact, we had less personal difficulty with Fred Busse than we had with any other mayor of Chicago in forty years. For one reason, we had very little to do with him. For another reason, Nano was as good a politician as he was.

In Busse's time, however, we had plenty of trouble with the Board of Education. The Dunne board members had not attained a majority before their removal by Busse and had left E. G. Cooley in office as Superintendent of Schools. Cooley thought that with Busse's election, he could retaliate upon the teachers for having opposed him during the Dunne administration. He used every means in his power to make life miserable for members of the Federation. Life in that time was, for the Chicago grade school teachers, a constant fight against the menace of demotion, of removal, of general oppression. The Busse Board and Superintendent Cooley did everything possible to discredit the teaching force.

One example of their methods was shown by the story of John J. Sonsteby, now Chief Justice of the Municipal Court of Chicago, then a member of the Board of Education. Sonsteby took to Springfield a bill designed to remove from the educational fund of Chicago the expense of repairs to buildings. The custom of charging these repairs to the educational fund cut down the salaries of teachers. In the school districts of Illinois outside Chicago, the cost of such repairs was charged against the school building fund and not against the educational fund. Sonsteby also took the statement of a certified public accountant which showed an error in the statement of the Board of Education. This error had been devised in order to defeat the bill which Sonsteby favored and which was also favored by the teachers. The teachers' bill also split the educational fund into two items, one for salaries, the other for incidentals but not for repairs. In Springfield, Sonsteby secured from Louis Larson, secretary of the Board of Education of Chicago, a sworn statement of the board's finances which Larson was handing around to members of the Legislature. This sworn statement contained an error—if you can call it that—of $600,000. Larson was endeavoring to show the legislators that the teachers had misinformed them in regard to the board's expenditures. Sonsteby spiked that story there, then came back to Chicago with Larson's statement and his own auditor's proof of its untruth. He asked the board to print both statements in order to clear the teachers.

Within a few weeks after its organization, the Busse Board had repealed the Post report and restored the Cooley scheme of secret marks and promotional examinations. It had cut 2,500 teachers fifty dollars a year each, giving "financial stringency" as a reason. It had thrown away a year's work of the architects' department on model schools. It had abolished the Dunne Board's model schoolroom plan of forty seats and had restored the old-type room with fifty-four seats. It had repealed the resolutions of the Dunne Board regarding the *Tribune* lease suit.

I did not realize how far I had gone along the wide but rough road of public work until I had conversation one day with Dr. John Guerin. Dr. Guerin, a Limerick-born Irish gentleman of the old school, a martinet, dictatorial but honest as the day was long, was one of the few hold-overs of the Board of Education, having been retained by Busse, not because of his political complexion but because of his high standing in the community. At the time when Otto C. Schneider and Alfred R. Urion were fighting for the presidency of the board, each had secured ten votes. Dr. Guerin held the twenty-first, the deciding vote. He came in to see me on the morning of the day of the election. He wanted to vote for Urion, not for Schneider. I didn't think it made much difference which man we got. Schneider belonged to the Busse school of politics. Urion was an employee of Armour and Company.

I said, "If you're going to vote for Urion—"

He said, "I don't have to vote for Urion, but—"

I said, "Doctor, you'll be good for something today. Today you're an indicating figure. Tomorrow you'll be a cipher. There's something you can do today. After you've done it, I don't care how you vote."

He said, "What do you want me to do?"

I said, "There's a motion before the board to cut the salary of the school principals. That salary should be cut, I'll admit. Their salary shouldn't have been raised. But we teachers are more opposed to the principle of cutting a salary than we are opposed to the big salary of the principals. If the board once gives a salary, it should never cut it."

Dr. Guerin said, "You're a damned little Irish politician."

"All right," I said, "you're a damned fool if you don't get something out of it. You're going to be a cipher tomorrow."

He stalked out of the room and I didn't think I'd see him again. In an hour, he came back and said, "What was that you wanted me to do?"

I told him again, and he said, "I guess you're right." He voted for Urion and his vote elected him. Urion kept out the report of the principals' cut.[24]

That wasn't what I was thinking about, though, when I went out into the sunlit Chicago street that afternoon. I was mulling over Dr. Guerin's taunt. I knew I was little and I knew I was Irish and I was afraid I was damned, but I didn't like the idea that I had become a politician. I didn't like politicians. I'd seen too many of them. I didn't want to be a public character. Appalled at the idea of myself which had suddenly been opened to me, I paused at the corner of Dearborn and Washington Streets. I realized that for nearly ten years I had been going along without thought of anything except causes and conflicts. What, I asked myself, was I going to do about it?

I did what almost any woman under eighty would have done. I walked over to a big store on State Street and bought for myself a blue lace dress.

[24]*Proceedings, Board of Education*, 1909-10, pp. 1-2. Urion was elected to the presidency on July 14, 1909.

N.E.A.

1

At the beginning of the century, the National Education Association was the Sanhedrin of the educational world of the United States. There was at that time no real reason why it should have been. It did not fairly represent its great body of membership, the grade teachers of the public schools. Its directorship was self-perpetuating and undemocratic. Its officers were allied and aligned with the powers that were fighting democracy in the public schools. Nevertheless, by virtue of their own self-constituted authority, the high officers of the Association managed to convey the idea that they and they only could speak for and to the educators of the nation.[1]

In 1899, Nicholas Murray Butler was chairman of the resolutions committee at the convention of the Association, which met in Los Angeles. Butler caused this clause to be placed in a resolution, "We deplore any effort, organized or otherwise, to keep incompetent teachers in their places." The resolution in itself was nothing but a magnificent generality, but Butler took occasion to state to the newspaper men of Los Angeles that it referred to the Chicago Teachers' Federation.[2]

[1]From its formation in 1857, the National Education Association had become the representative body of the teaching profession by the last decade of the nineteenth century. Yet, in 1900, there were only 2,332 active members, and they were primarily public school superintendents and principals together with normal school and university faculty members and administrators. These "scholar kings," who were almost exclusively men, gathered each year for an annual meeting at different locations throughout the country. See Reid, "Professionalization," Chap. 1 and 6. The standard account is Edgar B. Wesley, *NEA: The First Hundred Years* (New York: Harper, 1957).

[2]Nicholas Murray Butler (1862-1947), a faculty member and dean at Columbia College, was the leading advocate for school centralization in New York City during the "School War" of 1895-96. He became president of Columbia University in 1901. By 1911, it was the largest university in the world with an enrollment of 7,500. He retired from the presidency in 1945. Diane Ravitch, *The Great School Wars: New York City, 1805-1973* (New York: Basic Books, 1974), pp. 144-58, 184-86. Haley's assessment of Butler was in accord with that of Robert LaFollette, of Wisconsin, who considered Nicholas "Miracu-

Dismissal of incompetent teachers was, of course, not only the privilege but the duty of any competent board of education. The Chicago Teachers' Federation had never fought and has never since that time fought against the dismissal of any genuinely incompetent instructor. Our point, however, was then, as it still remains, that any such incompetency must be determined by fair and just judges and not by a venal superintendent or school board.

Those of us who were in attendance at the Los Angeles convention—and there were several thousand in the Chicago delegation—realized that the gage of battle had been flung at us. We had already had enough experience with the Harper bill to be ready to take it up. To our surprise, we found unexpected allies within the N.E.A. On the very night that Butler's resolution was being adopted, an organization of the National Federation of Teachers was being formed in Los Angeles as a protest against the domination of the National Education Association by the big interests of the country and their tools within the organization.[3] We teachers felt, although we could not then give adequate testimony to prove our case in court, that there was tremendous and threatening significance to us in the fact that the Butlers were stepping out of their schoolrooms into the arena of political life to take up cudgels against the ordinary teacher in the schools. We felt, although we could not then formulate the reasons, that there was an enormous power latent in the public school teachers of the United States, which must be used either for or against the movement toward democracy. We knew somehow that upon our academic freedom depended the actual political freedom of the children who were being taught in the schools and who would be taught in them in the years to come. We felt that we had upon our shoulders, sometimes overweighted by overwork, the heavy responsibility of doing our part to maintain the institutions of this republic.

We could not put all this emotion into words then. We were too new in the game of public life to know its phrases, but we did know its fundamental issues. We had to be free to fight; and the Nicholas Murray Butlers of the N.E.A. were trying to hold us down in the nation at large in the same manner that the Wiliam Rainey Harpers were trying to hold us down in Chicago. We Chicago teachers recognized that our experience was forcing us into leadership of the liberal forces

lous" to be "the handy man of privilege" and a "bootlicker of men of fortune." *New York Times*, June 22, 1922.

[3] The CTF attempted to establish a national organization in 1899 and again in 1902. Membership was 180 in 1903, with approximately half of the members from Chicago. The effort was abandoned in 1905. A new organization, the National League of Teachers' Association, was successfully created in 1912. See Reid, "Professionalization," Chap. 6.

within the national association. We didn't go out looking for it. It was just another of the heavily disguised blessings which were always being handed to us on pewter platters.

After our Chicago Teachers' Federation had started the tax fight in 1900, Nicholas Murray Butler came to our office in the Unity Building. Frank Fitzpatrick, the Boston representative of the American Book Company, had preceded him, with the statement that we had misunderstood Dr. Butler and that he had been misquoted by the Los Angeles papers. He said that Dr. Butler would like the opportunity to straighten the record with us. Dr. Butler, very pleasant in manner, reiterated Fitzpatrick's denial of the truth of the statement made to the newspapers, declaring that he had not said that the resolution referred to the Chicago Teachers' Federation. We talked a little at the time about the tendency, then at its height, to concentrate all power in the hands of the superintendent of schools and to give him absolute jurisdiction over appointments, promotion, and dismissal of teachers. I do not recall that Dr. Butler committed himself definitely on the subject, but I remember that Fitzpatrick appeared to be taking issue with him and protesting against the one-man power in education.

The next meeting of the Association was in Charleston, South Carolina, in July, 1900. I don't remember much about any important issues at that session. Strangely enough, my most vivid memory of that old town is the fact that I had to spend two weeks in it with no clothes other than what I had worn for travel. Somewhere along the way my own trunk had been lost. The one given me in its stead contained nothing but baby clothes. After the *dolce far niente* fashion of the sunny south, my baggage did not reach me until the day I was leaving Charleston.[4] I think, though, that even under the circumstances I should have recalled anything vitally important at the Charleston convention.

On the 8th of July, 1901, the N.E.A. met at Detroit. A general program was listed for the first morning session. Nothing of importance was scheduled upon it, and I certainly had no expectation of trouble when I strolled over to the Armory to listen to the speeches. Dr. William T. Harris, United States Commissioner of Education, "the Conservator of Education," was laboriously delivering a statistical account of the great increase in the number of schools of higher and secondary education in the nation. He boomed on about the enormous increase of the number of students in these schools, the number of teachers, the cost of equipment. I wasn't particularly interested in Dr. Harris. I knew that he had been a disciple of Hegel and that he had

---

[4]*Dolce far niente* is an Italian phrase meaning delightful idleness.

tried without success to impose the Hegelian philosophy upon the American educational system. Like Josiah Royce, Harris had already become a dodo in American educational philosophy.[5]

At the close of his speech, three other speakers were to discuss Dr. Harris' paper. Each one began with the statement that there was nothing to be said after Dr. Harris had spoken, since he always said the last word on his subject. In the usual fashion of speakers, however, they were managing to find words beyond the last. The first one expressed the hope that some Rockefeller or Carnegie would one day see the wisdom of extending his donations for educational purposes in the public schools. The third speaker said not substantially but literally that the audience should go home with the feeling of self-complacency after having heard Dr. Harris' paper, that the educational sky was now without a cloud, and that progress was assured. He told them to pat themselves on the back for their good fortune in living in such a wonderful age and time of progress.

When he had finished, the audience was almost as stupefied as he had been stupid. Afterward, a man who had been sitting on the platform told me that the presiding officer turned to him and said, "For God's sake, say something to awake this audience. I will throw the subject open to discussion." At any rate, he asked for discussion from the floor. It was a most unusual procedure in the National Education Association and, as far as I know, was the first time in the history of the organization when such a thing had been done in a general meeting.

The situation reminded me of the one about which Susan B. Anthony had told me. She said that the incident which held longest in her brain was one that had happened in her home town of Rochester, New York. The State Teachers' Association was meeting. The question before the meeting was how they could raise the standard of the teaching profession up to the standard of the law and the church and medicine. She stood up and asked for the floor. The chairman said, "What does the lady want?"

All the women were in the back of the hall and the men up in front. When Susan said she wanted the floor, the chairman was so lost in bewilderment that he looked at the men and said, "What are we going to do about it?"

One man said, "She has a right to the floor." His voice was a voice in the wilderness. He said, "I move that she be given the floor." They

[5]William Torrey Harris (1835-1909) was the U.S. commissioner of education from 1889 to 1906. This was the nation's highest educational post. He was formerly superintendent of the St. Louis schools. The standard biography is Kurt F. Leidecker, *Yankee Teacher: The Life of William Torrey Harris* (New York: Philosophical Library, 1946).

debated for half an hour and decided to give the floor to her by a majority of one.

Then she said, "Doesn't every mother's son of you know that, as long as you allow women into the teaching profession and shut them out of other professions, just so long will you keep that profession down to the level of women? You must either shut the women out and keep them out, or else you must let them into the other professions."

After the newspapers of Rochester had finished ragging the men for questioning the rights of the women members, who had the same rights as they, other papers took up the issue, and Susan awoke to find herself the banner bearer of a cause.

I had no expectation of awakening into any such fame when I made decision to lift my voice but I had, I think, something of the same feeling of the right of my sex to equal representation in an organization where we bore the heavier burden of responsibility and obligation.

I had been listening to the speakers with the thought running through my head, "are these men fools or are they knaves? Do they know the facts or are they simply uninformed? Are they consciously boosting big business?" The facts in regard to the inadequacy of revenue for school purposes had been written on my consciousness so indelibly by the tax fight, which we had just won in the Illinois Supreme Court, that the announcement of the discussion swung me up to my feet.

I called out, "Mr. President!" With a startled look, the President turned in my direction and, recognizing me, gave me the floor. It was the first time that any woman had spoken from the floor at a general meeting of the National Education Association and the first time that any grade teacher had dared to speak at all in the Association, although even then the grade teachers were paying about 90 per cent of the revenue which sustained it.

I began by saying that I hoped the hopes of the first speaker who discussed Dr. Harris' paper would never be realized. I trusted that no Rockefeller or Carnegie would ever contribute from their ill-gotten millions to the public schools. Such a gift would close the eyes and seal the mouths of the teachers, who of all people should have their eyes open and their mouths free to state the facts. The public schools should get their revenue and their support from public taxation and never from private gifts.

In regard to the other speaker, I said that I hoped that the audience would not do as he had told them. There was no reason why they should go home with any feeling of self-complacency. The number of schools and the number of students and teachers had increased enormously, as the United States Commissioner of Education had said, but, as he had not said, the revenue for school purposes had not increased to meet this expansion. There was no need, I added, of proving this point to a body composed as largely as was this audience of classroom teachers, for it was out of their pockets that the different increases had come. The classroom teachers, whose salaries were not being raised and whose classes were being made larger every year, were the ones who were really paying the price of educational expansion in the United States.

I had never before spoken in a hall of the size of the Armory, but my voice must have penetrated to the farthest corners of that big barn for, when I finished, the audience broke loose and stood up to cheer.

Encouraged by the applause, I added a few of the facts which I had learned out of the tax fight. I told them of the escape from taxation of millions of dollars' worth of property belonging to the public utility corporations in Chicago and railroads of Illinois. These facts disclosed in my own state existed, I was sure, in every other state in the Union in a greater or lesser degree. I spoke altogether for only four minutes, then I sat down. Had I thrown a bomb, I couldn't have rocked the pillars of that rotten old institution which the N.E.A. was at that time any more than I did by those few words of truth flung at time-serving place fillers.

Dr. Harris ambled to his feet; he pointed his finger at me. "Pay no attention," he rumbled, "to what that teacher down there has said. I take it that she is a grade teacher, just out of her classroom at the end of the school year, worn out, tired out, and hysterical. I have repeatedly said that these meetings held at this time of the year are a mistake. If there are any more hysterical outbursts after this, I shall insist that these meetings be held at some other time of the year." Again he pointed his finger at me. "Chicago," he roared, "is no criterion for other parts of the country. It is morbid, cyclonic, and hysterical. You never can tell what is going to happen in Chicago."

He went on to defend the railroads, declaring that by wise combination and judicious expenditure they had effected a saving. He shouted that he knew the Vanderbilts and their system. He yelled that formerly where there had been two parallel competing roads, there was now but one, and that the cost of maintaining the two roads was in that way eliminated. By this method, the railroads saved money for the public. He pointed to me again and said, "You should read—" and named a list of books, among them Adam Smith's *Wealth of Nations*.

Then he sat down.

Immediately Irwin Shepherd [Shepard], the secretary, was on his feet announcing the names of people for whom there were telegrams. I came to my feet too and again called out for the president. My voice

rang against the secretary's, but I won when Shepherd [sic] stumbled
over an address which he could not decipher. The president again gave
me recognition.[6]

I said, "I plead guilty to one charge made against me by Dr. Harris. I
am a grade teacher, but I am not just out of the schoolroom. I have
been out for two years, working on this tax question as it affects the
railroads and public utility corporations. I know what I am talking
about. I have the facts. Dr. Harris, you either do not know or you have
not stated the facts. This is no time or place to continue this discussion,
but I am ready to meet you at any time or any place that you may
name, here today or later, to continue this discussion on the issues you
have raised." I added, "If it be morbid to go into the courts and get an
opinion, which I have little doubt will be sustained by the higher
courts, ordering the taxing officers to assess property of five public
utility corporations, amounting to two hundred million dollars, that
for years have escaped taxation; and if it be hysterical to go before the
people and tell them these facts, then we in Chicago plead guilty to
your charge of being morbid and hysterical. But I think this audience
will be glad that there is one morbid place in the United States and that
they will hope with me that such hysteria will become contagious."

Dr. Harris made a poor attempt at apology, but he did not even
recognize my challenge. Afterward, I learned that it was only while I
was speaking for the second time that the "Conservator" had found
out that I was one of the teachers who had acted for the Chicago
Federation in the tax matter. By that time, he had realized that he had
made a mistake in running counter to the public sentiment of his
audience and he tried to retreat.

The meeting adjourned at that. The incident would have been
closed except for two results. One was that "Pa" McAuliffe of the
Record Herald was made so indignant by Harris' denunciation of
Chicago as morbid and hysterical that he sent Jimmy Bates down to
Detroit to cover the rest of the N.E.A. convention from the point of
view of the insulted Chicago teachers. The other result, not as immediate, was the arousing of the grade teachers in the audience and,
through them, of nearly all the grade teachers in the Association to
realization of their power. We, the elementary school teachers, had
found out that we were another Estate.

In 1902, the Minneapolis convention of the N.E.A. ordered a special
investigation on taxation and school revenue to be undertaken by its
national council, unofficially designated as the "national cemetery,"

---

[6]Irwin Shepard (1843-1916) was the president of Winona State Normal School in
Minnesota from 1879 to 1898. His service as secretary of the NEA lasted from 1893 until
1912. *Proceedings, NEA*, 1901, pp. 64-67. Shepard was able to keep the report of this
encounter from the annual published report. See CTF Files, Correspondence, 1901.

as it was the usual burial place of any disturbances in the Association. As usual, this investigation amounted to nothing, but it furnished excuse for any discussions of the subject at the general sessions and thereby prevented immediate recurrence of episodes like the challenge to Dr. Harris in the Detroit meeting.

The ordered investigation, however, did not quiet the demands of the grade teachers of the United States for action by the National Education Association in regard to teachers' salaries, tenure of office, and pension. So clamorous grew these demands that by 1903 the national council ordered a genuine investigation of the subjects involved and asked for an appropriation from the N.E.A. to pay the expenses of the investigation. The report prepared was unsatisfactory, as it contained a mass of data with no recommendations and little of any use for the purpose of drawing conclusions. The report was never printed and it was not until 1911 that the San Francisco convention authorized the appointment of another committee with an appropriation to pay its expenses, with instructions to make recommendations, and with an order to present the report at the next annual business meeting.[7]

2

By 1903, the conflict between the great body of members and the very small body of officers of the National Education Association had become sharply defined. At the convention, held in Boston in July, Charles W. Eliot, then president of the N.E.A. and also president of Harvard, presided at the business meeting, where Nicholas Murray Butler took the floor to present an amendment to the by-laws. The amendment provided that the president of the Association should appoint the members of the nominating committee. Under the existing by-laws, the active members of each state met at a designated place on the afternoon of the first day of the convention and selected from their state or territory a member of the nominating committee, there being as many members on that committee as there were states and territories of the United States. The president had power to appoint a representative from any state or territory whose active members failed to appoint their representative. Butler, however, proposed to take this power of selecting all members of the committee away from the active membership of the Association and vest it solely in the president.

At that time, a by-law could be amended by a two-thirds' vote of the

[7]Haley is not correct. A 466-page *Report on Salaries, Tenure, and Pensions* was published by the NEA in 1905. Catharine Goggin was a member of the committee. Haley was appointed to the 1911 committee whose *Report of the Committee on Teachers' Salaries and the Cost of Living* was published in 1913.

body without a year's notice. Even then, however, such dictatorial action as Eliot's and Butler's was unusual. I was the first one on the floor to attack Butler's amendment. I asked Dr. Eliot, "Is it proposed under Dr. Butler's amendment that the president shall appoint the nominating committee?"

He said, "Yes."

I said, "The nominating committee will appoint the president."

He admitted that.

"If the president appoints the nominating committee and the nominating committee appoints the president, this amendment establishes a self-perpetuating machine."

At that, S. Y. Gillan and Carroll Pearse explained that this was the same principle of ring rule which they thought they had killed in Milwaukee, but that evidently they had only scotched it, as it was sticking its head up again.

Dr. Butler said that his reason for presenting the amendment was that the active members in the different states did not attend the meetings. I told him that such a statement sounded very funny to me because on that day and year there had been 111 active members at the Illinois meeting.

When the vote was counted, Dr. Butler had lost. On the next day, the newspapers cartooned and lampooned him, although the Boston papers spared Eliot. The *Chicago Record Herald* had a cartoon showing a teacher seated at a desk with a lead pencil in her hand, saying, "Come right up here, boys," to two boys, one of them Butler, the other, Eliot.[8]

Just before this time, a child labor bill was pending in the Illinois Legislature. I was representing the committee of the Chicago Federation of Labor at the hearing of the house committee on the bill when [John Mitchell?] Levis, of the Alton Glass Works, appeared before that committee. He stated that if that bill were passed, his company would have to go out of business, as it could not get men to do the work being done by boys. Clarence Darrow, then a member of the committee, asked Levis what work boys did that they could not get men to do. Levis said that it was picking up a two-ounce bottle, walking a little distance with it, then going back and picking up another bottle, an almost automatic process requiring little thought but much repetition. He added that if the children were kept in school until they were fourteen years old, as that labor bill provided, they would be unfit to

[8]S. Y. Gillan was a normal school teacher in Milwaukee and the editor and publisher of an educational journal, *The Western Teacher*; Carroll G. Pearse (1858-1948) was the superintendent of schools in Omaha who later served in Milwaukee. Both were identified with the "progressive" or "insurgent" group within the NEA. See also *Proceedings, NEA*, 1903, pp. 24-31; *Chicago Record-Herald*, July 10, 1903. The cartoon is reproduced in the illustrations after p. 182.

learn the trade. Darrow asked him if boys could learn the glass blowing trade by carrying two-ounce bottles across the floor a couple of hundred times a day. Levis said that they saw the men blowing the glass and would learn it by that watching.

After the hearing, I met Levis in the Leland Hotel and talked with him for nearly an hour. I asked him if he had thought out why the children who remained in school until they were fourteen years of age were unfitted to learn a trade. He said that the literature, history, music, drawing, and other things of that kind which were being taught the children in the public schools unfitted them for that kind of work.

Not long afterward, Albert E. Winship, editor of the *Journal of Education* in Boston, and one of the most potent forces for liberal and progressive education this country has ever known, told me that the National Manufacturers' Association offered to duplicate the check which he received for every lecture that he gave if, in these lectures, he would attack the child labor bills then pending in the state Legislatures. Winship added that one of the lecturers at the State Teachers' Association had told him that she had received a check from the National Manufacturers' Association for striking at the child labor bill. I have cited these instances, not with any idea of dragging out old scores, but in order to show the underlying difficulties within the National Education Association during those years.[9]

Between the time of the Boston convention and the one which followed it in St. Louis the next year, the ruling powers of the N.E.A. cooked up the idea of a federal charter.

In 1904, with Frank Fitzpatrick, the book company agent, in the chair, the National Council of Education was removed from control of the active members. It was in this year that the motion to draw up a new federal charter for the Association was made and carried.[10] The association of Fitzpatrick with the passing of the charter idea was not coincidence. The organization had been so useful to the book interests and was becoming so useful to other big business interests of the country that some drastic measure had to be devised to keep control in the hands of the ring which still possessed it. The federal charter was designed to do this. In 1905, the convention at Asbury Park pushed

[9]Alfred Edward Winship (1845-1933) was considered the dean of educational journalists. He edited the *Journal of Education* from 1886 until his death. As Haley indicates, Winship was supportive of the insurgent movement within the NEA.

[10]This was the St. Louis meeting in which Haley spoke on the subject, "Why Teachers Should Organize." The "old guard" was represented by Denver's superintendent Aaron Gove (1839-1919), who followed Haley and spoke on the topic, "Limitations of the Superintendent's Authority and of the Teacher's Independence." *Proceedings, NEA*, 1904, pp. 145-57. See Appendix B for Haley's speech.

along the charter plan to such a point that it was ready to go before Congress in the early part of 1906.[11]

Dr. William T. Harris, speaking before the educational committee of Congress at that time, told its members that the business meeting of the active members of the National Education Association was always a "mob." He urged the committee to recommend the passage of the federal charter for the purpose of taking from the active members the dangerous power which they then had, of ordering appropriations from the accumulated fund of the National Education Association, which at that time amounted to $175,000. Dr. Harris started his speech in a panic. His panic increased as he pictured the horrible spectacle of this mob of teachers ordering expenditures of the fund, which they had created. His argument was the more ludicrous because he put it forward as an excuse by the trustees of the N.E.A., who were presenting this federal charter to Congress in violation of the constitution of the N.E.A.

I appeared before the Congressional committee for the purpose of explaining that the proposed charter made substantial changes in the constitution of the Association without one year's notice of such change, a time required by the constitution of the organization. The charter, which had been presented by Louis Soldan at the Asbury Park convention, would prevent reincorporation under the laws of the District of Columbia. It proposed to give to the trustees not only the custody of the fund of the Association, but initiative in the spending of that fund. Under the constitution, the trustees were merely custodians, with no power to initiate expenditure. The federal charter created a reserve fund not provided by the constitution. The charter also took the national council absolutely beyond the control of the active members of the Association.

Before I had gone to Washington, I had written for information regarding the membership of the educational committee of Congress to an old friend of mine. He went to James Monahan, then an officer in one of the government departments and one of the great ethnological authorities on the American Indian, evidently thinking that he would have information, as he had, on other aborigines. Monahan sent me the information. Just before I reached Washington, he was summoned to the White House by Theodore Roosevelt, then the President, who said to him, "What is this I hear about your interfering with legislation in which my friend, Nicholas Murray Butler, is interested?"

[11]The motion on the federal charter was made in 1904 and passed at the 1905 meeting. *Proceedings, NEA*, 1905, pp. 1-4; 30; 32-36; 46-49.

The influence of book companies in educational affairs is one of the themes found in Upton Sinclair, *The Goslings: A Study of the American Schools* (Pasadena: The Author, 1924).

Monahan said that he replied, "You give me credit beyond my deserts when you say that I could interfere with anything that you or your friend, Dr. Butler, are interested in."

Monahan said that he believed the President realized the absurdity of the affair, although he said, "Well, what is there in it?"

Monahan replied, he said, "At the request of a lady in Chicago, I informed her of the time and place of meeting of the committee of education in the house, giving her the names of the chairman and members of that committee."

The President said, Monahan related, "I do not see that you have done anything that any American gentleman would not be expected to do for any American lady."

Monahan replied, "I do not see that I have done anything that is not demanded by a square deal."

The President then said to him, he told me, "Yes; but I want you to understand that I do not want any head of a department to interfere with any legislation that I or any of my friends are interested in. Good day."

On the day of the hearing of the charter bill, the member from Massachusetts, who was chairman of the committee, was not present. A Congressman from Louisiana presided. John B. Pine, representing the board of trustees of the National Education Association, urged the committee to recommend the passage of the charter. The presiding chairman asked him how he could make claim that the federal charter did not make substantial changes in the constitution of the Association. Not Pine, but Dr. Harris, jumped into the breach to defend the board of trustees, as he had, five years before, defended the railroads for tax dodging. That was when he called the membership of the N.E.A. a mob. By his assertion, he let the cat out of the bag. Senile, superannuated, he had revealed what Pine had been trying to evade. The acting chairman showed clearly that he thought that Pine had been trying to impose upon the committee.

At the end of the hearing, I went to New York City to see Arthur Brisbane. I put the whole matter before him. On January 18, an editorial written by him, and one of the most brilliant ever presented on the subject, appeared in all the Hearst newspapers. It elucidated the federal charter scheme and stigmatized it as the attempt of a clique to take control of the affairs of the National Education Association out of the hands of the teachers of the United States and vest it in an oligarchy. Just after the appearance of this editorial, I had a letter from Brisbane, telling me that Butler had been after him, asserting that he had been misinformed. I sent Brisbane the printed material which I had presented to the committee of Congress and all other official documents and references necessary to show that his editorial was entirely in harmony with the facts.[12]

Congress passed the federal charter [June 30, 1906], but attached to it a referendum clause.[13] By this, it was sent back to the active members and was not in effect until it had been adopted by them. It would have been presented at the convention in San Francisco in 1906 but, on account of the fire, that convention was postponed until the next year in Los Angeles. I did not attend the Los Angeles meeting, but Ella Flagg Young told me that Dr. Harris heard that I was in the city and would be at the meeting. She said that whenever a woman arose in the hall, she could see Dr. Harris tremble. By the vote of the Los Angeles convention, the national council was placed back where the constitution had placed it and under the control of the active members of the Association. The provision, however, which permitted the self-perpetuation of the ruling powers remained. The little board of trustees, of which Nicholas Murray Butler claimed to be chairman, though he was never elected, continued to exercise major authority. It was to take several years for us to win our fight against that.

3

Ella Flagg Young, at that time Superintendent of Schools of Chicago, was elected president of the National Education Association at the Boston convention of 1910. For twenty years she had been one of the outstanding educators of the country but, in the long run, it was her moral courage rather than her mental capacity that made her a leader of women. She had left the Chicago schools back in the Nineties when "Bulletin Ben" Andrews had restricted the freedom of thought among his subordinates so terribly that she felt that she could not remain in the system without nullifying her own integrity. She had been brought back into the system by the Dunne Board, which had placed her in charge of the Normal school. When later [1909] the Board of Education wanted a superintendent to follow Cooley, its members called the candidates before them. They asked one question, "What would you do with the Chicago Teachers' Federation if you are appointed Superintendent of Schools?"

Mrs. Young replied, "I'd treat it as an educational institution."

All the rest of the candidates had sidetracked. Each one tried to guess

[12]Arthur Brisbane (1864-1936) was the editor of the *New York Evening Journal* from 1897 to 1921. This paper belonged to the Hearst syndicate. See editorials in the *New York Journal* and the *Chicago Record-Herald*, Jan. 24, 1906.

[13]U.S. Congressional Record, 59th Cong., 1st Session, pp. 9639-40. See also *Proceedings, NEA*, 1907, p. 1.

what was in the minds of the board members instead of expressing his own mind. Mrs. Young alone had said what she thought. She got the job.[14]

She once told me that any Superintendent of Schools would have to possess a trinity of personalities in order to attain success in that job. He'd have to be an educator, a politician, and a policeman. She must have been all three of them, for she attained a success in her work such as no one of her predecessors or successors has ever won. She was, I think, the nearest approach I have ever seen to thought in instantaneous action. She was an organism that took up thought with the most amazing speed. There never seemed to be a space of time between her grasp of a thought and her execution of the idea in action. Her intellect was a machine gun, but her sense of justice was so great that she only used that intellect in offensive when she was stirred by some terrible injustice against those too weak to hold their own.

By 1910, the great majority of the members of the N.E.A. realized her power, her strength, and her integrity. By that time, too, the Woman Movement of the United States had grown to such an extent that there was now a chance of electing a woman president. Thirty-nine thousand members of the organization went to Boston, at least 30,000 of them already convinced of the desirability of Mrs. Young's election. The opposition forces, however, did their best to prevent that election by raising a point of distinction between so-called active memberships and others not included in that category. To overcome their plot, we had to break down their artificial restrictions. We were successful in that, and Mrs. Young was triumphantly elected.[15]

By her election, she became one of the members of the board of trustees of the N.E.A. The members of the board, Nicholas Murray Butler, Carroll Pearse [of Milwaukee], [Henry B.] Brown of Valparaiso University, and a man named [Calvin] Woodward, attended in the early part of 1911 a meeting of the board of which Mrs. Young had not been notified. She had promised at the time of her election to call for an investigation of the permanent fund of the N.E.A., but Dr. Butler informed the trustees' meeting that such an investigation would not be conducted. There had been, a few years earlier, a breath taking scandal in the organization when one of the members of the board of trustees, Newton Daugherty, of Peoria, had been sent to the penitentiary for

[14]See note 2, page 23.
[15]Haley was the master strategist behind Young's election. Selected as the second choice of the nominating committee, Young received 617 of the 993 votes of the motion to elect. *Proceedings, NEA*, 1910, pp. 33-35. See also Reid, "Professionalization," pp. 224-30. It is likely that the publicity engendered by this election helped insure Young's continuation as superintendent.

misappropriation of certain funds; and possibly the board had decided that any question of investigation would be alarming to members of the organization.[16] Pearse, returning from the board meeting in the east to Milwaukee, came into our office in the Unity Building and asked me if Mrs. Young would not consider the possibility of receding from her position in asking for an investigation. He was, I know, speaking entirely as Mrs. Young's friend, but I knew that nothing short of death would prevent Mrs. Young from carrying through any moral issue upon which she had launched.

Just a week before the San Francisco convention of 1911, Mrs. Young was taken desperately ill. Her doctor, a nurse, and her faithful friend, Laura Brayton, Bertha Benson and one of the Walkers, those sisters who had always been Mrs. Young's devoted allies, accompanied her from Chicago to San Francisco. They occupied one Pullman car and kept it hung in wet sheets. Between sessions of the convention in San Francisco they kept her swathed in sheets dipped in cold water. By this process and by powerful medicine, they were able to bolster her strength so that she never missed a meeting of the convention.

The forces opposing her had gathered up material which they had expected to convict her of fraudulent election in Boston. When our Federation special reached Oakland, we were met by a crowd of women, all in a terrible state of mind. They had just discovered a difference in statement between the final program of the N.E.A. and its original program. The difference would have taken away the voting power of thousands of teachers. The final program stated that delegates would have to show both their blue badges of membership and their receipts for their dues. Very few of them had brought the receipts for dues, thinking that the blue badge would be sufficient to insure them the power of attendance and vote.

First of all, we told the reporters of the San Francisco newspapers about the situation. Then we got word to Mrs. Young that she must be at the first meeting of the convention, as this matter would come up at that time. It must have been torture for her to make the physical effort, but she came out on that platform as if she were not a desperately sick woman. Someone said, "I move that the secretary be permitted to tell why he took this action."

Mrs. Young said, "The secretary will be given the floor to tell what happened between the dates on which he issued the two programs." The secretary—Shepherd [sic], who was one of the old privileged group—never raised his head. She repeated her sentence, but Shepherd

---

[16]The Daugherty indictment and trial was reported in the *Peoria Star*, Oct. 5, 30, and Nov. 1, 1905.

[sic] said nothing. It was the time when the opposition might have brought in the whole attack against the legality of her election in Boston. Knowing the import of that silence, we held our breaths. I don't know how long it was, but time seemed to stand still. Then Mrs. Young said, "The regular order of business will be resumed."[17] The opposition to her had died aborning.

4

In 1912, the N.E.A. convention came to Chicago.

Unless you knew Chicago politics, you wouldn't believe that Tom Carey, Stockyards politician and leader of "Tom Carey's Indians," could be an instrument of grace for the general membership of the National Education Association. Tom Carey, though, was the agent of Providence who opened the doors to the grade teachers of the organization. And the joke of it was that he didn't know what he was doing when he did it![18]

At the Boston convention of 1910, a report of the committee on by-laws had been shuffled around so that it never came out upon the floor of that body. The report was the most reactionary recommendation anyone could conceive. Its purpose was to send back the ordinary membership of the organization into chains. There was no chance of getting it through while Mrs. Young was president and so it had been held until she was out of office. Carroll Pearse was then president of the Association. He was not in favor of the proposed amendment to the by-laws, but he evidently realized that without the support of the great body of members he would not be able to stop the steam roller.[19]

The situation was complicated by the candidacy of Grace Strachan, Assistant Superintendent of Schools in New York City, for the presidency.[20] Knowing the danger of establishing two battle fronts at a time

[17]A brief account of this meeting is found in *Proceedings, NEA*, 1911, pp. 49-53; 23-27.

[18]Thomas Carey (1863-1925) was an Irish Catholic political leader from the 29th Ward near the stockyards. Carey was the owner of Hawthorne Race Track. He was considered to be one of the "Gray Wolves," but Carter Harrison II was able to gain his support and loyalty during the early years of his administration. Harrison wrote that Carey was married to a school teacher and that "her better education made him see life differently." She helped persuade Carey to back Harrison. Harrison, *Stormy Years*, pp. 86, 155-156.

[19]The by-law discussed here was a proposal requiring thirty days advance registration to establish voting eligibility at the annual meetings. Its purpose was to curtail "packing" of the convention as the Chicago and Boston teachers had done in 1910. *Proceedings, NEA*, 1912, pp. 30-73.

[20]Grace Strachan was the leader of the Interborough Association of Women Teachers (IAWT). This was the largest organization of teachers in New York City. Strachan was a strong advocate of equal pay for women and published a book on the subject, *Equal Pay for Equal Work* (New York: B. F. Buck and Co., 1910). The failure of the Chicago teachers to back Strachan divided the progressive forces of the NEA and highlighted the

when we should be concentrating on one, I went to New York to see Katherine Blake. Katherine laid her cards on the table. She said that she wanted to have Grace elected president because if she were, she could be Superintendent of Schools in New York. Then Katherine would be Assistant Superintendent.

I said, "We've been fighting for years in the N.E.A. to keep the organization from growing more reactionary. We have tried to put some breath of democracy in it. Now we have an opportunity to get by-laws of our own formulation. Groups of progressive people have been working on them. We can't afford to lose our chance in Chicago, because there we can get out our teachers and fill the Auditorium. We couldn't do it in a small town, and the convention is likely to go next year to a smaller city. We must concentrate upon the issue, not upon the candidate this year. Our work is the liberalization of the by-laws." They laughed heartily at the idea of by-laws.

Later, at a meeting with Grace Strachan and some of her friends, a woman present, not a teacher but an employee of the Department of Apportionment and Estimate of the City of New York, said, "Miss Strachan, why don't you get your friend, the mayor of New York, to write a letter to the mayor of Chicago and tell him what he wants him to do?"

"Well," I said, "there isn't anybody in the Chicago schools whom I know who does what the mayor asks him to do. The mayor in Chicago wouldn't tell anybody what to do."

"Oh, nonsense! Is it Mrs. Young?"

I said, "I can't see the mayor of Chicago telling Mrs. Young what to do about the presidency of the N.E.A. No mayor of Chicago would try to do it. Maybe you can get away with that kind of thing in New York, but I'm telling you you can't get away with it in Chicago and I'm advising you not to try it because you'll fail. You'll fail miserably and you may do a great deal of harm. The teachers of Chicago will never stand for that."

I added, "I'm sorry if you're coming to Chicago to try to put over that kind of job. That will be the time to get by-laws for the National Education Association that are not reactionary, that will give the teachers a chance, that will take power out of the hands of the feudal lords who have, for a long time, run the N.E.A. All you can do is that one thing. We can't have any wrangle over it."

They laughed me out of court. A day or two before the convention,

---

problem of the voting system which allowed the local teachers to control the annual election. *Chicago Record-Herald*, July 9, 10, 11, 1912.

the New York delegation landed in Chicago with a letter from the mayor of New York to Mayor Harrison.

Just at that time, we learned that the old guard of the N.E.A. had appealed to the city government for a police cordon at the Auditorium. The officials intended to require some kind of a preferred admittance card that had never been required before; even badges and tickets of membership would not be sufficient to take in members of the organization. Only those passed upon by the old guard were to be allowed a chance to get on the floor when the vote on the by-laws would be taken.

Just at that time, Tom Carey came to see me. He had in tow a textbook agent to whom he owed some kind of debt, financial or political. This man believed that Carey could get the books he represented into the schools. Carey wasn't able to get by the Board. Somehow he got the idea that I could help him. Never in all my life had I or have I made any such agreement with anyone. The book agents could go to the devil as far as I was concerned. I steered clear of them and saw that they steered clear of me. This book man knew that he had no business coming to me, but he let Carey do the talking. Carey wanted to find out the cause of the row then going on between Harrison—who had come back to office in 1911—and the Board of Education. I told him that whatever it had been, it had been straightened out. "Now," I said, "as long as you're here, I might as well tell you that Harrison appears to be allowing his police department to run wild. They're going to have a lot of policemen down there at the N.E.A. meeting to keep the Chicago teachers out." I told him what I knew about it and said, "If that's done, you'll have Hell to pay."

He said, "I'll stop it. I'll take charge of it myself."

I said, "See that the doors are open. They're coming here from New York to force a political appointee into the presidency of the N.E.A. We're trying to get the by-laws amended. We'll lose if they win."

Carey said, "How'll I stop that?"

I said, "The mayor of New York is asking Harrison's help to put over the presidential candidate for the N.E.A. from New York."

Carey asked, "Does the mayor know that?"

I said, "He doesn't know it from me."

Carey must have told him immediately, for on the next night Mrs. Young received from Mayor Harrison a letter telling her that as long as she wanted to stay in the schools, she could stay there as far as he was concerned. Mrs. Young showed the letter at a dinner which she attended with the New York contingent. They knew then that the jig was up. Carey looked after the policemen too. There was no attempt to use them to keep out the Chicago school teachers or the other members of the organization who did not have the special admission tickets. We got the by-laws we wanted and licked the old guard.[21]

[21]Haley omits other developments that involved her efforts to open up the NEA to the classroom teachers and to women. Among these were the establishment, in 1912, of a new organization, the National League of Teachers' Associations, composed of urban woman teacher organizations which met concurrently with the NEA, and the creation of a Department of Classroom Teachers by the NEA one year later (1913). This increased recognition of persons who were in the classroom and who were of the feminine gender resulted in a pattern of alternating men and women presidents of the NEA beginning in 1917.

ₒₒ⟦ VII ⟧ₒₒ

Rothmann, Revenge, and Retribution

1

Peter Reinberg: You may talk very freely.

Mayor Harrison: Yes, Mrs. Young; tell me what they did to you to cause you to resign.

Ella Flagg Young: Mr. Rothmann wanted me to demote and dismiss teachers who lobbied in Springfield or wrote to members of the Legislature against the Board's pension bill. I refused to do what he demanded of me.

Mayor Harrison: You were right and Mr. Rothmann was wrong. But you must admit that Miss Haley hit Mr. Rothmann very hard.

Mrs. Young: Yes, I know she did, but I defended Mr. Rothmann.

Mayor Harrison: Well, I told them that the time to kill that Federation was when it first started before it had grown too powerful.

—Statement by Ella Flagg Young to representatives of the Chicago Teachers' Federation, 1913.[1]

The year 1913 was false dawn.

In both the nation and the state the Democrats went into office that year with promises for reform of popular government which were, in the end, to come to little. Some of these were defeated by corruption, both within and without the ruling party. Some were abrogated, as most campaign pledges of all political candidates are abrogated. Others were put into effect only to become converted, as the years passed, into systems hardly less deleterious than the ones they succeeded. Perhaps the World War thwarted, as Woodrow Wilson said it had, the national purpose of political reform which was then stirring the United States. In the commonwealth of Illinois, however, the cause of failure was

[1]This account of Young's resignation involves Mayor Carter Harrison II, Peter Reinberg, the president of the Board of Education, and Ella Flagg Young. Mrs. Young received a vote of confidence from the board and withdrew her letter of resignation. *Proceedings, Board of Education,* 1913-1914, pp. 572-73; *Chicago Tribune,* July 31, 1913; *Chicago Record-Herald,* Sept. 6, 1913; *Margaret Haley's Bulletin,* 8 (Dec. 10, 1930), p. 269.

nearer home. The same old "debbil" of human nature which had animated all the Legislatures of the state, notably the Legislature of 1901, and which was to dominate all later Legislatures, notably the Legislature of 1935, was once more at work in that year before Sarajevo.

There were great issues coming before that Legislature: Initiative and Referendum, woman suffrage, employee pension, school pension, vocational education. On the surface the outlook for liberal legislation seemed promising. Edward F. Dunne was Governor of Illinois. In addition to its Democratic members, the House of Representatives of the state numbered twenty-one Progressives and three Socialists. A liberal majority seemed assured; but, by that time, Catharine Goggin and I had cut our political wisdom teeth, and as legislative representatives of the Chicago Teachers' Federation, we gazed on the Springfield set-up with the jaundiced eye of doubt.

Through the greater part of 1911, I had campaigned the Pacific Coast for woman suffrage.[2] I had witnessed its victory in California, but in the course of a campaign when I'd almost literally leaped over the Sierras and the Coast range in bumping automobiles, when I'd seen the hate of men unleashed against every woman who took the stump to demand the vote, I had come to realize that woman suffrage was not an end in itself but a means to a more important end, the governmental establishment of fundamental justice to all men, women, and children of the nation. To my mind, the passage of the Initiative and Referendum was more important than the passage of the Woman Suffrage law. Upon the former, I felt, depended, for good or for ill, the fate of my native state for years to come.

The Initiative and Referendum bill [came] up for passage in the House with a Democrat, William McKinley of Chicago, in the chair. Back of him on the platform sat the Blonde Boss of the Republican party of Illinois, Billy Lorimer, later to be flung out of the United States Senate on the charge of having bribed the Illinois Legislature to insure his election to the Senate in Washington.[3]

[2]Haley wrote the major part of her autobiography in Seattle, Washington, following this campaign activity on the West Coast. This Seattle manuscript, consisting of twenty installments, was written between December 27, 1911, and February 13, 1912.

[3]This episode occurred in the 1913 legislative session. Dunne considered the initiative and referendum the most important issue of his administration. He blamed Hubert Kilens, the representative from the Fourth District, for betraying his trust and for bringing about the defeat of the bill, which was one vote short of the 102 needed. *Chicago Tribune*, June 22, 1913.

Haley is wrong when she states that Lorimer was "later to be flung out of the U.S. Senate." This had occurred earlier in July, 1912. That Lorimer continued to hold political influence is surprising; however, Haley was able to defend her charges, which led to an investigation by the Illinois House of Representatives. This episode is discussed further on pp. 161-62. For Lorimer, see note 4, p. 46.

Afterward execrated by his own party even more bitterly than by his former political foes, Lorimer was probably neither better nor worse than any other political boss of his time. He had come up from poverty—he had been a Chicago street car conductor—to power; and, just as do most politicians, forgot to take with him memory of what political oppression meant to the poor. He surely could have had no thought of the common people of Abraham Lincoln's state on that day when his cold blue eyes transfixed the representative of one of the Stockyards districts and caused the man to change the vote which would have carried the Initiative and Referendum.

Not until twenty-two years later when Edward J. Kelly, Mayor of Chicago and political boss of the state, sat on the same platform, directing by look and by tally-sheet the votes of the legislators, did such an outrageous performance again affront the basic traditions of American law-making. Lorimer's appearance on the speaker's dais, threat and menace to the weak-kneed, challenge to the stronger, struck the real keynote of that assembly.

From the moment when the man from Back of the Yards changed his vote under Lorimer's frown, we knew that, in spite of a liberal governor and a supposedly liberal Legislature, we were in for one of the most bitter contests we had ever encountered.

We entered the lists with the banner of school pension legislation. Our entrance was determined, once more, not by our own volition, but by the exigencies of the situation. Again we fought not from desire but from necessity.

2

The original pension law had been passed in 1895 and put into effect by the Board of Education on the 1st of January, 1896. In 1901 the Legislature had passed a law that permitted any teacher in the system to withdraw from the pension at any time she desired. There was no power given to the pension board, however, by the 1901 law to permit any teacher to return. Once out, she had to stay out.

About two-thirds of the teachers withdrew from the pension. All the contributions from 1901 to 1907 were voluntary. The fund went so low that by 1907 it became absolutely necessary, if the pension were to survive at all, to secure new legislation.

The Legislature of 1907 passed a law which made it compulsory for the teachers who came in to remain in the pension. It permitted all teachers who had withdrawn and who wished to return to pay into the pension fund what they would have paid if they had remained. It was a fairly good bill and had been pulled out of cold storage in the senate committee where the Busse forces had put it, by Eleanor Lewis Nowlan, known to and beloved by thousands of Chicago school teachers as Nellie Nowlan. She was one of the gayest, bravest, blithest souls who ever worked for any cause. She usually won her points not by battle but by cajolery, not by imprecation but by the telling of stories so funny that now, years after her death, men and women smile in happy remembrance when they chance to recall some one of the rare tales of Nellie's telling.

In 1909, a committee of the Legislature was authorized to codify the educational laws. This body had no authority to change any law nor to eliminate any. Edwin G. Cooley, then Superintendent of Schools of Chicago, was one of the members of the special body appointed by the Legislature to make this codification. When the result of the committee's labors was published, it was discovered that two sections of the pension law had been omitted. The first clause failed to give the pension board any authority to continue to pay the pensions of teachers who had retired under the law of 1895. The other clause gave the pension board the right to pay less than the maximum pension, that is, less than $400, which was the maximum of that time. The pension board was left to judge as to whether the funds of the board would permit the paying of that amount. If the pension board were compelled to pay the maximum at that time, it would have bankrupted the fund because there was not sufficient money at that time to pay even a $400 pension. Unless that clause was restored to the pension law, the pension board was helpless. The elimination of these two provisions from the code was disastrous to the pension. The situation was so dangerous that the people who knew of its existence did everything in their power to keep it from becoming generally known. Francis G. Blair, State Superintendent of Instruction, who had been chairman of the legislative committee, was appalled when he had called to his attention the omission of the two sections. He said that E. G. Cooley had taken the responsibility for certifying to him the Chicago portion of the law and that Cooley had assured him that nothing had been omitted.

The Chicago Teachers' Federation tried to secure legislation to nullify Cooley's so-called error. Senator John M. O'Connor—afterward Judge O'Connor—introduced a bill for that purpose in 1911, but it failed of passage. He introduced another in 1913. That bill, Senate Bill 299, was pending in the senate at Springfield when another, House Bill 203, was introduced in the lower branch of the Legislature by Seymour Stedman, one of the three Socialist members.[4]

[4]Seymour Stedman (1870-1948) was an attorney who served for one term in the Illinois House. He was an unsuccessful candidate for mayor in 1915, governor in 1916, and for vice president of the United States in 1920 on the Socialist ticket.

If there was one man in the lower house from whom we would have expected intelligent cooperation, Stedman would ordinarily have been that man. He had formed, however, a friendly association with three women who had gone to Springfield as lobbyists for an organization called the Chicago Teachers' Pension Contributors' League, later to be the Teachers' League. This organization had secured a charter from the state of Illinois some time around the beginning of November, 1912. At their request, Stedman had drafted the bill. Frank J. Ryan, who represented the Harrison forces in the lower house of the Legislature, introduced the bill in March, 1913. Later events made it clear that the real sponsors of the bill were William Rothmann and Alfred R. Urion, both members of the Chicago Board of Education. The combination of Rothmann, Urion, the three women representing the Pension Contributors' League, Seymour Stedman, and Frank J. Ryan is one of the most enlightening episodes in the long and dark history of Illinois politics.[5]

Seymour Stedman had been elected, as had been many other liberals, by the cleavage in the Republican party which had erupted into the Progressive movement. In his political beliefs, he was sincerely and earnestly an opponent of established privilege. It's queer, though, how so many political liberals are led astray from their convictions by personal relationships. Stedman unfortunately was one of these. Unwittingly, he let himself be made the tool of a group of people who, unlike him, knew exactly what they were doing and why they were doing it.

The three women who represented the Pension Contributors' League were in no way representative, however, of the Chicago teaching force. One of them was not even a member of the teaching body. Another became, shortly afterward, involved in a particularly nasty divorce suit. The third was already the central figure—although the story was not published until later—in a fantastic drama. She had come back to the school where she taught, after a vacation, with a story that the man who she had secretly married had died at sea on their honeymoon. She wore deep mourning for him and signed his name after her own in a legal proceeding which she brought to claim the estate of an old

[5]Alfred R. Urion (1864-1946), a Republican, was general counsel for Armour and Company from 1887 to 1917. He was president of the board (1909-1911) during the Busse administration.

William Rothmann (1866-1934) was a lawyer associated with the firm of West and Eckert. Roy O. West, the senior partner, was national secretary for the Republican party, a member of the Cook County Board of Review, and a close ally of Governor Deneen. See note 14, p. 64. Haley campaigned against the reelection of West to the Board of Review in October, 1914. She told her audience to "smash this alliance of coal and real estate interests with the tax office. Let us show these politicians that we have political memories, that we know who to punish, that we women voters remember our friends." *Day Book*, Oct. 28, 1914.

couple with whom she had lived. Legal heirs of the estate found, down in Peoria, the supposedly dead husband, who had in the meantime married another woman. She also had married again. The woman who wasn't a member of the school system had, for some time, been a resident of "Teed's Heaven," a communal experiment not recognized by the police which flourished for a while in Englewood. Of such strange stuff were the advocates of House Bill 203.

Urion and Rothmann, however, were the real backers of the bill. From Ella Flagg Young herself, I had learned that a condition of her appointment as Superintendent of Schools of Chicago was her promise to Urion to secure for the Board of Education larger representation upon the teachers' pension board. It is difficult for me to make this statement about Mrs. Young. She was, by all odds, the finest Superintendent of Schools the city has ever had and one of the greatest women who has ever been in American public life. It was unfortunate that she should have been tied in any way, but the exigencies of politics make it necessary for everyone who receives appointment from a political body to make some sacrifice. That was hers. She probably entered into it without realization of its eventual cost to the teachers. Before the battle was ended she was willing, even anxious, to forgo all her own personal ambition and personal advantage in order to rectify the situation that her promise had created.[6]

Urion, the attorney for Armour and Company, represented the idea, only too common with boards of education, that the teachers, who earned their money, were not competent to handle that money for themselves. His idea was the establishment of a paternalism by which the Board of Education would control the pension board, so that it might dictate how that board should be run. In spite of decades of political attack, the pension board had remained under teacher control. House Bill 203, the brain child of Urion and Rothmann, would have

[6]Rothmann's alleged misuse of the interest from the police pension fund was discussed by Ella Flagg Young in the *Chicago Tribune*, Dec. 13, 1913, and Jan. 8, 1914. See pp. 155-58.

The investigation of the police fund was conducted by a committee headed by Alderman Charles E. Merriam, which reported in 1911. A distinguished political scientist, Merriam (1874-1953) took an active part in civic affairs. He was the Republican candidate for mayor in 1911 and served as an alderman from 1909 to 1911 and 1913 to 1917. Merriam had great respect for Haley and wrote of the CTF: "As a well organized and aggressively led group the Federation has had no superior among all the social groupings of the city even among the professionally political organizations. If all the groups were similarly organized and deployed for action the politics of Chicago would take on a colorful hue and the problem of non-voting would become a memory." Merriam, *Chicago*, p. 126. Merriam is considered to be the father of the behavioral movement in political science. Karl, *Merriam*, p. viii.

taken away this control, vesting it in a body which could be manipulated by the Board of Education.[7] Urion's motive was unquestionably the Big Business idea of corporate direction of public affairs. Rothmann's was less pervasive.

All that we knew about Rothmann at that time was that he had been chairman of the policemen's pension fund and that he had retired from that office some time early in 1911. In the course of the next year Mayor Harrison, who had been re-elected in 1911, appointed Rothmann to the Board of Education. It was natural to suppose that Rothmann had an interest in pension funds. We didn't know, however, the depth of that interest until our battle with him had already started.

We had already induced Frank Ryan to turn his back on his own bill and had won the endorsement of the Federation of Labor for a pension bill approved by the Chicago Teachers' Federation. The Board of Education then tried to put over on us a confidence game. A meeting of the legislative committee of the Board of Education was called for the 5th of April. Representatives of the Chicago Teachers' Federation and of the Chicago teachers' pension board were invited to attend the meeting. Nothing was said in the invitations that the meeting was to be a conference. We went with the expectation of being merely sitters upon the sidelines. We found not only the members of the legislative committee and other members of the Board of Education but also representatives of the Pension Contributors' League.

John C. Harding, chairman of the committee, began the meeting by the statement that the Board of Education wanted the co-operation of all those present in getting through the Legislature a bill that would satisfy everyone. "Harmony John" was doing his best, but I had to upset his apple cart. When he said that the sponsors of House Bill 203 were willing to withdraw their bill and asked that the sponsors of Senate Bill 299 should do likewise, I said, "The sponsors of House Bill 203 have nothing to withdraw but a corpse. Their bill is dead. Our bill is very much alive and it is Senate Bill 299. Our bill is not going to be put in the hopper with any other bill. It is going right through." As a matter of fact, it had gone through that day, but I didn't know it.

Urion then presented a rough draft of a bill which could not possibly have been passed as one bill, but would have to be in two. Its clumsiness was not, however, our objection to it. It provided for giving the pension fund one dollar of public money for each dollar contributed by the teachers and made that payment compulsory by the Board. There was an optional clause giving the Board the authority to

[7]The Urion bill proposed a board of four school board members, four teachers, and the superintendent ex officio.

put in another dollar if desirable. The point which we opposed, however, was the provision that the six members of the teaching force should be reduced to three members and that the members of the Board were to be increased so that there would be six Board members and three teachers on the pension board. The chairman of the finance committee of the Board of Education was to be, ex officio, a member of the pension board. Rothmann was then chairman of the finance committee.

William B. Owen [principal of the Chicago Normal School], representing the pension delegate convention, declared that he would say nothing without a meeting of that convention. His opinion was backed by everyone present except Florence Deneen, sister of former Governor Deneen, and by the three women who spoke for the Pension Contributors' League. Harding then said that Urion made a motion that all pension bills in the Legislature be abandoned and that the Board of Education's bill be approved. I objected to Harding putting the motion in that way. He then apologized and said that the motion provided that the backers of House Bill 203 should abandon their bill and approve the Board's bill. They voted. No one else had any chance or desire to vote on anything.

When the meeting was over, I spoke to Rothmann. It was my impression that the meeting had sent the matter for discussion to the teachers, and I told him, "I will give you my word that I will not lift my finger to influence the judgment of the teachers on this bill." For, although I did not believe in some of the provisions of the bill, notably in the one giving control to the Board of Education over the pension fund, I felt that the matter might safely be left to the teachers themselves. To my amazement, Rothmann said, "It doesn't make any difference what the teachers do. You people approved this bill today."

I rushed out of the room and down the hall after Harding to get him back. Harding wouldn't come. Rothmann laughed at me. I told him, "The teachers didn't vote at all. They didn't have a vote." He kept on laughing.

The next day, the ballot went by mail to the teachers of Chicago. On it was a legend, "This conference bill approved by representatives of the Chicago Teachers' Federation, the Pension Contributors' League, the Pension Delegate Convention, and the Teachers' Pension Board." With the ballot was a communication from Mrs. Young and from Urion informing the teachers that they were to deposit the ballot in a mail box on a certain day about a week after that date.

John C. Harding, the Labor member on the Board, told me that the ballot had been prepared in Mrs. Young's office. Mrs. Young told me that she did not know what had happened at the meeting of the legislative committee of the Board of Education, which had been held in her office. Mrs. Young sought for the truth. Harding wouldn't back his own story (he never would have backed it had not Andy Lawrence, the publisher of the *Herald Examiner*, forced him to do it).

We got out word to the teachers through the correspondents of the Federation that the ballots were false. We told them that if they voted to approve the Urion bill, William Rothmann would probably become the head of the pension board.

Some of the teachers who had been warned happened to be attending classes at the University of Chicago. They chanced to mention to professors in that institution something of the immediate circumstances of the pension fight. To their amazement they learned from these professors, associates of Charles E. Merriam, who had been a member of the Chicago City Council, that there had been a City Council investigation of William Rothmann's activity as chairman of the policemen's pension board for seven years. This investigation had shown that during those years $20,000 a year in interest, $140,000 in all, had never found its way into the police pension fund. The disclosure had forced Rothmann out of office but had not found its way into the public prints.[8]

No one of us was crass enough to think that Rothmann had taken this money for himself. It was and continues to be a political practice, in Illinois at least, that the interest on certain public funds shall be used for the benefit of the political machine in power. Sometimes the officer, elective or appointive, in charge of such funds is apprehended in these transactions and brought to trial. Occasionally he is sentenced. Usually, however, the machine, which can control judicial as well as executive officers, gets him off without penalty. In Rothmann's case, there was no criminal prosecution. Rothmann had been originally a Harrison appointee, and when Harrison went back into office he put him on the Board of Education.[9] Possibly Rothmann could have stayed on that body in pleasant obscurity for many years if he had not revived his old interest in pension funds.

The teachers who heard the Rothmann story from the University of Chicago faculty kept coming to the office of the Federation and to Catharine Goggin's house all through the Saturday and Sunday which followed their discovery. Catharine and I held court all afternoon on the story. On the next morning at nine o'clock, I was in the office of the City Clerk, Francis D. Connery, seeking a certified copy of the report of the investigation of the Chicago City Council on the police

[8]*Chicago Journal*, Aug. 30, 1915; *Margaret Haley's Bulletin*, 8, (Dec. 10, 1930), pp. 269-70, gives a detailed account of this episode.
[9]*Chicago Record-Herald*, July 23, 1912.

pension fund interest story. I had to wait from nine in the morning until four in the afternoon in the outer office for this copy. Unfortunately for Connery, there was no other door out of his inner office but the one beyond me, and I kept him prisoner as long as he could stick it out. Finally, he capitulated and let me have the copy. It was the report of the Council committee, of which Charles E. Merriam had been chairman. Briefly and vividly it convicted William Rothmann of the use of the interest money on the police pension fund.

Catharine Goggin opposed the printing of the Rothmann report. I insisted that if he were to be the president of the pension board, the teachers had the right to know his record as the president of another pension fund. The board of managers ordered a general meeting of the teachers be held the next evening at the old Masonic Temple and appointed a committee of three, Miss Goggin, Mrs. Ida Fursman, the president of the Federation, and myself, to decide whether or not the report should be printed and the copies brought to the meeting. Mrs. Fursman voted with me and we had the report set up in type.

Just a little while before the meeting was held, Mrs. Fursman told us that Mrs. Young had called her up and asked her to come to her in the LeSalle Hotel, where she was living at the time. We had to start the meeting without Mrs. Fursman. The printed copies of the Merriam Commission report had not yet arrived from the printer, but they came before Mrs. Fursman's return, and were distributed to the teachers.

Mrs. Fursman did not come back until some hours later. She told us that, after considerable parleying, Mrs. Young had asked her to make ready a petition for a salary increase for the teachers and to present it the next day to the finance committee of the Board of Education. Mrs. Young advised her not to have the petition come from the Federation, but to have the teachers in one school sign it and get it in immediately. Rothmann was the chairman of the finance committee. Mrs. Fursman, however, did not add the two and two of political action. She told Mrs. Young how busy she had been all day and explained to her that the report of the Merriam Commission was even then being distributed at the teachers' meeting. She telephoned to find out if it had already been distributed. When she found that it had been, she said to Mrs. Young, "Now shall we go ahead with the petition for a salary increase?"

Mrs. Young said, "Go ahead with the petition."

Catharine Goggin never lost her equilibrium; but she came as near to it then as I ever saw her. When I regained mine and after we had explained to Mrs. Fursman the height of the mountain on which she had been taken, we decided that we would put in a petition anyway. We had Nano Hickey take it over from the Haven School to the finance committee the next day. Needless to say, it was never reported to the Board.

Copies of the Merriam Commission report on the policemen's pension fund were sent to every teacher in Chicago. On the day following this mailing, the pension delegate convention met. William B. Owen, its chairman, had just launched the proceedings when a principal leaped to his feet and waved a copy of the report about Rothmann, shouting, "This irresponsible anonymous report!—"

I was up in the gallery, but I walked down to the rail and called, "My name is not 'Anonymous.'"

He said, "Who is the father of this report?"

I said, "I don't know who is the father, but I am the mother."

Some one cried that I should be given the floor. I went from the gallery to the platform and showed the certified copy from the City Clerk. I also had the stenographic report of the hearing before the Merriam Commission, which had conducted the investigation. I also had—and this was the bombshell—Charles E. Merriam parked in the gallery. I asked permission of the house to ask Mr. Merriam if he would identify the copy of that hearing.

The moment I mentioned Merriam's name, Mrs. Young stood up. "I refuse," she said, "to remain in a meeting where a member of the Board of Education is attacked." She strode down the aisle, with Owen after her, trying to bring her back. Mrs. Fursman took the gavel and said she would entertain a motion that Rothmann be invited to come to the meeting. The motion passed unanimously. Mrs. Fursman sent a messenger after Owen to tell him of the action. He brought Mrs. Young back.

We waited for hours for Rothmann to come. He never came. Then for another hour the meeting discussed the question of having Merriam identify the report. Through that hour, he stood on the platform, waiting the chance to say one word. Even then we knew how momentous that word would be. We did not realize, to be sure, all that would come out of our action. But even if we had, we should have gone on just as we did. Finally, Merriam was permitted by the house to answer the question. At nine o'clock that night, he said, "Yes."[10]

Mrs. Young sent for Miss Goggin and myself the next day. She told us that the first meetings of the teachers' councils were to be held that afternoon. For the first time, the teachers were to meet alone, without principals or supervisors, for discussion of academic questions. She said that Mr. Urion had just discovered that these meetings were to be held and that he had gone into a panic, in fear lest they would be forums for the discussion of the pension bill. Mrs. Young had told him that the meetings would not go outside educational matters of discussion. She said, "If that pension bill is discussed in any one of those

[10]A record of the meeting is found in "Minutes of the Board of Trustees of the Pension Fund," Apr. 23, 1913, CTF Files.

centers, there will be no councils again." Miss Goggin and I went to work at the telephone, passing along the word that if pension were mentioned, the teachers' councils would die at sunset. Not a word about pension was spoken in any one of the councils.

Two days later, the teachers voted. When the ballots were counted, a majority was revealed against the Board of Education's bill.[11]

The next meeting of the Board passed a resolution calling on the State Legislature not to consider any further legislation unless they passed the Board's bill, and they called on the governor not to sign Senate Bill 299. On the following Sunday, I took that resolution to a meeting of the Federation of Labor. The Federation referred the matter to its executive board, which sent a copy of the Merriam report to every member of the State Legislature. By that time, we knew we had come into deadlock with the Board of Education, that they would try to block the enactment of our own remedial legislation unless we gave them control of the pension board. We realized, though, that the support of the Federation of Labor was not only our best but practically our only hold upon the Legislature. We went down to Springfield armed with a report from the Federation of Labor showing conclusively the justice of our fight.

Rothmann, Mrs. Young, and Angus Roy Shannon, the attorney for the Board of Education, went before the committee of the house in charge of the hearing. [Thomas N.] Gorman, of Peoria, was its chairman. He twisted Shannon into knots, and asked Rothmann if he could explain why, in the seven years of his presidency, $20,000 a year of interest failed to go to into the policemen's pension fund. Rothmann murmured something about a sick treasurer. Mrs. Young made a brief statement that was noncommittal. The committee recommended the matter to a sub-committee. A man named [Joseph A.] Weber, in the sub-committee, who was closely associated with Louis Larson, secretary of the Board of Education, tried to twist it out of shape there; but John P. Devine and Michael Igoe stood over Weber and forced him to put through the amendment on which we had agreed. The amended bill, which wasn't all we wanted but which was far better for us than we would have been given by the Urion bill, passed its final reading on the day when Governor Dunne signed the bill which made woman suffrage a law in Illinois.

Woman suffrage passed into law in Illinois because of Governor Dunne, the Bull Moose movement, and Ruth Hanna McCormick. There was, to be sure, a popular surge of desire for it; but the mechanics of victory operated through these three elements. Without a governor

---

[11]The vote was 1,683 to 1,397 of 5,500 contributors. *Ibid.*

of Dunne's type, the bill could not have been signed. Without the Progressive balance of power in the Legislature, it could not have come to him. And without Mark Hanna's daughter, the Progressive machinery could not have been put in motion.[12]

The impulse toward woman suffrage was not at that time as powerful as it seemed upon the surface of events. From my California experience, I had come to know that not only were the great corporate interests of the country opposing it, but that some of the Labor leaders of the United States believed that it would operate against the interests of Labor. Andrew Furuseth, probably the most determined of all American Labor leaders in devotion to the single purpose of Labor, had told me in San Francisco that he himself was convinced that woman suffrage would increase the difficulties of Labor. He felt that the promotion of the Labor cause was altogether a matter of education of the voters. It was hard enough to educate a body of men trained to voting into realization of what Labor meant to them, without taking on the education of millions of women entirely untrained in public questions. It was not that Furuseth had any desire to keep away from women any right or privilege they should have. It was merely that he believed the time not yet right for their participation in public affairs.[13]

I could not agree with him, but I saw that there was some justice in his argument of expediency. Right or not, that point of view influenced many men in Illinois politics who would otherwise have inclined toward woman suffrage. Combined with the old line opposition, their attitude would have held off the vote for women in the 1913 Legislature had it not been for the peculiar political make-up of that body.

The Progressive party platform of 1912 had included practically all the forward-looking political, social, and economic ideas of that time. Raymond Robins, originally a Southerner and a Democrat, turned from his own party and his own sectionalism in order to write that platform because it incorporated all the points in which he believed. He had already made alliance with Theodore Roosevelt, on Roosevelt's agreement to put Governor Deneen on the spot. Roosevelt gave Deneen

[12]Ruth Hanna McCormick Simms (1880-1947) learned politics early in life through her association with her father, Marcus A. Hanna, the national "boss" of the Republican party at the turn of the century. Her marriage to Medill McCormick, who became publisher of the family business, the *Chicago Tribune*, brought her to Illinois. The two of them were prominent leaders of the Bull Moose movement in the state, which split the Republican party in 1912. Mrs. McCormick was elected to the U.S. House of Representatives in 1928; two years later she lost her bid to win the Senate seat which her deceased husband had held from 1918 to 1925.

[13]Andrew Furuseth (1854-1938) was president of the International Seamen's Union of America from 1908 until his death.

a week to choose between Taft and himself. While Deneen still hesitated after the deadline, Robins, who hated Deneen viciously, wangled in Frank Funk, of Bloomington, as the Progressive candidate for governor, thereby insuring the election of the Democrat.[14]

The Progressives held the balance of power in the Illinois Legislature of 1913. There were twenty-one of them in the lower house. One of them was Medill McCormick. Like most of the Progressives, McCormick had a great deal to say, both on and off the floor. The real director of Progressive destinies, however, was his wife. She was very rarely seen around the capitol, going only occasionally to the gallery to listen to speeches, but she was certainly her father's daughter in her genius for organization. She furnished the sinews of war and the plan of warfare in the campaign for woman suffrage. She had able aids in Antoinette Funk, Grace Wilbur Trout, and Mrs. Sherman Booth, but it was her strategy and her organizing power that won the vote.[15]

From 1901 until 1913, there had been continuing attempts to push through the Legislature some sort of bill providing for a certain type of vocational training in the Chicago public schools. These vocational bills were uniformly vicious. All of them were predicated upon the idea of separating cultural education from industrial. The cultural idea and aim of education would be wholly absent from the industrial training which they provided. There is an undying feud between the industrial advocates of industrial education and the educational advocates of industrial education. To the educator, industrial training stands for the development of children through activities and sufficient manual training, not as preparation for manual effort but as development of the child, of his brain and his hand. The industrial advocates wanted nothing like the type of vocational training desired by educators. They wanted no subordination of the industrial to the educational. They wanted industrial schools to supplement and aid industry and to prepare children for it.

[14]Raymond Robins (1873-1957) had been a member of the Dunne Board. He and his wife, Margaret Dreier Robins, were friends of Haley and advocates of the rights of organized labor and of land value taxation. He was an unsuccessful candidate for the U.S. Senate, running as a Progressive in 1914.

[15]Medill McCormick (1877-1925) was the national vice chairman of the Progressive party. He later served one term in the U.S. House of Representatives and was elected for one term in the Senate. Both he and Ruth Hanna McCormick were strong opponents of the League of Nations.

Governor Dunne signed the suffrage bill on June 27, 1913. A photograph of the event featured three of the leaders of the women's lobby: Mrs. Grace Wilbur Trout, Mrs. Antoinette Funk, and Mrs. Sherman Booth. The fourth key individual, Mrs. Medill McCormick, was unable to attend the ceremony. Haley is shown seated at his desk across from the governor. Dunne stated that he wanted her in the picture since it was the work of Haley and the Chicago Teachers' Federation for good government that converted him to the cause of woman suffrage. *Chicago Journal*, June 27, 1913; *Chicago Daily Journal*, Feb. 2, 1914. See illustrations after p. 182.

You don't have to be told that the victims of this purely industrial education would be the poor children of the city. If the rich had industrial training for their children, you may be certain that it would be the kind that would supplement academic work.

All through the United States through those years, the battle went on between educational leaders and industrial leaders for supremacy in the schools. In some of the states, the industrialists won. In others, notably in Wisconsin, a type of vocational training was established that supplemented the academic. Wisconsin, with its dairy and agricultural interests, would not of course accentuate any purely industrial training. Illinois, on the other hand, is a combination of archaic customs of thought and of industrial domination. Even yet, it is a terrific struggle to maintain any real standards in our state. Springfield, below the line where the backwardness begins, is an antiquated town, having its effect upon the Legislature. Two-thirds of that Legislature is drawn from the rural sections outside Chicago, although on the basis of population Chicago should have a majority in that body. Even yet, the question of redistricting the state is a bone of contention in every Legislature. It isn't a matter of political parties. It's the agricultural against the urban.

Springfield is really a southern town. It's so hot down there and the town itself is so far down in a valley that you feel at times in the summer that you're at the bottom of a bowl set on a hot stove. Springfield is in warm weather two lines of tilted-back chairs and of cuspidors. In such an atmosphere it is difficult, under the best conditions, to get through progressive legislation. When you add to that the fact that the powerful Illinois Manufacturers' Association maintains an organization with direct influence upon a large part of the Legislature, you realize how almost insuperable the difficulty becomes.

Just as it is today, that was the situation in 1913, when the so-called Cooley Vocational Bill came up before the Legislature.[16]

I had come away from Springfield to let the members of the Legislature get over their mad at me. (I had written a resolution in the course of the Rothmann fight for the legislative committee of the Chicago Federation of Labor. This resolution attacked, with perfectly good reason, certain members of the Legislature. The Federation of Labor had posted it. Then a committee of the Legislature held session from ten in the morning until midnight, trying to find out who wrote it. I was ready to tell them any minute if they had called me, but they didn't. At midnight I sent word to the speaker that if the committee put on any more Labor witnesses, I'd get up without being called and tell

---

[16]For a detailed account of this episode, see Reid, "Professionalization," pp. 147-57.

the body that there wasn't a word of anything in that resolution that wasn't true. Then a big, bearded man from somewhere down-state moved that they cite the executive committee of the Chicago Federation of Labor for contempt of the Legislature. They voted to do it. Then I laughed. "That's a good joke on that old fellow," I said. "He hasn't the right rat. I'm on the legislative committee." I had laughed, though, too soon. Somebody tampered with the resolution and changed the indictment from the executive to the legislative committee. They summoned me before the bar of the house. I said what I had to say; they didn't like it; and, although they did nothing to me, I thought it would be just as well if I got out of their sight for a while.)[17]

While I was away, trouble started again. I felt like the little girl in the Jones School who had been led, greatly against her will, to take an unaccustomed bath. While she was in the tub, a circus parade went by. "That settles it," she said when she discovered her loss. "That's the last time I'll ever do anything like that."

I had been back in Chicago less than a week when Mrs. Young telephoned me that [Francis] Blair, the State Superintendent of Public Instruction, had just informed her that the Cooley vocational bill was coming up immediately. She said that she was sending William J. Bogan, president of the Midwestern Section of the Vocational Association, down that night and that she wanted me to go too.[18]

I said, "They'll pass that bill if I go down. It always takes them about two weeks to get over their mads."

She said, "I want you to go anyhow."

I found Governor Dunne at breakfast the next morning. I told him that the bill was on second reading in the senate that day and that it would be shoved through the house in the same manner. I gave him a line of talk that I thought would appeal to him and told him that he'd have to take care of the house. I said that we could look after the senate, but that it was his job to keep it from passing in the lower body. I told him where he'd get off if he let that bill go through; he'd be between

[17]Haley's resolution had called the defeat of the initiative and referendum "the most brazen, shameless, and anarchistic proceeding that ever disgraced even an Illinois legislature." This fight to defeat the will of the people "was personally conducted by Boss Lorimer from the seat of honor behind the speaker's desk." In response to the circular containing these charges, the Illinois House subpoenaed the officers and members of the Executive Board of the Chicago Federation of Labor to defend their allegations. The CFL indicated it had no intention of apologizing and added further factual support to the changes at the hearing. The House then voted to censure the leaders of the CTF. "Plain Speaking in Illinois," *Life and Labor*, 3 (July, 1913), pp. 199-202; *Chicago Tribune*, May 28, 1913.

[18]William J. Bogan (1870-1936) was the principal of Lane Technical High School from 1905 to 1924. He was assistant superintendent during the McAndrew years and became superintendent of schools in 1928 until his death eight years later.

the teachers and the business interests. He understood what the trouble would be, and he said he's stave it off in the house.

I found Dick Barr in the senate. I don't know what Dick Barr is in other connections, but for any bills we've ever had in Springfield he has always registered his stand with complete candor. He said, "Well, now, I promised these people—" but he added, "They'll be satisfied if they get it through second reading. If you make a fight on it, it may not go through. If you don't fight it, I'll promise it won't pass third reading in the senate.

Barr had courage to make even that compromise with me. He came from Joliet, a town controlled by the United States Steel Company. The steel company was backing the Cooley vocational bill. Urion was backing it. Lorimer was backing it. Urion and Lorimer sat together in the library of the capitol that day, sending for the legislators as the bill progressed. In spite of them, though, Barr was able to keep his word. By the time for adjournment that night, the Cooley vocational bill didn't have a wiggle left in it. Dunne had taken care of the house and Barr had taken care of the senate. Democrat and Republican, Trinity graduate and steel town man, they were gentlemen of their word.[19]

As far as we, the public school teachers of Chicago, were concerned, our work with the Legislature of 1913 was finished. We came back to Chicago with the sense of victory achieved. We did not yet know the price to be exacted from us for that victory. We did not apprehend that, because of 1913, in less than three years we would be forced to fight for our existence and for every ideal of academic freedom we championed, as a result of our actions. In other words, we underestimated William Rothmann.

3

We should have taken deeper heed of Rothmann's passion for revenge. We knew that he forced Ella Flagg Young's resignation a little while after the adjournment of the Legislature. She told me that he used to come into her office day after day, pestering her with questions of no importance to her or to the public welfare, but which had nagging value. Other people would have thrown him out, but Ella Flagg was a hold-over from a generation that couldn't let go of its sense of values of

---

[19]See note 10, p. 94 for Barr. The opposition of the CTF together with that of the Chicago and state Federations of Labor helped defeat this plan for a dual system of schools. The debate over vocational education received more editorial attention than any other school issue in the years from 1890 to 1920. John Beck, "Chicago Newspapers and the Public Schools, 1880-1920," (Ph.D. diss., University of Chicago, 1953), p. 284.

established authority. To her, a board of education was a board of
education, not merely an aggregation of men and women capable of
mistakes of judgment and method. She had lived through a period
where the board of education demanded not only service but subservience from a superintendent. It was part of a caste system. She had
broken away from it in many important ways, but not in the manner of
courtesy and, like many other punctilious people, she was always at a
disadvantage with those less punctilious than herself. All she could do
was suffer in silence until she could endure no more. Then she blew up
with a bang that shook Chicago.

Her resignation, flung out without prelude, startled everyone connected with the public schools, the Board of Education, the teachers,
the mayor, the civic organizations interested in educational welfare.
The mayor sent for her. With Peter Reinberg, then president of the
Board of Education, an honest old florist who never knew what the
pitching was about, although as president of the County Board he
originated and operated at the lowest possible cost the splendid Cook
County Forest Preserve system, Ella Flagg went to Harrison's office.
She told him that she had defended Rothmann, but she didn't explain
that she hadn't been able to stop the cannon ball from hitting him
because she hadn't talked fast enough to Mrs. Fursman in trying to
convey to her Rothmann's bribe to the teachers. Harrison realized the
situation, though, and urged her to reconsider her resignation. When a
mass meeting at the Auditorium Theater, presided over by Elizabeth
Bass, president of the Chicago Woman's Club and one of the grandest
fighters for women this country has ever known, demanded Mrs.
Young's retention, even the Rothmann crowd had to back down. Ella
Flagg stayed—but so did Rothmann.[20]

Robert M. Sweitzer and Carter Harrison were candidates for mayor
at the Democratic primaries in 1915. A clever politician named [Chris-
topher J.?] McGurn, who was an ally of Harrison and a long-time
enemy of Roger Sullivan, the Democratic boss of Illinois, sent a
delegation of Harrison's supporters to Sweitzer headquarters immediately after the primaries, knowing full well that the Sweitzer leaders
would be so cocky with their victory that they would repel all advances
of the Harrison adherents at that time. Just as McGurn had expected,
the Sweitzer headquarters leaders left the members of the Harrison
committee sitting outside the door cooling their heels. After an hour's
wait, the Harrison men left in angry mood. When they went back to

[20]The Board refused to accept this July letter of resignation by a 14 to 1 vote. *Chicago
Record-Herald*, July 30, 1913.

McGurn, he showed them how they could secure revenge by helping to elect William Hale Thompson, the Republican candidate.[21]

I do not know if William Hale Thompson, left to himself, would have been friendly to the cause of academic freedom. Thompson is, as everyone knows, a man of warring characteristics. At times, he has advocated and put across measures that were genuinely for the public good. At other times, he has worked directly against that good. An aristocrat by birth—as much as any American can be an aristocrat— Thompson has always been a gallery player in public life. He had accomplished enough good during his term in the City Council, principally through the establishment of playgrounds for children, to give an idea that he would be liberal toward the cause of education. Even after these years, it is not possible to estimate what his personal intention would have been, for he went into office with a political obligation to the Harrison forces. There were rumors, some of them fairly well substantiated, that Thompson, even before his election, was opposed to the Chicago Teachers' Federation. We could not know, however, how authoritative these rumors were until a few months after Thompson's election to the mayoralty.

Jacob M. Loeb, who had been appointed by Harrison to membership on the Board of Education, became the leader, although not the brains, of the new Board, making terms with Thompson and with Thompson's boss, Fred Lundin, who always called himself "the poor Swede."[22] Thompson could not appoint any members upon the Board until July 1, 1915, when the terms of seven members expired, but Loeb and his arch-instigator, our ancient enemy, William Rothmann, combined with the Thompson forces as early as June of that year in battle against the teachers.

On June 1, 1915, the City Council referred to its committee on schools a resolution from the Board of Education offering to pay half the expenses of a certified public accountant to audit the Board's books and accounts. Legally, the City Council had the right of supervision of

---

[21]William Hale Thompson (1869-1944) was a colorful politician who served three terms as mayor, 1915 to 1923 and 1927 to 1931. "Big Bill" exploited the religious issue in the 1915 campaign and reworked this in different guises in his subsequent campaigns. See Reid, "Professionalization," pp. 161-63; 177; 181-82, and Lloyd Wendt and Herman Kogan, *Big Bill of Chicago* (Indianapolis: Bobbs-Merrill, 1953) (hereafter cited as Wendt and Kogan, *Big Bill of Chicago*).

[22]Jacob M. Loeb (1875-1944) was president of a fire insurance firm, Eliel and Loeb, whose major client was Sears, Roebuck, and Company. His brother was a vice president of that company. A representative of the Jewish segment of the population, Loeb was a Democrat initially appointed by Mayor Harrison. *Chamberlins*, 15 (July, 1916), pp. 26-27.

accounts of the Board of Education; but the Board has for years insisted that the Council had no real jurisdiction over it. On the 19th of June, Samuel Ettelson, then a state senator but also the Corporation Counsel of the Thompson administration, had the Journal of the State senate "corrected," that is, mutilated, to show that a resolution had been adopted by the senate directing Barratt O'Hara, then Lieutenant governor, to appoint a senate commission, later known as the Baldwin Commission, to investigate the Chicago Board of Education. Later investigation showed that no motion for the appointment of any such commission had ever been made or considered by the senate. Ettelson's action was the perpetration of pure fiction upon O'Hara, who was certainly asleep at the switch when he let it go through. The commission, with Percy Baldwin as chairman, came at once to Chicago and began hearings in the LaSalle Hotel.[23]

The members of the commission were Baldwin, a Chicago real-estate dealer, George Harding, a leading Thompson supporter, [William S.] Jewell, a Republican from a mining district in Illinois, [Peter E.] Coleman, the mayor of LaSalle, and Steve Canaday. Canaday and the mayor of LaSalle were also from coal mining districts. Had it not been for the geographical setting of these three last named members of the commission, there is no knowing what might have happened to the Chicago schools out of that hearing.

The Baldwin commission gave only one day's hearing to the affairs of the Board of Education. During that day, they had Mrs. Young and Michael J. Collins, then president of the Board, upon the stand. Collins was there for the morning session. Baldwin treated him so badly that at noon I told him that, if he dared act toward Mrs. Young as he had acted toward the president of the Board of Education, I would throw the first thing at my hand, probably the water pitcher, at his head and that I would not stop my action there.

The rest of the sessions were all concerned with the Chicago Teachers' Federation. Jacob M. Loeb was the star witness. He proceeded to attack the Chicago Teachers' Federation, placing in evidence documents which purported to show: first, that the Chicago Teachers' Federation had urged the passage of a bill in the session of the 1913 Legislature to increase the tax levy in order to increase the educational fund; second, that the Federation had resisted a cut in teachers' salaries in May, 1915; and, third, that the Federation was composed of "lady labor sluggers" and citing as an example of their "labor slugging" the attack which had been made on one William Rothmann, his fellow member of the

[23]The City Council investigation tended to have a pro-labor orientation, while the illegally constituted senate commission was decidedly opposed to organized labor. See *Margaret A. Haley's Bulletin*, 1 (Oct. 7, 1915) and the *Day Book*, Apr. 14, 1916, for details on the Baldwin Commission.

Board of Education. With that, the three senators from the mining districts down-state arose as one man and swore to high Heaven that they were not against organized Labor or the Chicago Teachers' Federation. They quit that day and never reappeared at the hearings. Neither did George F. Harding. For want of official attendance, the commission folded up. For six weeks, the so-called commission had striven to discredit the Chicago Teachers' Federation and, through us, all the public school teachers of Chicago.

A few days after the adjournment of the Baldwin commission, I went for a much needed rest to a sanitarium in Milwaukee. On the night that I left the city, two events of deep importance, one to all the teachers, the other to me in person, took place. The *Chicago Tribune* ran a story which stated that for seven years, from 1900 to 1907, I had accepted two salaries, one from the Board of Education and one from the Teachers' Federation. The other event was the adoption of the infamous "Loeb Rule" by the rules committee of the Board of Education.[24]

I was so busy with the Loeb Rule and its consequences that I did not find time to file suit for libel against the *Tribune* until the last day allowed me by law. I had not wanted to file that suit, but I was driven to it by the failure of the *Tribune* to retract the story. Walter Howey, who was City Editor of the *Tribune* then, had promised me that he would run the retraction on the front page of the paper. On the day after I filed the suit, he telephoned me in rage and said, "I told you we'd print the truth on the front page."

"Oh, yes," I said. "You said you'd print the truth on the front page, but when did you mean to print it?"

He said, "You think you're privileged to take a fling at anyone, but just as soon as someone takes a fling at you, you begin to whimper. You took a fling at the *Tribune's* lease. You're never done whacking at that."

I said, "You'd better distinguish between me and the *Tribune*. I can take a fling at the *Tribune* on its lease and it can't defend itself on that."

Not only for my own self-respect but for the sake of the teachers whom I represented and the causes which I espoused, I had to bring the suit against the *Tribune*. When the suit was filed, a member of the *Tribune* legal staff, a man whom I had known from his boyhood, came to me with an offer of $10,500 in settlement of the action. I told him that if he offered the whole $50,000 for which I was suing, I wouldn't take it. What I wanted was not money but a verdict proving that I had been libeled.

[24]*Chicago Tribune*, Aug. 24, 1915.

My attorney was Frank Walsh, of Kansas City, who was then on the Joint Labor Board. The Labor Board consisted of five Labor men and five employers, with William Howard Taft representing the employers and Walsh spokesman for the Labor men.[25] From what I knew of Walsh and of Anton Johansen, another Labor member of the board, and from what they told of Taft, that board must have been the cussingest crew in the whole United States. Walsh could hold his own with everyone except Johansen, but he said that Taft could outdo Anton on any occasion and with any provocation. Taft, though, was so judicial and had such good sense that they deferred to him on all matters that they couldn't put over him.

Walsh thought that I was foolish not to take the money which the *Tribune* offered, but I knew that a verdict would mean more to me and to the people whom I represented than any amount of money could. I got the verdict finally, although it carried only a $500 award. Judge David, who tried the case, told the jury that I had such high reputation in the community that I couldn't be financially injured by any such publication. That was comforting, anyhow.[26]

When Rothmann had realized that we teachers had the Federation of Labor for our tribunal in any disputes with members of the Board of Education, he set out to break our association with that body. The tenure clause which Governor Altgeld had put in the pension law of 1895 had protected the teachers from constant fear of being dropped by the Board without proper cause and due procedure. The teachers believed that the tenure extended for the whole period of a teacher's service. Rothmann—or somebody bigger than Rothmann—had a different idea. He held that the teachers had to be elected every year and that no attempt by rule of the Board to give them a right to trial meant anything except a right to trial during the year. The Board, he held, could put them out without trial at the end of the school term in June. The Board could do this, he said, without trial or revision. Once out, the teachers stayed out.

This was the basis of the Loeb Rule, although the rule as it was first passed by the whole Board on the 1st of September, 1915, did not state this clearly. The Loeb Rule was directed against the affiliation of the Chicago Teachers' Federation with the Federation of Labor. On the day when it was passed, Ed Nockels, John Walker, president of the Illinois State Federation of Labor, and I went to Springfield.[27]

On the train, we met Senator Duff Piercey. He said, "I think I know

[25]William Howard Taft was the former president of the United States (1909-1913). The board was appointed by President Woodrow Wilson to help support the United States during the critical years before and during America's involvement in World War I.

[26]*Chicago Tribune*, June 21, 1918; *Margaret A. Haley v. The Tribune Company*, No. 324324 in the superior court of Cook County.

that you're going to see Steve Canaday. I'll go with you." While we waited for Canaday in the hotel across the street from his office, Piercey told us how the Ettelson resolution had been written into the senate records in order to create the Baldwin commission. He declared that he had been in the senate on the day when the resolution was supposed to have been carried and that he would swear that he had never been mentioned.

When we found Canaday, we asked him to deliver to us a letter which he had received from Myer Stein, an attorney of Oak Park, Illinois, who was sometimes known as the "bill carpenter" of the senate. The letter asked Canaday to send to Stein his bill for expenses on the commission.[28] It stated that philanthropic persons in Chicago were furnishing a fund to pay the expenses of the commission and that Stein would send Canaday a check. Canaday told us that Governor Dunne had advised him to release the letter to the State's Attorney of Cook County if he were requested to do this by that official. He said that he would accept a long distance telephone order followed by a telegram from the State's Attorney if we could get this communication to him.

We came back to Chicago that night and went directly to the office of Maclay Hoyne, the State's Attorney of Cook County. Frank S. Johnston, his assistant, telephoned Canaday an order for the letter. Within ten minutes, Canaday's answer, a copy of his letter from Stein, came over the wire. That night [September 8, 1915] I read the telegram at a great mass meeting in the Auditorium Theater, where Samuel Gompers spoke against the Loeb Rule.[29] On the next day, Senators Jewell, Coleman, and Harding came out with public statements that, although they had received letters from Myer Stein similar to the one sent to Canaday, they also had refrained from sending in their expense accounts to the unknown philanthropist.

The adoption of the Loeb Rule by the Chicago Board of Education did not merely menace the integrity and well being of every teacher in the Chicago public schools; it put in jeopardy the continued development of democracy in the United States. To the uninformed, the attempt to annihilate the Chicago Teachers' Federation, which was the basis of the Loeb Rule, may have seemed a chance occurrence unrelated to any of the great tendencies of the time. Even to those familiar with

[27]Passed by Loeb's rules committee on August 23, the Loeb Rule was accepted by the board on September 1. *Proceedings, Board of Education*, 1915-16, p. 734. Nockels was secretary of the Chicago Federation of Labor.

[28]Stein had acted as a "prosecuting attorney" for the Baldwin Commission hearings.

[29]"Stenographic Report of the Meeting of the Chicago Federation of Labor, September 8, 1915," CTF Files.

the facts, the issue might have seemed merely a clash of personalities between the executive officers of the Chicago Teachers' Federation and William Rothmann and his allies. It was not really that. The battle between the Rothmann forces, who were the Loeb forces, and ourselves was only a battle of personalities in so far as they stood at one pole of social thought and we stood at the other. The people whom they represented sought control not only of the public school system of Chicago but of the country. We sought to keep them from obtaining that control. We strove to hold not only academic freedom for the teachers but economic freedom for the children.

Their motive was simple. The great profits of huge corporate interests were being reduced by a growing governmental control. Democracy was already demanding that this control should become more powerful. The selfish interests of predatory wealth depended then, as now, upon the breaking down of the popular power. The fight of the teachers for life was as deeply based in genuine democracy as were the early struggles of the men who had founded this nation.

The immediate motive of the attack against the teachers was threefold. We were being punished:

Because we had defeated the Cooley vocational bill [1913 and 1915];

Because we had protested at the proposed cut of 7½ per cent in our salaries;[30]

Because we had exercised our rights and privileges as the citizens of a free nation.

It was this exercise of rights in appearing before the Illinois State Legislature which precipitated the crisis. We had shown during that session of the Legislature that we possessed, through our association with the Chicago Federation of Labor, a political power which influenced the legislators as no consciousness of the righteousness of our cause could have done. The men who sought to control public opinion as a weapon for their own exploitation of the masses knew that they must reduce the teachers of the public schools into feudal subservience to themselves. They knew that they could not do this while we were able to influence legislation toward insuring the freedom of the schools. They knew that they must divorce us from the general Labor movement if they were to win their war against us and against what we represented. They seized their opportunity in using the class consciousness of a Thompson, the stupidity of a Loeb, and the vindictiveness of a Rothmann.

---

[30]This proposal had come from an earlier committee chaired by Loeb, the committee on efficiency and economy. It was this report and salary cut recommendation that had led Aldermen Robert Buck and Charles Merriam to establish a City Council investigation. *Proceedings, Board of Education,* 1914-15, p. 1128; *Journal of the Proceedings of the City Council of the City of Chicago,* May 17, 1915, p. 259.

The Loeb Rule provided that "Membership by teachers in labor unions or in organizations of teachers affiliated with a trade union or a federation or association of trade unions, as well as teachers' organizations which have officers, business agents, or other representatives who are not members of the teaching force, is inimical to proper discipline, prejudicial to the efficiency of the teaching force, and detrimental to the welfare of the public school system. Therefore, such membership, affiliation, or representation is hereby prohibited."[31]

The rule provided that all members of the educational department who are now members of any such prohibited organization should forthwith discontinue their membership therein, and provided that no person should thereafter be employed in any capacity in the educational department until such person should state in writing that he was not a member and would not, while employed in the educational department, become a member of any such prohibited organization. It also provided that no member of the educational department should be eligible for promotion, advancement in salary, or transfer from school to school until he should have stated in writing that he was not a member of any such prohibited organization. A pledge was sent out by the secretary of the Board of Education to teachers that they would not join any of the prohibited organizations.

It was immediately evident that in order to hold their jobs in the Chicago schools, the teachers who were members of the Chicago Teachers' Federation would have to resign from that body. Loeb said that the enforcement of the rule would be the duty of the Superintendent of Schools. Ella Flagg Young said that it would be the duty of the Board. Rothmann said that any teachers who refused to conform to the rule would be tried by the Board and, if found guilty, would be fined, suspended, or dismissed from the service. The Board's action, he declared, was final and non-reviewable. It would not be necessary, he added, for the Board to deal with all the Federation members at one time. In all human probability, he thought that after fifty of the recalcitrants had been tried, found guilty, and dismissed from the service, the great majority of the remainder would conclude that their best interests would be conserved by announcing their willingness to obey.

On September 14, a petition for an injunction against the Board of Education to restrain the enforcement of this rule was filed in the Superior Court of Cook County in the name of the people of Illinois by Maclay Hoyne, State's Attorney, on the relation of Ida L. M. Fursman, tax payer, teacher, and member of five of the prohibited organizations. Mrs. Fursman was still president of the Chicago Teachers'

[31]*Proceedings, Board of Education,* 1915-16, p. 734.

Federation. On September 23, Judge John M. O'Connor issued a temporary writ of injunction, prohibiting the enforcement or any attempt to enforce the rule and any discrimination because of the rule against teachers in the service or candidates for teachers, affiliated with trade unions. Judge O'Connor made decision that the Loeb Rule, if enforced, would prevent teachers from membership in any of the following associations:

The National Education Association;

The Illinois State Teachers' Association;

The Chicago Teachers' Federation;

The American Federation of Labor;

The Chicago Federation of Labor.

He found the rule arbitrary, unreasonable, oppressive, illegal, contrary to public policy, and void. He found that the Board of Education could not create a monopoly by limiting the classes of citizens, as provided in this rule, which it might employ or refuse to employ.[32]

During the course of the hearing for the temporary writ, the attorneys for the Board of Education sought to delay the hearing in order to give time to the Board to send out the pledge cards to the teachers. Isaiah T. Greenacre, who was representing the interests of the Chicago Teachers' Federation, made protest against the attempted procedure, declaring that in the thirty years while he had been practicing law, "not sleight of hand," he had never before met an instance when a public body sought to trick a court by such a palpable device. "That a governmental body should try such a trick is inconceivable," he said. "That an educational board should do it is worse. Think of the Board of Education, by its example, teaching the children, the citizens of the next generation, to circumvent courts and law."

"The Court may trust the Board of Education," he added. "I cannot. If people fool me once, shame on them; if they fool me twice, shame on me."

On the 29th of September, the Board of Education amended the Loeb Rule, although it did not rescind the action.[33] Even after these years, the issue of Board of Education control upon the freedom of action of public school teachers remains so grave an issue that I believe it only right to set down the roster of those members of the Board of Education who voted for and against the Loeb Rule upon its adoption. They were:

---

[32]The legal protection, however, was limited to one year, since the board had tried to dismiss teachers that it had voted to re-employ at its June 23, 1915, meeting. See *Margaret A. Haley's Bulletin*, 1 (Sept. 23, 1915), pp. 13-16.

[33]The Loeb Rule was amended to read "membership in some teachers' organizations." The board had the power to decide which ones were "inimical, prejudicial, and detrimental." *Proceedings, Board of Education*, 1915-16, pp. 885-86.

Yeas: William Rothmann, Jacob N. Loeb, Charles S. Peterson, Mrs. George P. Vosbrink, Dr. Peter C. Clemensen, Ralph C. Otis, John W. Eckhart, Joseph A. Holpuch, Mrs. Charles O. Sethness, William Schlake, Ernest J. Kruetgen.

Nays: John J. Sonsteby, Harry A. Lipsky, Mrs. John MacMahon, Dr. Otto F. Warning, Mrs. Gertrude Howe Britton, John A. Metz, Dr. Stephen R. Pietrowicz, Mrs. William E. Gallagher, Michael J. Collins.

Of the rules committee, who had passed the Loeb Rule on the 23rd of August, 1915, Jacob M. Loeb, Ernest J. Kruetgen, and Mrs. Charles O. Sethness had voted for the measure. Michael J. Collins, the president of the Board, had told Loeb that he would be unable to attend the meeting when it was shifted from four o'clock that day to seven o'clock that evening. John A. Metz was not notified of the change of time in the meeting. Mrs. Gallagher was out of the city. Mrs. Sethness, who had been out of the city, came back in time to attend the meeting at the hour to which it had been postponed.

On October 16, attorneys for the Board of Education appeared before Judge Denis E. Sullivan in the Superior Court and made a motion to have the temporary injunction granted by Judge O'Connor dissolved. From October 26 until November 15, the hearing before Judge Sullivan was held. On November 29, Judge Sullivan rendered his decision, refusing to dissolve the temporary injunction granted by Judge O'Connor. In his decision, Judge Sullivan said:

> The Board of Education acts in a dual capacity—governmental and private. In its governmental capacity, it has a wide discretion in performing its duties and in controlling the school system, and one with which the courts are very loath to interfere; but when, in its private capacity, it enters into a contract for the employment of labor or the purchase of supplies and material, then the same rule of law applies to it that applies to an individual.
>
> It has been suggested by counsel for defendant that the court shall look beyond the pleadings and the record in this case for reasons why the Board of Education desires to pass this rule at this time. A court is not permitted to go beyond the record before it, to search for evidence, or to take cognizance of facts not pleaded or proven, aside from those which under the law the court should take judicial cognizance of. . . . Our Supreme Court has held many times that the right of labor to organization is a legal one, and that membership in such organizations is not in violation of law.[34]

Judge Sullivan's decision, in effect, enjoined the Board of Education from enforcing or attempting to enforce the Loeb Rule and from discriminating in any manner because of the rule and its contents and

---

[34]As found in I. T. Greenacre to CTF, December 9, 1915, CTF Files. The appellate court concurred with the refusal of the superior court to dissolve the injunction.

substance (and this also covered the amended rule, which contained no new but only slightly less contents and substance) in the treatment, discipline, employment, promotion or failure to promote or demotion, advancement and salary, transfer from school to school, suspension or dismissal from service or admission to the service of the Board of Education, or in any recommendation of teachers or other members of the education department. It enjoined the Superintendent of Schools from failing to recommend or the Board of Education from refusing to employ, the next June or at any time before or after June, any teacher because she was or was not a member of any of the organizations attempted to be prohibited by the Loeb Rule. The Board was also enjoined from enforcing any of the substance of the Loeb Rule, even though it should be incorporated into some new rule later passed.

It was a splendid victory, but short lived. We knew that the Loeb-Rothmann forces, backed by the Illinois Manufacturers' Association, would take other action against us, but we did not yet know what that action would be. Even our triumph in the lower courts did not make us too optimistic.

We knew our enemy.

4

On the 11th of December, Ella Flagg Young walked out for the last time from the office of the Superintendent of Schools.[35]

In the year that Lincoln died, a frail girl hardly out of her 'teens, she had begun her service to Chicago. Fifty years later, she resigned from the highest educational office ever held by a woman. She had found the public schools noble chiefly in intention. Steadily, throughout the years, she had devoted her splendid abilities to tearing down what was false and servile and to building up what was true and free. She had entered upon her calling youthful, unknown, one of undistinguished millions. She laid down her task, a leader famous throughout the world. Wherever women aspired to serve the race, wherever education was a liberating, soul-freeing process, wherever teaching signified the more abundant life, the name of Ella Flagg Young was known and revered. To struggling women everywhere, her career had been a beacon.

Her valedictory, spoken a little while before her resignation, voiced her creed:

> In order that teachers may delight in awakening the spirits of children, they must themselves be awake. We have tried to free the teachers.

[35]The board had rejected her on a 10-10 vote. *Proceedings, Board of Education*, 1915-16, pp. 1274-75.

Some day the system will be such that the child and the teacher will go to school with elastic joy. At home in the evening, the child will talk about the things done during the day and will talk with pride. I want to make the school the great instrument of democracy.

Before she left Chicago, Ella Flagg gave all her worldly possessions to two institutions, the Mary Thompson Hospital for Women and Children and the Chicago Public Library. To the people of Chicago, she left an infinitely greater gift, an ideal of democracy in education which has heartened the fighters for freedom through long and sometimes dreary years since she went away.

5

One of the first rules of any game is to keep your enemy from winning the rewards of his vice.

One of Rothmann's and Loeb's most active supporters was Ernest J. Kruetgen. In addition to his membership on the Board of Education, Kruetgen was, with John W. Eckhart and William Schlake, a candidate for the office of Chicago postmaster. The postmastership was open to a Democrat because Woodrow Wilson was in the Presidency. Wilson had held off from any appointment in the place, however, because of his bitter quarrel with Roger Sullivan. It was likely that some one of the Harrison faction would be given the postmastership, but the place was still open when, one morning on the street car, I met Dr. Frances Dickinson. With a gleam in her eye, she told me that she had just heard that Kruetgen was a likely candidate for the post.

"Is that possible?" I asked.

She said, "More than possible."

We had a Board of Managers meeting that afternoon. The next day, I went to Washington to see President Wilson. I told Wilson that it seemed to me the Democratic party must be terribly short of material for postmasters when its only candidates were all men who had taken a slap at the women teachers of Chicago for doing what they should have been doing, making the corporations pay their just taxes. I named those three bucks and asked Wilson if he thought that every man who had persecuted the teachers should think himself qualified by it for the postmastership in Chicago.

Wilson sat very quietly and seemed really interested while I told him how the candidates for the postmastership had tried to beat up the Chicago school teachers. He smiled a rather knowing smile every once in a while and showed a very sly kind of amusement. Of course, he was feeling mellow anyhow because he was going to be married the next week, but he seemed to be genuinely sorry for the teachers. I knew, of course, that he must be realizing that there was a political aspect to it, too. The teachers didn't have national suffrage then, but they had state suffrage in many places, Illinois among them. That gave them a lot of power. It gave them more power with the President than with the State Legislature. All offices that were named in the State constitution were offices for which women could not vote, but they could vote for any office that was created by the Legislature. The Illinois law also gave them the right to vote for presidential electors. Women had the vote for electors in enough states to constitute a balance of power in the electoral college in the forthcoming elections of 1916. The situation made women everywhere important to all politicians and made women in organizations more important then than they are now.

Even without sympathy, a President of the United States was bound to give some heed to the representative of a teachers' organization in the sovereign State of Illinois, where women would vote for the presidential electors the next November. I'm not saying that Wilson might not have given me courteous attention in any case. I'm only saying that he was playing a political game well when he did.

When I returned to Chicago, I found out that Kruetgen had gone to Ed Nockels and John Fitzpatrick to get their help for the postmastership.[36] He had come in and called Nockels by his first name and slapped him on the back. Catharine Goggin had been there. As she told me about it, she said to me, with her sly little wink, "If you'd been there, he would have slapped you on the back and said, 'Maggie, what can you do?'"

6

Catharine Goggin was killed on the night of January 4, 1916.

Less than an hour before she was struck by a speeding truck as she crossed a poorly lighted street corner on her way to her home, she had been sitting beside me in our office in the Unity Building at a meeting of the board of managers of the Federation. I had been presenting my report of my interview with President Wilson. She had made a motion to approve the report and to concur in its recommendation that the teachers stand by organized Labor in its determination that promotion to public office should not be made a reward for aiding the privileged interests and their beneficiaries in their efforts to destroy the citizenship rights of public school teachers. She spoke to her motion with a tinge of sadness and regret but with no trace of personal resentment toward the members of the Board of Education, who had outlawed the

---

[36]Nockels was secretary and Fitzpatrick, president, of the Chicago Federation of Labor. See note 9, p. 93.

organizations of teachers affiliated with the organized Labor movement and that placed under the same ban the organizations of teachers that had officers not members of the teaching force.

Just before she left the board meeting, she warned us of the necessity of guarding the interests of the classroom teachers, the rank and file, whom she knew, from her own long experience in the classroom, to be the hardest worked and poorest paid group in the service. Once more, she had explained that the discrimination against this group, on whom the heaviest burden of responsibility for the success or failure of the public schools must always rest, is due to the relatively large number in the group as compared to other groups in the system; and that this preponderance of numbers was at once the weakness and the strength of the group. Cocking her hat on the side of her head, as she always did when she was stirred by any emotion, she said, "Abraham Lincoln must have been thinking of them too when he said, 'The Lord must have loved them, He made so many of them.'" That was her farewell.

Never, I think, in the history of Chicago has there been such a spontaneous and sincere mourning for any woman as that which followed Catharine Goggin's death. All of us who knew her and who had worked with her had realized that she had been beloved by those who knew her well. We had no idea of how many people understood and appreciated her magnificent unselfishness, her self-abnegating fortitude. She had never thought of herself, and so a multitude of men and women thought of her when the time came to do her honor. All day and through most of the night, while her body lay in the Council chamber in City Hall, men and women, tens of thousands of them, passed through to take a last look on the face of the woman who had worked for other women. Judges of the courts, union Labor officials, representatives of the City administration, members of the Board of Education, Aldermen, principals of schools, and teachers made up the long line of mourners. Many wept as they passed.

On the next day, after a requiem mass in the Cathedral of the Holy Name, all that was mortal of Catharine Goggin was laid at rest in Calvary Cemetery. On her grave was set the great circular panel of roses, made to represent the seal of the Chicago Federation of Labor, above which were set the words, "Her spirit lives."[37]

Two weeks later, the board of managers of the Chicago Teachers' Federation sent a letter to the man who had driven the Marshall Field

---

[37]A forty-eight page issue of *Margaret A. Haley's Bulletin* was published on Jan. 27, 1916, in memory of Goggin. The issue of proper fender legislation was a continuing topic before the City Council for months and stories on this subject appeared often in the *Day Book* in 1916 and 1917.

and Company truck which had struck Catharine Goggin. The letter told him that the board had just learned of his grief over the accident.

> We want to lessen your grief (they wrote) by telling you that the teachers as well as the law hold you guiltless. Selfish greed in the lack of a fender, and the failure of the City to enforce the fender ordinance, and light and otherwise protect its dark and dangerous places—these were the cause—not you.

In death as in life, she was struck by the power that disregards everything in its brutal race for money.

7

From the time in 1895 when Governor Altgeld caused to be inserted a tenure clause in the pension law for teachers, it was believed that the public school teachers had security of position, which enabled them to improve their educational work. They believed that their tenure in office was guaranteed by state law and thought that the tenure extended for the whole period of a teacher's service. The Loeb-Rothmann forces, however, devised an idea that the teachers had to be elected every year. The Board of Education could, they decided, put out any teacher at the close of the term in June. Although the Loeb Rule had been thrown out of court, the Loeb cohorts acted as if it had been sustained by the judicial tribunal. On June 27, 1916, the Board of Education threw out sixty-eight teachers from their posts in the Chicago public schools. Thirty-eight of these—the thirty-eight whose records were above question—were members of the Chicago Teachers' Federation. Mary F. Dwyer, one of the best teachers in Chicago, was among them.[38]

The political manipulation by which the measure was carried through the Board was skillfully conceived and perpetrated. The original list, prepared by Rothmann and Loeb, of teachers not to be re-elected had seventy-two names. Nearly all of the "thirty-eight" upon the list were or had been officers of the Chicago Teachers' Federation. Those who had not been actively associated with the Federation were men or women credited to those Board members whom the Rothmann-Loeb group thought could be manipulated from their allegiance to the

---

[38]The federation continued to defend its right to affiliate with organized labor. In the midst of this crisis, eight associations joined together and formed the American Federation of Teachers on April 15, 1916. The CTF was the heart of the new national union and designated Local Number One. The other area locals included the two high school affiliates, which had developed with CTF encouragement, the Federation of Men Teachers (1912) and the Federation of Women High School Teachers (1914) and the nearby group organized in Gary, Indiana (1916). Organizations from New York City, Washington, D.C., Scranton, Pennsylvania, and Oklahoma City provided the eight locals required to obtain a national charter from the American Federation of Labor. See Reid, "Professionalization," pp. 248-50.

general teaching force by their desire to keep their friends in the schools. The Board members involved would normally have stood up for the rights of the seventy-two teachers; but, in order to save the four on the list for whom they were politically responsible, they sacrificed the sixty-eight. They did more than that, too, for "the 68" stood as symbol for all public school teachers. If they paid the price of their right to free speech and free thought by the loss of their jobs, it meant that every public school teacher in the United States would be under the same threat. The failure of these Board members to live up to their moral convictions was one of the greatest tragedies that I have ever witnessed.

The dropping of the sixty-eight teachers was signal for an uprising in the public schools. For the first time, all teachers in the system realized how precarious was their means of livelihood and how dependent they were upon the political, commercial, and economic motives of men who knew little and cared less about the fundamental principles of education. All over Chicago, meetings of protest were held, and it was with a united front that the teachers went into court action.

The battle ended with a decision from the Supreme Court of Illinois on the 19th of April, 1917, anniversary of the first battle for American independence. The decision, which Ella Flagg Young called the "Dred Scott Decision of Education," practically sustained the action of the Board of Education. The Supreme Court held that the Board of Education, so far as any law that existed was concerned, was free to elect any teachers or no teachers in the entire system. According to this decision, any board of education in the State of Illinois could refuse to elect anyone except blue-eyed teachers or red-haired teachers or tall teachers or short teachers or thin teachers or stout teachers or spectacled teachers or Ziegfield chorus girls. If any board of education in the state wanted torch singers instead of educators, it was at liberty to have them. The decision held, too, that under the law a teacher's term expired at the end of a school year in June. From the end of the school year until the time of re-employment, no teacher was in any system in the state of Illinois. The teacher, leaving her classroom at the end of the school year, had no assurance that she could come back at the opening of the next school year. It was, by and large, the most devilish, dastardly, and devastating opinion ever leveled against American public school education.[39]

On the day after the Supreme Court rendered this decision, Governor Lowden signed the Otis law. The law, called for its sponsor, Ralph C. Otis, member of the Chicago Board of Education and one of the heirs

[39]*The People* v. *City of Chicago*, 278 Ill. 318 (1917).

of the estate which held the Board of Education lease upon the immensely valuable southwest corner of State and Madison Streets, modified the Supreme Court decision for the City of Chicago. The law had been passed by the Legislature and had been awaiting the governor's signature. Had Governor Lowden signed it at any time before the Supreme Court decision, it would have been wiped out by that decision. His delay in the signing saved the city of Chicago from the condition which still exists in Illinois outside the city.[40]

The Otis law, which gave the teachers tenure, provided that they could not be dismissed except with a trial on charges. In case of such a trial, they must be given thirty days to prepare their cases, and the Board must, by a majority of the Board, approve any committee report upon such action, before the committee report could be effective. Trial must take place before the whole Board. A majority of the Board was required for approval of any verdict. The teacher so tried would have a right to appeal to the courts for a review.[41]

The teachers of Chicago gained in the long run by the Rothmann-Loeb Rule and the Rothmann-Loeb action of throwing out "the 68." For years, they had been taking their tenure for granted. The attack upon it, unjust though it was, stirred them into making that tenure something actual and established in specific terms.[42]

8

The entrance of the United States into the World War accomplished what Jacob Loeb and William Rothmann had not been able to do. It alienated the great body of teachers in the Chicago public schools from the American Federation of Labor.

If the road to war had been a straight one, teachers of the Chicago public schools would have gladly made common cause with the American Federation of Labor in defense of our nation. We knew, however, that tremendous forces outside the groups of organized Labor in the United States had been working to influence those Labor leaders who were advocating the entrance of the United States into the war.

[40]Frank O. Lowden (1861-1943) was a Chicago lawyer, gentleman farmer, and a former director of the Pullman Company, who served as governor from 1917 to 1921. The Otis Law also reduced the Board of Education from twenty-one to eleven members; this fulfilled one of the recommendations of the 1898 Harper Report. For a careful study of Lowden's career, see William T. Hutchinson, *Lowden of Illinois: The Life of Governor Frank O. Lowden*, 2 vols. (Chicago: University of Chicago Press, 1957).

[41]*Laws of Illinois, 1919*, p. 723. The governor signed the bill on Apr. 20, 1917.

[42]On May 20, 1917, the Chicago Federation of Labor adopted a report from President John Fitzpatrick recommending the withdrawal of the CTF. This report is in the CTF files. The following day the CTF sent a petition to the board requesting the readmission of the thirty-eight federation teachers and this was accepted. Those teachers who wished to return were able to do so in the fall of 1917.

In 1916, the American Federation of Teachers, a recently organized fledgling, sent, without consultation with any other group, a Chicago School principal [Charles B. Stillman] to a conference in Washington. This conference, purporting to be representative of American school teachers affiliated with organized Labor, was really less conference than springboard for the British propaganda.[43]

Early in 1917, Samuel Gompers, by birth an English Jew, and then president of the American Federation of Labor, called a meeting of the chiefs of the Federation and its affiliated groups. At this meeting, Gompers influenced these leaders to agree to back Wilson if he went into war. No declaration of war was made until this agreement was made.

A Labor lobby at Springfield held a closed meeting in order to get across the Gompers program of an approval of war.

The cumulative effect of the dissemination of this information was that the Chicago public school teachers lost confidence in the integrity of those Labor leaders who had either blindly followed Samuel Gompers or who had been willing to trade their moral opposition to war for the sake of material benefits which certain of their groups would secure from the waging of such a war. The feeling of betrayal, not always voiced but always present in the minds of those of us who knew the situation, accomplished what all our avowed enemies had not done. It destroyed the unity of Labor.

War has, however, its own unities. With the biggest battle of the world going on, it was not possible for anyone to carry on little local battles. We saw, though, even while it was happening, that a great war was eroding what little wars had not done. Woodrow Wilson once said that, for the United States, the war had turned back the hands of the clock fifty years. All the great liberal measures which he had advocated—among them those for which we had fought—were swept away by the mighty flood of conflict. Not merely the legislation of liberalism but the spirit of liberalism went down before it.

I knew something of this, although I saw it then through the darkened glass of contemporaneous vision instead of through the clear

---

[43]Charles B. Stillman (1885-1948) was the president of the Federation of Men Teachers, which had been organized in 1912 along the lines of the CTF. A woman high school teachers federation was established two years later. He was elected president of the American Federation of Teachers when it was formed in April, 1916. Haley was designated national organizer but local affairs kept her busy in Chicago. The opposition to World War I, shaped by her sympathies toward Irish independence, was so intense that she was permanently estranged from the AFL following this March, 1917, conference. Haley used this episode to explain the CTF withdrawal from the ranks of organized labor. While this may have been a factor, it seems more likely that the withdrawal was a condition for the return to the classroom of the ousted federation members in the fall of 1917. Haley to the editor of the *Christian Science Monitor*, Dec. 3, 1937, CTF Files; Reid, "Professionalization," pp. 247-52.

crystal of hindsight, as I stood beside Ella Flagg Young's grave on a cold, windy day of October, 1918. I had seen her a few months before in Pittsburgh at the convention of the National Education Association. As she had come out on the platform, the audience rose as one man in the most spontaneous tribute I have ever seen given to a human being. She spoke then with a spiritual power which swayed everyone there not only for the hour but for a long time afterward. Listening to her then, I had thought of her as symbol for the time through which she had lived, a woman of genuine greatness, of magnificent vision, of tremendous accomplishment. She had been the old America marching onward in hope, in courage, in clarity of vision. Now she was dead.

Even in the presence of death, emotions other than sorrow sometimes rise. Before the funeral cortege reached the cemetery, a group of teachers had already gathered there. One of them sighted a huge wreath which had been sent by Jacob Loeb. Indignantly, she snatched it from the place of honor which it had been given and put it on another grave, saying that Ella Flagg Young could not rest in peace under those flowers. Nellie Nowlan happened to see it resting against a headstone that bore an Irish name. She snatched it off once more and put it on a grave whose headstone indicated that a Nordic slept beneath. "No Irishman could lie under that," she said.

It was days afterward before anyone realized that the Comic Muse had walked hand in hand that day with the Muse of Tragedy.

Margaret Haley and other referendum petitioners, Springfield (from the *Times Magazine*, vol. 1, no. 3, (February 1907)

Catherine Goggin (courtesy of the Chicago Historical Society)

Ella Flagg Young, ca. 1911 (photo by Mabel Sykes, courtesy of the Chicago Historical Society)

Cartoon of the 1903 meeting of the National Education Association, *Chicago Record Herald*, July 11, 1903 (courtesy of the Illinois State Historical Library)

Cartoon against the *Chicago Tribune* from the *Public*, November 29, 1906, reprinted in the *CTF Bulletin*, December 7, 1906

THE BABES IN THE WOOD,
And the Dumb Watch-dogs of Chicago.

Cartoon on the issue of school lands from the *Public*, March 2, 1907, as printed in the *CTF Bulletin*, March 1, 1907

Margaret Haley (in white) campaigning for woman suffrage in California, ca. September-October, 1911 (courtesy of the Chicago Historical Society)

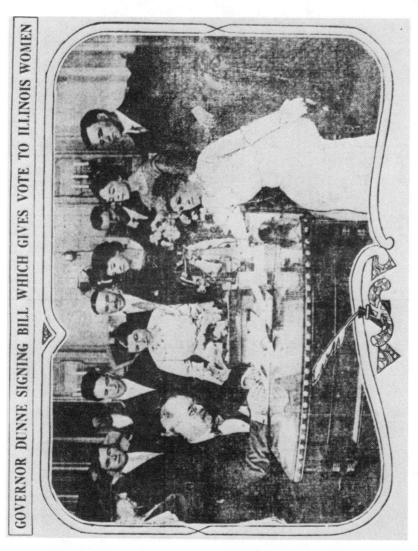

GOVERNOR DUNNE SIGNING BILL WHICH GIVES VOTE TO ILLINOIS WOMEN

Governor Edward F. Dunne signing the Illinois suffrage bill, June 26, 1913. Haley is seated across from the governor. *Chicago Record Herald*, June 27, 1913 (courtesy of the Illinois State Historical Library)

Campaigning against the proposed 1922 Illinois Constitution, Haley with telephone, ca. November, 1922 (courtesy of the Chicago Historical Society)

⚙[VIII]⚙

One War Is Over; Another Begins

1

The World War had shown the United States to be one vast and fallow field for all propaganda. The sowers of the seed—those agencies of power and prestige who already knew the methods and benefits of propaganda—realized during the war that the public schools of America were ideal engines for their purpose. As a result, the essential character of the public schools has been changed in these years which have followed the war. Institutions designed to be breeding places of free and individual opinion have been converted into proving grounds for experiments designed to aid and abet established privilege. Never in the history of the United States have the public schools been so harassed and circumscribed by influences trying to use them for private gain as they have been since 1918. The story of the schools of Chicago through the torrential Twenties and the troubled Thirties has been a story of siege. Students and teachers alike have been beleaguered by forces which have striven to make them merely ciphers instead of integers in education. The tendency of the times made the Chicago public schools nothing better than a battlefield. They would have been conquered territory had it not been for the American fighting spirit of the public school teacher.

The reactionary spirit of war was still in the air when Illinois' political leaders decided to call a convention for the revision of the state constitution [1920]. There is no doubt that the constitution of Illinois is one of the most restrictive ordinances with which a great commonwealth has ever been bound. The people of the state were aware of the necessity of changing those provisions which prevented intelligent progress. The time, however, was one of the worst which could have been chosen for such change. Probably that is exactly why it was chosen. Those state leaders who did not want change were astute enough to realize that they could make a showing of apparent progress while at the same time maintaining the old order.

183

At that, however, there might have been a chance of the establishment of a new constitution if the convention had not made such
fool mistakes on tax revision in the proposed legislation that they got
everybody in the state by the ears. Even at that time there were forces in
Illinois interested in genuine reform and with sufficient representation
at that convention to be able at least to arouse public interest in
forward-looking measures. One of the most significant sessions of the
body came on the day when David Felmley, who was the president of
the Illinois State Normal School, talked nearly all day.[1]

Felmley was an ardent Single Taxer and took delight in answering
the many questions—some of them incredibly stupid—that were hurled
at him by members of the convention. "Private Joe" Fifer, former
governor of the state and one of its most distinguished mossbacks, was
astounded to learn that a man like Felmley was head of a state normal
school. Fifer couldn't get away from amazement at the idea that a man
with Felmley's beliefs should ever be in a public school in any capacity, even in a one-room school. It was beyond Fifer's comprehension
that a Felmley could ever have become head of a normal school.
Although neither Felmley nor any other reformers were able to make
any constitutional change in the state, nevertheless 1920 was not altogether a lost year since it gave them opportunity to keep alight their
torch of regeneration.[2]

[1]Haley was a member of the Advisory Council of the Constitutional Convention
League of Illinois. Founded in 1914, the goal of the league was to modernize "our
outgrown and repressive State Constitution of 1870." George E. Cole, president, to Otto
J. Krampikovsky, August 18, 1914, Otto J. Krampikovsky Papers, Illinois State Historical Society.

The Constitutional Convention, which was convened by Governor Frank Lowden on
January 6, 1920, completed its work in September, 1922. Three major issues in the
debates were home rule for the city of Chicago, the initiative and referendum, and tax
reform. Each of these represented concerns of urban reformers which were shared by
Haley and her colleagues in the CTF during the organization's formative years. Haley's
disappointment with the results of the convention reflected the failure to resolve these
continuing issues which were basic to Chicago and its relationship to the state of
Illinois. Janet M. Clark, "Constitution Making in Illinois: A Comparison of Two
Conventions, 1920 and 1970" (Ph.D. diss., University of Illinois, 1973), p. 81.

On March 10, 1920, several speakers including the superintendent of public instruction, Francis J. Blair; the superintendent of schools in Chicago, Peter C. Mortenson;
Mrs. Ida Fursman, president of the CTF; and Robert C. Moore, the secretary of the
Illinois State Teachers' Association, presented testimony on the subject of the public
schools. In their presentations both Haley and David Felmley (1857-1930), who served as
president of Illinois State Normal from 1900 until his death, gave major attention to tax
reform and presented arguments for rates which would tax increases in land values
higher than other forms of property. For Felmley's testimony see *Debates of the Constitutional Convention of the State of Illinois*, 1920-1922, vol. I, pp. 527-54. Haley's
remarks are found on pp. 562-77.

[2]Joseph W. Fifer (1840-1938) was one of the eighty-five Republican delegates to the
102-member Convention. He had served as governor of Illinois from 1889 to 1903. The
proposed new constitution was defeated by a margin of more than five to one in a special

Another steam roller went into operation during that same year. The forces of reaction within the National Education Association, believing as did the Illinois leaders that the time was ripe for reassertion of their doctrines, had selected Salt Lake City as the place for its annual convention, knowing that the geographical location of that place would prevent an SOS call to the grade teachers of any large city, an action which had saved situations in earlier years in Milwaukee and Chicago.

The city and state superintendents of Utah had assured panic-stricken officials of the organization—the old guard had come into control again after the death of Ella Flagg Young and after ten years of absence Dr. Nicholas Murray Butler was again in attendance—that they could keep the teachers of their state under control. The official pronunciamento of the organization solemnly announced that the meeting of 1920 was "for the especial purpose of saving education for all time to come from the horrible wiles and the witchery of the one little woman," according to A. E. Winship, editor of the *Journal of Education*. Although Dr. Winship overestimated, I think, their fear of me, none the less some fear seemed to exist since with the first meeting the steam roller advanced upon me according to prearrangement so that I was immediately denied a hearing.[3]

By another prearrangement, a thousand voices in the great Tabernacle took up the cry, "Question, question, question." David E. McKay, head of the educational interests of the Latter Day Saints, tried to protest against the reiterated shouts, but Dr. Richard R. Lyman, his co-official, demanded that I be heard. The steam roller went into intermediate, and I was called to the platform. All that I asked was for a re-reading of a sentence brought in by the resolutions committee. The sentence stated that the committee "had resolved that the unrest of the times must not invade the teachers' ranks." I asked what had become of a resolution on tenure, which was a little dearer to the hearts

state election held December 12, 1922. In recalling this campaign, Robert C. Moore, secretary of the Illinois State Teachers' Association, described Haley's role and said, "Many of the advocates of ratification placed the *blame* for this defeat on the teachers,— but we call it the *honor.*" *Haley Memorial Booklet*, p. 49.

A new constitution for the state of Illinois was ratified by the voters on November 18, 1970, following the state's sixth constitutional convention. Robert P. Howard, *Illinois: A History of the Prairie State* (Grand Rapids, Mich.: Eerdmans, 1972), pp. 563-67 (hereafter cited as Howard, *Illinois*).

[3]Winship's report of the meeting is found in *Journal of Education*, 92 (Aug. 19, 1920), pp. 119-20. He referred sardonically to Haley as "the Holy Terror." The success of the NEA's membership campaign resulted in an organization with more than 100,000 members. The reorganization plan called for a representative assembly of 600. Haley and the Chicago teachers had been able to block this at the meeting in Milwaukee in 1919 but were unable to do so in Salt Lake City. The plan brought the system of local domination which Haley had been able to use to advantage to an end.

of grade teachers. The answer was unsatisfactory, even to the women who had been skillfully loyalized by the Great Leaders. A new resolution on tenure was then written. I was asked to present it but I said, "You would be suspicious of the Lord's Prayer if I offered it." My refusal safeguarded the passage of the resolution, for it went through unanimously. The battle of Salt Lake City had been won by a laugh.[4]

The cost of living had risen so high in the years following the war and salaries of teachers had remained so low that, with the high prices, the public school teachers of Chicago were in a state of constant anxiety. They had a maximum that, by guess and by gosh, had been put up to a figure of $2000. They'd had to fight like fiends for that, but it was no longer adequate. Two thousand dollars a year meant far less in 1921 that it would have meant in 1911. There was only one way in which the situation could be handled. It was necessary to go before the Illinois Legislature to ask for a tax rate increase.

Just as soon as we began to talk about the need of the increase, politics, high and low, thrust themselves into the picture. The high school men teachers went down to Springfield with a request for a tax rate increase, but they lied about the reason why they were asking it. Instead of saying that they wanted more money for themselves, they said that they wanted it to decrease the number of children to a teacher. Their maximum salaries were $3400 a year at that time. The grade teachers were getting a maximum of $2000. Therefore, we grade teachers were not afraid to talk about the real issue. In 1921, $2000 did not represent a living wage for men and women who had the responsibilities and obligations of the Chicago public school teachers. In addition to their teaching work, the grade school teachers were then part-time mothers. So many women were working outside their homes that tens of thousands of children were being left to the care of teachers not only throughout the entire school day but through recreation time as well. When the mother works away from the home, a great part of her natural burden falls upon the grade school teacher. The teachers knew that they were earning and entitled to a higher salary than they were receiving. They wanted it clearly understood, however, that they asked only that to which they were entitled.

We took a stand at that time: This, we said, is the last tax rate increase for which we shall ask the Legislature. The tax rate increase, we declared, is not essentially the right method of procedure. The method of assessment of property is wrong. There is a lack of equalization—the same old thing that we started out to fight about when we tried to make the State Board of Equalization assess the corporations.

[4]The "battle of Salt Lake City" was the passage of the reorganization plan.

We do not want the burden to fall upon the shoulders of the people least able to bear it. There should be, we said, a correction made in the assessment. The burden of taxation falls most heavily on the people who don't and won't get their taxes fixed. The whole tax fixing business keeps secret from the people what the assessors are doing. The whole process is wrong.

We made our declaration publicly. We believed then, as we believe now, that no honest and genuinely democratic government can exist without an honest method of taxation. As citizens and tax payers as well as teachers and public servants, we have crusaded for honesty in tax legislation and tax administration.

In 1921, William Hale Thompson was still mayor of Chicago. By that time, the tendency of some of his lieutenants was so well known that the Legislature, at least that part of it which was anti-Thompson, feared to give any tax rate increase lest the Thompson Board would gobble it up for some other purpose and not make any increase in the teachers' salaries. I was called before the house committee on revenue in the Legislature when the tax rate increase bill was being considered. Its members told me that they had no assurance at all that the money from the tax rate would be used to increase teachers' salaries.

I said, "If you don't give the increase in the tax rate, there won't be any increase in the teachers' salaries, and you've admitted that their salaries are too low for present prices. If you do give it and there's any indication that the Board will squander it, you won't be to blame for that. I'll give you my word that we'll put up a fight and we'll get the money for the teachers or we'll put that Board where it belongs."

The committee on revenue recommended the bill. The Legislature passed it. The governor signed it. But it was the next year before we received the increase for which this bill provided the funds. We nearly had to send the Thompson Board to jail to get it. That Board wanted to use the money for other purposes. They tried to make terms with the teachers to bring them into the political machine. We had a stiff fight with the Thompsonites but we won it.[5]

[5] The perennial school financing problem created by an expanding school population and the lagging response of the local tax structure was exacerbated by the inflationary impact of World War I. One study indicated that, nationally, teachers' salaries rose 16 percent from 1914 to 1919, while the cost of living increased more than 100 percent. E. S. Evenden, "The Payment of American Teachers," *Nation*, 109 (Aug. 30, 1919), p. 295.

Both the building fund and the educational fund were increased by the 1921 legislature. The CTF pointed out that the Thompson Board increased expenditures for teachers' salaries from approximately $14.6 million to $20 million, a 36.6 percent increase, while monies for other purposes went from $4.376 million to $8.7 million, a 100 percent increase, in the years from 1919 to 1921. *Why The Chicago Teachers Are Irritated and Dissatisfied*, March 29, 1922, pamphlet, CTF Files.

William Hale Thompson had missed a fine opportunity of establishing an honest and efficient Board of Education in Chicago. He had
been mayor for two years when the Otis Law was passed [1917],
changing the membership of the Board from twenty-one to eleven.
Under the law, he might have thrown out, by the 1st of July, all the
hold-overs from the old Harrison Board, thereby breaking down that
organization with its traditions of antagonism to the teaching force.
The teachers of Chicago were not unfriendly to Thompson. They
recognized that, although his methods were sometimes crude and
absurd, the man had a certain fundamental democracy of intention.
His ridiculous declarations against the textbooks which failed to vilify
George III of England to the extent the mayor thought desirable had
made him an object of opprobrium to the world at large; but there
were large numbers of Chicago school teachers who realized even then
that there was a certain measure of justice in his attacks. They knew
even better than he did how widely and deeply war propaganda had
sapped some of the old established ideals of American patriotism.
Thompson's misfortune was his inability to phrase his contentions
with clarity and dignity. In public he was a clown; in private, as an
official, he was the tool of a ruthless and unscrupulous machine. "The
Poor Swede," as Fred Lundin called himself, Dr. John Dill Robertson,
Al Severinghaus, and a dozen others engineered the Thompson policy—and landed it in a ditch.[6]

Thompson had let the old Harrison Board of Education remain in
office longer than its legal term under the Otis Law. He had refused to
reappoint Rothmann, but he had reappointed Jacob Loeb. He had also appointed to fill a vacancy Mrs. F. E. Thornton. John D. Shoop,

[6]Lundin, Robertson, and Severinghaus were political associates of Thompson. Big
Bill had won a second four-year term in 1919. Fred Lundin (1868-1947) was considered to
be the brains behind the machine; reportedly, he told board member Hart Hanson, "To
hell with the public. We're at the trough now, and we are going to feed." Wendt and
Kogan, *Big Bill of Chicago*, p. 210.

The sordid scandals of the Thompson school board during his second term in office
forced the mayor to bow out of the 1923 election campaign. Haley's comments about
Thompson's war on textbooks refer to his successful campaign for reelection in 1927
when Thompson denounced McAndrew as a tool of King George. Her sympathetic
treatment of Thompson indicates the effectiveness of his nativist tactics. Haley's strong
identity with the cause of Ireland seemed to overshadow the graft and corruption of the
Thompson years.

Following Thompson's defeat in his bid for a fourth term in 1933, a *Chicago Tribune*
editorial included the following: "For Chicago, Thompson has meant filth, corruption,
obscenity, idiocy and bankruptcy. He has given the city an international reputation for
moronic buffoonery, barbaric crime, triumphant hoodlumism, unchecked graft, and a
dejected citizenship. He nearly ruined the property and completely destroyed the pride of
the city. He made Chicago a byword of the collapse of American civilization." Apr. 8,
1931. *Ibid.*, p. 333.

appointed under the old law as Superintendent of Schools after Ella Flagg Young's final resignation, remained in that office until 1918, when he was succeeded by Peter A. Mortenson. In July, 1917, the Thompson Board of eleven members was appointed and confirmed by the City Council. Some time later, it developed that Thompson had promised to give Jacob Loeb a Board that he would control and of which he was to have been president. Instead of that, however, Thompson left Loeb on the Board, but put on no one to support him. Edwin S. Davis became the president. Then the ousted members of the old Board took the matter into court and won reinstatement, and in 1918 Loeb returned to the presidency through the votes of those old members who had been reinstated by court order. In 1919, however, the Thompson Board, including Loeb, was back. For four years it functioned as one of the most efficiently political of all the Thompson administration political units.[7]

It had, however, one member whom I could never in honesty or fairness group with the others. Dr. Sadie Bay Adair remains in my mind as one of the truest and most loyal friends whom the public school teachers of Chicago ever had. Personally honest, absolutely courageous, she was held by no class consciousness and by no dread of offending any of those interests who sought to dominate the public schools. She had a freedom which Jane Addams never enjoyed and she used that freedom as Jane Addams had never been able, for the furtherance of the deeper interests of both teachers and students in the schools. She was hampered, of course, by her associations with the Board of which she was a member, but she remains in my memory as an outstanding woman citizen of my city.[8]

The majority of the Board, however, had little interest in things academic. Most of them rendered unto Caesar everything that was his and a little bit more. New schools went up like mushrooms on the prairies, not because they were needed, but because their building was part of the political system, benefitting builders, contractors, and other friends of the machine. New supplies were poured in to replace others that were in no way worn out. The situation finally became public scandal to such an extent that the Democratic leaders of the city realized that exposure of the methods of the Thompson Board would

[7]In addition to Shoop and Mortenson, a third superintendent, Charles Chadsey, also served for a brief period during these years. The chronology is correct. A board whose membership was not legally contested was finally constituted on October 20, 1919. The Thompson members were characterized as the "Solid Six." *Proceedings, Board of Education*, 1918-19, pp. 14-26, 1919-20, pp. 1-3, 853. See also Counts, *School and Society*, pp. 251-53.

[8]Sadie Bay Adair (1870-1944) was a physician appointed to the board by Thompson. She opposed the actions of the "Solid Six" during her years of service.

make excellent campaign material for the election of 1923. It was the plan of the Democratic leadership to nominate as a candidate for the mayoralty Judge Dever, who was a jurist above reproach. With his impending nomination, the Democrats went into action to indict the Thompson Board and, in the last days of August, 1922, brought the matter to a head by Grand Jury action.[9]

2

The attacks, led by the *Chicago Daily News*, on the Thompson Board came so thick and fast that on Labor Day, 1922, Robert Emmet Crowe, State's Attorney of Cook County and one of the leaders of the Thompson machine, asked Isaiah T. Greenacre to accept a position of Assistant State's Attorney in the preparation of cases against the Board.

Throughout the latter part of August, Crowe had been handling before the Grand Jury an investigation of the Thompson Board. Our Federation had been criticizing not only the Board of Education but also the method in which Crowe's office had been conducting the investigation. The public demand for competent and honest legal direction grew so great that Crowe was forced to take cognizance of it. He finally agreed to ask Greenacre to take a place as Special State's Attorney. That position would have given him considerable freedom of action in the investigation. Instead of that, however, Crowe made him an Assistant State's Attorney.

Greenacre asked us, the officers of the Chicago Teachers' Federation, what we thought he should do. He said that he realized he was being given the position in order to embarrass us, but that he thought it would be a serious mistake not to take it. Unless he was asked by us not to do it, he would accept the appointment.

At the end of his first forty-eight hours in the State's Attorney's office, Greenacre had found out about a "slush fund" gathered by the engineers of the Chicago public schools for distribution to certain

[9]A series of grand juries were convened in the summer of 1922. They found gross irregularities and misconduct in the purchase of school lands and equipment and furnishings. The board attorney, William Bither (1867-?), was sentenced to a one- to five-year term for conspiring to obtain school funds fraudulently. The board president, Edwin S. Davis, and vice president, Albert Severinghaus, were indicted, along with Fred Lundin and several others, for defrauding the schools of more than one million dollars. In the midst of this scandal, Thompson withdrew from the 1923 campaign. Wendt and Kogan, *Big Bill of Chicago*, pp. 201-2, 206-15.

William Dever (1862-1929) was a longtime jurist and an Irish Catholic who was identified with the reform element of the Democratic party. His strict enforcement of prohibition together with the controversies surrounding the administration of superintendent of schools William McAndrew brought about his defeat in his campaign for reelection in 1927. Thompson was returned for his third term as mayor of Chicago.

members of the Thompson Board. The money had been delivered to these members of the Board at what was called the "teapot party." The purported occasion of the party was the giving of a silver service to Albert H. Severinghaus. In the silver service was the collected money.[10]

I also know something about the gathering of that fund and I was summoned to appear before the Grand Jury. I hated to tell some of the things which had been told to me and in the Grand Jury room I hesitated for a long time. I told the members why I was hesitating. I was trying to think whether I'd be of more benefit to the public by destroying my usefulness as a confidant of people who were accustomed to bring to me material for the bombs that they themselves were not in a position to make or throw. I thought, if I tell some things about how I learned of certain affairs and what I learned, I shall never be useful again in exactly that way. I may never be able to learn anything again. I hesitated for quite a long time and the jurors did not push me. Finally I decided that I'd better tell them what I knew.

I said, "I'm not going to give you any names except those that are in the public press and I'll tell you who else knows what I'm going to tell you. You can go to the Chief of Police, Charles Fitzmorris, and ask him to give you the names of the two policemen who were in the Masonic Temple building for an entire day." I told them the date as nearly as I knew it. It was the day on which the engineers were coming down to the Masonic Temple to deliver the slush fund money for members of the Board of Education.

I told them, "Mr. Fitzmorris knows the two members of the police force whom he assigned to that building; Mr. Fitzmorris can tell you who they were." The police had been guarding while the engineers had been putting that money in. Either they or other policemen similarly assigned had guarded it all night.

The next morning, the *Chicago Tribune* and the *Herald and Examiner* ran stories that I had "dealt in glittering generalities" when I had talked to the Grand Jury. Was I hot under the collar? I called up Richard Burritt of the *Daily News* and said, "I want to be sure that you don't print the same story."

Burritt said, "I wouldn't have printed it. I knew it was a lie."

I said, "I'll tell the other afternoon papers. I'll go right over there to the court and stand up Gorman (he was an Assistant State's Attorney at the time) and tell him he lied. I'll get hold of Judge Kickham Scanlan (the judge in charge of the Grand Jury session)."

Burritt said, "Get over to Scanlan and tell him that you want to get in again to that Grand Jury."

[10]Albert Severinghaus was one of the "Solid Six" and the vice president of the board.

I called all the afternoon papers, told them that the *Tribune* and *Herald and Examiner* articles were untrue and that I was going over to Judge Scanlan and the Grand Jury to tell them.

There was a very important meeting of the Board of Education at two o'clock that afternoon. I had to tell Mortenson, the Superintendent of Schools, that I'd be there as soon as I could. I told him, "Don't let John Dill Robertson (the president of the Board) put anything over you today. Don't let him bluff you. He will if he can." John Dill, who had been Commissioner of Health with Thompson and who had been shifted over to the Board of Education, was one of the slickest workers of the Thompson regime. He was neither educator nor administrator, but he was carrying out the will of his particular group on the Board. He was afraid I'd take him before the Grand Jury and so I was able to outbluff him. The Board of Education was going to adopt a whole new set of rules. Peter A. Mortenson, the Superintendent, was fighting the change, which was certain to militate against the welfare of the schools. Eventually the changed rules went through. Neither a good superintendent nor a Grand Jury investigation was sufficient to stop that Thompson Board from putting over whatever it intended.[11]

Then I went to Judge Scanlan. A legal question of vital import had just arisen: The question of whether an August Grand Jury could hold over as a Special Grand Jury for the month of September. The August Grand Jury was a particularly good investigating organization. I told the judge that Greenacre thought that the jury could hold, although he realized that there would be a legal question about its continuance. Judge Scanlan told me that he would act on whatever Greenacre would present to him, but that he must have the material early that afternoon as his office expired at five o'clock. I didn't know what to do, whether to get to Greenacre at once and let my private fight go by the board. My private fight had grown, too, with something that Judge Scanlan had told me. He said that Gorman had denied that he had given to the newspapers the story about my appearance before the Grand Jury.

I said, "I think Gorman's lying."

"Well," he said, "I can't help that."

I said, "I'm going behind it."

"Well, go to it. I can't do anything about it."

I said, "He lied about me and I'm not going to let him get away with it."

[11]Robertson was president of the board following the indictment of Davis in 1922. He was a former associate of William Lorimer and a prominent advisor of Thompson. The former mayor used Lundin and Robertson as foils to explain the administration problems of his previous terms to the voters in 1926 and 1927. Wendt and Kogan, *Big Bill of Chicago*, pp. 226-28.

When I went out of Judge Scanlan's office, a group of newspaper reporters—Hilding Johnson of the *Herald and Examiner*, John Herrick of the *Tribune*, Frank Cipriani of the *Post*, Richard Burritt and Gregory Dillon of the *News*, and A. L. Sloan of the *American* among them—were standing Gorman up against the wall.

They all turned toward me as I said, "Hello, Mr. Gorman. So you called my statement before the Grand Jury 'glittering generalities?'"

He said, "No; I didn't."

I said, "Mr. Gorman, you did."

He said, "I wasn't the only one in there."

"You were the only one except the Grand Jury. There was no one on that Grand Jury who would tell it. I know it was you. I'm going in there to find out, to put it up to them."

Gorman said, "I didn't say *that*."

Every newspaper man there howled, "You *did* say that."

Herrick said, "I wrote the *Tribune* article because you told me that."

Cipriani piped up, "You told me that, too."

Hilding Johnson shouted, "You gave me that story."

They all stood by one another, and Gorman stood stolid while I said, "Do you call it 'glittering generalities' to tell the Grand Jury where the slush fund was collected and to tell them where it was deposited? Didn't I tell that Grand Jury where it was?"

If he hadn't said "Yes," I'd have gone right back to the Grand Jury room to verify my statement. But Gorman said, "Yes."

"Didn't I tell you about the Masonic Temple?"

"Yes."

"Didn't I tell you that Fitzmorris would tell which policemen he had sent to guard the money?"

"Yes."

"Didn't I tell you that the money came from the engineers of the public schools.?"

"Yes."

"Do you call those 'glittering generalities?'"

"I didn't."

Then I went to find Greenacre. Greenacre was able to get word to Scanlan that the jury could continue into September as a Special Grand Jury. Indictments were returned against those Board members who had taken the slush fund money and these men were brought to trial; but the indictments were finally knocked out. Crowe, Thompson, and John Dill Robertson were a trinity of power. It is not a good thing for any one party to be so deeply entrenched. Perhaps, though, it isn't as bad to have one party taking all the blame as it is to have the bipartisan alliances which have always held in Illinois. Nowhere has it shown more plainly than on the Board of Education. There the two parties always play both ends against the middle and the middle is the public.[12]

Unbelievable though it would seem, John Dill Robertson had been put on the Board of Education with an idea of rehabilitating that body. The Thompson crowd knew that some of its members on the Board had gone too far, and Robertson was chosen to save the pieces. In common with most people of the city, we teachers knew little of him beyond the fact that he had ᐧbeen Commissioner of Health, a post which at that time was ordinarily supposed to mark at least an ordinarily good professional record for its holder. We did know, however, that he would be no better than any other machine politician on the Board of Education and we were opposing the ratification of his appointment by the City Council, although we had nothing particularly definite to base it upon until one day a telephone call came to me.

A man who refused to give his name asked, "Are you against John Dill Robertson?"

"Yes."

He said, "If you want the record of his diploma mill, go over to the American Medical Society." He directed me to a floor and a room in that building. "On the table there," he said, "you'll find the *Journal of the American Medical Association*"—he said the date—"and in it you'll find the whole story."[13]

I went immediately to the building and up to the room he had designated. On the table, open at the page where the story began was the magazine containing an article about John Dill Robertson. I secured photographers and obtained a photostatic copy of the record for every member of the City Council. I saw that it was put into the hands of every member before the voting for Robertson began. The members of the Council certainly voted for him with their eyes wide open. Robertson had been found guilty of issuing diplomas to people who had no right to them. With the photostats, I sent to the members of the Council a letter which declared, "If you vote for Robertson as a member of the Board of Education, you're taking the whole responsibility on yourself."

For many years, it had been the established custom of Chicago mayors to secure the signed resignations of their appointees on the

[12]The silver teapot incident with the $78,000 slush fund was discussed editorially by the *Chicago Tribune*, Sept. 9, 1922. Haley's comment regarding bipartisan relationships refers to the alliances across party lines which assisted both Thompson and the later Cermak-Kelly-Nash machine to control the city. Howard, *Illinois*, p. 475. See also pp. 203-4 of this narrative.

[13]The specific reference to the *Journal* is difficult to trace. The editor's search of the indexes for the period 1915-22 was unsuccessful.

same day when they appointed them to office. This, of course, was to keep the appointee from any continuing action distasteful to the mayor and to take away from that executive the onus of dismissal. Thompson followed the custom but he failed to secure some of the resignations of his members on the Board of Education before he had made public announcement of their appointment. After the Council had ratified them, they were "sitting pretty," and some of them refused to make out the formal resignations. One of them was a Democrat, Francis E. Croarkin. Another was a Republican, J. Lewis Coath. Thompson secured the resignations of the rest of his Board, including that of Dr. Sadie Bay Adair, who wanted to recall her resignation after she had given it but found that she couldn't. Thompson did not report the resignations to the City Council because he was waiting for Coath's and Croarkin's so that he could send in a complete new batch of names at one time. As a result, the old Board stayed in as long as did Thompson; but by his action he left a situation which rose like Banquo's ghost at the banquet of his successor.

3

In May, 1921, four bills vitally affecting the interests of the teachers, the children, and the public, were pending in the State Legislature.[14] They were:

Chicago teachers' pension bill;

Bill providing a minimum and minimum-maximum salary for Chicago teachers;

School revenue bill;

School land sales bill, authorizing the Board of Education to sell school lands without the consent of the City Council.

Until May 10, the Board of Education and the teachers worked harmoniously together for the passage of the school revenue bill, which provided for an increase in the tax rate of the Chicago educational fund from $1.20 to $2.92, an increase which would have brought thirteen million dollars to the educational fund.

On the 10th of May, I spoke in behalf of the Chicago Teachers' Federation to the senate committee on education against a motion to recommend the passage of the school land sales bill. This bill had been introduced at the request of the man who was then attorney for the Board of Education, William A. Bither, who spoke that day in favor of its passage. The committee did not recommend its passage. It remained

[14]Chronologically, Haley has moved from the end of the second Thompson administration in 1923 back to 1921. This material (pp. 195-202) is drawn from *Margaret Haley's Bulletin*, 4 (Sept. 30, 1926), pp. 27-38.

in the committee until the end of the session, with the result that the law remained unchanged and the legal power and responsibility of final approval of all sales of school lands remained in the City Council, the elected representatives of the people, a body whose members can be held directly responsible to the people for their acts.

The school land sales bill, if enacted into law, would have transferred that legal power and responsibility to an appointed body, the Board of Education, a body whose members can be held to no direct responsibility to the people for their acts.

On Friday, May 13, three days after the senate committee meeting at which the school land sales bill was put to sleep, Bither, the attorney for the Board of Education, sent me a letter threatening to cut $500,000 from the teachers' salaries if the teachers insisted on opposing that school land sales bill. Bither wrote that it would cost the Board of Education $500,000 a year to hold in its present condition the vacant property under consideration for lease and that the school fund would be depleted to that amount each year. It seemed to him, he said,

> but fair that said amount should be deducted from the salaries of the teachers and prorated equally among the salaries of the teachers. Under no other consideration could I recommend to the Board of Education that they hold this vacant property.
>
> If this proposition meets with your approval, we will abandon the bill now pending in the Legislature and immediately take steps to have $500,000 deducted from the salaries of the teachers for next year and prorated among the different teachers.[15]

The Chicago teachers' pension bill, which had been introduced at the request of the Teachers' Pension Board, had been recommended for passage by the senate committee on education and was on the calendar for second reading.

For more than twenty-five years, whenever the Chicago teachers had attacked a wrong, such as the school land sales bill, or tax-dodging and tax fixing, there had been one sure sign that a backfire against the teachers had started: their pension law was always attacked.

On Tuesday, May 17, four days after the receipt of the threatening letter from the Board's attorney, a representative of the Board of Education [Bither] was discovered outside the door of the senate chamber, just before the senate convened, urging the senator who had introduced the teachers' pension bill to have that bill sent back to the committee on education that day in order that arguments against it might be heard.

Immediately I began to show individual members of the senate a

[15]William A. Bither to Haley, May 13, 1921, as reprinted in *Ibid.*, p. 33.

photographic reproduction of Bither's letter to me. I told them that the teachers of Chicago needed that pension bill, but that they needed their self-respect and integrity and intended to keep those and their pension law as well; and, further, that those teachers would not stand for that school land sales bill in order to get their pension bill or any other bill they favored through the Legislature.

One of the senators showed the copy of the letter to a member of the Board of Education who happened to be in Springfield that day. The member took it to Bither, who was also in Springfield, and told him that the teachers considered that letter as a notice served on them that the Board was fighting through him against their pension bill. Bither left Springfield. The pension bill stayed on the calendar. It was never sent back to the committee. Later it passed the senate, then the house, and was signed by Governor [Len] Small in my presence after I had spent a long night chasing and checking an erroneous legal opinion against the bill which had been filed in the Attorney General's office after the Legislature adjourned. This opinion had been filed without notice to the attorney of the Teachers' Pension Board. We had to prove, and did prove, to the satisfaction of the Attorney General and Governor Small that the opinion was erroneous as charged.[16]

With the teachers' pension bill safe and secure out of the senate committee on education and the school land sales bill safe and secure in that committee, the fight veered to the teachers' salary bill. True to form, the attack on that bill was made through padded estimates. The attorney for the Board of Education again became the battering-ram.

On May 25, eleven days after the receipt of the threatening letter, the Board's attorney presented to the house committee on revenue an itemized estimate which had been prepared in the office of the Board of Education. It showed the itemized and total estimated expenditures from the educational fund for each of the five years, 1921 to 1925. In presenting this estimate, the attorney explained that it was figured on the basis of getting a thirteen million dollar increase from the increased tax rate provided in the pending revenue bill, and on the basis of continuing to pay through those five years the salary schedules then in force, $1600 to $3400 for high school teachers, and $1200 to $2000 for regular elementary teachers, from the kindergarten through the eleventh grade (with all bonuses as then paid).

[16]By legislative act in 1909, all statutes pertaining to the public schools were brought together in the Illinois School Act. The 1921 amendments to this act raised the mandatory contribution of the Board of Education from a matching basis to a requirement that public funds equal $2 for every $1 contributed by the teachers. In addition, in the event that payments should exceed income, the board was authorized to appropriate sufficient funds to balance. *Chicago Teachers' Pension Law*, fourteen-page pamphlet, Aug., 1921, CTF Files; *Laws of Illinois, 1909*, p. 343, *1921*, p. 821.

Against Bither's itemized estimate, we set for comparison the actual expenditures from the educational fund as shown by the official *Proceedings* of the Board of Education for the five-year period of 1917 to 1921. A comparison of these two sets of figures presaged the facts which we afterward proved by 1926, that Bither's estimates had been padded and that the padding was being done to make the legislators believe that the Board could not pay the salary specified in the teachers' salary bill, even if the revenue bill were passed. We told the house committee to pay no attention to Bither's estimate. The members of the committee were confused by "variances" in the statements of the teachers and of Bither, who was aided and abetted by other representatives of the Board present at the meeting. The teachers believed, and showed then, that the estimated expenditures for each year indicated sufficient money to increase the salaries to the amount provided in their salary bill, $1500 minimum, $2500 minimum-maximum. The representatives of the Board denied it, but time later justified us.[17]

The members of the Legislature feared that if that estimate were even approximately correct and the Legislature passed that revenue bill, there might not be money to pay the salary increases provided in the salary bill. The teachers were perfectly honest in stating to the members of the Legislature that they needed the revenue bill in order to pay needed salary increases, and asked its passage for that reason. The house committee on revenue reported the bill out on May 25 with the recommendation that it pass, and it was put on the calendar.

The next day, the Chicago Teachers' Federation held a mass meeting after school hours in the Olympic Theater. The threatening letter of the Board's attorney was read. The teachers retorted by reasserting emphatically their opposition to the school land sales bill. They publicly disclaimed responsibility for the padded estimates and urged the passage of the school revenue bill, to insure the increased revenue, and the teachers' salary bill in order to insure the teachers the payment of the belated increase in salary specified in the bill and needed to pay the post-war prices for the necessities of life.[18]

A few days after the meeting, the pension bill passed the senate. The "variances" and padded estimates, however, defeated the salary bill. Charges were made on the floor of the house that padded estimates and misrepresentation were being used to influence the passage of the revenue bill. The bill was sent back to the revenue committee. There

---

[17]Bither's estimates are compared with actual expenditures for the years 1921 through 1925. In each year the actual expenditures were less than the estimates. The conclusion was that 1927 expenditures would not be likely to reach Bither's estimate for 1925. *Margaret Haley's Bulletin*, 4 (Sept. 30, 1926), p. 34.

[18]*Ibid.*, p. 29.

the teachers demanded a showdown. For four hours, a heated discussion of the situation continued. The members of the Legislature became convinced during that conference that the teachers had no responsibility for any padding that had been done and were entirely opposed to such methods of attempting to secure legislation.

The fate of the revenue bill caused an unofficial but stringent order from the Board of Education that teachers were not to be allowed to go to Springfield. That prohibition, secretly or openly, has been one of the major issues in the war for freedom which we teachers have waged. Time and again, active members of the teaching body who have appeared before the State Legislature to ask for their just dues or for needed reforms have been told by school officials to return to their schools and warned that failure to do so would be cause of their discharge from the system. It has not been possible for a man or woman within the school system to wage the fight absolutely necessary for the maintenance of his rights. Just as the old straw bosses used to penalize the men in their employ who spoke for the unions to which they belonged, so the members of the Board of Education have sought to intimidate the teachers who used their rights and duties of citizenship. The same method of human defence had to be used in both cases, the employment of a man or woman whose means of livelihood could not be taken away from him or her by their enemies. To many people, the term "business representative" may connote what the old term "walking delegate" did; but the result of the method has insured to Chicago teachers a freedom of expression and action that would have been otherwise impossible.

The [Revenue] bill was again recommended to pass by the house committee on revenue. It went back on the calendar and passed the house in almost the last hour of the last day of that heated session.[19]

After the adjournment of the Legislature in 1921, our Federation started a salary campaign to get the Board to increase the teachers' salaries with the increased revenue provided by the Legislature for that purpose. A petition was presented to the Board on November 19, 1921, signed by 6,767 teachers asking for a $1500 minimum and $3000 maximum. The Board paid no attention to the petition, but started to spend the appropriated money like drunken sailors. The teachers grew angrier as the orgy of spending for "incidentals"—purposes other than teachers' salaries—continued. The money being spent was the money which the teachers had secured from the Legislature for the express

---

[19]The bill increased the school tax law to 2 percent of assessed valuation and added approximately thirteen million dollars to the Chicago school fund. Robert C. Moore, "The Moral Jungle," address delivered to the CTF, May 13, 1922, CTF Files.

purpose of paying increases in their salaries. The Board was diverting it to its own—and manifestly illegal—uses.

On March 11, 1922, the first gun in the war on this reckless spending was fired at a meeting of the Federation. On March 31, a mass meeting ordered by the Federation was held in Woods Theater and an overflow meeting around the corner in the Garrick Theater. At these meetings, ten thousand copies of a sixteen-page pamphlet entitled "Why the Teachers Are Irritated and Dissatisfied," which had been prepared and printed by the Federation, were distributed. A committee was authorized to present this pamphlet to the mayor on behalf of the teachers' petition for salary increase.[20]

The committee of teachers authorized for the purpose called on Mayor Thompson on the 6th of April. He showed them a typewritten paper containing a table of percentages which he said that Bither, the Board's attorney, had that day brought to him. He said that their table of percentages was at variance with Bither's percentages, and asked the teachers' committee to go back and check on their percentages.

Although they felt that they were being handed another stone instead of the bread for which they asked, they took Bither's estimate and checked it with their own percentages, which were based upon official records of the Board of Education as shown in its printed *Proceedings*. While they were doing this, some one thought to compare Bither's estimates to the mayor with the estimates he had presented to the Legislature a year earlier. They found that Bither's two sets of percentages were not only at variance with the teachers' percentages but were at variance with each other. They decided that, instead of setting the teachers at the job of reconciling their figures with Bither's, Mayor Thompson would have done better to put Bither at work reconciling Bither's variance with Bither.

Mayor Thompson asked the president of the Board of Education to call in the teachers' committee for discussion at a conference of the so-called "variances." The teachers' committee agreed to enter a public conference as soon as the Board of Education had published its expenditures for the educational fund for the year 1921. The Federation had already discovered that "conferences" of peers behind closed doors may be all right for peers, but when the heavyweights on one side of the conference table have all the guns—six shooters and army pistols at that—and the lightweights on the other side of the table are not allowed to bring even a popgun, such "conferences" become confidence games in which the guns win. Evidently the president of the

[20]The pamphlet reported that Chicago teachers' salaries ranked twenty-fourth of urban school systems while the city ranked second in wealth. CTF Files.

Board of Education wanted no public meeting, for there was no more talk of conference.

A final gun against the teachers in the skirmish was set off by the representative of the Board of Education [Bither], who issued on June 9, 1922, a long wail against the teachers which stated:

> It is probably sufficient to say in regard to salary matters that another wait is in store with a possible deflection entirely, unless our cause is handled carefully, of which we confess doubt in the face of recent experiences. . . .
>
> Let us not permit the Bolshevicks [sic] to turn aside the chance of reason and equity to prevail.[21]

Whether he had taken a random shot at the "Bolshevicks" or whether the school administration had changed its mind and failed to notify him is not known. Be that as it may, he had misfired again, for on June 14, 1922, the Board of Education adopted a salary schedule ranging from $1500 to $2500 for elementary teachers and $2000 to $3800 for high school teachers with a bonus for special teachers and a revised schedule for principals.[22]

In 1913, the Legislature of Illinois had amended the teachers' pension law by making mandatory the appropriation from the educational fund of the amount of public money which the law of 1911 had made permissive, and also by adding a new provision authorizing in addition thereto a new permissive appropriation equal to the teachers' contributions. This had made mandatory the payment of one dollar of public money for each one dollar of teachers' contributions and had authorized, but did not compel, the payment of an additional dollar.

From the 1st of January, 1912, to the 1st of July, 1921, the total public money paid into the teachers' pension fund was one dollar for every dollar deducted from the teachers' salaries and paid into the fund. The additional dollar which the law of 1913 permitted, but did not compel the Board of Education to pay from July 1, 1913, to July 1, 1921, was never paid into the teachers' pension fund.

The amendment of 1921 made the amount of the public contribution two dollars for every one dollar deducted from the salaries of teachers and paid into the fund, and made the payment of this two dollars mandatory.

Beginning January, 1922, a tax of three-tenths of a mill was levied annually on each dollar of assessed valuation of property in Chicago.

---

[21]*Margaret Haley's Bulletin*, 4 (Sept. 30, 1926), p. 32.

[22]*Proceedings, Board of Education*, 1921-22, p. 1160. This was one of the most substantial increases the teachers had secured. However, this schedule was not paid in full for twelve of the next twenty-one years. Herrick, *Chicago Schools*, p. 143.

The amendment of 1921 provided that if the expenditures in any year exceed the income of that year the Board of Education shall, the following year, appropriate from the educational fund and pay into the pension fund the amount of the excess of such expenditure over such income.

We had come a long way from the first pension legislation of 1895, but we were still a long way from the millennium, and no one knew it better than we did. We realized that we had won something of victory in these post-war years, but we recognized that the method which politicians had used to give us that to which we were rightly entitled was not the right method. Even though we were entirely justified in our salary and pension increases, we were aware that the taxation methods used to provide for those increases were not fundamentally just. We had reason to know then—as we knew twenty years earlier and as we know now, fifteen years later—that the one right way of taxation was not by increasing the tax rate and putting additional burden upon the little fellow but by revising the tax method so that the big fellow would pay his share. Long before the politicians realized it, we teachers knew the public temper and the reasons for that temper: for, after all, we teachers are like the three tailors of Tooley Street in writing, "we, the people . . . ."[23]

[23]The phrase "three tailors of Tooley Street" is attributed to the British statesman George Canning (1770-1827), who told of three Londoners whose petition of grievances to the House of Commons began "We, the people of England. . . ." According to E. C. Brewer, the phrase describes "any pettifogging coterie that fancies it represents the nation." E. C. Brewer, *Brewer's Dictionary of Phrase and Fable*, centennary ed. (New York: Harper and Row, 1970), p. 1059. Carl Sandburg immortalized the three tailors in his poem "Three Ghosts," published in *Smoke and Steel* (New York: Harcourt Brace and Co., 1920), p. 102.

°⟦ IX ⟧°

Carpetbagger

1

Reaction against Thompsonism elected Judge William E. Dever mayor of Chicago in 1923. Dever had made a splendid record on the bench, and the liberal-minded voters of the city expected that he would continue it in the mayor's office. He failed, however, because he let himself be dominated by George Brennan, then the Democratic "boss" of Illinois.[1]

Brennan, who was a realist in politics as all bosses have to be, probably earned more opprobrium than any other holder of the title. That was probably due less to his manner of personal reserve than it was to the fact that he had come up from circumstances which usually create a different type of leader. Brennan had worked in his boyhood in the coal mines of Illinois. He had been injured in one of them and had then become a teacher in a country school. He was later a district superintendent of schools. From that, he went into the statehouse in Springfield, where he was a clerk during John P. Altgeld's administration, sitting at a desk beside Brand Whitlock, later wartime Ambassador to Belgium and one of America's foremost liberal writers.

In spite of these associations, Brennan was the leading exponent in Illinois of the bipartisan alliance system. The *Chicago Daily News* is responsible for the story that Brennan counseled Joseph P. Savage, who had a desk in the office of the insurance company which Brennan represented in Chicago and who was supposed at that time to be a

[1]Carpetbagger refers to William McAndrew, who came to Chicago as superintendent of schools following Dever's election in 1923. A classic account of the McAndrew years is George S. Counts, *School and Society in Chicago*. The author brings together political, sociological, and historical analyses in this study.
George Brennan (1865-1928) succeeded Roger C. Sullivan as Democratic party boss in 1920. As Haley indicates, Brennan was an acknowledged master of bipartisan politics and he maintained a working relationship with the corrupt Thompson administration. See note 9, page 190, for Dever.

Democrat, to make alliance with Marshall Field III, whom he had known at a southern training camp, and leap on the Leonard Wood bandwagon before it got by.[2] The Wood bandwagon didn't go far, but it took Savage into the Republican party, where he made association with Robert E. Crowe. Savage, however, kept his desk in Brennan's office.

The shadow of Brennan was not yet showing full length upon the floor of Dever's office when Dever started out to rearrange the Board of Education. He came up at once against the difficulty which Thompson had created. Croarkin's term had expired, but Coath's had not.[3] Thompson had not reported to the city council the resignations which he held of the other members of the Board. When Dever went into office, I called his attention to that fact and asked him, "Can't you take those resignations?" He adopted that course, but made his new appointments gradually.

He tried to get Coath's resignation, but Coath declared that he would not turn it in except on the request of Judge [Michael Louis] McKinley. McKinley had no reason to ask Coath for the resignation unless Dever made the request of him. Raymond Robins and I together urged Dever to ask McKinley to press the point with Coath; but, whatever happened, Coath remained the last of his line upon the Board, holding office throughout Dever's entire term and remaining to become the president of the Board when Thompson went back in 1927.

Dever appointed as his private secretary one Arthur O'Brien, who had been a clerk in Judge Rush's court. There he had been in charge of some records of divorce cases which had been entered in such a way that some of the newspapers had lost important stories. When the reason for this failure became known, one of the newspapers, the *Journal*, attacked O'Brien and started a feud, which grew in strength with Dever's appointment of him to a place where he could either give or block news. Continuing the feud, the *Journal* went after other matters connected with the Dever administration. One of them was the condition of the schools.

The buildings were so crowded that children were packed in like sardines. There were some places where the school grounds were so wet and muddy after rains that you almost had to get a derrick to pick you up and carry you across. While the Thompson Board had built unnecessarily in some districts, they had failed to make provision in those places where the new schools were most needed. The *Journal* not only

[2]Leonard Wood was a candidate for the Republican presidential nomination in 1920.
[3]See pp. 194-95. See also Francis E. Croarkin, *Ninety Years: The Autobiography of Francis E. Croarkin* (Chicago: The Author, 1952), pp. 234-37.

ran stories but showed pictures of the condition. The Dever administration went jittery over the situation, for the parents of the children were demanding action.[4]

Francis X. Busch, Dever's corporation counsel, found a solution of the difficulty. The Board of Education had the power by resolution to call on the City Council to put a proposition to the people to raise the taxes for the purpose of increasing the number of schools.

Charles M. Moderwell, president of the Dever Board through its first two years of existence, jumped at the idea.[5] Because Dever was still the white-haired boy of the teachers, they threw themselves into the campaign and got the tax rate increase over. Moderwell did not wake up to what he had done until the precedent had been established. He set going an engine that appalled him when he saw what it could do. The Moderwell precedent was the method demanded by the teachers ten years later, when the Board of Education was declaring it had no power to do anything about teachers' salaries.

In December, 1923, Moderwell appointed a commission for the ostensible purpose of investigating school housing conditions. As the commission worked in 1924, three phases developed: first, the reorganizing of the school system educationally to introduce the platoon system, which would allow two sets of children to occupy the school buildings at the same time; second, the question of whether existing school buildings should be removed and new buildings erected; third, the question of revenue for building and repairs to schools and for paying teachers. Too late, we saw that the Moderwell commission was doing exactly what the commission of 1898 had tried to do: determining its educational policy by available revenue instead of determining it by educators, putting the cart before the horse. Its work was

---

[4]A series of articles on school conditions ran from Sept. 10 through Oct. 4 in the pages of the *Chicago Daily Journal*. Each article was illustrated with a photograph. Representative headlines included: "Chicago Education Board Condemns 48 Little Ones to Pass Their Days in Gloomy Basement," "Class Meets in Teachers' Restroom," "2100 Children in Building Designed for 1200," "Chicago Houses Northwest Children in Firetrap; Others into Unsanitary Portables," and "West Pullman Wins First Prize for Wretched Class Conditions in Public Schools; 22 children and teachers in space six by fifteen feet." This latter space was a former cloakroom!

[5]Charles M. Moderwell (1868-1955) was a businessman associated with coal operations in West Virginia and the Peoples Gas Company. He was an active member of both the Union League Club and the Association of Commerce. Four other members appointed by Dever also belonged to the Association of Commerce. Counts, *School and Society*, p. 160.

The Association of Commerce was organized in 1904. Its major effort in educational affairs had been the attempt to secure a dual system of schools with the Cooley vocational bill. Controlling school expenditures and, as a consequence, keeping the tax rate low were other aims. The natural antagonist of the association was the Chicago Federation

made easier by the fact that the Dever Board had, by that time, brought in as superintendent of schools William McAndrew.[6]

2

William Bishop Owen, principal of the Chicago Normal school and one of the real educators of the city, seemed to stand first in line to become superintendent of schools.[7] Owen had been a professor of Greek at the University of Chicago, where his personality and methods had won him the friendship of Charles E. Merriam. Merriam was Dever's choice for the presidency of the Board of Education; but the University senate hesitated to give sanction to his acceptance of the place, and Merriam chose to remain at the University. Had Merriam chosen to enter the public school battles, the history of the four years that followed would probably not have been written in red ink. As a member of the City Council, Merriam had given the best service of any man ever in that body. He knew the schools. He knew the problems of educators and the objectives of education. Merriam as president and Owen as superintendent of schools would have made a team which might have saved the schools from the depredations of the so-called business interests which almost wrecked the institution.[8]

Owen, however, had by one unconsidered action, in the summer of 1923, managed to antagonize almost all the classroom teachers in the United States. Owen was known to be parliamentary adviser to Charl Williams at the session of the National Education Association in Boston in that year. Against his advice, although this was not generally known, she called an extra session of the classroom teachers after the regular meetings. Owen presided at the meeting and so, in spite of his

of Labor. Thus, with the Cooley bill in the background, later proposals identified with school reform which were linked to business interests immediately engendered the opposition of organized labor. *Ibid.*, pp. 133-64.

[6]*Proceedings, Board of Education,* 1923-24, pp. 1265-71, 1453-60 contain the reports on the platoon system and junior high schools.

Edward Krug, in the second and final volume of his *Shaping the American High School, 1920-1941* (Madison: University of Wisconsin Press, 1972), describes McAndrew's fate as a "classical tragedy." He writes that McAndrew brought to Chicago "the most approved developments in education" and that "his fate was a major shock to pedagogical leadership throughout the country," pp. 36-39.

Haley resumed publication of her *Bulletin* in 1925. Originally published as the *Chicago Teachers' Federation Bulletin* from 1901 to 1908, it appeared for one year, 1915-1916, as *Margaret A. Haley's Bulletin* and then again from 1925 to 1931 as *Margaret Haley's Bulletin.* Both the *Bulletin* and her lengthy speeches found in the stenographic reports of the CTF for the 1920s and 1930s are excellent sources for her assessment of the McAndrew years.

[7]William B. Owen (1866-1928) was a member of the faculty of the University of Chicago from 1892 until 1909. He then became president of the Chicago Normal School and remained there until his death.

[8]See note 6, p. 152, for Merriam.

protest to Charl Williams, had to assume the deserved blame for the procedure, which almost broke up the organization at that time. Owen knew that by his Boston mistake he had lost the superintendency in Chicago.[9] When he came back to the city, he telephoned to me and talked for nearly an hour, explaining and regretting his action, but insisting that he had no other course except to remain silent and take the blame. It was all unfortunate because Owen would have made a splendid superintendent. Instead, Chicago suffered from one of the worst superintendencies in its checkered history of education.

A mayoralty election in the city of New York sent William McAndrew to Chicago. McAndrew had at one time done good work as the principal of a New York school and had then established a reputation for educational ability far beyond his deserts. When he was being kicked out of New York for interference in a political campaign there, he maneuvered himself into the limelight so effectively that he became a candidate for the superintendency of the Chicago schools.[10]

Peter A. Mortenson, who had been a good superintendent—he had made the teachers' councils an integral part of the educational system—was slated to go, probably because he would not be amenable to the intentions of the big business interests controlling the Board. McAndrew, who had many years before been the principal of the Hyde Park High School in Chicago, still had friends at court. They recommended him to the extra-governmental committee which was considering candidates for the superintendency, not on the ground of their educational qualifications, but on the matter of their potential subserviency to what was already becoming the invisible rule of Chicago. McAndrew was summoned to a meeting held in the Union League Club, one of the high altars of privilege, and presided over by Charles M. Moderwell, president of the Board of Education. Moderwell, who was fairly liberal in his public ideas, was nevertheless a non-union operator of West Virginia coal mines.[11]

[9]The issue had to do with an attempt to increase the influence of the Department of Classroom Teachers through the enactment of a constitution for it. Haley and her followers opposed the convening of the special meeting. Material on this is found in the July-August, 1922, folder, Box 48, CTF Files.

[10]William McAndrew (1863-1937) had served as a teacher and administrator in Chicago at Hyde Park School during the years 1889 to 1891. A native of Michigan, McAndrew was associate superintendent of schools in New York for ten years before assuming the Chicago post. Following his Chicago experience, he was an editor of the *Educational Review* and the *School Review* until his death. Haley seems to have supported the choice, for she praised him as one of the three foremost educators in the country. *American Educational Digest*, 43 (Feb., 1924), pp. 264-65. McAndrew came at a salary of $15,000. *Journal of Education*, 99 (Jan. 17, 1924), p. 59.

[11]The Union League Club had its origins in a secret society formed during the Civil War. Chartered in 1879, this patriotic civic organization had 2,356 members in the 1920s. Through its interest in honest, efficient government, the club provided significant

The first that we knew of the situation was when James Mullenbach, a member of the Board of Education, came to our office one Saturday night. He said, "McAndrew of New York was in town today. He was entertained at the Union League Club by Moderwell. The Board members are considering him for superintendent."

I said, "The hell they are!"

Mullenbach added that McAndrew had told the men present at the Union League meeting that the platoon school was still in existence in New York City. That was contrary to what [William E.] Grady, who was Acting Superintendent of Schools in New York and who had come to Chicago a little while before to debate on the platoon system with Wirt of Gary—Wirt didn't appear at the debate but sent substitutes—had said on that occasion. I told Mullenbach, "I'll bet on Grady."[12]

Mrs. Fursman [a past president of the CTF] and I went to New York. Grady told us that the platoon school had been established. The New York schools, he said, had never been built for such an arrangement. Grady said that the platoon school system had been defeated in New York by this circumstance: The parents of the children in attendance usually didn't know whether or not the children were learning anything, but they did know, when the children came home complaining of lost mittens, that they would have to buy them new ones. They knew there was no place in the platoon school for children to keep their books or other possessions and that they were constantly hauling everything around. The consciousness of parents that their children were forever tramping and forever losing something drove the platoon schools out of New York. McAndrew had lied to the meeting at the Union League when he had said that the platoon schools had not been abolished. He had also failed to tell that meeting that he would draw a pension of $2500 a year from the New York school system even if he became superintendent in Chicago. We knew then the kind of man we'd have to deal with if McAndrew were elected.

---

financial support for the investigation of the Thompson school board and supported Dever for mayor in 1923. Its continuing interest in school affairs was demonstrated during the McAndrew years. Bruce Grant, *Fight for a City: The Story of the Union League Club of Chicago and Its Times, 1880-1955* (Chicago: Rand McNally, 1955), pp. 224-26, 230.

[12]William Wirt (1874-1938), the superintendent of schools, introduced this plan, which sought to use fully the school facilities beginning in 1908. It was popularized in 1915 through a series of articles by Randolph Bourne, who saw the plan as a progressive, humane approach to the problems of urban school systems. The attempt to introduce the Gary plan in New York failed in 1917. Chicago proponents tried to avoid association with Gary, which was a factory town of the U.S. Steel Corporation. The terms "platoon," "Detroit," and "work, study, play" were used to describe the system. The opposition to the plan in Chicago was led by the CTF and their friends from organized labor.

The best study of the Gary plan is Ronald D. Cohen and Raymond Mohl, *The Paradox of Progressive Education: The Gary Plan and Urban Schooling* (Port Washington, N.Y.: Kennikat Press, 1979).

McAndrew must have impressed the Union League tycoons, however, for he was elected superintendent in December, 1923. His first
public appearance in Chicago was marked by a significance which we
did not understand until later. The reporters seeking him for picture
and interview found him in the Peoples Gas Light and Coke building,
the building where Samuel Insull had his private offices, over which
Bernard F. Mullaney, who had been Fred Busse's secretary, stood
guard. McAndrew evidently didn't want to be caught in the gas building, for he kept dodging in and out among the high pillars.

In the years through which he served as superintendent, McAndrew
played the devil in the schools. He had everybody in the system by the
ears. The principals hated him. The high school teachers despised
him. And the elementary teachers abominated him. The teachers'
councils, which had been established in 1913 on the recommendation
of Ella Flagg Young and which had been re-established in 1919 on the
recommendation of Peter A. Mortenson, were maintained until September, 1924, when the Board of Education abolished the rule providing for the meeting of these bodies.[13] The councils had been the
official organization of classroom teachers for free, uncontrolled discussion and expression of educational policy. Their abolition was one
of the worst blows ever administered by an administrative body to the
academic freedom of the schools. The Board offered an insulting
substitute, which excluded any real criticism of the system by the
teachers. In February, 1925, the Board passed an amendment to its
rules, denying to members of voluntary organizations of teachers the
right to freedom of communication on school grounds, outside of
school hours, in regard to the business of their organizations.[14]

As always, effect had followed rapidly upon cause. The Board was
penalizing the teachers' councils because the teachers' councils [thirty-
nine in number] had unanimously voted against the platoon schools.
A platoon school is a plan of organization by which more children—
from 10 per cent to 70 per cent—are enrolled than there are seats for in
the classrooms. This is done by "dumping" the 10 per cent to 70 per
cent on the school playground or in the auditorium or basement and
by keeping all the children rotating from room to room, from teacher
to teacher, so that the same 10 per cent to 70 per cent may not be kept
waiting longer than thirty consecutive minutes to get into classrooms.

By this method, even six-year-old children have six or seven teachers
a day and, in some cities, from twelve to thirteen teachers a week.
Teachers handle as many as four hundred different pupils a day and a

[13]Report of the Elementary Teachers General Council, pp. 289-92; *Proceedings, Board of Education*, 1924-25, pp. 259-61.
[14]*Ibid.*, 1924-25, pp. 769-70.

thousand a week. Educationally the platoon schools are frightfully destructive. Even under the best physical conditions, they are evil.

The schools, which had been successful in Gary, a completely industrialized town, were being advocated in Chicago by the industrialists and their minions. Just before Dr. John Dill Robertson left the presidency of the Board, he declared himself "sold to the idea" of the platoon school, but added that it might be impossible for the Board to put it over because of the opposition of certain educators. He thought that the platoon system would save the tax payers one hundred million dollars—he didn't say in how many years—and advocated the projection of the idea through a school plan commission.[15]

In the same month that McAndrew appeared at the Union League Club, an educational commission was appointed for investigation of the results of the platoon schools in Detroit, Pittsburgh, Akron, and Gary. One of that commission was Rose Pesta, at that time an elementary school principal. With fine courage, she brought in a minority report against the platoon system. In spite of that report, which showed the difficulties, dangers, and inadequacies of the platoon method, the Board continued its steam-roller operation.[16]

The Federation printed the reports of the nine Chicago teachers [a CTF committee], the elementary school principal, and the district superintendent who visited the Detroit schools, this report declaring, "the platoon school is exactly the factory system applied to education." Notwithstanding those reports and the testimony of all the great educators of the country against the method, the Board adopted the platoon school in July, 1924, with the declaration that it was to be an experiment to be tried in a few schools and carefully watched. By June, 1925, McAndrew announced that sixty schools were running on the platoon plan.

By November, 1926, the platoon school system was so well developed that public opinion against it had become genuinely aroused. The Marys and Johnnys of Chicago were losing their gloves and their rubbers, and their fathers and mothers were telling the aldermen of their wards what they thought of the system. On November 24, the City Council unanimously passed a resolution directing the Council's committee on schools to investigate the platoon schools of Chicago, on the ground that they were educationally unsound and that they were violating health and fire ordinances. The Board of Education took no action, however, and throughout the rest of the time William McAndrew remained in Chicago the platoon school hung like Mohammed's

[15]*Ibid.*, 1923-24, pp. 1453-60, contain the majority and minority reports on the platoon system.
[16]*Ibid*, 1924-25, pp. 14-20, 59-61, report this action of July, 1924.

coffin. Only after his enforced departure did the noble experiment fade into oblivion.

Another of McAndrew's experiments was the junior high school. This, like the platoon school, was designed to industrialize the public schools. The idea was that boys and girls who did not expect to finish a high school course would be better equipped if they were separated before the end of the grammar grades from those children who would probably take a complete high school course. It was in essence the most undemocratic process possible in an American school. It divided, at the end of the sixth grade, the children whose parents lacked money to insure them six more years of school from the more fortunate children who had such insurance. It was the sharpest line of demarkation on the basis of wealth and privilege ever established in any school system. Economically it was planned for the purpose of turning youth into industry with the greatest possible speed. It was a system for the advantage of the factory owner and operator, not for the child in the schools. It was an exemplification of the idea that the owner of the Alton Glass Works had stated a quarter of a century earlier: that the less children knew about cultural values, the better automata they became in factory service. It was a fundamental denial of the basic constitutional rights of every citizen to equal opportunity.

The junior high schools were to last, unfortunately, longer than did McAndrew in the school system. When they were thrown out in 1933, it was by a method which badly confused the real issue, so that their elimination carried with it an element of injustice to many individuals in that division of the system. In principle, however, they were educationally, morally, and socially wrong.[17]

The McAndrew regime brought to the schools a confusion so dire that only the teachers who lived through it have been able to estimate its probable effect upon the children who were the ultimate sufferers from its mistakes and misdeeds. The abolition of the teachers' councils had established Fascism on the teaching force. The establishment of the "hundred per cent or nothing" rating system on the children lifted the spear heads of the legions at the front of every schoolroom.[18] Insisting upon a method of marking which every honest educator in the country knew by that time to be an absurdity, McAndrew put into effect a machine as disruptive as an army of tanks. Children who took home reports on which they were marked according to the superintendent's order brought back protests of furious parents. Added to the

[17]The report on junior highs is found in *Ibid.*, 1923-24, pp. 1265-71.

[18]This reference is to intelligence testing, which McAndrew introduced. This was associated with "sorting" students for the junior high schools and vigorously opposed by organized labor. *Illinois State Federation of Labor Weekly News Letter*, July 26, 1924, pp. 1-4.

anger already aroused by the losses of the platoon system, public rage against the little, bearded Scotchman rose to the point where it could no longer be ignored as a political factor in the city. The man who had been brought to town by the group seeking to control the public schools for their own industrial benefit had overshot their mark as well as his own.

Some superintendents might have kept the Board of Education in good humor, even while they were doing the Board's dirty work in the schools; but William McAndrew was not by temperament a diplomat. With his amazing faculty for stirring up trouble on every front, he even projected difficulty into the last place where he needed to have it, the Board of Education itself.

In 1925 [October 14], the Board refused to re-elect William H. Campbell [73 years old], the member of the board of examiners recommended by the superintendent of schools to that post [examiner], which action automatically returned him to the principalship from which he had been taken for the examiner's position. The Board directed McAndrew to make another recommendation. McAndrew declined to do so. He wrote a report yards long explaining why he could not recommend anyone else to take Campbell's place. His refusal precipitated a clash between him and the Board. For a little while— although it was not known then outside the Board rooms—there was danger that the Board would discharge McAndrew if he insisted on upholding Campbell. The two Scotsmen might have gone down in defeat had it not been for the diplomatic service of Don Rogers, principal of the Smyth school, who was in and out of the superintendent's office.

Rogers went to the Men's City Club and told the chairman of its schools committee that the difficulty between the Board and the superintendent would result in McAndrew's dismissal unless some outside influence would intervene. Willis Thorne, the chairman of the committee, asked his group to appoint Rogers as one member of the committee on education who would have power to offer to the Board the good offices of the chairman of that committee to try and settle the difference between McAndrew and the Board. Rogers then went to the Union League Club and persuaded a committee there to appoint him as a representative of that organization for the same purpose. He then returned to the Board and, on behalf of these two clubs, tendered his services as intermediary in the case.

Somebody's service ameliorated the situation, although McAndrew held stubbornly to his determination to save face for his friend Campbell. Evidently, though, he realized that the Board was determined to shift the examiner back to a principalship and he set out to pad a pillow on which his friend might fall with ease and grace and, at the same time, prevent himself from being branded with defeat. The result was a plan which he called the emeritus service.

The emeritus service was to be a branch of the educational service of the Board of Education to which all members of the teaching force should be assigned when they had reached the age of seventy years. Each person transferred to the service was to be paid annually a sum equal to one-half his average annual salary during the ten years preceding his transfer and no person was to receive less than $1500 nor more than $2500. The emeritus service would automatically take out Campbell from his post as examiner, thereby giving apparent victory to the Board of Education, even though it also seemed to leave McAndrew as a political victor in the struggle. As a mere incident, it also took out of the educational into the emeritus branch 119 teachers and principals of both elementary and high schools who had been in no way concerned with the Board of Education fight against the superintendent.

The Board had been working on an age retirement bill which had already passed the 1925 Legislature [Miller bill] but had not been signed by the proper authorities to put it into effect as law. This bill, which because of that lack of signature could not become law until some time later, was not as arbitrary as the emeritus rule in cutting off teachers and principals at the age of seventy; for although seventy was the age set for retirement, the time was staggered. This bill provided that all persons in the Chicago public schools who reached the age of seventy-five in 1926 should be retired, but that the age of retirement should be seventy-four in 1927, seventy-three in 1928, seventy-two in 1929, and seventy in 1930 and thereafter. Those retiring were each to receive $1500 a year, regardless of salary or position previous to that time.

Under this bill, which would become law as soon as it was properly signed, Campbell was not liable to immediate retirement and that was why McAndrew had to fix up something to take care of his situation. It made no difference to the superintendent or to the Board of Education that other people would suffer injustice from this procedure. It made plenty of difference to the sufferers, who were thrown out without notice. The Board passed the rule on the 9th of December, 1925, providing that it was to go into effect in 1926.[19]

The second semester of the schools begins on February first. On January 12, McAndrew presented to the Board a list of teachers and principals who were to be placed in emeritus service on February 1.

[19]*Proceedings, Board of Education,* 1925-26, p. 561.

The Board passed the recommendation for such transfer. On January 25, the retired principals and teachers received notices of this action. The next meeting of the Board of Education, where the successors of the retired teachers and principals would be appointed, was scheduled for Wednesday afternoon, January 27. If anyone were to bring suit against the Board, it would be necessary to have a hearing for injunction take place between the time of the Board's action on Wednesday and the following Monday, when the new appointees would take office.

Someone told me that James E. Armstrong, principal of the Englewood High School, one of those deposed by the McAndrew order, was going to bring such a suit and that Judge Dunne was his attorney. I called Judge Dunne, but found that he was out of town. His son-in-law, William J. Corboy, told me that Armstrong had been there to see Judge Dunne and that they were considering a suit, although no definite action had yet been decided upon. I asked him if he would consult with Isaiah T. Greenacre and he said that he would be glad to do it. Greenacre agreed to talk with him. I called back to Corboy, but he had gone to a banquet. The bill had to be filed the next morning. Greenacre said, "There's nothing else for us to do but go ahead. Get somebody who can bring the suit and get your data together."

I got hold of Mary Hecox, who was also on the list, and took her with me to Greenacre's office about nine o'clock that night. We found there, consulting with Greenacre, the last man whom anyone would expect to discover under the circumstances, Willis Thorne, who had helped Don Rogers get the Men's City Club back of McAndrew. Thorne was furious at Rogers' use of him. He had never for a moment thought that he was pulling chestnuts out of the fire for the superintendent and he had expected that Rogers would return to him with a report of his activity, which of course Rogers had never done. Thorne's fury had been aroused most of all by the fact that his own sister was on the list which McAndrew had sent in for retirement. It was Thorne who secured a public stenographer for us in the building where he and Greenacre both had offices.

Together, we all worked on the preparation of the petition for injunction. Mary Hecox signed her name to it, but she was a modest woman and signed on the lowest line. She left space above her own for other signatures. That was how it became known as the "Armstrong case." Armstrong signed the petition after Thorne and Greenacre had communicated, the next morning, with Judge Dunne's office. Chester C. Dodge, another high school principal, also signed the petition at Thorne's request.

The petition for injunction went before Judge Hugo Friend on

Wednesday morning, January 27. On the same afternoon, the Board of Education filled the places of the twenty-seven principals on the emeritus list. On Thursday morning, these principals received notices from McAndrew directing them to report that morning to the schools to which they had been elected or transferred on the previous day. In accordance with this notice, these principals reported for duty Thursday morning and again Friday morning to their new posts of duty, so that in about forty schools there were two principals on those days while in nearly forty other schools there were none.

On Saturday morning, January 30, Judge Friend started the hearing. Frank S. Righeimer, attorney for the Board of Education, made a motion that the case be continued to a later date. His request was granted, and the delays always associated with such cases began. Finally, Judge Friend refused to issue an injunction against the Board, but he did this on the promise of the Board of Education's attorneys— especially of Righeimer—that if the teachers had been illegally dismissed they would be returned and would get their money for the time they had been out. When the case came back to Judge Friend, remanded by the Appellate Court, we had the stenographic record of that promise to show the judge. Before that time came, however, the emeritus service had been superseded in law by another provision for age retirement.

In the meantime, Armstrong and Dodge had located the age retirement bill that had been passed by the Legislature and lost in transit. They found that Bert McCann, clerk of the house of representatives at Springfield, had left it in his desk when he had gone to California. They made him come home and take it out so that the lieutenant governor ([Fred E.] Sterling) could sign it as president of the senate. Sterling probably cursed them roundly when he had to do it, and Sterling was one of the most virile cursers in Springfield. Then they secured the signature of the speaker of the house. Finally, Len Small, the governor, signed it [May 19], and the age retirement bill became a real law, going into effect July 1, 1926.[20]

Judge Friend's denial of the injunction against the emeritus service rule had been appealed to the Supreme Court of Illinois. It was December, 1927, before the Supreme Court transferred the case to the Appellate Court, holding that it had no jurisdiction of the appeal. In February, 1928, the Appellate Court gave a decision reversing the ruling of the Circuit Court and directing the Board of Education to restore the complainants to their respective positions. The group

[20]Another, more detailed version of the enactment of the Miller Law is found in Chester C. Dodge, *Reminiscenses of a Schoolmaster* (Chicago: Ralph Fletcher Seymour, 1941), pp. 100-11.

thrown out by the rule claimed their back salary, while the Board contended that they owed it money. When the case returned to Judge Friend, however, for rehearing by the order of the Appellate Court, the people on the emeritus service were granted their money.[21]

Three years of controversy, projected by McAndrew to satisfy his own vanity, had brought back the Board to its starting point. Everybody had gone all the way around Robin Hood's barn.

3

One of our points of opposition to McAndrew appeared when he started out to increase the tax rate, a procedure that we teachers had promised the Legislature we would not take. He put in to the Board a report on teachers' salaries which was a slovenly piece of work and diabolically wrong. It provided for the principals a salary schedule that named the increases they should get from the beginning to the end of the schedule. It did nothing of the kind for the teachers. The McAndrew schedule was, as so many others had been, a scrap of paper. It was worse than most of the others because, as a matter of fact, it actually lowered the salaries of the largest number in the teaching group, the elementary teachers.

In 1897, the maximum salary of a primary teacher in Chicago had been $800 and of a grammar school teacher $825. In 1898, each maximum salary was raised $75. Ten years later, in 1908, the primary school teachers received $875 and the grammar school teachers $900. Through successive raises, fought, bled, and almost died for, during the succeeding years, the primary grade teachers were receiving $1,355 maximum and the grammar grade teachers were receiving $1,380 maximum in 1917. The 1921 Legislature brought the 1922 salaries up to $2,500 each for maximum for both primary and grammar grade teachers. In that year, 3,339 teachers were being paid this maximum salary. The others, excluding 959 on a special maximum of from $50 to $250 more, received from $1,500 minimum upward to the $2,500. There were at that time 8,602 elementary teachers, 266 elementary principals, and 2,466 high school teachers in the Chicago public schools.

The McAndrew salary schedule planned to cut off from $300 to $1,175 from the aggregate salary then paid every entering classroom teacher for the first five years. It added, however, $5,500 each to the aggregate salary of entering principals for the five years of the "lower

[21]The decision of the appellate court, together with a review of the case including earlier legal opinions, is reprinted in *Margaret Haley's Bulletin*, 5 (Mar. 31, 1928), pp. 119-32.

group" of their schedule. It piled up higher salaries at the maximums of the schedules, with no assurance that the large group of experienced classroom teachers, almost 50 per cent of the entire body, who were then at the maximum of their schedules, would be allowed to reach these new heights of salaries or that there would be any money to pay them if they did. It provided no increase in salary for any classroom teachers then in the "lower group" of the schedule. These were about 30 per cent of the entire force. It would increase immediately the salaries of all principals in the "lower group" from $1,000 to $1,200 and of all the principals in the "upper group" from $950 to $1,300. It would cut the salaries of more than 1,500 teachers in the "lower groups" of the schedules. It was a raise that was not a raise, with a cut at the bottom and no money at the top.

The McAndrew schedule of increases (?) was presented to the Board of Education in March, 1925, and referred to the finance committee of that body. The Board was already in deep financial difficulties, difficulties which eventually took it into the deep waters of the great political problem of unjust taxation. It had not the money to make honest raises of salaries, especially to the large group of teachers, who were finding with the increase of living cost the need of higher salary, but who were not asking for it because of their knowledge of the Board's finances. The McAndrew schedule had for concomitant a demand for increased tax rates. The Chicago Teachers' Federation, representing not only its own membership but also those teachers who felt as its members did that they had not the right to take money—no matter how much they needed it—at the cost of an unfair taxation measure, made protest to the Board. For months, the Federation fought against the McAndrew salary schedule and against the method of providing money to meet it. On April 27, 1925, after a secret conference of Board members where a letter from the executive committee of the Chicago Association of Commerce approving the schedule was presented, the Board in open meeting adopted the salary schedule.[22]

The resolution putting the schedule into official effect called for the authorization of a referendum on the question of a tax rate increase from $1.92 to $2.92 to every $100 of assessed valuation. The Board had authorized it on a gambler's chance that the revenue for it would be found or would be authorized by the tax payers. The principle established by this procedure—that of increasing heavily the school payroll before the money necessary for the increase over a period of years is in any way available—was one of the most dangerous elements of the entire proceeding. In spite of having cut down the largest number of

---

[22]*Proceedings, Board of Education,* 1924-25, pp. 1409-14.

teachers, the schedule would have added a heavy expenditure from an educational fund already burdened with a deficit and without visible means of support.

This resolution, even though it included amendments that ameliorated some of its worst features, was still dynamite. Isaiah T. Greenacre had given us the opinion that the resolution did not protect from diminution the salaries of teachers then teaching and that there was no provision for their protection in the schedule. Mayor Dever, who had been a jurist for many years, sustained Greenacre's opinion on all points presented, including the point that the Board was not enabled to delegate to the superintendent any right to retard the salaries of individuals. On the same day that the Board passed the resolution, Mayor Dever appointed new members of the Board, who were confirmed by the City Council on the 13th of May. On May 22, the new Board reconsidered the vote taken on April 27 by the old Board and sent the resolution back to the finance committee, where it remained in cold storage for nearly two years. Just before Dever was coming up for re-election in 1927, the McAndrew report again rose above the horizon.

By this time, the finances of the Board had become a matter of general political as well as of particular educational attention.[23]

As early as December, 1923, the Federation had known that the Board of Education had not sufficient money to give teachers any further salary increase. Although the teachers remained inadequately paid, particularly in comparison with all other service or labor in that time, the Federation declined to make any request for another tax increase. Robert C. Moore, president of the Illinois State Teachers Association, had said to me after the tax rate increase of 1921 had been secured: "This thing of increasing the tax rate has come to the end of its rope. The work must be addressed now to getting the right kind of assessments. The assessment values are so uneven that the taxes almost murder some people, while others are getting out. The people of this state have got to work for reassessment. The situation has gone to the place where it is correcting its own evil."

The City Council didn't want [an] increase in the tax rate any more than did the Chicago Teachers' Federation. The Board of Education, however, held to its old policy of advocating a raise in the tax rate in order to secure additional funds. As usual, a proposal to increase the teachers' salaries was only the smoke screen behind which the Board could secure money for other purposes. The Dever Board, however,

---

[23]Beginning in 1915, the board shifted to a credit system of finance based on the sale of tax warrants. By 1926, almost eleven years of tax income had been spent in ten years. Thus, in 1927, the board's only source of funds was the 1927 taxes, which were yet to be collected. Herrick, *Chicago Schools*, pp. 179-80.

"the business men's Board," was the first one to make budget padding a wholesale rather than a retail process. In February, 1926, Edward B. Ellicott, president of the Board of Education, and six other members of the Board appeared before the schools committee of the City Council and urged that committee to recommend that the City Council submit to the voters at a primary election a tax rate increase of one dollar for the educational fund of the Board of Education. In presenting to the committee "a statement of proposed revenue and expenditures for the year 1926," Ellicott said that a total of $3,800,000 additional expense would be added to the school system for the operation of thirty-six new schools which were going into service that year. A sub-committee of the schools committee of the Council found, however, that the regular budget of a little more than $41,000,000, which did not include the $3,800,000, provided for the entire cost of operating for the entire year all the schools opened in 1926, including teachers' salaries; and that therefore this additional item of $3,800,000 as an item of expenditure for 1926 was nothing but padding. The explanation of Nelson B. Henry, secretary of the finance committee of the Board of Education, was that the error was entirely typographical, which had set down 1926 instead of 1927.[24]

By September of the same year, the Chicago Principals' Club was representing to the City Council that "bankruptcy faces the schools unless immediate financial relief is granted" and asking the Council to put a tax rate increase on the ballot at the November election. The Chicago Teachers' Federation opposed the increase on the ground that it was not the proper method of procedure and also that the Board had sufficient money without its use. In October, Ellicott sent to Mayor Dever a report showing that there would be a surplus of over $5,000,000 of revenue in the educational fund on December 31, 1926, but that $2,500,000 of this might not be received on that date and another $1,500,000 might not be received at all. By December, Nelson B. Henry was making report to the same effect, although authentic official sources showed that there would be a $4,500,000 surplus on December 31. Patrick J. Carr, treasurer of Cook County, showed that the $2,500,000 which Henry insinuated might be held back by the County treasurer from payment to the City treasurer on the legal date of December 31, would be turned over to the City treasurer on or before December 1 of the same year. Carr proved that there would be more than $5,300,000 surplus in the educational fund on December 31.

The misrepresentations of facts about the educational fund would

---

[24]Elliot B. Ellicott (1866-1926) was an electrical engineer. A Democrat, he was appointed to the board by Dever and died during his term as president.

undoubtedly have defeated a referendum on the tax rate increase had the City Council been stampeded, through such misrepresentations, into submitting that proposition to the people. Such a defeat would have been a great misfortune to the schools as well as to the people at large, who were paying unjustly spread taxes. The schools committee reported, however, that the entire controversy over the condition of the educational fund in 1926 was due to inaccurate and misleading financial statements made by the Board of Education. It sustained the charge that there was $3,800,000 padding in one item of proposed expenditure and told the Board to clean house. The committee's report made it clear that the way to get the needed revenue for the schools was through co-operation between the City and the County. It advised that the City co-operate with the president of the Board of Cook County Commissioners, Anton J. Cermak, in his efforts to get an appraisal of all the lands and buildings of Cook County as a means of securing a fair, equitable, and uniform assessment of real estate at the quadrennial assessment to be made by the Board of Assessors and Board of Review of 1927.[25] In December [6], the County Board took action for a County-wide appraisal. Ellicott, who like Edward J. Kelly, afterward mayor of Chicago, had been an engineer of the Sanitary District from the time when Colonel Robert Rutherford McCormick, publisher of the *Chicago Tribune*, had been a dominant force in that afterward malodorous body, died suddenly in Henrotin Memorial Hospital.

Throughout that time, the Chicago Teachers' Federation kept reiterating its stand: The way to secure larger public revenue was not through tax increase but through a scientific, uniform, and equitable appraisal of the lands of the entire city and county. There were teachers outside the Federation, however, who did not feel as we did. They believed that a tax rate increase would be carried by the politicians. [Charles B.] Stillman voiced that idea at a harmony meeting in Victor Olander's office.[26] Mary Abbe, president of the Federation, who weighed about a hundred pounds, came down off a stool as if she weighed a thousand when she cried to Stillman, "Would you accept that sort of way of putting it over on the people?"

[25]Anton (Tony) Cermak (1873-1933) was an experienced politician who gained control of the Democratic party following Brennan's death in 1928. Cermak was elected mayor of Chicago in April, 1931, following a successful campaign against Big Bill Thompson. He was the victim of an assassin's bullet in February, 1933, while riding with President-elect Franklin D. Roosevelt in Florida. See Alex Gottfried, *Boss Cermak of Chicago: A Study in Political Leadership* (Seattle: University of Washington Press, 1962.)

[26]Stillman had served as first president of the American Federation of Teachers. He was a principal of the Burr Elementary School in the 1920s and a spokesman for the principals at the meeting. See note 43, p. 181. Victor Olander was the secretary-treasurer of the Illinois Federation of Labor.

Olander, who was trying to find a way for the public out of the tax impasse and who was working with the City Council finance committee toward that end, asked me if I knew how a reassessment could be correctly done. I told him that I knew the way. I happened to know it because immediately after the City Council had turned down the tax rate increase proposition, Henry M. Ashton, who was then representing the high school men teachers, had said there was no way by which an assessment could be equalized. The City Council, he said, could do nothing about it. I was as mad as a wet hen when I left the Council chamber. On the way over to the Unity Building, I met William H. Holley, now a judge of the United States District Court. Holley said, "You'll never have equalized assessments until you get the Somers system." I wired to Cleveland, where the Somers system was in operation, asking for a copy of the law under which it operated. Some fool there wired back that the Somers system wasn't a law.

Then I sent for [Emil O.] Jorgenson, one of the leading advocates in Chicago of Single Tax. Jorgenson brought me the report of the Cleveland assessor, which was the basis of the Somers system. The Somers system had been effective in Cleveland from the time of its establishment under Tom Johnson. There was no reason why it could not be effective in Chicago. We prepared a statement from it and sent it to the finance committee of the City Council, asking them to get a reassessment of the Loop on this basis and to get the necessary help to make it. The City Council voted on appropriation for a sample survey and directed the Manufacturers' Appraisal Company to do the work. Harry Cutmore directed the job for them.

This appraisal fixed value on fifty-two buildings on three typical streets in the Chicago Loop district. From these appraisals, charts were made, which revealed instances of the gross inequalities in assessment of Loop property and which showed wide divergence between the values set by the Board of Review and those of the appraisal company. It was recognized that these inequalities could be remedied only by a scientific appraisal, which would wipe out the deceptive, secretive, unequal assessments which permitted much property to escape taxation altogether or to pay only a small percentage of its share in the burden.

The Teachers' Federation then asked the City Council to appropriate $100,000 for a scientific, uniform, and equitable appraisal of the lands of the entire city. The Board of Commissioners of Cook County had already appropriated $50,000 toward the same purpose. The Federation offered to provide for an insurance fund of $100,000 to insure the payment of the same amount appropriated by the Board of Education for the same purpose, in the event that for any reason whatsoever this money would not be available from the funds of the Board. The situation stood there at the time of the mayoralty election of 1927.[27]

During three years in Chicago, William McAndrew had alienated almost every group of people with whom he came into contact. He had antagonized the Board of Education. He had offended the business interests who had depended on him to do what he had promised them. He had docked, clocked, and smocked the teachers. He had upset them, not only by fake salary schedules and absurd rulings about methods in classrooms, but also by alliance with Charles H. Judd, then director of the School of Education of the University of Chicago, who had characterized public school teachers as "a mobile mob of women meditating matrimony," and who had consistently opposed them. He had thrown out the teachers' councils, thereby destroying the absolute essence of democracy in the public schools of Chicago. He had confused the children. He had thrown the town into turmoil, which was bound to express itself politically.

The primary elections early in 1927 showed that McAndrew was Dever's principal liability. So many teachers known to be Democrats voted in the Republican primaries for William Hale Thompson that precinct captains rushed into City Hall with protests against the situation which had caused them to take this action. Something had to be done at once to allay the resentment of the teachers. In the same old way, the same old method was taken out of the mothballs.

On March 26, 1927, just a little while before the April election for mayor, Mrs. W. S. Hefferan, one of the trustees of the Board of Education appointed by Mayor Dever, made public announcement that on April 8 the finance committee would approve the McAndrew salary schedule and that on April 13 the Board of Education would pass it.[28] The schedule hadn't been changed at all before its burial and it looked even worse in its grave clothes. I didn't know that it was being resurrected until after I had entertained some distinguished visitors, who were a little slow in telling me the object of their calls.

[27]The board voted to make available $100,000 for this purpose on Mar. 12, 1927. The CTF voted to guarantee to provide this amount if the board was unable to do so. *Margaret Haley's Bulletin*, 4, (Mar. 31, 1927), p. 204.

The members of the CTF voted to pay $25 each to help raise the funds at a mass meeting held at the Studebaker Theater, Sept. 23, 1927. *Chicago Tribune*, Sept. 24, 1927; Margaret Haley to J. Lewis Coath, president of Board of Education, Oct. 25, 1927, as reprinted in *Margaret Haley's Bulletin*, 5 (Oct. 25, 1927), pp. 43-50.

[28]Helen M. Hefferan (1865-1953) had been a student of Colonel Parker at the normal school. An active Democrat, she was the first president of the Illinois Congress of Parents and Teachers. Initially appointed in 1923 by Dever, she served on the board for eighteen years.

Heading the parade were Charles E. Merriam and Donald C. Richberg. Merriam did the talking.[29] He said that Dever intended to appoint Victor F. Olander, of the Chicago Federation of Labor, upon the Board of Education. I said, "What assurance have you that he will, and what good will it do? If Olander goes on the Board now, it's too late."

Merriam looked sad. Richberg blew up. I told him to blow up all he liked. They went out.

Then Quirk, of the *Tribune*, came in. He said that he had come from Dan Sullivan, the political editor of the *Tribune*, but that his errand wasn't newspaper business. Sullivan, he said, wanted me to keep quiet.

"What am I doing that Sullivan wants me to keep quiet? Tell him I'll go out and yell my head off. What does he mean by keeping quiet?"

Quirk wouldn't tell me.

I said, "You'll have to come back here later because Mary McDowell is coming over now and I don't want to leave her waiting for one minute, or she'll think I'm high-hatting her."

Mary McDowell was then the head of Dever's Department of Public Welfare. She had a hard job there and she was doing it well.[30] She had done all her jobs in the town well, for she was right on fundamental questions, not sacrificing principle to expediency. Even then, she was advocating Dever's re-election because she continued to believe in him. She asked me if I couldn't arrange to have her talk with the teachers about the school situation.

I said, "Mary, I can't help you very much. You could do nothing with the teachers. They've been crying to high Heaven and nobody has heard them. Now they've got to protect themselves."

She went away not in anger but in sorrow. Merriam came back alone. After he had talked a while about Olander, I asked him, "What is this all about?"

"We want you to keep quiet."

"What do you mean? I'm not opening my head." He didn't tell me, but said he'd come back at nine o'clock that evening.

Then Quirk returned. He was a good trader and he knew that at other times I'd be the source of front-page news for him. He put his

[29]Donald Richberg (1881-1960) was a lawyer who was active in Republican politics. Later, he co-authored the National Industrial Recovery Act in 1933 and served as general counsel for the NRA under Franklin D. Roosevelt.

[30]Mary McDowell (1854-1936) was the head of the University of Chicago Settlement from 1894 to 1929. Active in a variety of reform causes, she was a major voice in support of legislation limiting hours of employment for women and children. Dever appointed her commissioner of public welfare in 1923. See Howard Wilson, *Mary McDowell, Neighbor* (Chicago: University of Chicago Press, 1928).

cards on the table. The Board of Education, he said, was going to drag
out the McAndrew report the next day and didn't want me to lift my
voice in protest. Would I, he asked me, keep quiet?

"When did I ever keep quiet under circumstances like these?"

He said he couldn't remember and went out.

Merriam came back at nine o'clock. He said again that Olander
would go on the Board. I said, "I know what you want. You want me
to keep quiet tomorrow when they drag out the McAndrew report. You
want me to stay away from the meeting of the Board of Education. I
know why Richberg was here with you and I know why you're here
again. Well, I won't keep quiet. That report is no good. It hasn't been
fixed up as it should have been by its amendments, and you know that
there isn't any money for an increase now. The teachers are not
demanding an increase in salary. They want peace. They want that
damned fool kicked out and some kind of peace restored to the schools."

Then Merriam went out.

Mrs. Hefferan had been right. On April 8, the finance committee of
the Board of Education passed the revived McAndrew schedule. Even if
the schedule could have been passed at an earlier meeting, it would not
have had enough political effect to change the result of the election.
William McAndrew had been the cause of the defeat of William E.
Dever.[31]

4

Less than two weeks after the election, McAndrew spoke at a dinner of
the University of Michigan Club in Chicago.[32] There he said, "I was
brought to Chicago for a distinct task—the loosening of the hold of the
'invisible empire' within the schools, a weird system, a selfish system,
doing everything to indicate a selfish purpose and demanding the
right to govern the schools." Just a little while before, Mrs. M. V.
Ayres, speaking before the Woman's City Club, had said that Mc-
Andrew had been placed at the head of the public school system as a
result of the interest of a "public spirited body" made up of groups of
powerful men in certain Chicago clubs.

[31]Haley campaigned openly for Thompson in 1927. To defeat his opponent, Mayor
Dever, Thompson returned to his old campaign tactics of fostering prejudice. He
attacked the school board and McAndrew for endorsing unpatriotic history texts. This
"America First" approach was a sorry spectacle, which included Thompson's threats
against the King of England. However, it brought victory to "Big Bill." See Wendt and
Kogan, *Big Bill of Chicago*, pp. 222-70.

[32]McAndrew acknowledged that he had been brought to Chicago to "steamroller" the
Chicago Teachers' Federation. *Chicago Daily Journal*, Apr. 18, 1927.

The "invisible empire" was, of course, the Chicago Teachers' Federation. Who, though, were the "groups of powerful men" interested in having its hold loosened?

The City Council wanted to know the answer to the question. On the first meeting in April, after William Hale Thompson and the newly elected aldermen had been inducted into office, a resolution was introduced into the Council requesting McAndrew to appear before the Council committee on schools. He didn't appear as ordered but he didn't completely avoid trouble by that absence.

There is a section of the school law for Chicago, numbered 129, which read:

> The superintendent of schools, the business manager, the attorney, and assistant attorneys are exempt from civil service law. All others are subject to the provisions of the civil service law.

That section, which is law, was invoked by a stationary fireman, named John J. Brennan, who asked the Superior Court of Cook County for a writ of mandamus to compel the Chicago Board of Education to stop violating the school law and the civil service law, and to force the Board to fire the firemen who were being hired illegally and to hire the firemen it should hire legally. The Superior Court granted Brennan his writ of mandamus. The Appellate Court confirmed the decision on March 2, 1927. The Supreme Court of Illinois refused on June 20, 1927, to review the decision of the Appellate Court. The Board of Education had no course open except obedience to the decision.

Under that decision, the Board was compelled to shift back to the teaching force those graduates of the Normal school who were occupying positions as clerks. The Board, at a meeting on August 3, passed a resolution directing the superintendent "to forthwith make requisition for the services by the Civil Service Commission of such employees as may be necessary to carry on the clerical and business administrative activities of the education department."

McAndrew not only refused to carry out the order but gave aid, counsel, and comfort to the group who were bringing legal action against the Board to prevent the consummation of its order. McAndrew gave the Board the chance it wanted to throw him out. He was immediately ordered to trial before them on the charge of insubordination. The case against him dragged on for months, with a hearing one half day a week, but it never came to a head because McAndrew's term expired before a verdict was reached. With his carpetbag in his hand and an albatross hung around his neck, he left the Chicago he had turned upside down and inside out.[33]

I met him just as he was leaving the offices of the Board of Education. He said, "Good-by, Miss Haley. I hope I'll see you again."

I said, "I hope I'll never see you again."

[33]In the aftermath of Thompson's America First campaign, the McAndrew "trial" came to focus on patriotism and school textbooks. The superintendent was suspended in August. The official charges were presented in a letter from a member of the board, James A. Hemingway, dated Aug. 29, 1927. It is reprinted in *Margaret Haley's Bulletin*, 5, (Sept. 17, 1927), pp. 7-11, 23. After several weeks of hearings, McAndrew stopped attending and retired from the superintendency in January, 1928, with the expiration of his four-year term. Several items in the Otto L. Schmidt Papers at the Chicago Historical Society are valuable for this episode. Dr. Schmidt and Mrs. Helen Hefferan were the only members who supported McAndrew. See also Counts, *School and Society*, pp. 276-84.

ₒ⁰[X]⁰ₒ

Nero Fiddles

Even back in Babylonia and Egypt, where the first historical tax systems originated, there must have been difficulties in administration. There was one difficulty, however, which the publicans of those days did not project. That was the iniquity of secret taxation. The markings on bricks found in ancient ruins show that these peoples used methods of publicizing the tax declarations.

That was exactly what the Assessors of Cook County were not doing.

The Legislature of 1898 had created a Board of Assessors that went to work in 1899. This board superseded an old method, by which each town within the County had its own assessing machinery. The new Board of Assessors, numbering five, took over the assessment of the County. Instead of beginning a new system and setting up new machinery and new methods, the Board of Assessors went right on reproducing the old township books, with all the errors and all the inequalities and all the lack of uniformity as to what percentage of the total value the assessed value of each one represented.

The law of 1898 also provided that the quadrennial reassessments should be published by the Board of Assessors. The Board of Assessors obeyed that law once. They published the lists of 1899. This publication showed such terrible and glaring inequalities in the taxation of Chicago property that succeeding boards dared not continue the practice for fear that the town would blaze into revolt against their methods. For more than a quarter of a century, the assessing body, one of the principal legal organizations of the County, was breaking the law.

After twenty-five years of struggling for our political, economic, and academic rights, we had discovered that the lack of revenue to run the schools of the city was due to the utter lack of equity, uniformity, justice, and fairness, or even common sense and common honesty, in the assessment of property. The tax rates were already too high. A few instances of equitable assessments in other cities—Cleveland, Ohio, and Jamestown, New York, among them—had shown that tax rates had been reduced when the assessments had been equalized and put on a uniform basis; and that haphazard guess work, favoritism, fraud, and mysterious methods had disappeared; that the public had been made acquainted with general conditions, and that fair assessments had been approved by the people of those communities. Where the people knew that the taxes were equitable, they were willing to pay their taxes without protest. It was the knowledge, already growing among the people of Chicago, that the methods of taxation were unjust and unfair, particularly to the small tax payers, that was even then beginning to create an attitude of protest against the existing machinery and its operators.

No less culpable than the Board of Assessors was the Board of Review, which had the duty and privilege of revising the taxes established by the Assessors. The appraisals made by the Manufacturers' Appraisal Company showed valuations of Loop property in 1926 greatly in excess of the valuations set by the Assessors and approved or revised by the Board of Review. This sample appraisal showed valuation of $555,972,415 above that of the tax setting bodies. This was the equivalent of the taxation necessary on 110,794 little homes of $5,000 value each. It meant that more than 100,000 small tax payers were making up the deficit caused by this underassessment of high priced Loop property.

Although appraisal had not yet been made of districts outside the Loop, everyone who knew anything at all about the tax situation in Chicago knew that fearful injustices were being done. Sometimes in the same block upon houses built exactly alike at exactly the same cost, different valuations would be set because of the tax fixing custom that has been part of all civic politics. Two houses, each worth $10,000, might have—and usually did have—assessments of wide variation. One might be assessed on a full value of $6,000, the other on a full value of $8,000. Upon the first, the tax payer would pay $270 a year; upon the second, $360 a year. A tax rate increase of one dollar a thousand would force the first tax payer to pay $300, the second $400 a year. If, however, the assessments were equalized, each one of the tax payers would pay $360.

As the tumultuous Twenties rose to climax, with tremendous fortunes being piled up by a limited number of individuals and with political power tending to centralize in small groups controlled or at least influenced by great financial, commercial, and industrial combinations, the City of Chicago nevertheless started sliding away from solvency. As early as 1923, the officers of the local government realized that something had to be done about adjustment of the tax situation. Dever appointed a committee soon after he was made mayor to report on methods and measures designed to ameliorate the difficulty of collecting sufficient taxes to meet municipal bills. The City Council passed a resolution calling on citizen groups of every kind to cooperate with it in making necessary changes in the tax levy set-up, particularly in the matter of assessment.

Out of this request developed two movements, both apparently headed in the same direction, but widely differing in fundamental intention. One of these groups, the Joint Tax Commission, headed by George O. Fairweather, assistant business manager of the University of Chicago, was an honest, whole-hearted crusade to remedy the terrible abuses known to exist in the offices of the assessing machinery of Cook County.[1] The other group, which came into power as an aftermath of the genuine effort of the people to correct the evils of Cook County assessments, had an altogether different basic intention. The Fairweather group and its allies wanted justice for the people at large secured by genuinely democratic methods. The subsequent group, best known as the Sargent Committee, wanted change in the taxing machinery; but the change it desired was a substitution of Fascist methods for existing taxing machinery.[2] If we had not been so concerned in our immediate object of securing equitable taxation, we would have realized even then that we were facing in our own community a situation which has broadened and deepened through these intervening years.

There's no question in my mind that the assessing of buildings and personal property is antiquated to a point that's practically unbelievable. It's older and more useless and out of date than the tallow candle or the prairie schooner, in an age of automobiles and airplanes. It's unsound, dishonest, and unintelligent. Wherever an attempt has been made to put it into practice in any way that could be called honest, its essential futility and unsoundness is demonstrated. To me, there is no doubt but that land values should be the subject matter of taxation. My belief, however, had nothing to do with my action through that period, for I knew that it was not yet possible to secure a system that

[1]The official name for this body was the Joint Committee on Real Estate Valuation. Following attempts by the Board of Education, the City Council, and the organized teachers to secure an appraisal in 1926, the Cook County Board of Commissioners appointed this committee in January, 1927. While it included representatives from the Board of Assessors and the Board of Review, these members declined to participate; therefore, it acted as a citizen's advisory committee. Herbert D. Simpson, *Tax Racket and Tax Reform in Chicago* (Menasha, Wis.: The Institute of Economic Research, Northwestern University, [1930]), pp. 124-27 (hereafter cited as Simpson, *Tax Racket and Tax Reform*). Simpson, a professor of finance at Northwestern University, was a member of this Joint Committee.

[2]The Sargent committee is discussed in chapter 11. Composed of businessmen who had served on earlier tax study groups, including the Joint Committee on Real Estate Valuation, it was officially called the Citizens' Committee on Public Expenditures. Its chairman, Fred W. Sargent, was president of the Chicago and Northwestern Railroad.

would be even 90 per cent workable. Those of us who wanted to improve conditions had to do the best we could with things as they were. The American public was not yet ready for any revolutionary change in taxing system, although the Chicago public was more than ready for revision of the method under which it suffered.

Even before the 1927 quadrennial assessment was spread by the Cook County Board of Assessors, everyone who knew anything at all about the tax situation knew that radical measures of change must be instituted to secure something like equalization of Cook County taxes. The first step was, of course, an honest appraisal of values. If the old practice of secrecy were to be continued, no honest appraisal was possible. Nothing but the fear of an aroused public opinion would have any effect upon the Board of Assessors or the Board of Review.[3]

The Chicago Teachers' Federation did not go into the war for honest tax valuation merely for the sake of fighting. Year after year, the teachers of Chicago were being warned that the City, and consequently the Board of Education, faced a deficit, which would result in the lowering of salaries and the possible non-payment of salaries. The only way by which the teachers could insure themselves the money they were earning was by seeing that the City received enough money from taxation. As far back as 1900, we had found out that the trouble lay in the failure of Big Business to pay its proportionate amount into the public treasury. The great corporations, particularly the utilities, were constantly corrupting Legislatures and officials to save themselves from just payment of what they owed the communities from which they acquired their wealth.

A little while after "Big Bill" Thompson had been re-elected mayor of Chicago in 1927, I met him in Springfield, where he and I were both witnesses at a Legislative hearing on the tax situation. I had said that the basic trouble with Board of Education finances was with the assessment of property in Chicago. Big Bill rose, crossed the room, shook hands with me, and said that I was right. I asked him why he did not take his "big stick" and go after the Board of Review and Board of Assessors instead of going after the school children's building fund to meet the approaching deficit in the educational fund and to increase the City's corporate fund. He said that he could not do it. I told him I did not know anyone who knew better than he how to use the big stick. I said I wished that I had it for a short time. I could and would use it. I didn't have a big stick, but I had a little one with nails in it. I took

[3]To illustrate the gravity of the situation, the yearly increase in assessed valuation in Chicago averaged 29 million dollars per year, while building permits averaged 200 million. Real estate taxes collected per capita doubled between 1915 and 1925, but the increase was not sufficient to keep up with the demands of the expanding school system. Herrick, *Chicago Schools*, pp. 177-81.

it out when we learned that the Board of Assessors and the Board of Review were giving no real relief to the community by their 1927 quadrennial. The County Board had made an appropriation of $250,000 to be used by the Assessors for the assurance of an equitable assessment. The City Council appropriated at different times during the year of 1927 another $100,000. The Board of Education, prompted by the offer of the Chicago Teachers' Federation to raise $100,000 for that purpose, appropriated another $100,000. Four hundred and fifty thousand dollars was therefore available for the making of a fair appraisal of Cook County property.

For nearly thirty years, the machinery for the making of an honest appraisal was right there in the County building. The public treasury was paying viewers to estimate all real properties of the town every four years. They might have viewed, but they never returned any information to the office that sent them out. Nobody ever required them to return any. Possibly their superior officers did not want them to bring in information because, if the information were not followed, the higher officials could be condemned. Through ignorance, through political favor, through graft, direct and positive, things went from bad to worse among the 3,300,000 pieces of property on the rolls. The 1927 assessment, no better than some of its worst predecessors, ranged from 5 to 500 per cent of actual values. Like other abuses, it had grown so terrible that already it was on the way to rectify itself.

The quadrennial assessment roll of 1927 was so fraudulent that anyone who knew an iota about taxing law knew that just as soon as it was attacked in court it would collapse. The teachers of the town had an advantage of being so closely in touch with the ordinary public that they were aware of the tense spirit of public protest against the injustices of that assessment. The Federation knew that thousands of attacks—as a matter of fact, more than 40,000 protests were filed as soon as the assessment notices were sent out—would be made upon the legality of the assessment. We knew that these attacks would not only wipe out the source of revenue for the current year but also for the four years following. If any civic department were to have any money at all for functioning until 1932, something had to be done and done fast.[4]

Back in 1919, the Legislature had established a State Tax Commission, which had the power to bring about an interim assessment. The Tax Commission had no power to make such an assessment, but it had

[4]Mary Herrick, then an active member and later president of the Women High School Teachers' Federation, wrote that the first major confrontation between the high school teachers and the CTF took place on this issue. The high school unions wanted to follow the traditional CTF tactic of instituting legal action. Given the enormity of the financial crisis, Haley pressed for the reassessment approach which she believed would avoid the long delays which pursuit through the courts entailed. *Ibid.*, p. 184.

control of supervision. If it ordered the taxing bodies to make a reassessment, those bodies would have to obey the order under the law. Therefore, on October 25, 1927, in anticipation of the legal action which would knock out the assessment of 1927 on grounds of general fraud, the Federation filed a petition for reassessment with the State Tax Commission.[5]

Why did the teachers of Chicago take on this leadership of the fight for equalized assessment?

The theory of relationship between the Board of Education and the teaching force is that the Board of Education looks after all business and financial arrangements concerning the public schools and that the teachers merely teach. The theory is excellent. Possibly, if it were ever worked out, it might result in a public school system that was educational. The world—and particularly Chicago—being what it is, the theory has never had a chance to work out in this bailiwick. The teachers, except for the period when teachers' councils were permitted, have never had opportunity to establish any real educational system. The Board of Education has failed woefully to make proper provision for the finances necessary to run the schools. It has, in the hundred years of its existence, given away land which, if kept, would pay the entire cost of the schools every year. It has, both in its internal and external relationships, willfully wasted millions of dollars; and it has consistently failed to acquire many other millions due it in taxes which have never been collected.

In 1925, the Board, apparently spurred by the need of money, joined with the Federation in a fight to bring tax dodgers to time. The case in question was one seeking a reassessment of 135 acres of land owned by the Union Stockyards Company, valued by that company at $130,000 an acre for rate making purposes but fixed at a full value of $11,000 an acre by the Board of Review for taxation purposes. The Federation turned over its data concerning the value of these 135 acres of Stockyards land to Henry M. Ashton, an attorney appointed by the Board of Education as its special counsel in this case. Ashton appeared one morning before the State Tax Commission on behalf of the Board of Education and urged that Commission to increase the assessment of the Union Stockyards Company in conformity to its own declaration of the $130,000 an acre value. In the afternoon of the same day, Ashton returned with the attorney for the Stockyards corporation and asked the State Tax Commission not to increase the assessment.

[5]The State Tax Commission was created in 1919 as part of a reorganization of state government under the administration of Governor Frank O. Lowden. The new three-member commission replaced the twenty-five-member State Board of Equalization. *Laws of Illinois, 1919*, p. 718; Hutchinson, *Lowden of Illinois*, I, pp. 314-318, II, p. 400. See also note 2, p. 430.

Between the years of 1913 and 1921, the increase of genuine valuations in Chicago was five hundred million dollars. Eighty million dollars of this got on the tax books. Four hundred and twenty million dollars escaped. Four per cent of that escaping amount would have been sixteen million dollars. Forty per cent of the sixteen million dollars, and this would be the amount due the schools, would have been six million dollars. Every year from that time onward, the Board of Education was missing that six million dollars and other collectible millions.

Was it any wonder that the teachers themselves had to take up the fight?

William H. Malone, the chairman of the [State] Tax Commission, was almost as picturesque a personality as James Hamilton Lewis. Later he was to be involved in difficulties that made him an exile from his own country, but through every step of the reassessment battles he was fair, honest, and efficient.[6] Quite as well as anyone else, he knew the tremendous influences which were fighting against a reassessment, but he held steadily to his duty as a public official. On the 10th of November, 1927, he started the hearings before his Commission. On January 25, 1928, the Illinois State Tax Commission entered an order for the publication of the 1927 assessment lists.

A little more than a month later, the Board of Commissioners of Cook County appropriated the money to make that work possible and, on the 1st of May, adopted the Jacobs plan of publication, approved by George O. Fairweather for the Joint Tax Commission and by myself for the Chicago Teachers' Federation.[7]

The Board of Assessors and the Board of Review had done everything in their power to prevent that publication. They knew that, just

[6]William H. Malone (1877-1956) had been elected to the State Board of Equalization on the Progressive ticket in 1912. He became chairman in 1916 and served until the board was abolished. Appointed by the governor to the State Tax Commission in 1921, he served as chairman of that body from 1929 to 1931. He resigned over a disagreement with the governor regarding proposed legislative changes and campaigned in 1932 for the state's highest office as an independent. In 1933 he was indicted for income tax evasion and served a nine-month sentence before he was pardoned. A twenty-four page pamphlet, *They Got Their Man* (Park Ridge: n.p., [1937]) is located at the Chicago Historical Society.

James Hamilton Lewis (1863-1939) was a colorful Democratic politician who served as corporation counsel during the mayoral administration of Edward F. Dunne. He was elected to the U. S. Senate in 1912 and again in 1930 and 1936.

[7]The Jacobs plan was a systematic approach to valuation. As she indicates, Haley worked closely with the Joint Committee for Real Estate Valuation. *Margaret Haley's Bulletin*, 5 (May 16, 1928), pp. 184, 186; Simpson, *Tax Racket and Tax Reform*, pp. 130-33.

J. Louis Jacobs (1885-1965) was a tax consultant and efficiency expert for Cook County from 1924 to 1932, when he became the first county assessor.

as soon as the ordinary tax payer realized how he had been overtaxed in order that holders of privilege might be undertaxed, there was likely to be a complete overturn of the political personnel of Cook County. Anyone who advocated this publication was as popular with the assessing and reviewing bodies as Necker had been with the nobility of France on the publication of his *Compte rendu*.

The State Tax Commission, on May 7, issued its order for reassessment. On May 15, a conference was held between the Board of Assessors and attorneys representing a dozen other organizations. Among them were Isaiah T. Greenacre. representing the chairman of the State Tax Commission, and Charles Center Case, representing the Joint Tax Commission. Opposed to them were eight attorneys, one of whom, Henry M. Ashton, announced that he represented the Federation of Women High School Teachers. Hayden Bell, attorney for the County Board and one of the most valiant battlers for fair assessments in office within the County, was also present. The question at issue between the attorneys was this: the Assessors' advisors told that before starting to reassess they should get a Supreme Court decision as to the constitutionality of the State law authorizing the State Tax Commission to order a reassessment. Greenacre advised them that their oath of office required them to assume the constitutionality of the law and obey it, that it was not for them to question its constitutionality. The Assessors agreed to make the reassessment.

Immediately, the Board of Review raised the question that the Assessors and they lacked sufficient money for the reassessment. The State Tax Commission met the objection by giving them Rules 14 and 15. Rule 14 required that the viewers, those men who for thirty years had been paid to view the different properties, should actually do the work the law required of them. Rule 15 required that the Board of Assessors and the Board of Review should use the information that Rule 14 had brought in to their offices. For nearly a week, it looked as if the reassessment were actually going into immediate operation.

Was it?

No.

On May 29, the Attorney General of the State of Illinois, Oscar Carlstrom, published an opinion finding the order for reassessment of Cook County real estate issued by the Illinois State Tax Commission "premature and of no force and effect."[8]

The Supreme Court had as yet made no decision whatever upon the law. There had already been three reassessments in three other counties of the state. No one of these had been successfully challenged. Carl-

---

[8]The basis for this ruling was that the Board of Review had not completed the process of holding hearings to receive complaints. *Chicago Tribune*, May 30, 1928.

strom's opinion was not legally binding. It was merely one man's idea, but it certainly threw a monkey wrench into the machinery of progress.

Len Small was governor of Illinois. It has been the fashion in certain civic groups of Chicago to regard Small as a machine politician with little public vision. From my experience of association with every governor the state has had for forty years, I can say without qualification that, with the exception of John P. Altgeld and Edward F. Dunne, Len Small was the most public spirited executive of all that time. He had what few elective and no appointive officers ever have, a sense of nearness to the people whom he served. More shrewdly than either Altgeld or Dunne, he knew all the moves that the opponents of the people at large would make, in the great game we make of politics. He knew then just what the crisis meant.

I knew when I went to him that he wouldn't throw me out of the office; but I didn't expect all that I really got from him. He listened intently while I outlined the matter to him. "What do you want?" he asked me.

"A special session of the Legislature."

"All right," he said. "If you will get a majority of both houses to ask me to have them come back for another special session, I'll issue the call."

Armed by his promise, I went into the house of representatives and asked someone there to get me a unanimous consent to speak to the house. The house gave it. I told them they should change the law so that the Assessors and the Board of Review couldn't wabble out of it. Then the Tax Commission would order the reassessment.[9]

The house knew the Chicago situation pretty well by that time. An investigating committee, headed by Senator John Dailey of Peoria, had held sessions for several months over the irregularities of Cook County assessments and had reported to the Legislature that the town certainly needed a revaluation. Both house and senate agreed on the special session, which was the shortest on record, five days, and which Governor Small always called "Margaret Haley's session." It enacted legislation to put teeth in the State Tax Commission order.[10]

[9]Len Small (1862-1936) served two terms as governor from 1921 to 1929. A Republican, he was considered a close political associate of Mayor Thompson. His administration was noted for its aggressive highway construction program. Small was charged with embezzling state funds; the legal actions ended with his payment of $650,000 to the state treasury. Howard, *Illinois*, pp. 465-66, 490.

[10]The legislation gave the State Tax Commission authority to order reassessments and required the publication of the names and addresses of property owners in each quadrennial assessment. Simpson, *Tax Racket and Tax Reform*, p. 134. Haley pointed out that the last time such a list had been published was 1899. *Margaret Haley's Bulletin*, 5 (May 31, 1928), p. 204.

That was June, 1928. Nine months later, on March 6, 1929, the
regular session of the next Legislature passed a law validating certain
measures which the tax levying bodies of Cook County insisted were
necessary before they could proceed with action. By September 30,
1929, there was on file in the offices of the Board of Assessors a
permanent property record card for every one of the 1,200,000 parcels
of land and more than 900,000 buildings in Cook County, the first
official record of its kind ever to be established in that office.

The State Tax Commission had ordered the Board of Review to
begin its revision of assessments on October 1 and to proceed not as
individuals, as heretofore, but as a body. The Board met on October 1,
but did not begin the actual work of hearing complaints until October
21. Two days earlier, the Supreme Court of Illinois had handed down a
decision declaring that the Tax Commission law was constitutional
and the order to reassess was legal. What Mrs. Wiggs of the Cabbage
Patch would have called "debatin' and decidin' time" was over. On the
afternoon of Monday, October 28, official announcement was publicly
made by the Board of Review that the Board would sit as a board and
hear all complaints.[11]

And did they pour in?

By that time, the Jacobs plan list, showing the inequalities, discrepancies, and dishonesties of Cook County taxation, was public property.
Every tax payer knew what his neighbor paid. He also knew what the
big buildings of the downtown district, the big hotels and apartments
of Streeterville, the residences of the "Gold Coast" paid. He knew for
the first time just how badly he had been gypped. The Third Estate
had arrived in force at the tax windows of Cook County.

Official testimony given under oath before the Illinois revenue committee authorized by the Legislature of 1927 showed that the Cook
County Board of Review had cut off $537,000,000 from the Assessors'
1927 quadrennial assessment. The joint commission on real estate
valuations appointed in 1927 by the County Board estimated that the
Board of Assessors had cut off another half billion dollars from its own
1927 assessment before turning that assessment over to the Board of
Review.

The billion dollars that had been cut off from taxation by these two
Boards was more than the assessed values of fifty counties in the State
of Illinois in the same year.

In addition to the loss of the billion dollars in assessed valuation in

---

[11]The October activities of the board coincided with the beginning of the Great
Depression. One of the early events was the break in the stock market on October 24
(Black Thursday), when stock prices fell dramatically.

1927, there was another unprecedented loss suffered in the collection of the taxes based on that reduced assessment. The educational fund alone lost nearly six million dollars of the forty-one million dollars that should have been collected on what was left of the assessment after the Boards had finished chopping it down. Instead of collecting the forty-one million dollars for the educational fund on the quadrennial assessment, the collection officers took in only a little more than thirty-five million dollars.

For that reason, the Board of Education found itself unable to meet its salary obligations in November and December, 1928. It then asked the City Council to authorize it to borrow from City funds $4,500,000 with which to complete the payment of the November and December pay rolls of the teachers. That was after the banks had loaned the Board the full legal limit of 75 per cent against its 1928 tax levy for the educational fund. To return that loan, the amount was taken illegally out of the legal income of the educational fund for the following year, 1929. Then the Board found itself in difficulties and rushed down to Springfield with a bill proposing to increase the tax rate for the Chicago educational fund from 96 cents to $1.47 in 1929 and to $1.35 in 1930. The same bill contained provision that the educational fund rate should automatically go back to 96 cents in 1931 and that the building fund rate should automatically go out of existence in that year and stay out.

The president of the Board of Education, H. Wallace Caldwell, rushed into action with a letter, of which 600,000 copies were sent out to fathers and mothers of public school children. The letter pleaded that the parents should send to members of the Legislature an expression of their agreement with the Board's policy. Caldwell declared in the letter that "such outstanding citizens as Elmer T. Stevens, George F. Getz, James Simpson, William Wrigley, Jr., George M. Reynolds, W. Rufus Abbott, John Hertz, Silas H. Strawn, and Thomas E. Wilson," as members of the executive committee of the Mayor's Committee, had been responsible for the production of the bill.[12]

The bill, known as House Bill 633, had never been presented at any open meeting of the Board of Education. I had heard that Caldwell had been working on something of this type and I asked to be permitted to see a copy of any bill that might be presented to the Legislature. I was told that there was no copy of a bill and no bill. The bill was, however, introduced in the house on the day following their refusal to show it to me by Representative [Calvin T.] Weeks.

[12]H. Wallace Caldwell (1895-1940) was a real estate man described as a young booster of Mayor Thompson. Wendt and Kogan, *Big Bill of Chicago*, p. 302.

The next day, Geraldine Daly, my associate on the *Bulletin* which we were then issuing, called me from Springfield, where she was looking after some of our reassessment bills. She said, "Representative Weeks came to me today and asked me if I could tell him what was in that bill he had introduced for the Board of Education yesterday. He said the newspaper men were asking him, and he didn't know what was in the bill."

Knowing that the bill had been smuggled to Springfield, I read it carefully as soon as she sent it to me, wondering what joker had been tucked away in it. I had a queer feeling when I began to realize that I could find no provision for a school building tax rate after 1930. I called up Hayden Bell, who told me that the County Clerk would not apply the new tax rate under the language of that bill, and that if he did, it could not be collected; that the bill was so worded that the old tax rate would have to stand for 1929.

I took my belated copy to Greenacre, the wise, faithful counsellor for thirty years of the little group of us who were fighting for what we knew was a great, but seldom a winning, cause. He caught instantly the omission of the building fund rate, but went over the bill carefully before he gave his written opinion. I went to Springfield as soon as I received that.

By the time the bill came up for hearing, Frank Righeimer, attorney for the Board of Education, had brought in explanation for an amendment, which Weeks presented to the committee that day. Righeimer's statement said that there had been a typographical error in getting up the bill. A downstate representative who was a county superintendent of schools wanted to know why the Chicago Board of Education had come to Springfield to ask the Legislature to vote a tax rate increase, which the people of Chicago could grant on a referendum. Caldwell told him that the law for Chicago was different from the law downstate. His information was a great surprise to the legislators.

The bill was in sub-committee when I met Thomas J. Courtney, then a member of the state senate and later State's Attorney of Cook County, who had been helping us. Courtney told me not to worry about anything the sub-committee did. The committee, he said, would do what we wanted. I told him that I was glad to hear that, as the sub-committee had certainly bashed in my head.

"Did you ever hear," he asked me, "the story of the man who was brought into a Tipperary court to show how badly he had been hurt? The prosecutor called the judge's attention to the witness, but the attorney for the defendant won his client's release when he asked, 'Your Honor, what was a man with a head like that doing in Tipperary?'"

When House Bill 633 reached the senate, its sponsors—and in almost every instance they were the same men who had been fighting the reassessment—found that they could not get it through that body without amending it again by inserting a budget provision. They had drafted no budget provision and they had little time in which to make one. Thomas V. Sullivan, another attorney for the Board, came to me to find out if Greenacre had drafted a budget, if I had a copy of it, and if I would give it to him. Three weeks earlier, one of the state senators had told me that Sullivan had only found out that day, that House Bill 633 could not get through the senate without the budget amendment. Greenacre had made the budget amendment in the meantime, and Sullivan took it.

The Greenacre amendment saved the Keeler amendments, which contained the Keeler budget. Sullivan and I went together over them. I showed him the parts of the Keeler amendment that should be stricken out—that were other than budget provisions—and where certain of Greenacre's words would probably be better than Keeler's. Sullivan put those in. That afternoon, Senator [John T.] Joyce introduced it. The bill passed with the Greenacre amendment plus the Keeler amendments. That evening, I asked Joyce if he knew whose budget he had introduced.

He said, "The Board's attorney drafted it."

I told him it was the Keeler budget.

He said he understood that they had drafted it at noon that day.

I said, "You misunderstood. They copied it at noon today."

If it had not been for the vigilance of the people whom the Board was opposing, the Board measure would never have passed the Illinois Legislature or, if it had, the building fund of the Chicago schools would have been completely out after the next two years.

Harris Keeler, who was all there was to the Bureau of Public Efficiency, an unofficial, tax considering organization, which had been fostered by Julius Rosenwald, head of one of the great mail order businesses of the United States [Sears and Roebuck], had devised a plan for saving large sums of public money yearly.

Until that time, the tax levy had been divided in this fashion: 10 per cent was estimated to be lost in collection; 75 per cent could be anticipated by borrowings from the banks. This left 15 per cent. Keeler's plan involved the use of this 15 per cent as a revolving fund. It had to trail behind the warrants, but it gave to the Board of Education a financial loophole at the time when it was most needed. The Keeler amendment provided for an appropriation for a working cash fund to retire tax anticipation warrants. By this plan, the Board would eventually get back to a cash basis and gradually decrease the amount of loans and thereby decrease the payment of interest on loans from banks, and eventually wipe out that interest.

For years, under the existing law, the Board of Education had been borrowing from big banks, usually the banks of Chicago, on tax anticipation warrants and paying them in interest such huge yearly sums that the situation had become grave. The law permitted these borrowings up to 75 per cent of the taxes anticipated. It did not make such borrowings compulsory, but through the torrential Twenties the practice had grown appallingly.

As late as 1929, H. Wallace Caldwell got through the Legislature a bill authorizing the Board of Education to issue tax warrants for that year amounting to more than thirteen million dollars more than they had money to repay, with interest at the rate of 6 per cent. Now, seven years afterward, not a dollar of money has been collected to pay them. Not one bank in Chicago held any of these 1929 warrants; all were held by eastern banks. The Supreme Court decision of 1935 held that warrants above 90 per cent of the total tax levy are of no value. This is one of the few instances when the banker, not the public, is holding the bag.

No one who has known the Board of Education can imagine that it was the Board's intention to defraud the banker. Caldwell did his best to persuade the City Council that it should provide that the bank which bought the warrants should be the depository for the Board's educational funds as they were being collected. This would have insured the bank, but it would have broken the spirit of the law and withdrawn the money from the working cash fund.

Governmental agencies had joined the great spending orgy of the western world. The Sanitary District "Whoopee Board" had set the pace for all local expenditures. Chicago was on a spending spree and, to pay for it, Chicago had to go on a borrowing spree. Already, officials were robbing Peter to pay Paul. The trouble was, by the end of the Twenties, that Peter had awakened to the fact of how he was being robbed and was protesting against his unwilling part in the transaction. The tax payer was refusing to be mulcted. Reassessment had delayed tax payments in Chicago, but the condition held more serious elements than that of delay. Small home owners, small business men, small tax payers of all kinds, had learned that they were the men and women who paid, not only the expenditures for City government, but also the interest on the loans which the City, including the Board of Education, was receiving from the great banks.

Had other conditions been normal, the Keeler plan would have done away with the millions of dollars a year in interest. Even under the appalling conditions of the Thirties, the working cash fund established by law that day in Springfield has been one of the few bulwarks of security held by the Board of Education.

There has existed a venerable, if not venerated, precedent, which was taken out of the cupboard by the Board of Education in 1930. Assuming that the City Council would provide for the issuance of 1930 tax anticipation warrants against the educational fund tax levy, the Board might print educational fund tax warrants in small denominations, called scrip, corresponding to the salary payments of the teachers and issue these to the teachers in lieu of their regular pay checks. These warrants would draw 6 per cent interest until paid, but would not be paid until the 1930 taxes could be collected in 1931. The teachers would have to "hawk" the warrants to find a purchaser and take the price the purchaser would be willing to pay. The practice had been used in earlier years until Corinne Brown had raised such protest about it that the Board had taken back its warrants and paid the teachers in cash.

In spite of new protests, the Board revived the custom. They had no power under the law to do it. We took the matter to the courts. Judge Philip Finnegan declared the process outside the law. His decision was so definite that both the Board and the City Council stood in danger of being held in contempt of court if they made any effort to subvert it. Even after Judge Finnegan had issued his decision, however, the Board of Education continued to issue these warrants. Judge Finnegan had to call in Lewis E. Myers, who by that time was president of the Board, to tell him that the scrip could not be handled, but that the Board must find a way to pay the teachers. Myers gave up the scrip idea reluctantly. The utilities, gas and electric, had been particularly friendly to their use. The handling of them gave big local corporations a chance to make money even when they purchased them at par. They could exchange them later for actual warrants, which they could use for payment of their own taxes and on which they drew interest. For the teachers, however, they were a losing proposition.

The Board was still owing the teachers their May and June salaries for 1931 when the scrip was withdrawn by court order. The Board had, however, three million dollars in tax warrants which it had intended to work into the scrip. We made a gentlemen's agreement with them that these warrants should be used for the teachers' pay. Then, just before the last meeting for the summer of the Council finance committee, I discovered that the Board had broken its agreement and turned over the warrants for sale. John S. Clark, chairman of the finance committee, helped us save the day.

Then the Board of Education found that it had about three million dollars of bills to pay, mostly coal bills. It took action that they could use any warrants available to pay those bills. The warrants we had won back under duress had not yet been given to us. Now the Board was going to give them to the coal companies. Cermak, by that time mayor of Chicago, had to sign the warrants.[13] I went over to his office in the City Hall to tell him that if he put his signature on them, he would be in contempt of court.

Cermak could see around a corner about as well as any man who ever sat in the mayor's chair. He never took his ear far away from the ground. He had a sense of closeness to the people whom he represented that, in spite of other elements in his administration, kept him from being the worst mayor the city ever had. Cermak knew fairly well that he wouldn't sign those warrants, but he was upset and indignant about something else—he was having a fight over the telephone with Henry Horner, afterward governor of Illinois, yelling at him, "Chase them out. What have you got men in your office for?"—and he was also annoyed about another incident. Being the good horse trader he was, Tony brought up the incident before he'd tell me that he wouldn't sign the warrants.

A teacher had sent him a letter. He had it in his hand as he talked to me. She was, she said, cold and hungry. She was without her salary. She had no money. She had no possessions but a pair of blankets. She was going to come down to the City Hall with those blankets and go to sleep in the mayor's office, which, she understood, was warm and comfortable. Tony had imagination enough to see how such procedure would be reported in the newspapers. The teachers were desperate enough by that time, because of non-payment of their salaries, to do anything that might embarrass the public officials whom they thought were in any way involved in preventing that payment. He wanted me to take this particular teacher off his hands. He said she should be fired.

I said, "I think it would be a mistake to fire her."

Remembering the newspapers, he thought so too.

I didn't know the woman and I couldn't agree that I'd do anything about it. I think, though, that Tony must have visualized a couple of thousand other women with blanket rolls on their backs trudging into City Hall, for he didn't sign the warrants.

By 1931, the finances of Chicago had come into such a state that the banks were refusing tax anticipation loans. Bad administration, due to an impossible system of assessment and review, had destroyed faith in

[13]See note 25, p. 220.

general taxes as a source of credit and stopped purchase by the banks of anticipation warrants.

Even the Citizens' Committee, of which Silas Strawn was chairman, recognized the need of new taxation methods.[14] The Committee had raised the borrowing power of the City seventy-four million dollars early in 1930 to prevent payless pay days for public employees of Chicago and Cook County, and had also sponsored financial relief legislation for Chicago in the 1930 special session of the Legislature. One of these measures was the working cash fund, which enabled the Board of Education to borrow twenty-five million dollars without the payment of interest. All this, however, was being nullified by the delay in tax collections and the absence from the assessment roll of six hundred million dollars of taxable real and personal property which the existing system had improperly omitted. With tremendous labor, a tax machinery substitute was devised, taken to the Legislature, and, with the addition of several amendments and the subtraction of many features, finally carried. It is the system now in use in Cook County, a better system than the old one but far, far short of perfection.

The mountains had labored and brought forth a mouse.

[14]This was a group of fifty-eight citizens, organized by the Joint Committee on Real Estate Valuation, to help raise money in the form of emergency loans. Strawn (1866-1946) was a prominent corporation lawyer and former president of the Chicago Bar Association. In 1931-32, he served as president of the U.S. Chamber of Commerce. Several members of this committee served on the Sargent Committee (Public Expenditures), which is discussed in the following chapter. Simpson, *Tax Racket and Tax Reform*, pp. 185-86.

⚬⧘ XI ⧙⚬

Rome Burns

Cavalier.
Pioneer.
Racketeer.
Buccaneer.
The history of Chicago.

Into the valley of LaSalle and Joliet, of Lincoln and of Altgeld, had come forces of destruction. Goth and Vandal were beleaguering the defences of civic integrity. From Cicero, that town on the outskirts of Chicago, which unfairly and unfortunately for itself became synonymous with the fostering of lawlessness, whirled the bandit bands of Al Capone. From the heights of the Civic Opera building, that tall fortress beside the river, descended the cohorts of Samuel Insull. Both of these powers threatened Chicago, one by violence, the other by peaceful penetration.

The Citizens' Committee, which was supposed to be a financial savior of the City and which has proved to be one of the most insidious sappers of genuine civic spirit, had Samuel Insull for one of its first members. Its first chairman, Silas H. Strawn, was one of his leading attorneys. Strawn went into something like civic retirement after Insull, a fugitive from justice, had cruised the isles "where burning Sappho loved and sung," [the Mediterranean] but the spirit of Insullism remained. The Committee represented big business with two capital B's. Fred W. Sargent, president of the [Chicago and] Northwestern Railroad, became its chairman. Ernest R. Graham, one of the leading architects of the United States, became his coadjutor. John O. Rees became their seneschal.[1] The Sargent-Graham-Rees combination went into action to cut down the expenditures of the public schools.

[1]The title for this chapter was inspired by Mayor Cermak, who told the press that the U.S. Congress was "fiddling as Rome burns." This followed an unsuccessful trip to Washington in which the mayor sought a direct loan for the city from the Reconstruction Finance Corporation. *Chicago Evening American*, June 23, 1932.

The Citizens' Committee on Public Expenditures, formed in March, 1932, was also

244

From the beginning of the century, the public schools had been spreading out into broader activities. They have taken on the teaching of blind, deaf, dumb, crippled, and other handicapped children. Every one of these departments costs from three to ten times as much as the care of normal children. By the time of the low depression years of the early Thirties, the public schools had to help underfed children. The Citizens' Committee opposed these expenditures. It was trying to cut off fifteen million dollars from the educational fund for each year. It had no official standing, but it had for a time power far and away greater than that of any elected body in the city of Chicago.

Through the first five months of 1933, the school teachers of Chicago went without pay.[2] Through that time, men and women who had undertaken responsibilities and obligations went without the ordinary amenities of life. Even worse than their own plight, however, the teachers had to see, day after day, the miseries of the children whom they were trying to teach. It was a teacher in the Chicago schools, Anna Twohig, who said, "What the most intelligent people want for their children is what the teachers want for every child." The teachers of Chicago were seeing the children of Chicago going down in the ruins of a social collapse. They were asking themselves what was going to happen to these children and what would happen to society through the failure of the community to meet its obligations to its children. Through that time, I've seen teachers cry like children over their inability to save the children in their charge from the consequences of

known as the Sargent Committee. Another in the series of businessmen's committees which attempted to deal with the question of municipal finance, several of its members had served on the Strawn Committee discussed on p. 243. Of major concern to the Sargent Committee was a balanced budget for city government and this included a reduced level of school financing. The chairman, Fred W. Sargent (1876-1940), was chief executive of one of the midwest's major railroads. The teachers resented the fact that he was able to secure an eight-million-dollar loan for his Chicago and Northwestern Railroad from the Reconstruction Finance Corporation but would not support attempts to secure a federal loan for the public schools of Chicago. Sargent's views were expressed in an article, "The Tax Payer Takes Charge," *Saturday Evening Post*, 205 (Jan. 14, 1933), pp. 21, 74, 78, 80-82.

John O. Rees (1893-1973) was a tax expert who came to the city in 1926 from the Cleveland Bureau of Municipal Research. He served as director for the two major tax commissions, the Joint Commission on Real Estate Valuation and the later Sargent Committee. Herrick, *Chicago Schools*, pp. 260, 218.

[2]Between December, 1929, and August, 1934, Chicago's teachers received only nine paychecks on time with delays ranging from one week to ten months. Salaries were reduced 23 percent during this period. Penny J. Lipkin, "Payless Paydays: The Financial Crisis of the Chicago Board of Education, 1930-1934," (M.A. thesis, Columbia University, 1967), p. 1. See also "Disemboweling Chicago's School System," *School Review*, 41 (Sept., 1933), pp. 483-91. An extensive school survey was conducted by a team led by George D. Strayer of Columbia University in 1932. It gave considerable attention to financial matters, including high administrative costs, in discussing the plight of the city's schools. *Report of the Survey of the Schools of Chicago*, 5 vols. (New York: Teachers College, Columbia University, 1932).

the ruthlessness of an official program which had been inspired by unofficial greed. Away and beyond any record, they were bearing a load which was not rightly theirs. William J. Bogan, superintendent of schools at that time, asked the teachers in all the schools to make a list of all their humanitarian activities in the system. You never saw such a rebellion in your life as that which flared at his request. "No child should be labelled as a pauper," rose the teachers' howl of protest. Bogan, essentially a just man, withdrew his request. The teachers kept on providing food and clothing for the children. They kept on teaching them, not knowing when or if they would ever receive pay for their service. I still think that it was the finest example of public spirit that any group ever showed, the finest gift any profession ever tendered to its community.[3]

Did Chicago reward them?

And how!

Through the late months of 1932, the city surged in the restlessness of human misery. Through days of cold and rain and snow, men trudged the streets looking for work they could not find. In the long lines of those who still had hope enough to wait for the early editions of the newspapers, on the chance that some "help wanted" ad might open an opportunity, they talked to each other of what they thought might be the cause of their distress. On street corners, in little parks, at every point where a half dozen came together, workless men strove for some solution. Naturally, they turned to government with the idea that government could help them. While the national presidential campaign was being fought, largely on the issue of prohibition, local governments—particularly the government of Chicago—were becoming more and more conscious of the more fundamental economic and financial issue on their doorsteps.

The mayor, the City Council, the Board of Cook County Commissioners, had no more idea what to do about curing the situation than had the officials of Hamlin Town. Their only idea was alleviation. The County Board considered ways and means of establishing some kind of local currency. A method, something like a commutation ticket with stamps attached by each user, had been tried in some German communities and in a place out in Iowa, and at Irving Fisher's suggestion the Board considered its use in Cook County. The idea didn't get through, but the Chicago Teachers' Federation devised a coupon plan that had, for a time, a measure of success and that might have been much more successful could it have run for a longer time. The Stockyards companies and the Standard Oil Company worked with us on it.

---

[3]The morale of the teachers was recorded by an unknown author who wrote "Spasmodic Diary of a Chicago School Teacher," *Atlantic Monthly*, 152 (Nov., 1933), pp. 513-26. Entries run from March to Sept., 1933.

Orville J. Taylor was ready to work with us in it during his brief presidency of the Board of Education; but circumstances over which none of us had any control took Taylor out of office and blockaded further enterprise on that line. The City also was seeking some method of betterment in the condition of the people, who were already storming the doors of City Hall.

Thousands of unemployed men and women were seeking a permit to parade in protest against the futility of a civilization that denied them work. [Mayor] Cermak passed the buck to the City Council. Instead of giving to those unemployed who sought it a permit to parade through the Chicago streets, he referred it to the Council. Then came the deluge.

I had been in Chicago and of Chicago for fifty years. I had seen strikes, riots, all kinds of public demonstrations. I had watched men and women, aroused to protest against intolerable injustices, flame into righteous rages. Never, though, in all those years, had I seen anything like that scene in the City Council chamber on that November afternoon. Down the long sweep of the marble corridors stood uniformed policemen, shoulder to shoulder. A solid phalanx, they circled the dark walls of the chamber. At their desks sat the members of the Council, most of them worried men inspired by an honest desire to do whatever could be done to help the people who were appealing to them but fearful of the consequences of any public demonstration. Before them stood [as many of] the representatives of the Council of the Unemployed as the police permitted to come into the vast room.

Once, as Barnet Hodes, the corporation counsel, stabbed viciously at the sensitive consciousness of the representatives of the Council, a growl of rage rose from the crowd. One girl, a dark, blazing-eyed youngster, hardly past her childhood but already scarred by woe and worry, blazed out at him. Hodes returned with a fusillade against her and the other seekers of the permit. Once more, that menacing growl resounded under the crystal chandeliers. Then, like the Swiss Guard, the Council members surrounded Hodes and removed him from action. The immediate danger was averted, although the cause of it still remained.[4]

In February [1933], in Miami, Florida—far from his own gang-ridden city—Anton J. Cermak, mayor of Chicago, was shot by a man said to have been attempting the assassination of Franklin Delano

---

[4]This incident may have occurred on Oct. 26, when the City Council granted a permit to the "United Front of the Unemployed" for a parade through Chicago's loop. *Proceedings of the City Council*, 1932-33, p. 2994. The editor found no newspaper account describing this event at a council meeting; the parade took place on November 1, and "thousands participated" according to the *Chicago Daily News*, Nov. 2, 1933.

Roosevelt, president elect of the United States. On March 9, five days after Roosevelt took office, Cermak died.

He was the last elected mayor that Chicago was to have for more than two years. Had he lived a few weeks longer, the city would have continued in its unbroken tradition of democratic government. The law would have required a popular election to determine his successor. As it was, the City Council, directed by the Democratic County Central Committee, directed by Patrick J. Nash, directed by God knows whom, first named as temporary mayor one of its own members [Frank J.] Corr, whose only claim to fame was the fact that he had only a one-way signature—to put money into the banks but not to take it out—and later named for mayor Edward J. Kelly, one-time chief engineer of the Sanitary District and later president of the South Park Board. Not until two years later was Kelly elected by popular vote, and even the size of that vote could not change his essential characteristic of regarding political questions from the point of view of an appointive rather than of an elective officer.[5]

Tony Cermak had his faults, but he had also a sympathy with humanity which could not endure the sight of wretchedness. Sometimes, like nearly all public officials, he made the mistake of ducking his head to avoid that sight. I think, though, that for his epitaph, instead of the widely quoted words ascribed to him, "I'm glad it was me instead of you, Frank," he'd rather have my honest declaration that I'd rather have had him than Kelly as mayor of Chicago in the terrible time that followed.

From January to April, 1933, there was continued controversy between the Board of Education and the teachers over an agreement which the Board had made with bankers not to issue more than two-thirds of the total amount of 1932 educational fund tax warrants which, under the law, the Board could have issued. This cut off twelve million dollars from the money that should have been available for teachers' salaries. At the same time, the City Council provided for the full amount allowed by the law to pay other City employees. The Board denied that there was discrimination against the teachers, but the discrimination showed on the face of the evidence.

[5]Cermak died on March 6. The political power which he had consolidated for the Democratic party was extended by the Kelly-Nash machine. Frank J. Corr (1877-1934), a member of the City Council, served a term of twenty-eight days as mayor. Edward J. Kelly (1876-1950), former chief engineer of the sanitary district, was elected by the City Council to complete the unexpired term in April, 1933. He served as mayor from 1933 to 1947. Patrick Nash (1863-1943) was the influential sewage contractor who managed the operations of the powerful Democratic organization. Revelations of school board mismanagement were critical factors in bringing about Kelly's retirement from the mayoral office in 1947. Mary Watters, *Illinois in the Second World War*, 2 vols. (Springfield: Illinois State Historical Library, 1951, 1952), II, pp. 510-13.

On March 31, 1933, an overflow mass meeting of teachers, called by the Chicago Division of the Illinois State Teachers' Association, was held in the Auditorium Theater. This meeting authorized a committee, which came to be known as the Steering Committee, to go to Washington to seek federal aid.[6]

I went to Washington as a member of that committee. We went first to the Reconstruction Finance Corporation, but we didn't get to first base on that call. Then Senator Lewis, who like myself had learned a lot since the morning I'd found him breakfasting with Judge Grosscup, took us to Marvin McIntyre, one of President Roosevelt's secretaries. McIntyre had to see us whether he wanted to or not, for Lewis put his foot in the door and wouldn't take it out until we'd secured entrance. McIntrye said that the President couldn't possibly see us, but he sent us back to the Reconstruction Finance Corporation and told us to come back and report to him what Jesse Jones, the chairman of that body, would tell us. There wasn't much to report. Jones gave us serious consideration, but assured us that we'd have to come back to Chicago and make arrangements through the Chicago banks for the loans which would pay the teachers' salaries. We had been thrown back to the wolves, but thrown with such beautiful courtesy that we couldn't cavil at the manner of it.[7]

The great financial interests of the city were, of course, determined to prevent the Board of Education from paying to the teachers their back salary in bulk. They wanted to cut salaries. They regarded teachers' salaries as a community standard which determined other salaries and which should therefore be lowered; and they regarded teachers as enemies of the system which had propagated and fostered them. The banks were, and are, among the owners of property escaping proper taxation. Any fight for equitable taxation disturbed them. Some of them were also among the profiteers of school land fund leases. Any attack on the legality of these leases also disturbed them. Having the power, they were going to punish the teachers for past deeds, thereby erecting signposts of warning against future deeds.

The banks refused to lend the money to the Board of Education.

The Board called, for April 10, a conference of all heads of organizations of teachers and other employees, to discuss the question of getting money to pay their salaries, some of these already more than eight months in arrears.

---

[6]*Chicago Tribune*, Apr. 1, 1933. This was the steering committee of the Conference of Teachers and Principals.

[7]Harold Ickes, a Chicagoan serving in the Roosevelt administration as secretary of interior, recalled this episode in his autobiography. *The Secret Diary of Harold L. Ickes: The First Thousand Days, 1933-1936* (New York: Simon and Schuster, 1953), p. 22.

At that conference, the Board admitted discrimination against Board employees and showed willingness to rescind its agreement of tax warrant shortage with the bankers, if the banks would agree to buy the Board's warrants. The conference showed, however, that the Board was helpless. The bankers were in the saddle and riding hard. At the close of that conference, the nineteen representatives of the employee organizations went to the office of the Principals' Club. There they unanimously approved a communication to the Board of Education drafted by Isaiah T. Greenacre at their request. They asked the Board to take action at its meeting on April 14 to rescind its own 50 per cent limitation resolution. It notified the Board that they were asking the City to purchase the additional Board warrants up to 25 per cent of the Board's 1932 levy.

The next morning, Aaron Kline, of the Principals' Club and chairman of the Steering Committee, notified the teachers' representatives to appear that evening at the office of his club. When they arrived, Charles B. Stillman, one of the principals, announced that he had a report he wished to make. He said that on the evening of April 10, Fred Sargent, president of the Northwestern Railroad and acting head of the Citizens' Committee, had telephoned him an invitation to come at once to his home. He had talked there until midnight with Sargent, he stated. Sargent had asked him to have a small committee of teacher leaders brought to his office at nine o'clock the next evening. I was opposed to going to Sargent's office. I said so. I did not go then nor at any other time. I felt strongly that the teachers would be tricked. They were. It was during those conferences that Sargent "sold" to those teacher leaders the Ten Million Dollar "fake" deficit in the 1933 educational fund which the Board of Education later made the apparent reason for its school wrecking program. The leaders who went to that Sargent conference and to a later dinner which he served them did not, however, report what Sargent had told them until weeks after that wrecking had been accomplished. The only inference I could draw was that, even with a chart, they didn't know a bog when they saw it. I did not know the inside story of the Sargent meeting until months later. Then Aaron Kline told me that the Rees report, which was the basis of the school wrecking action, had been delivered by Sargent to the teacher leaders on that night of the 11th of April, 1933; that those leaders had turned that report over to Charles B. Stillman; that Stillman then checked up that report with Dr. Douglas in the office of the auditor of the Board of Education and thought that he had been shown an actual ten million dollar deficit.

Was there a ten million dollar deficit?

Not on your life.

The working cash fund had advanced to the educational fund at that time $14,862,717.60. This amount would in time be reimbursed. The date fixed in the law for that reimbursement was October 1, 1936. Then the amount of the 1931 educational fund taxes actually collected, up to that date, was to be ascertained and the amount of such deficiency was to be determined as of that date. An appropriation equal to the amount of such deficiency would then be set up in the budget of 1937.

The auditor of the Board of Education, however, some time around May 24, 1933, made a conjecture that there would be a deficiency in the 1931 educational fund tax collections of $6,828,057 below the amount necessary to reimburse completely the working cash fund for loans made to the educational fund in anticipation of the collection of the 1931 educational fund taxes. The law permits no conjecturing in regard to any such deficiency. It definitely provides that the exact amount of the taxes actually collected shall be ascertained on a definite date and that the deficiency, as of that date, is then and there to be determined. The law provides that an appropriation to cover that deficiency shall be made in the budget of the year specified in the law. The auditor of the Board of Education was misstating both law and facts when he made such a statement. Also, the auditor of the Board of Education was following the trail marked by John O. Rees, the financial factotum of the Citizens' Committee.[8]

Sometime in May, the Legislature had passed a bill which was an amendment to this law. This amendment was signed by Henry Horner, governor of Illinois, on July 11, 1933.[9] It provided that the amount of such deficiency so found on December 11, 1934, was to be staggered over a period of six years, and specified percentages of the total deficiency to be appropriated in the respective budgets of those six years, beginning with 1935 and ending with 1940. The years 1933 and 1934 were to have no appropriations from the educational fund to reimburse the working cash fund.

By the 12th of July, 1933, there was no deficit in the educational fund of the city of Chicago. The Legislature knew it. The governor knew it. Before the public could know it, however, the Board of Education flung out thirteen hundred principals and teachers from the schools, with the claim that the existing deficit made the action necessary.

Through the changing weather of that Chicago springtime, the

[8]A copy of the Rees Report dated "on or about April 12, 1933" is available in CTF Files. The role of the business community, in particular attention to bankers, during this crisis is discussed in Stephen D. London, "Business and the Chicago Public Schools, 1890-1966," (Ph.D. diss., University of Chicago, 1968). London includes pertinent information from an oral interview conducted in 1967 with John O. Rees.

[9]Henry Horner (1879-1940) was a Chicago native who served as probate judge of Cook County for eighteen years prior to his election in 1932. A Democrat and the first Jewish governor, he was reelected in 1936 and died in office near the end of his second term.

teachers of the city trudged to their schools, with little hope of ultimate reward and no hope at all of immediate pay. Finally, driven by necessity, they rose in public protest. Logically, they directed this protest against the banks that controlled the situation and that were blocking payment of their salaries by the Board of Education. When public officialdom broke down, the victims of the breakdown sought redress from the people whom they knew to be the controllers of the officials. The superintendent of schools said that he could do nothing. The Board of Education said that it could do nothing. The mayor of Chicago said that he would do what he could, but whatever he did brought no visible result. The solution lay with the bankers; and so the teachers went to the bankers.

They did not go as suppliants pleading for favor. They went as men and women demanding a just due. Five divisions of unpaid teachers paraded through the Chicago streets, then separated so that each one went to a different bank. The division which went to the First National Bank created such consternation among the officials there that the bank guards were disarmed in the fear of violence. Melvin Traylor, president of the bank at that time, was sensitive to the publicity sure to follow the demonstration, and sought to allay the anger of the teachers. The issue flamed almost into riot when the teachers paraded the streets, gathered in front of City Hall, and held protest meetings every Saturday morning in Grant Park, almost in front of the grounds where the Century of Progress Exposition was being rushed to completion. One of the teachers, Raymer, who might have posed for the "Citizen of Calais" at the Art Institute, was injured in a parade that was on its way to the Morrison Hotel, where it was understood that Patrick Nash and other politicians were holding a conference on the situation. A policeman at the corner of Clark and Madison Streets gave the right of way to a street car while the teachers were crossing the street. Someone broke a car window with a banner. The broken glass cut Raymer but, holding up his bloody arm, he held to his way. That was the spirit of the Chicago Teachers in that critical time.[10]

On the 12th of July, 1933, there was not a dollar of deficit in the

[10]Through the spring the teachers held parades, mass meetings, and protest actions at the Board of Education building. These culminated in late April with marches on the major banks in the Loop during spring vacation. These demonstrations were halted following a conference with Mayor Kelly on May 4. "Spasmodic Diary," pp. 520-21. See also "Walks in Chicago," *Time,* 19 (May 8, 1933), p. 34, and Milton S. Mayer, "When Teachers Strike: Chicago Learns Another Lesson," *Forum and Century,* 90 (August, 1933), pp. 121-25. Melvin A. Traylor (1878-1934), one of the most powerful bankers in the city, was a close advisor to Mayor Cermak. William H. Stuart, *The Twenty Incredible Years* (Chicago: M. A. Donahue and Co., [1935]), p. 473.

educational fund of the City of Chicago; but on that day ten members of the Kelly Board met behind closed doors in a room at the Skyline Club on North Michigan Avenue. Mrs. W. S. Hefferan [Helen], the one woman member of the Board and a hold-over from previous administrations, was kept out of the meeting.[11] At that informal meeting, the program of action was made out; then the ten members walked over to the Board rooms, went into formal meeting, and passed the wrecking program.

This program removed from the service of the Chicago public schools all of the teachers of manual arts, household arts, and manual training, and physical education. It eliminated half the kindergarten teachers, half the principals, and all of the junior high school teachers except those who had high school certificates that could be placed in the high schools. All the junior high school teachers lacking either high school or elementary school certificates were to be sent to the Normal school. Thirteen hundred teachers were put out of their positions, with only a warning from July to September.[12]

The teachers who were thrown out were specialists and, therefore, the least likely people in the school system to have unity of organization. Left to themselves, they might not have been able to raise the tremendous reaction which swept like a tidal wave over the town. The action of the Board, however, came at a time of high emotion among all the teachers. It threatened the tenure that has been one of the essential principles for which we have fought ever since Altgeld had incorporated it into the school law through the pension. The thirteen hundred teachers who were thrown out, in common with all the other teachers, were still unpaid after five months. They represented to other teachers and to the entire city what might happen to all public employees if complete power rested with a small, arbitrary, and appointive group of public officials. Had the city enjoyed the political privilege of Recall—a privilege denied it by "Blond Billy" Lorimer's bossism in Springfield in 1913—the Kelly administration would have gone out of power, even though few people knew as yet that there was no deficit to justify the Board in any such action.

[11]Hefferan worked closely with the Citizens' Schools Committee during this crisis. Herrick, *Chicago Schools*, p. 235. See also note 28, p. 222.

[12]*Proceedings, Board of Education*, 1933-34, pp. 24-28. The new president of the board, elected in May, was James B. McCahey (1890-?). *Ibid.*, 1932-33, p. 1342. The president of a fuel company, McCahey guided a school board which was subservient to the Kelly-Nash machine until his resignation in May, 1947. McCahey dominated both the board and the superintendent. Investigations by the National Education Association and the North Central Association of Schools and Colleges brought unfavorable publicity which helped to bring an end to Kelly's term as mayor. McCahey was forced to resign following the election. For an informative account of these years, see Herrick, *Chicago Schools*, chapter 14.

In the public indignation resultant from the action of the Board rose the voice of Robert Maynard Hutchins, youthful president of the University of Chicago. In a series of noteworthy articles published during July of that year Dr. Hutchins declared that the Board of Education had been motivated by political rather than by educational motives in effecting the change in the schools and pointed out the damage done the children of the city by the action. In one article issued during that period he stated that the Board of Education had willfully, wrongfully and fraudulently abandoned its own freedom of mind, substituting the judgment of outsiders for its own in the crisis.[13]

The first public statement of the lack of deficit was made at a great mass meeting in the Stadium on July 21 by Charles H. Judd. Judd, who had at one time fought against the interests of the Chicago public school teachers, came to their defense at a time when his aid was most valuable to them. With Hutchins, he lifted the banners of academic freedom at a time when that freedom was most damnably threatened. They were the only two men of high academic standing in the city outside the public school system who came out and told the truth. In [his Stadium speech] before the thousands of people packed into that great auditorium, [Judd] defined the real difficulty. [He agreed with] Hutchins [who had] said that the issue between the school board and the people was not economy. It was public education versus political jobbery. "Those who are fighting the school board are fighting for the schools. Those who are upholding the board are consciously or otherwise helping to maintain a political organization at the expense of the children of Chicago." Judd declared that the deficit was not real but manufactured.[14]

Hutchins' indictment of the Board of Education was so masterly that Greenacre incorporated it in his petition for legal relief. It was while we were talking over that petition in Carter's office on July 30, Greenacre, Carter, Aaron Kline, Irving Wilson, and I, that Carter began to read the report which John O. Rees had made for the Citizens' Committee, the report which purported to show the ten million dollar deficit in the educational fund. It was dated April 1, 1933. Aaron Kline had given it to Carter. Kline said that Fred W. Sargent had given it to

[13]Hutchins's articles were printed in the *Chicago Herald and Examiner*. He concluded by stating that the board's action was based "either on a complete misunderstanding of the purpose of public education, a selfish determination that its purpose shall not be fulfilled, or an ignorant belief that a system which has been wrecked can still function. The economic and social condition of Chicago will be worse for twenty-five years because of what the Board of Education has done." July 16, 1933.

[14]*Chicago Herald and Examiner*, July 26, 1933. The audience was estimated at more than 30,000 persons. No representative from the Sargent Committee or the business community spoke.

him on April 10. It contained the pretended justification for the wrecking program.

I said, "I can prove to you that's a lie. The Legislature enacted a law and it was signed by the governor. That law wiped out whatever deficit may have been claimed to exist prior to the enactment of that law and the signature of the governor."

I left the room, went to the telephone, and called up Springfield. From the secretary of the Illinois State Teachers' Association, Lester Grimm, I secured a copy of the *House Journal* of the date when the bill had been passed by the house. The Secretary of State sent me a photographic reproduction of the bill with Governor Horner's signature.

The publication of that legislation revealed to the public the dishonesty of the Board's action. It was the most deliberate and outrageous attack that was ever made on any body of educators. There was no question but that it was an attack of the big interests of the city upon the spirit of the teachers of Chicago. It was retaliation for whatever protests any teachers had made against their lack of payment through nearly all that year. It was the blackjack of power cracking on the heads of the little people.

Had it not been for Victor Watson, managing editor of the *Herald and Examiner*, for Hutchins, for Judd, the voice of the community, raised in howling protest, might have been less effectively articulate. Under their direction, the huge force of an aroused community showed what it could do and what it was likely to do under such oppression. For it was not alone at the livelihood and at the freedom of the teachers that the Board action struck. It hit the children of the public schools and, through them, their parents. Men and women who were striving to make their children good citizens knew how much they were being helped by the subjects that were being eliminated. The household arts section was a vital part of the Americanization plan in the foreign districts. Crane College, closed by the order, was giving opportunity to hundreds of boys who would not otherwise enjoy it. Ten men, sitting in a luxurious room in a fashionable club, had lifted barricades against the children of the city. In answer, they heard a voice that is seldom heard, the voice of the little people, and they were sufficiently political minded to know that its reverberations would be heard long after they had expected it to be forgotten and overlooked.

A petition, signed by 950,000 people, went to the next session of the Legislature in Springfield, asking for legislation to cure the situation that had been raised for excuse by the Board of Education. The petition had been circulated in the schools under the direction of a committee headed by Irving Wilson. The circulation of that petition almost brought into entire harmony the differing groups within the school system. For once, they had a common cause. It was the misfortune of the schools then, as earlier and later, that the opponents of genuine education have been able to divide the teaching forces. Not until there is unity of purpose among all the teachers of the city will there be complete success of action. Men and women, blinded by flattery or by a mistaken idea of self interest, break away from the ranks and make terms with the enemy. They hurt their own cause as much as they hurt those whom they leave; but they don't realize this until it's too late. I suppose that lawyers will say that their group is the hardest on earth to unify. Ministers will say it's their group. Doctors will declare that medical men are impossible to unite. I'll say, after the experience of a lifetime, there isn't any group on earth harder to get in line for common action than the educational group.

The lack of unification was evidenced by the number of suits brought in the courts that summer, all in a common cause, but all as varied in intent as there were petitioners. There were ten suits in all, four of them in one August day before four judges, and not one of the four stood up under hearing. Nothing but the ability of Edward Woods, attorney for the Hearst papers, and the wisdom of Isaiah T. Greenacre saved the situation from complete destruction. Woods prevented disaster in one case by taking charge of it just as the judge was dismissing it. He leaped in with a declaration that he was not the attorney of record but that he would be, and asked time to prepare his amendment. He won another, the suit brought by the *Herald and Examiner* to make the Board keep open the Parental School.

Out of lack of unity, nearly all the cases went off like duds; and out of the same lack of unity our own case—the one into which we had gone with the principals' and the high school teachers' organizations—also failed.

It was the only court failure that Isaiah T. Greenacre has endured for the Chicago Teachers' Federation in his long years of association with us. I do not enjoy telling the reason for its failure, but I feel that, in justice to him and in order that teachers everywhere may realize the need of genuine unity, I must set down the story. Greenacre, representing the Chicago Teachers' Federation, was associated with Allan J. Carter, for the Teachers' Federation and also for the Principals' Club, and Leo Hassenauer, for the Federation of Women High School Teachers. Greenacre had put into his petition for an injunction the charge made in a newspaper article by Robert Hutchins, that the Board of Education had "fraudulently, willfully, and knowingly abandoned their intellect." In legal terminology, it was a statement that the members of the Board had surrendered their judgment to someone with no right to use judgment. In other words, the members of the Board had divested themselves of their own intellect and taken the intellects of the Sargents and the Grahams of the Citizens' Committee. This constituted a charge of fraud. It was the axle of the entire action, which sought to force the Board to restore the thirteen hundred teachers. It was a serious charge against any public official, for public officials are expected and compelled to exercise judgment, their own rather than that of any unofficial adviser. They are also expected to have judgment to exercise.

Judge [William V.] Brothers heard the petition. He asked Allan Carter, "Where have you stated cause for action here? Do you charge fraud?"

Carter said, "Indirectly, yes."

"Not indirectly. Directly," Brothers insisted.

Then he denied the petition.

Not until it was over did Greenacre and I find out what had happened or why it had happened. Hassenauer, who was Donald Richberg's law partner, was awaiting a federal appointment, which he received a few days after he was out of the case. The statement of fraud against the Board of Education would have been a charge against one branch of the Democratic party, which was giving him an office, and, as Misther Dooley said, "A Dimmycrat is a Dimmycrat always." Hassenauer wouldn't sign the petition with the charge of fraud left in it.

Carter, representing the Principals' Club, was told by the representatives of the Principals' Club that it would be advisable for them to withdraw the charge of fraud from the petition.

Just before the hearing and after Greenacre and I had looked over the petition, Carter and Hassenauer agreed to withdraw the fraud charge. I did not know that it had been done. We would not have been parties to that petition had we known it. I thought Judge Brothers was wrong in his insistence about a direct charge of fraud. I knew nothing whatever about the change until nearly a year afterward.

The battle had been lost for the lack of a shoe; and the shoe was the realization by the representatives of the principals that, in order to save themselves, they had to stand shoulder to shoulder with the teachers.

The school wreckers had intended, it was apparent, to use their own discretion in throwing out the two hundred principals whom they had chosen for slaughter. I dug up for Westlake, of the *Herald and Examiner*, however, the seniority list of the principals. Its publication forced the Board to drop principals not as they had intended but according to rule. Some of the principals who had by that time striven to save their own skins at the expense of others in the same plight but lower in the system were caught by that publication. The Board had to drop them even when it didn't want to do it.[15]

Some of these principals went back to the high schools; others were completely out or went to Normal. All the dropped teachers who lacked certificates had to go back to Normal, so that the Normal school was thrown completely out of joint and has never again returned to its own normality. For years, girls who have finished there have been held out of the system and many of them for so long a time that they have lost their eligibility as teachers. The whole Chicago school system was thrown out of plumb by the action of the Board. Even later individual readjustments have failed to bridge the chasm that was created by that earthquake. It will take another decade before the damage done on that July day in the Skyline Club can be fully estimated by the people of Chicago.

Judge Brothers had to deny the injunction to keep the Board of Education from dropping the Thirteen Hundred. Legally, he had no choice when the charge of fraud had not been contained in the bill. Had I known that the petition had been emasculated, we would not have remained in the suit in any capacity. That removal of the fraud charge was made, however, between four-thirty on the afternoon when we saw the bill and the moment, a little before five o'clock, when the bill was filed. Not until the case was dismissed did we learn the truth.

The responsibility for that change rested not as much upon the two attorneys, Carter and Hassenauer, as upon the officers of the Principals' Club who authorized it through Aaron Kline. The principals of that organization sacrificed the whole cause of the Thirteen Hundred in their desire to save themselves with the Board of Education. It was the irony of fate that an unforeseen event caught some of them in the revolving machinery of decapitation. Their fate did not expiate their fault. The fact remained and still remains that, for their own selfish ends, a small body of school principals put in jeopardy not only the means of livelihood of more than a thousand of their fellow-workers in the school system but also the essential principle of contract between teacher and school board. As far as they were concerned, the rest of the Thirteen Hundred might have been entirely eliminated. The right of tenure, which kept the dropped teachers in the system at all and which in time found place again for some of them, was something which even the legal jugglers could not abrogate.

The loss of that suit and the consequent loss of place to the thirteen hundred teachers rests, however, as squarely upon their shoulders as

[15]The economy measures were reported at the July 12th meeting and the list of 145 principals was adopted on September 13. *Proceedings, Board of Education*, 1933-34, pp. 24-28, 156. The seniority list was published in the *Chicago Herald and Examiner* on August 26, 1933.

upon the shoulders of the wrecking crew of the Board of Education. It was the clearest instance of the devil-take-the-hindmost attitude of a large number of principals. To save themselves they launched a life-boat, leaving the rest of the passengers on the ship of education to sink or swim; and, until every teacher and principal in the public schools of Chicago and every other American community realizes that his or her interests are essentially the same and require common guarding, the same kind of incident is going to happen over and over again.

For forty years I had been a grieving witness of the fact that the force of intrenched privilege invariably sought to drive a wedge in the opposing force of democracy. At no time, though, was I harder hit by the practice, for this time I had trusted the other organizations with whom the Chicago Teachers' Federation had cast its strength.

On the day when I discovered that the charge of fraud, the nub of the action, had been left out of the bill for injunction against the Board, I felt—not in any symbolic sense but in physical truth—that my heart was breaking.

The financial stringency of the Board was not solved, however, by the discovery that there was no deficit. It still owed the teachers for the payless months of 1933, but it seemed to have no constructive idea for that repayment. It was a teachers' representative, not a member of the Board of Education, who secured legislation that eventually paid the teachers that back salary. Robert Keenan, who had been a member of the committee who went to Washington in the previous year, went alone to Washington in the early part of 1934, and got through Congress a bill permitting the Board of Education to issue bonds on the security of school fund land leases in order to pay the back salaries of the teachers for the time they had been withheld.[16]

The City Council, the State Legislature, and the Board of Education then passed enabling acts, but the banks hesitated to take up the bonds. Keenan returned again to Washington and persuaded the officers of the Reconstruction Finance Corporation to lend twenty-two million dollars to the Board of Education upon the security of the rentals of school fund lands.[17]

[16]This was an amendment to the "Loans to Industry" bill which passed Congress on June 16, 1934. President Franklin D. Roosevelt signed it four days later. The amendment authorized the Reconstruction Finance Corporation to loan up to $75 million to public school districts upon "adequate security." This limitation, together with its restrictions to cities of more than 500,000 population, meant that only Chicago, with its valuable school land holdings, could qualify. Jesse H. Jones, the head of the RFC, saw this as an opportunity to pay the back salaries of Chicago teachers, who "were in a truly pitiable plight". Jesse H. Jones, *Fifty Billion Dollars: My Thirteen Years with the RFC, 1932-1945* (New York: Macmillan, 1951), pp. 176-78; *New York Times*, May 24, June 17, 1933.

[17]On August 27, 1934, the Chicago teachers and school board employees received more than $26 million in back pay. This was made possible by a loan from the Reconstruction Finance Corporation of approximately $22,300,000, secured by the more than $35 million

The Reconstruction Finance Corporation bought bonds based on these rentals from the Board and resold them to the banks of Chicago. The banks are drawing about $750,000 a year interest on these securities. They will continue to draw that amount each year for nearly twenty years more. For that twenty-year period there will be no rental paid to the schools.[18] That's the price the public is paying for the payless months the Board gave the teachers.

Everyone but the tax payer is making money on those bonds. The Reconstruction Finance Corporation made money on them. The banks continue to make money on them. The Board of Education must provide for a sufficient appropriation every year to take care of the interest for that year on these bonds. They are also expected to make an appropriation to take care of the principal, $22,300,000. But here is the difficulty: None of the tax rates now in force provide the amount of money the appropriation calls for, because only about 75 per cent of the total of the tax levy of Cook County is collected. The school fund lands, which produce nearly a million dollars of income every year, are thereby impounded. The rentals are held to make up for any deficiency in the taxes to pay the principal that is due—and the bank which holds most of this interest money is the First National Bank of Chicago, which also is a lessee of school fund lands. Not a dollar of the lease money will go into the educational fund for the next twenty years. This creates a situation which will require constant watching if the public interest is to be considered. It is a fever box that cures one disease and creates another.

The school fund lands have been almost decimated by the processes of the Board of Education through the time of its existence. The provisions for reappraisement, at first every five years and later every ten years by appraisers appointed by the Board of Education, have been upheld more in the breach than in the observance. Once, after the appraisal of 1915, the Board of Education itself attacked its own appraisers' valuations as far too low, but court proceedings sustained the action of those appraisers. The Dunne Board was the only Board to make a definite policy to secure anything like rightful compensation from the lessees. It was twenty years later before any other Board of Education made any sustained effort to increase the valuations of school fund lands. Then the Dever Board appointed as one appraiser Albert H. Wetten, Judge Henry Horner of the Probate Court of Cook County named Benjamin F. Lindheimer, and the three judges of the

---

of school land property. Each teacher received fourteen checks, two for each of the seven months they were behind in pay. *New York Times*, Aug. 26, 28, 1934.

[18]Further information on this is found in *Chicago's Schools*, 1 (Jan., 1935), p. 1. This monthly newsletter was published by the Citizens' Save Our Schools Committee.

United States District Court for the Northern District of Illinois selected Paul Steinbrecher. These appraisers agreed upon an appraisement that meant an increase of almost 80 per cent in values as compared with the 1915 appraisal. This, of course, meant a corresponding increase in rentals. Nine of the lessees refused to pay rent on anything but the 1915 basis. Their tenders were refused by the Board of Education.

The lessees started proceedings in the Superior Court to contest the new appraisement. Judge Joseph B. David granted injunctions restraining collection of the increased rentals. The nine cases were referred by Judge Denis E. Sullivan to Master in Chancery Sidney S. Pollack, who made a report upholding the validity of the 1925 appraisal; but in April, 1932, the Illinois Supreme Court handed down an opinion reversing the decree which Judge Sullivan made in accordance with the Chancery recommendations. The ground of the reversal, as stated in the opinion, was that the appraisers, in fixing the value of the land, had made their appraisement excessive by taking into consideration the fact that the school fund properties were by law exempt from taxation. The Court said, "While it is true that the land, as long as it remains school land, is tax exempt, this is not an advantage that can be passed along to anyone who might choose to buy the land from the Board of Education."

Immediately after the Supreme Court had declared the 1925 appraisement invalid, the special attorney in charge of the litigation for the Board, Edward R. Johnston, recommended to the Board that no time be lost in presenting evidence to Judge Sullivan which would enable him to make a new valuation in compliance with that decision. For that purpose, he filed a cross bill. At that juncture, Samuel A. Ettelson appealed to the court on behalf of certain lessees for an extension of time in filing an answer, in order that he might have an opportunity to "negotiate" with the Board of Education.

The negotiations, which continued through the waning months of the Thompson Board, were blocked by Mayor Cermak. Cermak's death preceded their revival. Another set of school appraisers made out another basis of appraisal. The increase in rentals provided in their sliding scale is only 5 per cent every ten years for ninety-nine year leases. On one piece of land alone, the land on which McVickers Theater stands, the sliding-scale lease advocated by these appraisers would bring an average rental each year of $105,072, whereas the rental for 1925 on the basis of the school board appraisal made in that year would have been $122,023. The annual rental estimated by the sliding scale from 1983 to 2032, on a ninety-nine year lease beginning 1933, would be $199,726, nearly $3,000 less than the rental appraised by the Board for 1925. They certainly had little faith that Chicago was going to grow any better and its downtown property any more valuable. The entire appraisal was on the same basis of low estimates. This matter is still in litigation, with the Board of Education having little promise of getting anything like fair rental values on its property as compared with the privately owned property in the vicinity.[19]

By the original grant, the Board of Education owns the square mile of land located between Cicero and Central Avenues and between 55th and 63rd Streets. This property, the only original piece of the grant left intact, has now been leased by the Board of Education to the City of Chicago at a rental of twenty dollars an acre for the next twenty years. The City rents it at almost equally low price to aviation companies for an airport. These leases run for fifty years. The rental charged by the companies for one hangar is as much as the Board gets for a whole year for the whole square mile. The Board and the City Council acted together, at the behest of certain local groups interested in commercial aviation, thereby defeating the idea of the founding fathers of the Republic that this land was to be used for the education of American children. In order to clear a space for this enterprise, the Board of Education condemned a school building, which had been erected only a few years earlier. The protests of the parents of children who would have to walk for miles to the school to which they would have to be transferred prevented the consummation of that closing. The Hale School reservation remains intact upon the property.[20]

Only the other day, however, action by Edward J. Kelly, the mayor of Chicago, removed from the airport property the tracks of a railroad which, with the school reservation, had been allowed to remain on the property, so that the tenure of the school now seems more than a little uncertain. If the railroad tracks can be put off, the school can be put off, and the children of a district whose parents voted to come into the city of Chicago so that they might save the school fund land that was in their independent township of Clearing will have to trudge long blocks through all kinds of weather to another school.

God moves in a mysterious way, however, and the processes of nature may one day retrieve for the school children of Chicago a large part of the money stolen from them by Boards of Education through the last hundred years. The Ordinance of 1787 provided that every thirty-sixth square mile of the Northwest Territory should be used for

---

[19]Haley's comments reflect her conviction that, the depression experience notwithstanding, the valuations were set too low.

[20]This complete section of Clearing Township was acquired through annexation and is the site of Midway Airport. On August 19, 1981, the City Council voted unanimously to purchase this land, which it had leased in 1931 from the Board of Education. The purchase was intended to help alleviate the continuing financial distress of the public school system. *Chicago Tribune*, Aug. 20, 1981.

the purpose of raising money to provide for public education. Bit by bit, the Chicago Board of Education has practically given away these various pieces of land. There is, however, one piece of land within the city of Chicago that is rapidly becoming one of its most valuable sections. That is the section between Irving Park Boulevard and Lawrence Avenue east of Clarendon Avenue. At one time, this was an extremely narrow strip; but the filling in of that shoreline has extended it already several blocks eastward of Clarendon Avenue, so that it is now a considerable part of a square mile. Some of it is park property. Other parts of it are private properties held by people who have taken the chance, knowingly or otherwise, that they have proper title to it. By federal legislation, however, it is theoretically at least the property of the school children of Chicago, to be administered for their benefit only by the Board of Education.

By the legislation of 1934, the federal government is again in direct control of the school fund lands of the city of Chicago. The destiny of the school fund lands has gone right back where it started from; and if the legislators of 1937 have anything left of the enlightened vision of the legislators of 1787, there may yet be hope that the Chicago schools may one day be freed from the financial domination of greedy corporations and grafting politicians.[21]

In June of 1934 at the end of the school year, I went to California. I was so ill that sometimes, as the train sped westward, I wondered why I had chosen to leave Chicago to die. I went straight from the train to a hospital in Los Angeles. Months later, I came out of the hospital, but I was still so thin that with a loin cloth I would have looked like Mahatma Gandhi. The sunshine and the spirit of California revived me. The west coast, at least, has attained a degree of democracy superior to that of any other part of our United States. Thanks to Hiram Johnson, California has legislation which gives it a check on incompetent and inefficient public officers. Its Initiative, Referendum, and Recall give its people a boon greater than its vaunted climate.

I was reveling in leisure and freedom when I was recalled to Chicago by a situation in the Federation that had arisen with Mary Murray's death. For long years, Mary Murray had been treasurer of the Chicago Teachers' Federation. She had given to it service that could not even be estimated. We had all grown so dependent upon her wisdom and fortitude that her passing found us unprepared for the necessary readjustments. Against the advice of my friends in California, I insisted upon returning to Chicago. Grieving for our loss in her death, I was

---

[21]The reference is to the amendment to the "Loans to Industry" bill and the RFC loans to Chicago based on the school lands.

on my way to the train on the 22nd of May, 1935, when my friends told me that my youngest sister, Eliza, had died two days before. They had kept the news from me in the belief that I was unable to travel. It was now too late for me to reach Chicago in time for her funeral, for I was forbidden to attempt a journey by plane, and I came back in the knowledge that I should never see Eliza again.[22]

David Shanahan, going on eighty, is the veteran member now of the Illinois Legislature. I'm seventy-five, and the veteran of the lobby. We've seen many changes in the world since we first met in the State House at Springfield, wars, and booms, and depressions, but one thing has remained unchanged. That is the truth that Shanahan told me more than thirty-five years ago: that politicians punished or protected teachers according to the attitude of the teachers toward Big Business.[23]

As usual, the Board of Education was hitting back at the teachers for their civic activities when it inaugurated the legislation of 1935 on pensions and retirement age. The bill for the relief of the educational fund from immediate repayment into the working cash fund was of another character. It was based on absolute necessity. It should have been enacted two years earlier, but protest at that time was merely a Cassandra cry. Now, if the schools were to re-open in September and run through the year, it had to be passed.

Harold Ward, representative to the State senate for one of the Chicago districts, introduced more bills in the Fifty-ninth General Assembly of the State of Illinois than any other three men.[24] As the legislative whip of the Chicago administration forces, Ward brought in, among multitudinous others, so many bills for the Board of Education that at one time he told reporters that he didn't know the content of the sheaf he was holding in his hand. Among the bills introduced by him were two of vital importance, one of them brought in on May 21, Senate Bill 496, the second on May 22, Senate Bill 528.

Senate Bill 496 amended section 134½ of the school law and repealed the provision that, unless money received and applied to reimbursement of the working cash fund prior to a certain time shall be sufficient for a complete reimbursement of money borrowed in anticipation of the collection of taxes, the working cash fund should be reimbursed to the extent of the deficiency from any revenues accruing

---

[22]Haley spent almost a year in Palos Verdes, California. During this time, she resumed work on her memoirs. She lived at the home of her close friend Frances Harden, who had retired to California in 1929. Harden served as corresponding secretary of the CTF for twenty-one years and was one of "sixty-eight" ousted by the Loeb board. *Margaret Haley's Bulletin*, 7 (Oct. 31, 1929), p. 160.

[23]See note 20, p. 72.

[24]Harold Ward was considered to be Mayor Kelly's spokesman in the upper chamber. *Chicago Tribune*, June 30, 1935.

to the educational purposes fund, and that the Board of Education should provide for the same.

In other words, it left the reimbursement of borrowings from the working cash fund to be paid from the tax levy of the educational fund for the year against which the money was borrowed and from no other year and from no other resources. This bill gave freedom for the future to the educational fund. Repayment to the working cash fund would have to await the collection of taxes beyond the legal 75 per cent for whatever borrowing on tax warrants had been made for that year.

The borrowings in particular question were from 1930 and 1931. The Ward bill stopped the practice of charging against the regular educational fund for any year borrowings that were due to be paid for another year. It confined the payment of the loans to the taxes collected for the year in which the loans were made. The 1930 loans would have to be paid by the belated taxes for 1930 and not from any taxes of any other year.[25]

Senate Bill 528 provided for retiring teachers at the age of sixty-five and reduced the annuity paid by the Board of Education from $1,500 to $500.

These two bills were, by all odds, the most important that had been before the Illinois Legislature for many years.

The first bill, being a financial bill, seemed to have escaped the vigilance of the teachers' organizations, who had evidently fallen into the habit of leaving matters of that kind to me. The second bill, however, aroused immediate agitation among all the teachers of Chicago. Some of them had unfortunately assumed that the emeritus pension given by the Board to them was as permanent as the pension to which they subscribed.[26] They had not realized how completely this extra $1,500 rested upon legislative favor. Even at the time of its enactment, some of us had wondered about the ultimate legality of that provision and had sought to secure a more certain method of additional payment. We felt that the teachers should have a pension arrangement of such surety that no part of what they received could be taken away by the whim of any political boss who controlled a Legislature. We knew that, roughly, the teachers pay 47 per cent and the tax payers 53 per cent toward the fund of their regular pension, which does not include the emeritus payment; that firemen and policemen pay 30 per

[25]This released the board from paying old warrants for previous years with current income and provided an additional nine million dollars to the school fund in 1936. Herrick, *Chicago Schools*, p. 225. *Chicago Tribune*, June 30, 1935, indicates that approximately 375 bills passed the legislature; the two Ward bills are listed in the summary of legislative action. The most contentious issue seen in years was the increase of the sales tax to 3 percent.

[26]See pages 212-16 for a discussion of the emeritus pension.

cent to the tax payers' 70 per cent; and that other municipal employees pay 37 per cent to the tax payers' 63 per cent. We saw no reason why there could not be a readjustment of the regular pension so that the teachers would receive a somewhat larger amount and whereby they would be insured continuing payments.[27]

The provision to reduce the emeritus payments by the Board of Education to the teachers from $1,500 to $500 a year was a compromise between the Citizens' Committee and the City administration. Fred W. Sargent, of the Citizens' Committee, wanted the payment entirely eliminated. James B. McCahey, president of the Board of Education, favored the payment of $250 a year to teachers who would retire at the age of sixty-five. Edward J. Kelly, mayor of Chicago, either from natural generosity or political sagacity, passed on the order that the payment be set at $500.

The Chicago Division of the Illinois State Teachers' Association sent representatives to Springfield at once. One of them, George E. Anspaugh, principal of the Bryant School, was chairman of the legislative committee of the Association. On May 29, the day before Memorial Day, he attended the session of the Legislature. It was his last appearance in Springfield during that session.

On his return to Chicago on the night of May 29, he caused a meeting to be held at which representatives of a large number of groups of teachers were asked to be present. Isaiah T. Greenacre was invited to the meeting. At that meeting, Greenacre was asked what he would do if he were in Anspaugh's place. Anspaugh, he was told, had met in Springfield President McCahey of the Board of Education, who had told him that, in effect, he should have been in Chicago in his own school and that thereafter he would have to choose whether he would remain in Springfield or return to the school.

Greenacre advised that, in his opinion, McCahey would be within his right in reporting Anspaugh to the Board as absent from his place and in proceeding against him.

Anspaugh did not appear again at Springfield during that session, nor did any other teacher during the time while school was in session.

Being the business representative of the Chicago Teachers' Federation and not a teacher in the schools, I was free to go to any and all sessions of the Illinois Legislature.

I did.

The retirement and pension bill was delayed by what Senator [Richard] Barr called a "breach of promise." He had been told that a

[27]H.B. 4168 increased regular pensions for Chicago teachers from a maximum of $1,000 to $1,200. *Chicago Tribune*, June 30, 1935. It is evident that Haley supported this and did not consider the emeritus pension an issue of central importance.

bill which he had introduced should run simultaneously with the Ward bills. When these two Ward bills started ahead of his, Barr raised a row and stopped them, so that they waited for his bill to catch up with their two. The bills went through the senate at the third reading on June 4, were introduced in the house on the 5th, and passed on the 13th. Then they hung fire, waiting for Governor Horner's signature.

On Monday, June 17, a meeting of teachers was held in Chicago. George Mahin, who was acting as representative of the Chicago Division in Springfield in lieu of Anspaugh, brought before that meeting a document containing a report of the vote in the senate on the passage of the bills. At the top of this document was a cartoon of Mayor Kelly with a crown on his head and a whip in his hand. Members of the Legislature were depicted in poses of humility. The document was distributed at that meeting. A copy of it arose at a critical moment to plague its authors.

On June 19, Governor Horner gave a hearing to all the teachers who desired to speak on the retirement and pension bills. Susan Scully, then president of the Chicago Division of the Association, presented a typewritten document of several pages outlining objections to the bills. The governor stopped her once or twice to say that she was reading too fast and that he couldn't follow her. She slowed her pace, but the governor still insisted that he could not follow. Then he asked what the vote was on the bill in both houses. That was not, evidently, in her record. As she stopped reading, McCahey, president of the Board, rose and said, "Here's the vote, Governor, on these bills." He walked up to the governor's desk and put on it the document containing the cartoon, with the vote under the cartoon. He said, "This is the way we do things in Chicago." Then he walked back to his seat. It was good psychology.

Then a white haired principal arose to tell the governor that he would receive only $500 a year for the rest of his lifetime if the bill were signed. That seemed a shock to Horner, who had evidently not realized that there were teachers in the system who had not contributed to the regular pension fund and would therefore be limited in their annuities to the amount of money that the Board of Education pays to the teachers at the retirement age. That brought everyone up short. It was a confusing situation that had come to an awkward pause.

Then I jumped in. Senate Bill 496 was my job and I had to see that he realized at once, before he took action on anything else, the gravity of the crisis which it met. I said, "There will be a debt of between forty-four and forty-seven million dollars in the educational fund which the Board will have to meet out of current revenue, and it will be more than they'll get in any year, and the schools will have to be closed for a year unless you sign this bill."

He brought up objection after objection. I met them as he made them. Then the other representatives working on the other bill cut back in again. I went over and sat down in a big leather chair a little way from his desk. When they all finished, he looked around at me as if expecting me to follow them out of the room. Remembering how Tony Cermak had been appalled by the idea of the teacher who was going to invade his office, I said, "I'm going to stay here, Governor, until you promise me that you'll sign that bill."

He must have read determination in my eyes for, after a little more objecting, he said, "All right, I'll sign it."

Governor Horner did not sign the bill. Characteristically, he wavered, and let it become law without his signature. The schools didn't have to close that year. I've no quarrel with Harry Horner; but, for the sake of the record, I'll have to say that I'd rather have in the governor's chair a man like Frank Lowden who'll slap me straight in the face when he's against me.

Franklin Delano Roosevelt once said that after nearly thirty years of political experience he had come to believe that his first political mentor, Judge Alton B. Parker, had been right in characterizing Illinois as "a Commonwealth for Sale."

If it is, the Illinois State Legislature has been the counter over which it has been sold.

For more than thirty-five years I have attended every session of that Legislature. I have watched its public procedure and ferreted out much of its star-chamber method. I have seen the Tweedledum and Tweedledee differences between Republicans and Democrats. I have seen change come in the manners of the Springfield body with the presence of women in its membership. Men wash their faces now, even if they don't go back of their ears; but the Legislature of 1935 was just as subservient to bossism as the Legislatures of 1901 and of 1913. The only real difference that I could see was that the members of the 1935 Legislature were more restive under Kelly's dictation than the 1913 legislators had been under Lorimer's. They went with the machine but they didn't always want to go. At times, they were outspokenly relieved when a cog slipped in the machinery and an order for steam-rolling was countermanded.

One of these occasions came with the attempt to pass the Loyalty Oath Bill.

The Loyalty Oath Bill was, by one of the anomalies of politics, fathered by William Randolph Hearst and mothered by the Chicago administration forces, although that machine usually fought and was fought by the local Hearst newspapers. The two apparently diverse elements had been brought together by a high flare of Fascist passion.

Both of them wanted to put over a measure totally unnecessary and entirely dangerous. The teachers of Illinois were the last group of people in the community to need any such oath, and they resented the measure because it inferred that they, more than any other professional group, required it.[28]

It was easy to understand why the Chicago machine wanted to punish the Chicago teachers. It was harder to understand Hearst's insistence on the measure, especially after the years when the Hearst newspapers in Chicago had given yeoman aid to the cause of the teachers.

The Loyalty Oath Bill came up for passage in the senate on the last day of the session. In the house, Mayor Kelly of Chicago was sitting beside the Speaker, checking off the members as the roll call proceeded on some of the bills he had sponsored. In the senate, Sally Rand, the fan dancer, sat on the platform. [James J.] Barbour, the senator from the district housing two universities, Northwestern and Loyola, who didn't want the Hearst bill, was to speak against it. It was a hot day, though, and Barbour drowsed a little. When someone prodded him, he arose and began a speech, but it wasn't about the bill. It was about Sally. He wanted the senate to invite her to speak; but while he talked, Dick Barr, who was presiding, faded out of the picture. Tom Donovan, the lieutenant-governor, came on, and snapped into roll call on the Loyalty Oath Bill. It went down to complete defeat—at the last moment, the organization had released its cohorts from voting for it—just as [Edward P.] O'Grady, who had introduced it, came rushing on the floor.[29]

Ten minutes later, the Fifty-ninth General Assembly ended. It had, by and large, considered more bills of economic and social importance than any other Legislature in the history of the sovereign State of Illinois, the State of John Peter Altgeld and of Abraham Lincoln.

Sally Rand led in the singing of its recessional.

[28]The Board of Education supported this measure (H.B. 226) as well as a bill urging all teachers to live within the city (H.B. 188). The loyalty oath bill passed the house but was defeated in the senate by a 29-8 vote. It was opposed by the Citizens' Save Our Schools Committee. A review of the legislative session and educational matters is found in *Chicago's Schools*, 2 (Sept., 1935), pp. 1-4. Additional information on the subject of loyalty oaths is found in Howard K. Beale, *Are American Teachers Free?* (New York: Scribner's, 1936), pp. 65-74. Beale states that "requiring 'patriotic' oaths of teachers is an old expedient used recurringly in times of great stress."

[29]A *Tribune* reporter wrote that Sally Rand's presence was "said to have quickened many an assemblyman's pulse." *Chicago Tribune*, June 30, 1935. Rand had established her fame in 1933, with her sensational fan dancing at the Chicago World's Fair.

◦[XII]◦

The Darkling Plain

Chicago, like London, mirrors the eye of the beholder. To Jane Addams it was forty times forty playgrounds, a huge social experimental station for the children of the city streets. To Clarence Darrow it has been [the] arena for forensic debate of legal conditions. To Theodore Dreiser it has loomed a background of pale gray immensity before which move dun-colored men and women. To me Chicago is the proving ground of American democracy.

Upon its retention or rejection of basic democratic ideals depends not only its own future but the future of the nation. In the way of no other city, Chicago has been, through the past fifty years, battle ground of the two great opposing forces of American life: the defenders and the exploiters of true popular government. The war of privilege against people has been waged in and around the public schools of Chicago. The teachers of Chicago who have opposed special privilege have fought far more than their own fight. They have sustained the cause of liberalism. But for them the field of their city's democracy would long ago have been surrendered; and the loss of that redoubt might have already determined the outcome of the struggle. As it is, they have held the line at one of its most crucial points.

They have done, however, little more than hold it. After nearly a half-century of struggle they sustained, in 1933, an almost overwhelming defeat.

Will they be able to withstand the attacks that are sure to continue?

If I did not believe they could, I should not have written this book. I have set down my memories of the battles I have fought with no intention of that extension of personality which is, they say, the desire of all autobiographers. I have tried to tell my story with as little of my own personality as is humanly possible. My "We" is not editorial. I have usually visioned myself as so integrally part of the teaching force that, although I have not been in a schoolroom for almost forty years, I record myself, almost unconsciously, as a teacher. It is as a teacher now that I want to emphasize to other teachers, particularly to the teachers of my own city, what they must do to hold their heritage of freedom.

Those of us who labored in the heat of the day are coming to the evening of our lives. We shall not be able to bear much longer the burdens we assumed so buoyantly and which we have borne so long. Some day soon the last bell will ring for us. Then some one else must take up the knapsack of service. It is only in the hope that my experiences may be a field map that I have marked them down. For men and women die, but the old, old war of might against right goes on. Perhaps it will go on till the end of the world; but I believe that, long ere that, it may be won. It will only be won, though, by education— education, first, of the teachers, then education by them of the children in those affairs concerned with the common weal.

If our democracy is to continue, the teachers of this nation must teach the children of the nation the obligations of citizenship in a true democracy. They must teach them the essential issues of government, not passing political issues but those fundamental and basic principles that are the foundation of our system. They must translate for their pupils into understandable terms the enduring questions of economic and social existence: taxation, the land system, the money system.

There is in our United States a deliberate, continuing effort to befuddle the people by the cluttering nomenclatures of economics and of social and political science. As long as the public regards matters concerned with taxation, land, and money systems as Delphic mysteries, clear only to a few initiates after lifetimes of study, there will be no real and lasting improvement in the public weal; but taxation, land, and money are really simple matters if only they are presented with honesty and simplicity.

I was only a child when I read Alexander Campbell's booklet on monetary questions and understood from it what our monetary system was. What I could understand then any child could understand now. It should be the teacher's job to see that the child has the chance to understand these systems and to get them in their proper relationship to each other. One of the troubles of reform is that reformers all put their own isms into airtight compartments. Educators will have to be the engineers to relate and balance the issues.

Politicians will not do it. Political parties today would be jokes if they were not such tragic failures. Political programs are only accidentally right, if they are right at all. Political campaigns are nothing but ballyhoo. Partisan action, usually controlled in both parties by great and greedy financial interests, is seldom of any value to the people. At its best, it's no more than salve on the saddle sores. At its worst, it's a tightening of the domination of the many by the few.

Newspapers will not do it. Their owners and publishers are, for the most part, so involved with great corporate interests, especially in the big cities, that they will not, directly or indirectly, attack those interests. To the eternal credit of the editorial group of the Chicago newspapers, however, I must record the enlightened and courageous service which so many of them have given the cause of the Chicago school teachers, which has been the cause of the Chicago public. Men and women have, I know, risked their jobs to write or print the truth. With the development of chain newspapers, however, with the growing Fascist tendencies of William Randolph Hearst, and with banking domination of publishing enterprises, the American newspaper grows farther and farther away from the spirit of the American people.

There remains, therefore, for leadership in public affairs only the teaching body of the United States. The Fifth Estate, "Old Bob" LaFollette used to call us. As long as he lived, he watched our Chicago battle with the keenest interest and deepest sympathy. We were going, he thought, in the right direction. So deep was his feeling for our struggle that, when he died, the one floral tribute which his wife placed on his bier was the wreath sent by the Chicago Teachers' Federation.

We have, however, taken only a few faltering steps on the long road of human betterment that should be our destiny. If the teachers are to teach children of the nation how to think clearly and constructively on matters of national importance, they must first learn their own lesson.

Instead of running like hares to classes which give them nothing but promotional credits, they must study intensely and intensively the real problems of our time and our country. They must learn the essentials of money, land, and taxation systems. They must familiarize themselves with the methods and purposes of public utilities. They must find out who are the enemies of the republic, both in and out of office. They must scan the existing laws, discover why some of them can't be changed, and devise methods for their revision. They must find out what Initiative and Referendum and Recall mean, and how these methods may be exercised to secure better laws and put out dishonest administrators and legislators. They must inform themselves about the thieves and the thieveries which are putting the high burden of taxation upon the little man and letting the big fellow escape.

Then, having learned their lesson, they must teach it. If they'll send out one generation of thoughtful children, able to think, knowing something of the fundamental principles that are so widely misunderstood and disregarded, they will have accomplished what no revolution can ever wholly accomplish. They will have changed without bloodshed those conditions which must be changed somehow. One generation of properly taught children can do that—and our American democracy will survive. This is the high call of destiny to the American school teacher. Upon her rests the obligation to save our nation from revolution.

For the achievement of this purpose the teaching force must be unified. There can not be one group of teachers fighting another group of teachers, a condition we have too often suffered. The entire teaching body must develop the spirit of the corps. It will require sacrifice of snobbery on the part of the higher-paid groups, and, possibly, sacrifice of the higher pay: for it may be necessary to establish the Single Salary Schedule before teachers become aware of their real unity. There's no just reason why it shouldn't be done. Elementary school teachers require now quite as high a standard of education as do high school teachers; and it's always been true that the teaching of first grade is quite as important as the teaching of fourth-year high school. More important, really. The younger the child, the greater the need of a good teacher. The high-school teachers won't like the idea, but, unless they see in time on which side their bread is buttered, the day'll come for them when they may not have any bread to butter.

Like all great causes, the crusade of the Fifth Estate will demand its martyrs. Every cause does. Mrs. Pankhurst once told me in London that the death of Inez Millholland Boissevain, that bright spirit of courage who was trampled by the horses of the London police, had done more to plead the cause of woman suffrage in Great Britain than all the speeches ever made for it. Padraic Pearse, himself a teacher, said to me, as we stood at the door of his school, Saint Enda's, "I hope that some day I may die for Ireland." He did—a few years afterward. Today Ireland is a Free State.

Ever since the World War, the great forces of reaction have recognized the advisability of controlling the thought of the children who were passing through the public schools. They have known that, if these children learned the true answers to the true questions of our modern civilization, they, grown into manhood and womanhood, would change the system which continued special privilege for the few and injustice for the many. Therefore, the Fascists—and every man who wants to use government for the power and privilege of any one class or group is a Fascist—have striven unremittingly to prevent public school teachers from becoming educators in any true sense. They have sought to hold them down into being mere purveyors of manifest and innocuous information. And of what use is it to a boy or girl to learn that three time three is nine if all his so-called education merely turns him out into a community where, on what he earns, he's going to pay, in proportion, three or thirty or three hundred times as much in taxation as the big public utilities companies? Where he's going to find out sometime that the creed of nearly all Boards of Education is "the public be damned"? Where he'll discover that state legislatures have been little but hot pie counters? Where he'll realize that everywhere along the line he's been sold out? That's when the American public will blame, with reason, the American public school teacher unless the teacher takes up her responsibility now.

The teacher must realize, too, that the human heart seeks beauty as much as the human soul seeks justice. She must work, both as an individual and as a member of an Estate, to develop beauty as a factor in education. It was, I believe, Jane Addams' permanent contribution to American life that she recognized the value of trying to keep the social customs of the peoples from other lands. For beauty is an essential of all real education. I remember seeing, in a glass factory in Copenhagen, young men and women working in a setting of such beauty that they naturally expressed their appreciation of it in their work. I thought, as I watched them, of the Illinois glass manufacturer who wanted children to be given such limited educations that they would accept without protest the dull routine of the tasks given them in his factory. The Danish factory was the answer to those who declare that the Machine Age must sacrifice beauty to efficiency. There beauty and efficiency went hand in hand; but it was brains, as well as humanitarianism, that had put them together.

Teaching must be lifted to the high plane of a genuine profession. Councils of teachers must be re-established. Teachers—and teachers only—must undertake the task of setting and enforcing by law the standards for admission to their profession and of discharge from it. Teachers, not boards of education, should be the judges of the fitness or unfitness of their fellow-workers.

Above all, the teachers of the nation must discard the doctrine of *laissez-faire*. A member of the City Council once said during a discussion about buying gondolas for a city park, "Why not buy two, and let nature take its course?" Apathy may have its right in city councils and political parties, but not in education. Teachers have the obligation, by virtue of their position, to fight against that machine civilization which tries to extinguish all leadership other than its own. They must throw off the inferiority complex which they have developed under school systems which have oppressed them. The worst thing that can be said against the present school system of the United States is that it kills real leadership. No man or woman dares lift a hand against a board of education if he wants to hold his job. All leadership has had to be outside the teaching force; and yet America will swiftly deteriorate unless its public school teachers regain and reassert their freedom of opinion and of action.

This is the real problem of American education. The teachers require a code of ethics, not one enforced upon them from without, but one developed from within. The councils would have done that. That's why they were wiped out by order of a board of education. The development of an ethical consciousness in teachers is the vital need of the nation. Pension, tenure, salary—all of these are far less important than the fact that the teacher must be made to realize that she is a free human being. That's the real meaning of academic freedom.

Hopefully, there is a reviving movement for a demand for that freedom. Already the National Education Association is working on it, and, although I continue to believe that the wolves are still hovering around that organization, I know that there has been a great change in the general outlook of the body in the past forty years. In time, it may be the lot of that association, once the almost impregnable stronghold of the Harrises and the Butlers, to take up the cudgels of a great cause and make a nation-wide fight for freedom in the public schools. The world do move.

Luckily, ours is still a world in the making, and we are its makers. Sometimes I wonder if there aren't other places in the universe where people have gone further in the development of human consciousness. Perhaps their derelicts come here to grow a little better—or a little worse.

Who knows?

Sometimes I have thought that I had travelled a long way from my childhood on the Illinois prairie; but, a little while ago, on my way to Springfield, I passed the farm where I had spent my earliest years. It looked, at first, strangely different from my memory of it. Then, suddenly, I realized how little changed it really was. Its wide acres green in the springtime sunshine, its blossoming orchard, its blue immensity of sky—all these seemed as they had been when I, a wondering child, had gazed at them from the window of the farm house. They made, I thought, the one unchanging scene in a swiftly shifting world, a scene of peace, of beauty, of quietude, of freedom. And I, who saw it, was much the same child, staring out in wonder upon a wider but not a greater universe.

I had gone forth from it to the village, the town, the city. I had fallen in with the surging cavalcade of my generation. I had joined the army of women laboring for daily bread. I had fought for what I felt was right on a gory battlefield. That is the sum of my story.

To me—because it has always been [a] quest—life has been high romance. The circumstances of living may have been difficult at times, but life itself has been a great glowing adventure. Work has been more than compensation. It has been thrilling joy. Sadness has come to me often. My father's death, my mother's, my brother's, Eliza's, Catharine Goggin's, Mary Murray's, struck me like blows. I did not survive them. I lived through them. I have met, too, treacheries that leave a deeper sadness than does loss. Always, though, I have met the next day with the courage to take up the banner again.

I have been, I realize, merely a scout from the ranks of the besieged. If my work has any value to any one but myself, it will be because, at one point of the battleground, I have given service to my comrades-in-arms. Now that my work must be nearly done, the one service I can still give is my plea that they hold the field.

It is something, after all, to have lived for forty years upon a battle-ground, to have been even a small part in the gigantic struggle for justice; but, as the plain grows dark, I realize that I, like the land, have changed but little. Fighting Irish I was then, child of generations of men and women who had battled for something beyond immediate gain, beyond material welfare, perhaps a little beyond their own finite understanding. Fighting Irish I am yet—at seventy-five. And fighting Irish I shall be if, God willing, I may be looking down from some high rampart of eternity when the last war for man's freedom has been won.

Appendix A

To Jacob M. Loeb:

You are one of the Jews sore at Georgia for the way they hanged Leo Frank and called him a damned Jew there in Atlanta.

And you're talking a lot about liberty and the rights of school children.

You came from Kovno in Russia and you ought to know some thing about liberty;

And how school boards, police boards, military boards and czars have gone on year after year,

To choke the Jews from having societies, organizations, labor unions,

Shoving bayonets into the faces of the Jews and driving them to the ghettoes.

You know what I mean. You know these European cities where they call the Jews a despised race;

And anybody who spits in a Jew's face is not touched by the police.

D'ye get me? I'm reminding you what you already know.

You're the man who is leading the school board fight on the Teachers' Federation.

And you forget, your memory slips, your heart doesn't picture

How you and your fathers were spit upon in the face,

And now [sic] the soldiers and police misused your women—

Just because they were Jews, and in Kovno

Anybody could get away with what they did to a Jew woman or a Jew girl;

And now you, a Jew, stand up here in Chicago and act proud

Because you have in effect spit in the faces of Chicago women, accused them, belittled them.

First you tried to cut their wages, back there in May, a seven and a half per cent cut,

And now you're going to make it a law that teachers can't have a labor union;

And they got to take what you and Rothmann and Myer Stein hand 'em.

I don't think you'll get away with it.

Sam Gompers, an English Jew, will speak tonight at the Auditorium,

And Jacob LeBosky and Sam Alschuler and other Jews in this town

Are against the game of shackling the teachers and repeating Kovno and Kiev and Odessa here in Chicago.

In fact, five hundred Jews are already in revolt at your Kovno trick

Of slamming the door on free speech at the Hebrew Institute.

These five hundred are the real blood of the Jew race

That give it a clean flame of heroism.

You belong with the trash of history, the oppressors and the killjoys.

Carl Sandburg
Day Book, September 8, 1915

The *Day Book* misspelled Sandburg's name in the title of the poem but spelled it correctly at the end.

Appendix B

WHY TEACHERS SHOULD ORGANIZE

Margaret A. Haley, President of the National Federation of Teachers, Chicago, Ill.

The responsibility for changing existing conditions so as to make it possible for the public school to do its work rests with the people, the whole people. Any attempt on the part of the public to evade or shift this responsibility must result in weakening the public sense of civic responsibility and the capacity for civic duty, besides further isolating the public school from the people, to the detriment of both.

The sense of responsibility for the duties of citizenship in a democracy is necessarily weak in a people so lately freed from monarchical rule as are the American people, and who still retain in their educational, economic, and political systems so much of their monarchical inheritance, with growing tendencies for retaining and developing the essential weaknesses of that inheritance instead of overcoming them.

Practical experience in meeting the responsibilities of citizenship directly, not in evading or shifting them, is the prime need of the American people. However clever or cleverly disguised the schemes for relieving the public of these responsibilities by vicarious performance of them, or however appropriate those schemes in a monarchy, they have no place in a government of the people, by the people, and for the people, and such schemes must result in defeating their object; for to the extent that they obtain they destroy in a people the capacity for self-government.

If the American people cannot be made to realize and meet their responsibility to the public school, no self-appointed custodians of the public intelligence and conscience can do it for them. Horace Mann, speaking of the dependence of the prosperity of the schools on the public intelligence, said:

> The people will sustain no better schools and have no better education
> than they personally see the need of; and therefore the people are to be
> informed and elevated as a preliminary step toward elevating the schools.

Sometimes, in our impatience at the slowness with which the public moves in these matters, we are tempted to disregard this wise counsel.

The methods as well as the objects of teachers' organizations must be in harmony with the fundamental object of the public school in a democracy, to preserve and develop the democratic ideal. It is not enough that this ideal be realized in the administration of the schools and the methods of teaching; in all its relations to the public, the public school must conform to this ideal.

The character of teachers' organizations is twofold. Organizations on professional lines existed before the necessity became apparent for those for the improvement of conditions. The necessity for both is becoming increasingly evident, and the success of the one is dependent upon the success of the other. Unless the conditions for realizing educational ideals keep pace with the ideals themselves, the result in educational practice is deterioration. To know the better way and be unable to follow it is unfavorable to a healthy development. To have freedom in the conditions without the incentive of the ideal is no less harmful. It is, therefore, opportune that the occasion for organization in the newer sense, the sense understood in the subject of this paper, should be coincident with the formulation of the most advanced educational theory in a practical philosophy of pedagogy.

Modern educational thought has been dominated by the element of inspiration and the element of science; the former enthroning the child, displacing the subject-matter of knowledge as the center of educational theory; the latter founded upon the faith in underlying laws of human development in harmony with which it is possible to evolve a rational method of eliminating waste in the educational process.

How far the educative influence of teaching under these two motives tends to produce a teaching body capable of the highest kind of organized activity it is not possible to determine. Neither is it possible not to perceive the harmony between the principles underlying a rational system of teaching and those underlying the movement for freer expression and better conditions among teachers.

There is no possible conflict between the interest of the child and the interest of the teacher, and nothing so tends to make this fact evident as the progress in the scientific conception of educational method and administration. For both the child and the teacher freedom is the condition of development. The atmosphere in which it is easiest to teach is the atmosphere in which it is easiest to learn. The same things that are a burden to the teacher are a burden also to the child. The same things which restrict her powers restrict his powers also.

The element of danger in organization for self-protection is the predominance of the selfish motive. In the case of teachers a natural check is placed upon this motive by the necessity for professional organization. The closer the union between these two kinds of organization, the fuller and more effective is the activity possible to each.

Freedom of activity directed by freed intelligence is the ideal of democracy. This ideal of democracy is slowly shaping our educational ideal, and making its realization the function of our educational agencies.

The public school is the organized means provided by the deliberate effort of the whole people to free intelligence at its source—and thru freed intelligence to secure freedom of action.

Misdirected activity is proof that the educational agencies are not properly functioning. This may be because these agencies have not freed intelligence, or it may be because the intelligence which they have freed is denied free activity.

Misdirected political activity in lowering the democratic ideal, reacts to lower the educational ideal. On the other hand, a false or incomplete educational ideal fails to free the intelligence necessary for the work of constructing a democracy out of our monarchical inheritance.

That the public school does not feel its responsibility in the matter of political corruption, for instance, nor realize the effect upon the schools of this corruption and the misdirected activity of which it is a symptom, is proof that the public school is not yet conscious of its own vital function in a democracy.

When Ida Tarbell and Lincoln Steffens in lightening flashes, disclosed to the American people indisputable facts concerning the business methods of our so-called "good business men" and their relations to politics, they showed a condition of affairs that must make every thoughtful citizen stop and ask: "Whither are we going?" How many public-school teachers, on reading these disclosures, said to themselves: "We must take our share of the blame. The public school, that great agency of the people for freeing intelligence, has failed to do its whole duty." The public school is not wholly to blame. There are other educational agencies. There is the press, for instance. But the press does not belong to the people; it is a private enterprise. The schools do belong to the people, and they are free.

We teachers are responsible for existing conditions to the extent that the schools have not inspired true ideals of democracy, or that we have not made the necessary effort toward removing the conditions which make the realization of these ideals impossible.

We recognize anarchy in the act which takes the life of the chief
executive of a city, state, or nation; but there is another kind of anarchy
in our midst. It is the anarchy which sends the railroad and corporation lobby to the legislatures and to the taxing bodies—yes, even to the
bench—and in whose hands these servants of the people are as wax and
obey the command of the lobby, and defy the law they were elected and
sworn to uphold. This is the anarchy we need to fear in America, and
whose meaning the public-school teachers need to comprehend.

It was indeed an invaluable public service which the teachers of
Chicago rendered when they established in the courts, and in the
minds of the people, the fact that thru the connivance of public
officials five public-utility corporations are enabled to rob Chicago of
ten million dollars annually thru the free gift to these corporations of
the use of the public streets. Think what that means: the second city in
the Union compelled to pay to five corporations, her own creatures, an
annual tribute of ten million dollars; more than the combined cost of
maintaining the public schools and the public library—at the same
time her board of education closing the schools, cutting the teachers'
salaries, increasing the number of children in each room, and otherwise crippling the service for want of money!

America's motto once was, "Millions for defense, but not one cent
for tribute," and we teachers may continue to teach that it is still our
motto; but the children will learn, in spite of our teaching, that
"Millions for tribute and not one cent for defense" is nearer the truth.

The significant thing in the tax crusade of the Chicago teachers was
not the disclosing of these humiliating facts, nor the forcing of the
corporations to return to the public treasury some of their stolen
millions; it was that the public school, thru the organized effort of the
teachers, was the agency which brought these conditions to the attention of the public and showed how to apply the remedy.

Nowhere in the United States today does the public school, as a
branch of the public service, receive from the public either the moral or
financial support needed to enable it properly to perform its important
function in the social organism. The conditions which are militating
most strongly against efficient teaching, and which existing organizations of the kind under discussion here are directing their energies
toward changing, briefly stated are the following:

1. Greatly increased cost of living, together with constant demands for
higher standards of scholarship and professional attainments and culture,
to be met with practically stationary and wholly inadequate teachers'
salaries.

2. Insecurity of tenure of office and lack of provision for old age.

3. Overwork in overcrowded schoolrooms, exhausting both mind and
body.

4. And, lastly, lack of recognition of the teacher as an educator in the school system, due to the increased tendency toward "factoryizing education," making the teacher an automaton, a mere factory hand, whose duty it is to carry out mechanically and unquestioningly the ideas and orders of those clothed with the authority of position, and who may or may not know the needs of the children or how to minister to them.

The individuality of the teacher and her power of initiative are thus destroyed, and the result is courses of study, regulations, and equipment which the teachers have had no voice in selecting, which often have no relation to the children's needs, and which prove a hindrance instead of a help in teaching.

Dr. John Dewey, of the University of Chicago, in the *Elementary School Teacher* for December, 1903, says:

As to the teacher: If there is a single public-school system in the United States where there is official and constitutional provision made for submitting questions of methods of discipline and teaching, and the questions of the curriculum, text-books, etc., to the discussion of those actually engaged in the work of teaching, that fact has escaped my notice. Indeed, the opposite situation is so common that it seems, as a rule, to be absolutely taken for granted as the normal and final condition of affairs. The number of persons to whom any other course has occurred as desirable, or even possible—to say nothing of necessary—is apparently very limited. But until the public-school system is organized in such a way that every teacher has some regular and representative way in which he or she can register judgment upon matters of educational importance, with the assurance that this judgment will somehow affect the school system, the assertion that the present system is not, from the internal standpoint, democratic seems to be justified. Either we come here upon some fixed and inherent limitation of the democratic principle, or else we find in this fact an obvious discrepancy between the conduct of the school and the conduct of social life—a discrepancy so great as to demand immediate and persistent effort at reform.

A few days ago Professor George F. James, dean of pedagogy of the State University of Minnesota, said to an audience of St. Paul teachers:

One hundred thousand teachers will this year quit an occupation which does not yield them a living wage. Scores and hundreds of schools are this day closed in the most prosperous sections of this country because the bare pittance offered will not attract teachers of any kind.

Professor James further maintained that school-teachers are not only underpaid, but that they are paid much less proportionately than they received eight years ago.

It is necessary that the public understand the effect which teaching under these conditions is having upon the education of the children.

In reacting unfavorably upon the public school, these wrong conditions affect the child, the parent, and the teacher; but the teacher is so
placed that she is the one first to feel the disadvantage: she is held
responsible by the child, by the parent, by the authorities, by society,
and by herself because of her own ideals, for duties in the performance
of which she is continually hampered. The dissatisfaction and restlessness among teachers are due to the growing consciousness that causes
outside of themselves and beyond their control are making their work
more difficult. Some of these causes of irritation are inherent in the
school system. Such proceed from the failure of the system on the
educational and administrative side to adapt itself to the growing
ideals of education and the demand for rational methods of realizing
them. These inherent causes of trouble include the limitations of the
teachers themselves and the failure of the system either to remedy these
deficiencies or to remove the deficient.

Where friction is minimized by enlightened supervision and administration, the pressure of outside causes is less keenly felt. But
where the system is so administered that inherent weaknesses and
outside causes combine and reinforce each other to produce dissatisfaction, the double pressure increases the irritation, and correspondingly
hastens the time when sheer necessity impels the teachers to seek a
remedy or leave the profession.

The first and crudest form of expression that dissatisfaction with
these conditions takes is the reaction against the nearest and most
obvious cause of irritation—unsatisfactory supervision and administration, which are later recognized as effects rather than causes. The
last causes to be assigned are the real ones, and only when every
individual effort to better conditions has failed does the thought of
combined effort for mutual aid—in other words, organized effort—
suggest itself.

And yet organization is the method of all intelligently directed
effort.

Within the last decade in a few cities of the United States organization has been effected among those on whom devolves the responsibility of applying scientific principles to the actual work with children
in the school-room, the purpose of such organization being to secure
conditions under which rational teaching may become possible.

Such organization is at once the effect and the cause of a broadening
of the intelligence and the educational outlook of the teachers, for to
such organization they must take not only a reading acquaintance
with the best in educational theory and practice, but a practical knowledge of what constitutes scientific teaching. Nor is this all, tho it may
suffice for the professional equipment of those whose duties are merely

supervisory. The class-room teachers in addition to this must have the ability and skill, given fair conditions, to do scientific teaching. More than this, they must know the conditions under which scientific teaching is possible, must know when and in what respects such conditions are lacking; and then, most difficult of all, because it includes all these and much more, they must know how to reach the public with accurate information concerning the conditions under which teaching is done and their effects on the work of the school.

Such are the prerequisites of teachers who would successfully engage in the work of securing better conditions for themselves, and for the schools, thru organization.

A word, before closing, on the relations of the public-school teachers and the public schools to the labor unions. As the professional organization furnishes the motive and ideal which shall determine the character and methods of the organized effort of teachers to secure better conditions for teaching, so is it the province of the educational agencies in a democracy to furnish the motive and ideal which shall determine the character and methods of the organization of its members for self-protection.

There is no possible conflict between the good of society and the good of its members, of which the industrial workers are the vast majority. The organization of these workers for mutual aid has shortened the hours of labor, raised and equalized the wages of men and women, and taken the children from the factories and workshops. These humanitarian achievements of the labor unions—and many others which space forbids enumerating—in raising the standard of living of the poorest and weakest members of society, are a service to society which for its own welfare it must recognize. More than this, by intelligent comprehension of the limitations of the labor unions and the causes of these limitations, by just, judicious, and helpful criticism and co-operation, society must aid them to feel the inspiration of higher ideals, and to find the better means to realize these ideals.

If there is one institution on which the responsibility to perform this service rests most heavily, it is the public school. If there is one body of public servants of whom the public has a right to expect the mental and moral equipment to face the labor question, and other issues vitally affecting the welfare of society and urgently pressing for a rational and scientific solution, it is the public-school teachers, whose special contribution to society is their own power to think, the moral courage to follow their convictions, and the training of citizens to think and to express thought in free and intelligent action.

The narrow conception of education which makes the mechanics of reading, writing, and arithmetic, and other subjects, the end and aim of the schools, instead of a means to an end—which mistakes the accidental and incidental for the essential—produces the unthinking, mechanical mind in teacher and pupil, and prevents the public school as an institution, and the public-school teachers as a body, from becoming conscious of their relation to society and its problems, and from meeting their responsibilities. On the other hand, that teaching which is most scientific and rational gives the highest degree of power to think and to select the most intelligent means of expressing thought in every field of activity. The ideals and methods of the labor unions are in a measure a test of the efficiency of the schools and other educational agencies.

How shall the public school and the industrial workers, in their struggle to secure the rights of humanity thru a more just and equitable distribution of the products of their labor, meet their mutual responsibility to each other and to society?

Whether the work of co-ordinating these two great educational agencies, manual and mental labor, with each other and with the social organism, shall be accomplished thru the affiliation of the organizations of brain and manual workers is a mere matter of detail and method to be decided by the exigencies in each case. The essential thing is that the public-school teachers recognize the fact that their struggle to maintain the efficiency of the schools thru better conditions for themselves is a part of the same great struggle which the manual workers—often misunderstood and unaided—have been making for humanity thru their efforts to secure living conditions for themselves and their children; and that back of the unfavorable conditions of both is a common cause.

Two ideals are struggling for supremacy in American life today: one the industrial ideal, culminating thru the supremacy of commercialism, which subordinates the worker to the product and the machine; the other, the ideal of democracy, the ideal of the educators, which places humanity above all machines, and demands that all activity shall be the expression of life. If this ideal of the educators cannot be carried over into the industrial field, then the ideal of industrialism will be carried over into the school. Those two ideals can no more continue to exist in American life than our nation could have continued half slave and half free. If the school cannot bring joy to the work of the world, the joy must go out of its own life, and work in the school as in the factory will become drudgery.

Viewed in this light, the duty and responsiblity of the educators in the solution of the industrial question is one which must thrill and fascinate while it awes, for the very depth of the significance of life is shut up in this question. But the first requisite is to put aside all prejudice, all preconceived notions, all misinformation and half-information, and to take to this question what the educators have long recognized must be taken to scientific investigation in other fields. There may have been justification for failure to do this in the past, but we cannot face the responsibility of continued failure and maintain our title as thinkers and educators. When men organize and go out to kill, they go surrounded by pomp, display, and pageantry, under the inspiration of music and with the admiration of the throng. Not so the army of industrial toilers who have been fighting humanity's battles, unhonored and unsung.

It will be well indeed if the teachers have the courage of their convictions and face all that the labor unions have faced with the same courage and perseverance.

Today, teachers of America, we stand at the parting of the ways. Democracy is not on trial, but America is.

Addresses and Proceedings of the National Education Association, 43rd Annual Meeting, St. Louis, 1904 (Washington, D.C.: The Association, 1904), pp. 145-52

Appendix C

MAYORS OF CHICAGO

Carter H. Harrison II	1897-1905
Edward F. Dunne	1905-1907
Fred A. Busse	1907-1911
Carter H. Harrison II	1911-1915
William Hale Thompson	1915-1923
William E. Dever	1923-1927
William Hale Thompson	1927-1931
Anton J. Cermak	1931-1933
Edward J. Kelly	1933-1947

SUPERINTENDENTS OF CHICAGO SCHOOLS

Albert G. Lane	1891-1898
E. Benjamin Andrews	1898-1900
Edwin G. Cooley	1900-1909
Ella' Flagg Young	1910-1915
John D. Shoop	1915-1918
Peter A. Mortenson	1918-1919 (Acting); 1919-1924
Charles E. Chadsey	1919
William McAndrew	1924-1928
William J. Bogan	1928-1936

Index

MARGARET A. HALEY was a grade school teacher who left the classroom to serve as a full-time representative for the Chicago Teachers' Federation, the nation's most militant association of teachers at the turn of the century. Through her leadership, the CTF played an active role in the public affairs of Chicago and Illinois. Haley and her supporters, who were women grade school teachers, campaigned for such causes as tax reform, municipal ownership, teacher benefits, elected school boards, woman suffrage, and democratic school administration. Haley brought her organization into the ranks of organized labor in 1902. Several years later, in the midst of a struggle with the Board of Education, the CTF was the key local in forming the American Federation of Teachers. Haley worked to broaden the orientation and membership of the National Education Association. One measure of her influence was the election of Ella Flagg Young, the first woman president of the NEA, in 1910. Margaret Haley's story ends during the demoralizing experience of the Great Depression, with its "payless paydays" for the teachers of Chicago.

ROBERT L. REID, a native of Red Wing, Minnesota, holds a B.A. from St. Olaf College and M.A. and Ph.D. degrees from Northwestern University. He has taught at Miami University in Ohio and held administrative assignments at Sangamon University in Illinois. Currently, he is professor of history and vice president for academic affairs at Indiana State University Evansville. He has previously published "William E. Gladstone's 'Insincere Neutrality' During the Civil War" in Civil War History (1969) and "Organizing the Teachers: Women Activists in the Progressive Era" in *Sex, Race, Ethnicity and Education*, edited by Michael V. Belok and Ralph Shoub.